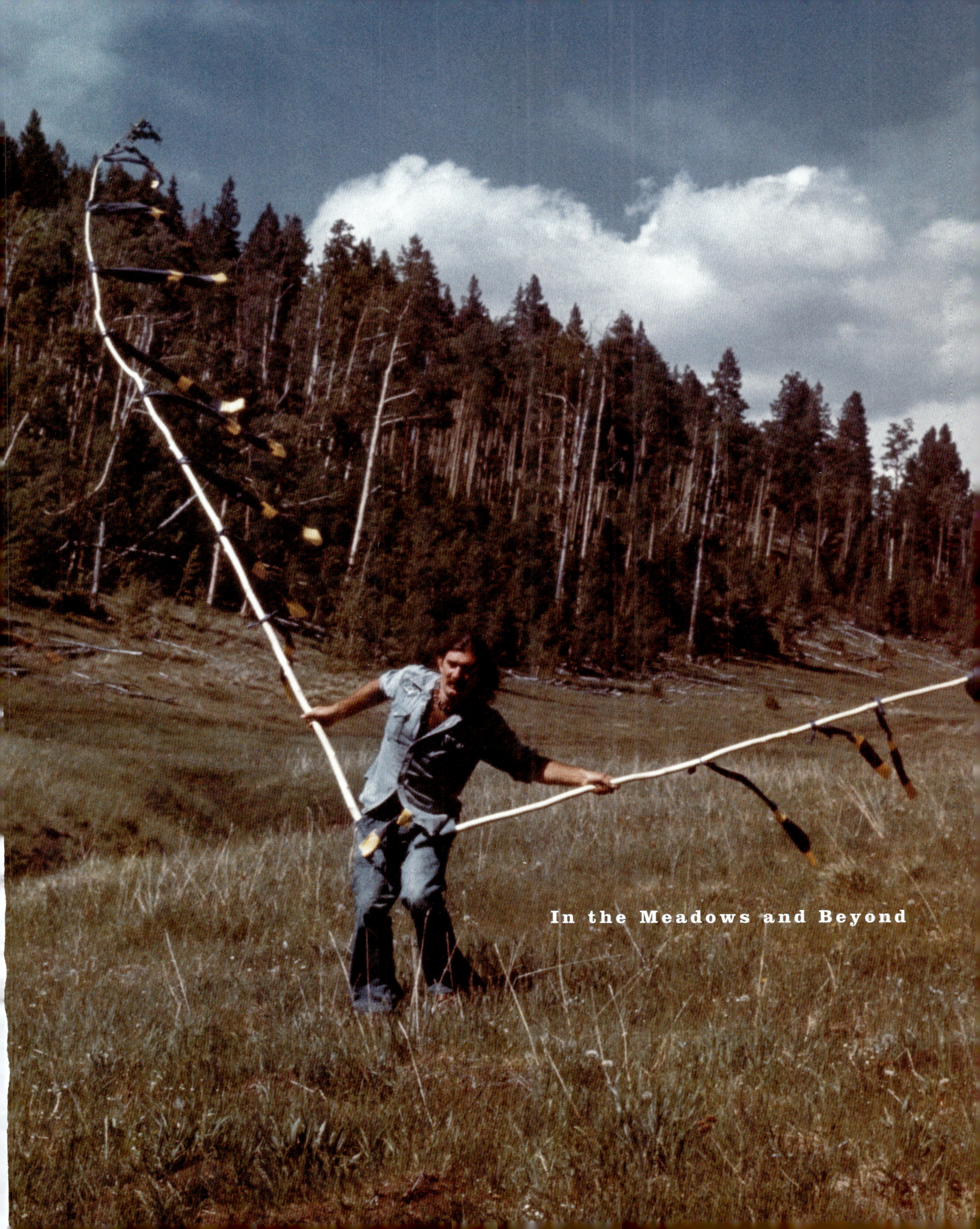

In the Meadows and Beyond

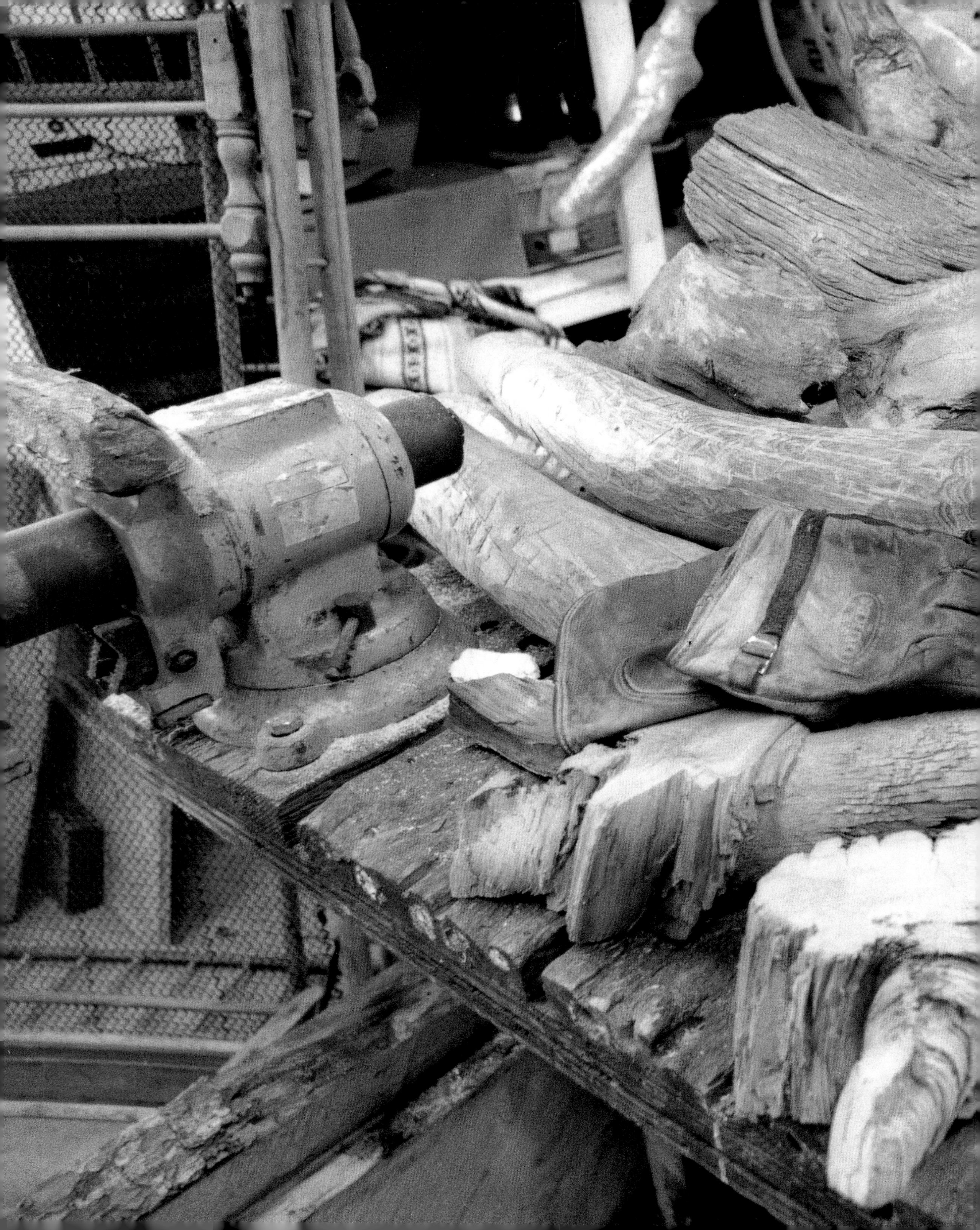

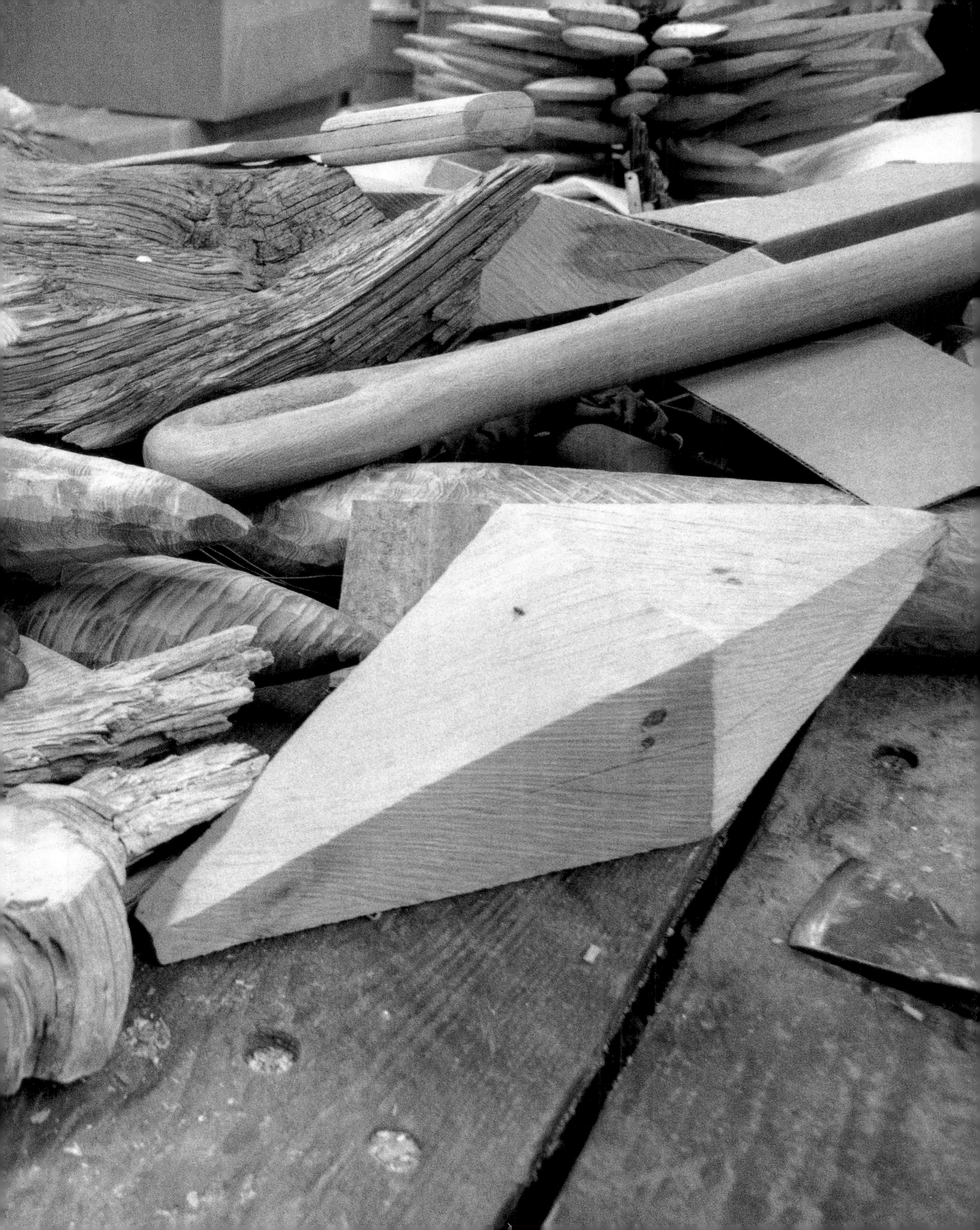

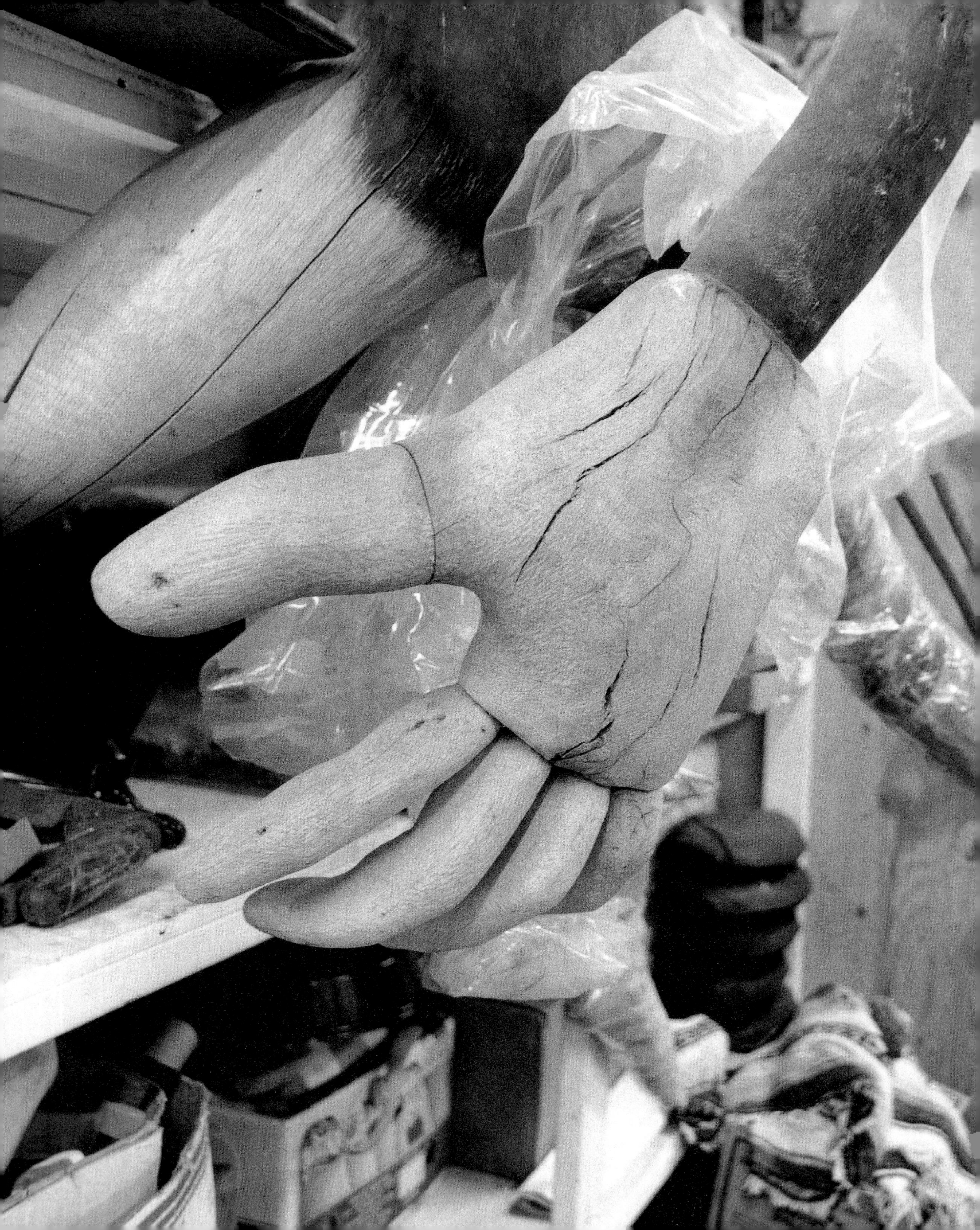

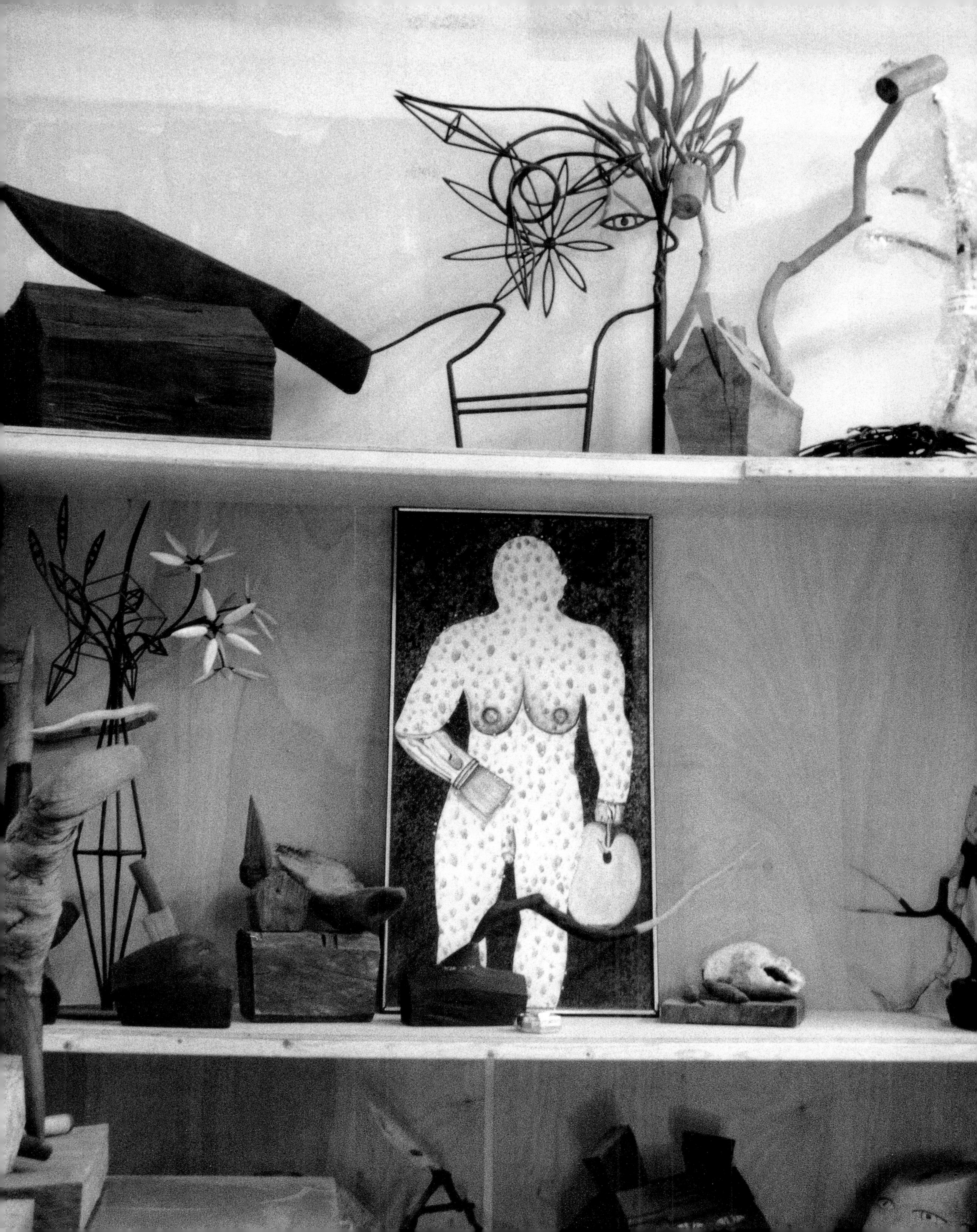

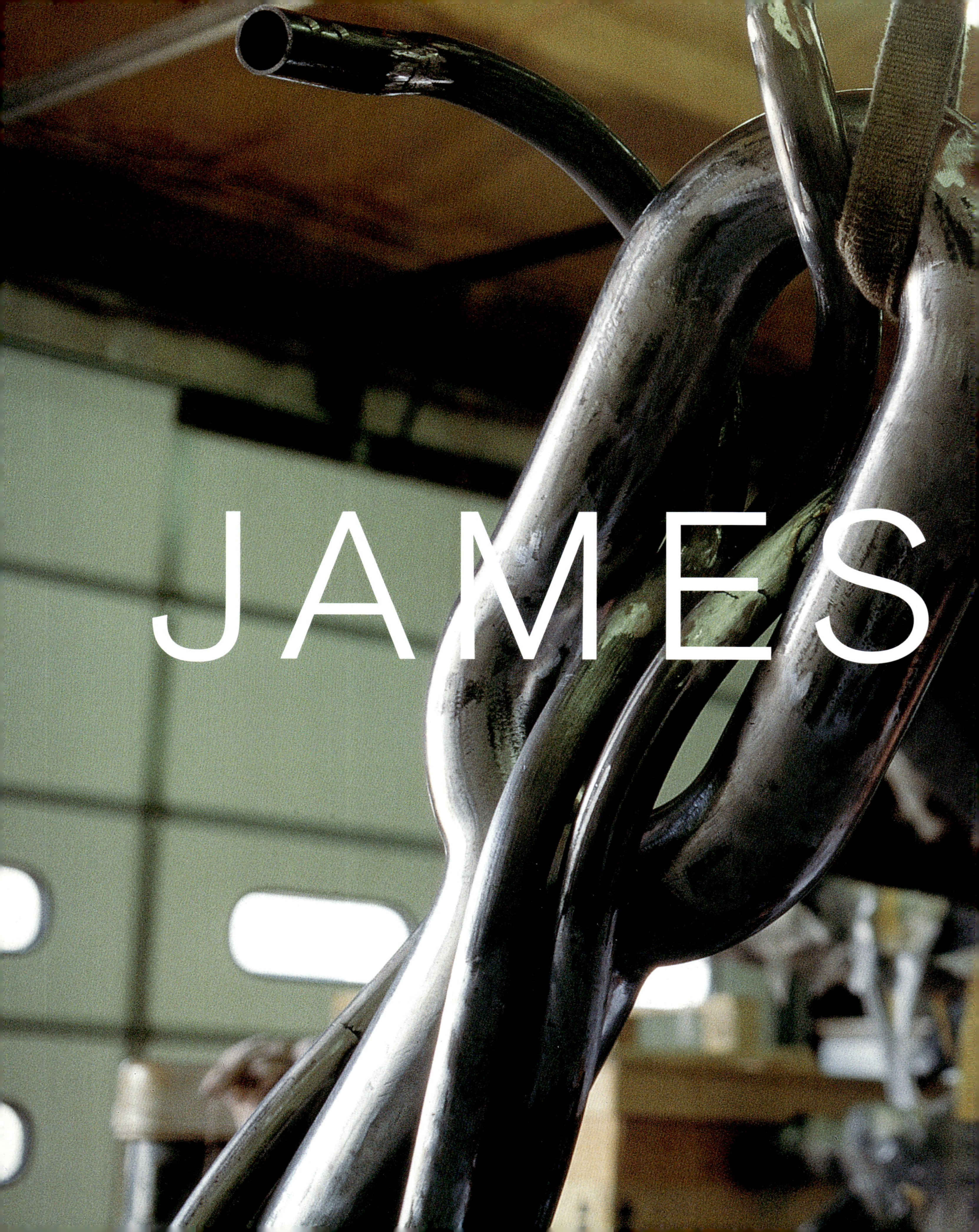
JAMES

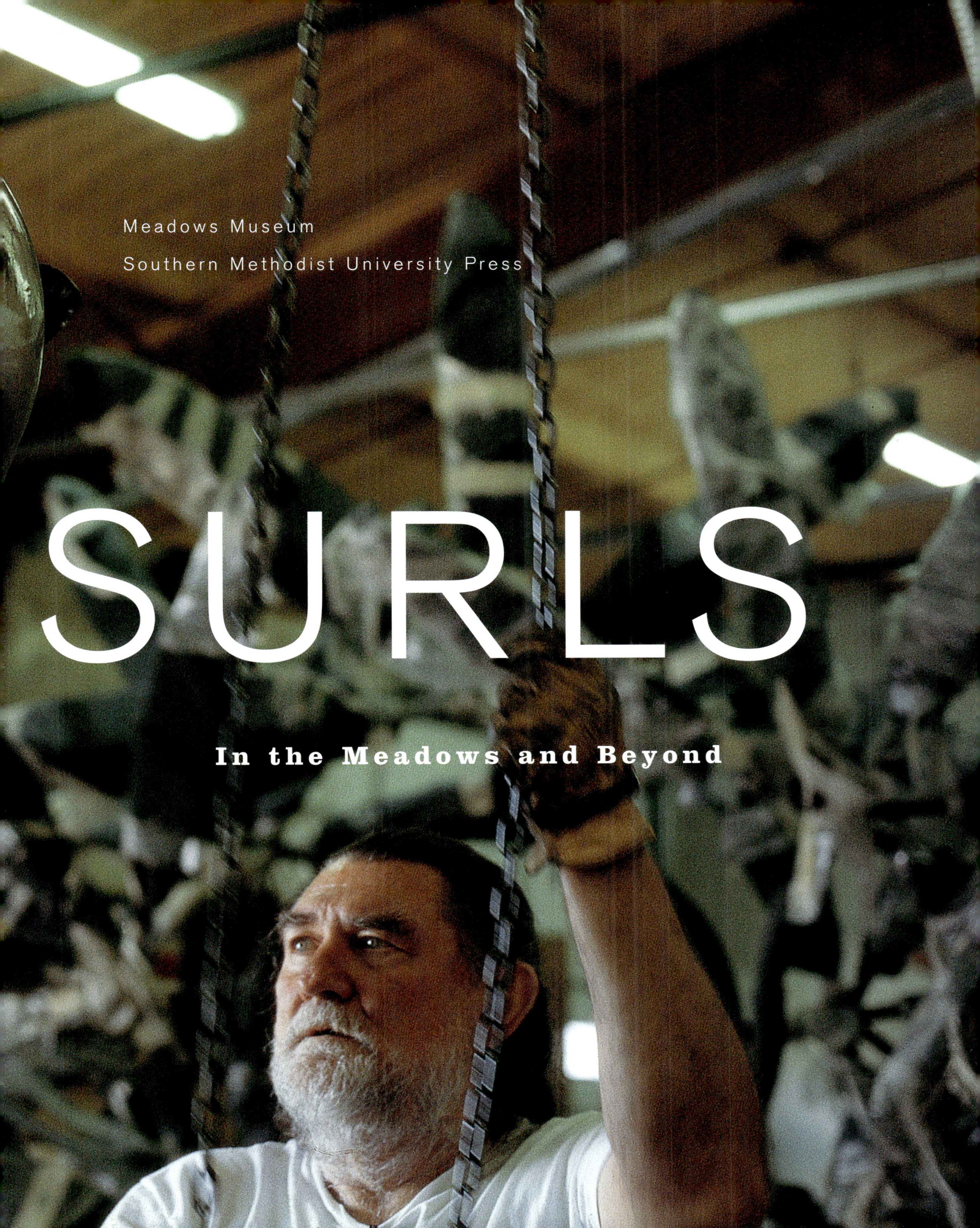

Meadows Museum
Southern Methodist University Press

SURLS

In the Meadows and Beyond

This book celebrates the achievement of James Surls and documents the exhibition entitled *In the Meadows: Recent Sculpture, Drawings and Prints of James Surls* held at the Meadows Museum, Southern Methodist University, Dallas, January 24 – April 20, 2003.

Special thanks go to Ambassador Kathryn Hall and Mr. Craig Hall, whose generosity made this exhibition and this book possible, as well as the following individuals, whose steadfast support of the artist and this project was invaluable: Nona and Richard Barrett; Linda and Bob Buford; Jim and Carolyn Clark; Kaleta Doolin; Christopher Gongolas; Patricia B. Meadows; Marilyn Oshman; Mr. Frank Ribelin; Jay Shinn; Julie and George Tobolowsky; Donald and Barbara Zale.

Editor: Jeanne Lil Chvosta with the assistance of Fronia W. Simpson
Coordinating editors: Courtney E. Kennedy and Bridget LaRocque Marx
Book Design: Greg Dittmar/Dittmar Design and Tom Dawson
New Photography: Michael Bodycomb

Printed and bound in Hong Kong

Library of Congress Cataloging-in-Publication Data
Surls, James, 1943–
James Surls : in the Meadows and beyond / [editor, Jeanne Lil Chvosta, with the assistance of Fronia W. Simpson].
p. cm.
Catalog of an exhibition held at the Meadows Museum, Southern Methodist University, Dallas, Texas, Jan. 24–Apr. 20, 2003.
Includes bibliographical references and index.
ISBN 0-87074-490-9
1. Surls, James, 1943–Exhibitions. I. Chvosta, Jeanne Lil. II. Simpson, Fronia W. III. Meadows Museum. IV. Title.

N6537.S93A4 2004
730'.92–dc22

2004049599

COVER
Into the Flowers (detail), 2002 (**PL. 13**)
Painted steel, wood
86 x 159 x 24 inches

FRONTISPIECES
1. *Five Minutes of Blue in Wind River*, 1974
Kit Carson National Forest,
Taos, New Mexico
2–4. The artist's studio, Basalt,
Colorado, 2002.

TITLE PAGE
James Surls in his studio, Basalt,
Colorado, 2002.

THIS PAGE
The artist's worktable, Basalt,
Colorado, 2002.

PAGE 12
The artist in his Tremont Street studio,
Dallas, Texas, 1975.

CONTENTS

The Voice out of the Whirlwind

One of the great pleasures of helping organize the exhibition *In the Meadows* and being part of this book has been the opportunity to get to know James Surls. Before this enterprise I knew the work but did not know the man, and it has been my good fortune to find that I respect the man as much as I do his art. James Surls is the genuine article, a man who believes in himself and his art, a "true believer" in the best sense. This is all well and good, but, of course, the reason for this book is the art itself.

Why is Surls's work so special, so appealing, and so engaging? I have had well over a year to ponder this question, and I have had the opportunity to get to know some of the work firsthand, to watch it be assembled and installed, to hear James Surls talk about it in a lengthy interview. You will have the opportunity to see the work for yourself in this book, and to hear from others who are far more knowledgeable than I am about Surls and his work. I am a classicist by profession, and my realm is made up of the stone, bronze, and terracotta remnants of antiquity, seemingly a world apart from contemporary sculpture. Yet, while Surls's work is contemporary in a chronological sense, he is an artist who has chosen to avoid the mainstream and to literally create his own path through the contemporary art world.

Quite simply, the art of James Surls has a universal appeal. It connects on a visceral level. Surls will argue that he is a Romantic, and he certainly is in the way he appeals to our collective emotions on a very personal level and invests his art with his own individual sensibility. For me, his most compelling works are the ones where there is an undercurrent of the fundamental and atavistic forces that lie beneath the surface, forces that are part of an irrational world that we moderns would prefer to ignore. And while it is not all about irrational undercurrents, for James Surls is a reasoned and thoughtful creative force who negotiates the tensions between the seen and the unseen, he is also an artist who, like a shaman, to use Surls's own metaphor, can control those unseen forces. Or, in the words of Loren Eiseley, the great anthropologist and historian of science, he is an artist who hears the voice out of the whirlwind:

> "Man is at heart romantic. He believes in thunder, the destruction of worlds, the voice out of the whirlwind. . . . Man has always had two ways of looking at nature, and these two divergent approaches to the world . . . (are) traceable far into the primitive past. Man has a belief in seen and unseen nature. He is both pragmatist and mystic."

P. Gregory Warden
Professor of Art History
Meadows School of the Arts
Southern Methodist University

ARTIST'S STATEMENT

An exhibition has its own parameters, a beginning and an end. I see this as a spot in time, like a world in a grain of sand, reflecting a surface that is everywhere, and everywhere the same distance from its center. A sphere filled with singular thought, in a state of being whole, not injured, not broken. A work of art should be whole in and of itself, a complete thing; but when taken as a component of a show, it is a fragment, only a part of a whole, and yet complete as a moment in life.

I am sincere in my intent to look out as far as my eyes can parallel-track the contradictions of my being. Paradox is the godmother of my soul, giving me the difference between dark and light, marking the tight line stretching from the heavens in a flower, to the relativeness in the palm of my hand. Meaning comes only in connection with something that exists out there.

How many grains of sand are there? How many worlds, heavens, and palms can we look through? When is the crystal clear enough for us to see eternity in framed time? Joseph Campbell said, "We are tigers in the goat pen." Are we then forever caught between the lamb and the beast? I would as soon run with the wolves, and be eaten by crushing jaws breathing low guttural growls, than be run over by an endless sea of sheep.

For all the poets who cleared the brush from the bower, so that I may go nutting my way towards mature sleep, I say thank you. Here now, I lay the sieve aside, and gather my honey in a wooden bowl, and eat the gift with honor to the giver. I owe so many, close and distant, family and friends who understand my flaws, and forgive me my faults; colleagues and collectors who lay blocks of stone at my corners so that I may expand with deliberateness and speed. I say thank you to them all. First, to the Meadows Museum as an institution for its willingness to undertake something of this magnitude, and second to George and Julie Tobolowsky, and Kathryn and Craig Hall, for here is the core of this endeavor. From the Museum: Carole Brandt, Greg Warden, Mark Roglán, Jeanne Chvosta, Kay Johnson and Will Johnson. From the community: Mark Thistlethwaite, Patricia Meadows, Ted Pillsbury, Marilyn Oshman, Nona and Richard Barrett, Barbara and Donald Zale, Linda and Bob Buford, Laura and Dan Boeckman. I would also like to thank Jim Baker and the staff at Anderson Ranch Arts Center for their part in making it possible for me to create a large portion of the work for the exhibition.

It is with a warm heart that I give special thanks to two people: one is my mother, Martha Sebastian, who gave me a creative spark and the will to use it. The other is Charmaine Locke, who has been a light in my life for thirty years.

I smile and say, I wish to dedicate this book to my wife and soul mate, Charmaine Locke.

James Surls

2003

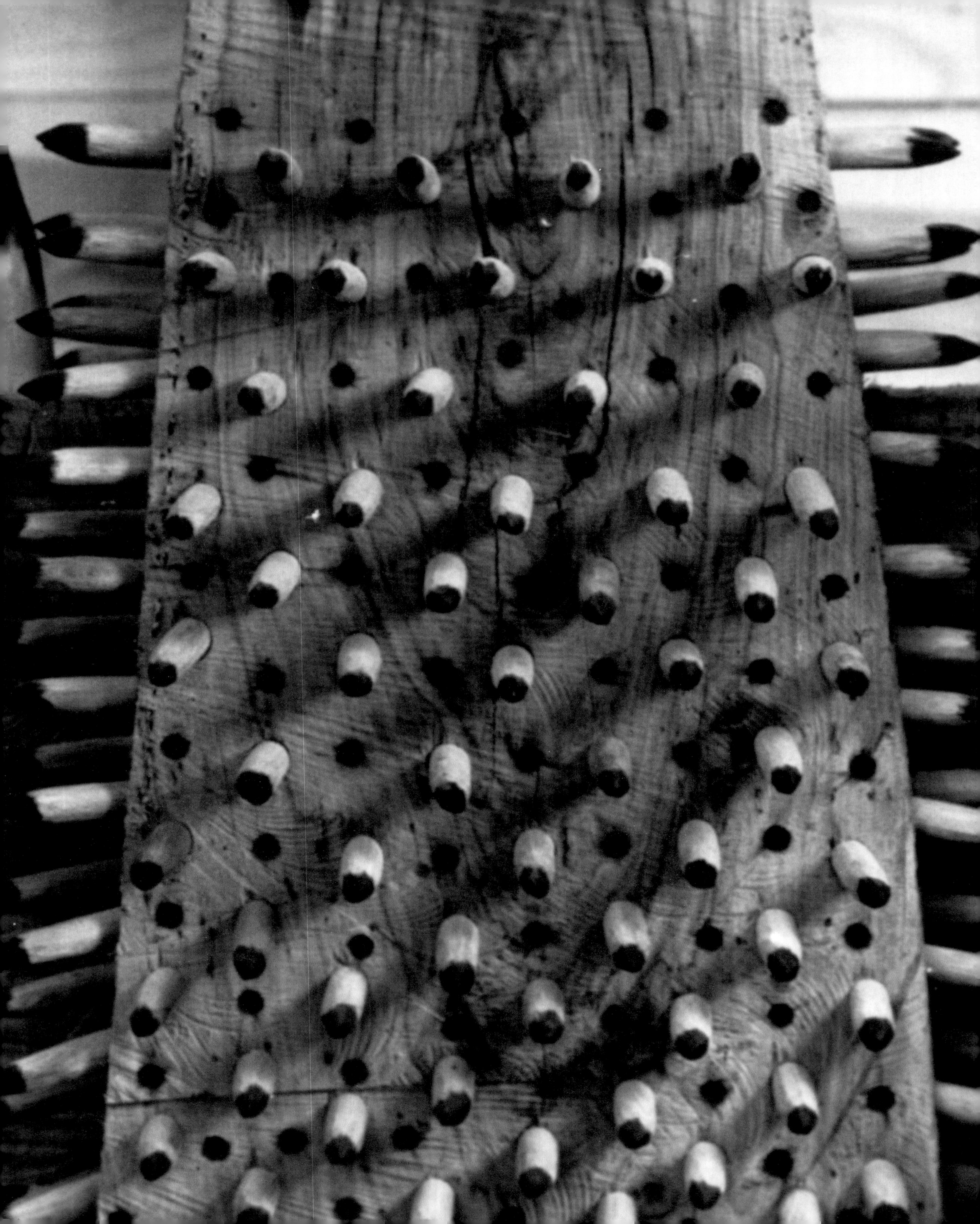

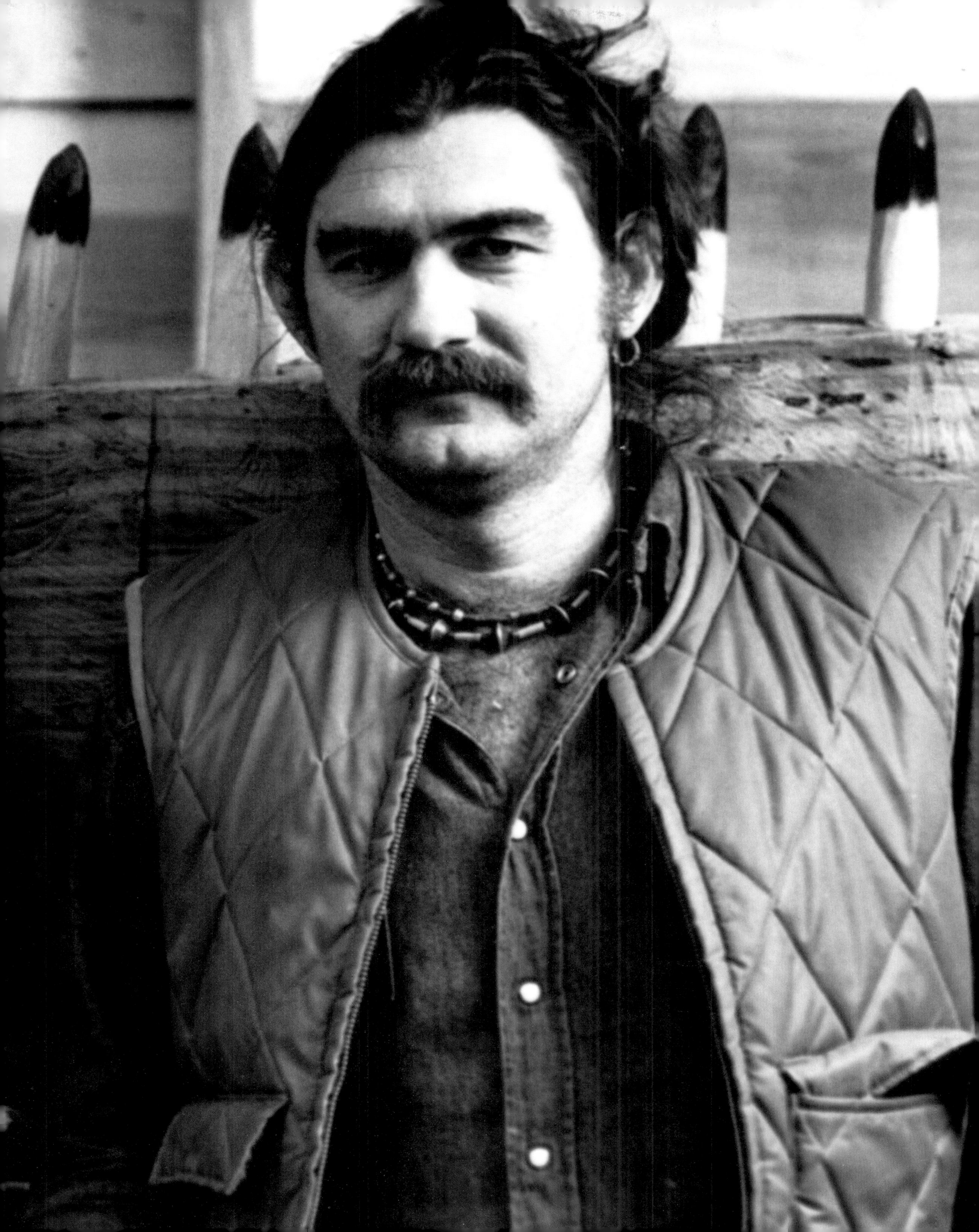

Me, God, Evolution, Love, Relationship and you

Me, God, Evolution, Love, Relationship and you.
What if what God knows is change?
Now is change going slow.
We think it is still.
The blink of an eye—one life,
times itself a thousand times.
The beginning is the beginning.
A burst of heat and belief
change, change, change.
A quasar is in the shoulder bone
of a giant, and Orion is real, and forever
or a fireball in its dying moments,
still real, but not forever.
Forever is slower than we can perceive.
All things end. Over.
When is forever over?
Or is forever never over?
Unless one is there in its overness,
to see the end.
When is over forever?
When does existence become nonexistence?
Where does love go when it is gone?
Which is more real, Love or no love?
Does God know love or not?
Does God have it to lose?
We do.
What if all God knows is change?
That's it. That's the fireball,
burning out there on the horizon for a time,
not all time, not forever,
just for a period of time.
A long now or a short now?
We being me and you,
have a short now.
Yours is yours, mine is mine.
Two centers touch and the heat rises.
To be touched.
Can't touch that.
Time has left its mark.
The mark of time.

Why are God and evolution not the
same thing?
Do we measure People stuff
in the same way we measure
God Stuff? Did God create us?
or did we create God?
Do we create love? or
Do we end love?
If we do, to both
then why and how?

What is the process which gives
rise to the beginning or
to the end of the existence of Love?

James Surls

I Never Knew

I never knew
until the sunrise
when the light layers came
and measured spaces hill to hill
true beauty comes in time
three hundred million light years
across
The best life I've ever had.

Great gobs of flowers
Hang over the garden wall.
Visual pie, topped with a soft hue
red and yellow, kill a fellow
where are all the snakes?
I always thought the snake got screwed.
Eve got the blame.

Space time my ass
It's here and now
and the sun is shining around the edges,
and the shadows have
Life about them
and rocks faces, looking out
through the houses of history
and sticks power, swung round
and round
another full turn, and darkness comes,
there is a quasar in the shoulder bone
of Orion, exploding on the horizon
No way is this just
A fireball in its twilight
and Adam turned into something
less than "that he could be"
Developing a king complex while
sleeping in a suit of armor.
The snake did ok—even though
he was and is hated to the teeth.
Eve became the juggler in a
Three ring circus.
While firing ovens
and wearing steel underwear,
when the armored man
was out conquering nature
or just killing something.
So much for harmonics
and the balance of the neutron Core
Blood Red and midnight Black,
Breathe deep
Don't Look Back
just like a man
eyeing forever
while his feet are stuck in plowed earth
just like a woman
imbuing the stone
giving it life
Firm, voluptuous and full
A new now
a beginning
Please God,
Give me just one more shot
I promise I'll do better.

James Surls

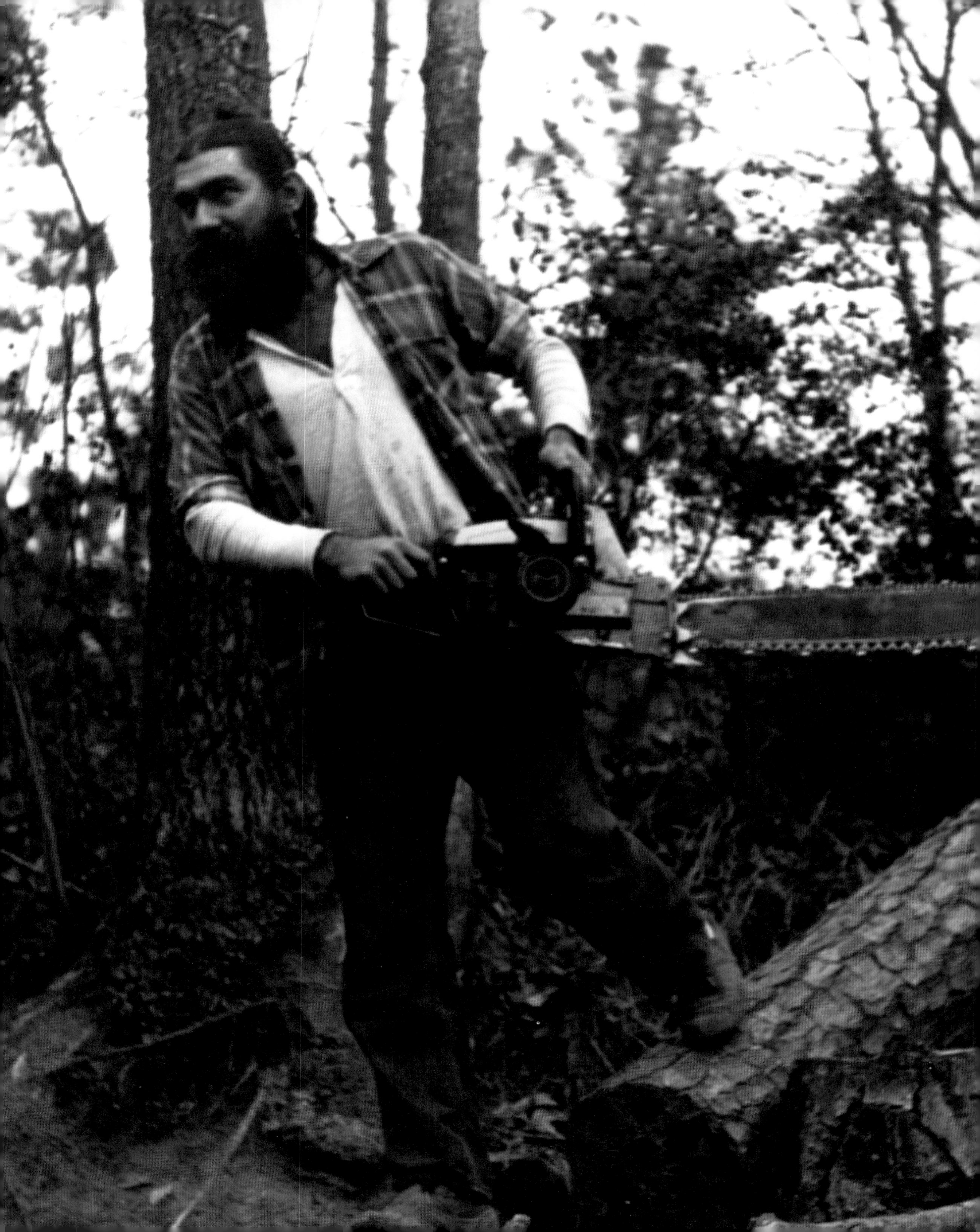

CHARMAINE LOCKE

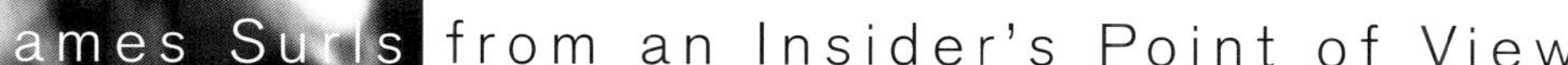

James Surls from an Insider's Point of View

The generation of artists that was working in New York City and being prominently displayed in galleries, museums, and magazines during the time James Surls defined himself as an artist was interested in reduction and simplicity, paring away surface "reality" to find the core "reality" of basic elemental forms, colors, spatial relations, and objects containing no overt "meaning" unless it was a "purity" of mental experience.

James Surls and the art he has produced for more than thirty years revel in complexity, the complexity of human nature, the multiplicity of experiential references, the dense network of interplays found in the human mode and the exponentially expanding possibilities of the natural world. There are also suggestions of the world beyond our sensory abilities to confirm, the realm of magic and spirit to which James gives credence, the world of myth that Joseph Campbell so eloquently and intelligently elucidated.

The work of this artist is not still or static or quietly fulfilling an academic credo. It is not sitting in repose, emptied out to receive a viewer's meaning. The works of sculpture as well as the drawings and prints are vital and animated, full of vigor, energy, and fire, and brimming over with information. James is charged up (and sometimes consumed) with the drive to build, to be productive, to be actively involved in learning and change, growth and expansion, for himself and for others. He has been an inspiring teacher of many inquiring minds for three decades, whether in the academic setting of the classroom or in lecture halls of universities and museums around the country.

I met James through one of his sculptures, an early piece that unfortunately no longer exists that was on display in a faculty exhibition in the SMU gallery. As I stepped into the gallery, I was captivated by a delicate aspen cradle suspended in space that was obviously more than a cradle. The quality that radiated from it, its "vivifying principle" or life energy, is the property that eludes the embrace of so many aspiring artists, and for teachers it is the most difficult aspect of art to convey. Technical skills, principles of composition, art theory, and history are elements of process that are more accessible. The elusive ability to breathe life into an object is another type of skill, something that James is very successful in incorporating into his own art as well as in imparting to others. James encourages students, then and now, to connect with their personal life experiences to inform their sculptures and to give them meaning and power, to dig into their own psyches as sources. This process affirms their experiences and elevates the act of making art into an arena that is liberating. He talks more about inspiration and how ideas are derived from experience than he does about tools and how to set the depth of a saw, or how to run the shop. He sets the tone

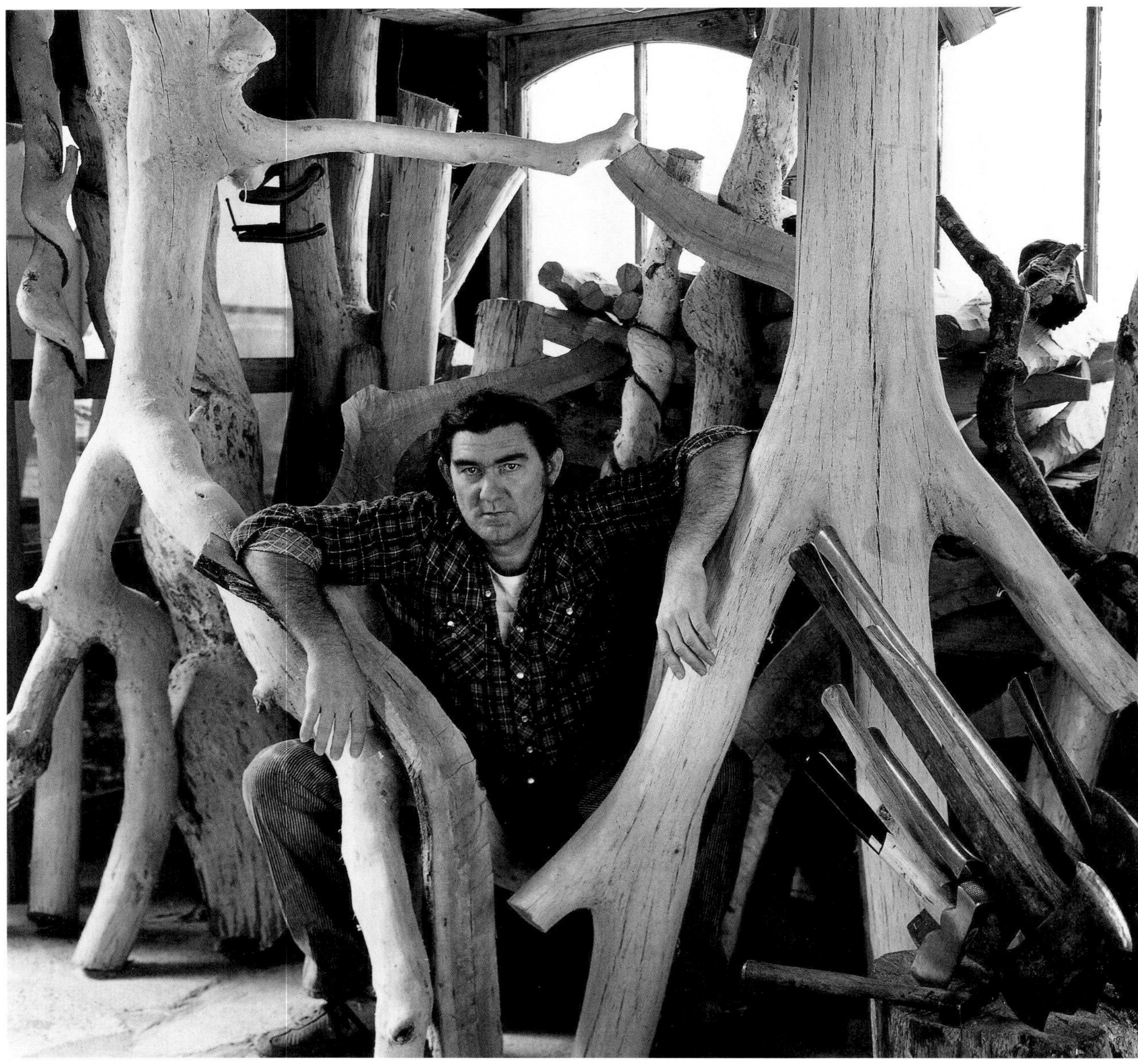

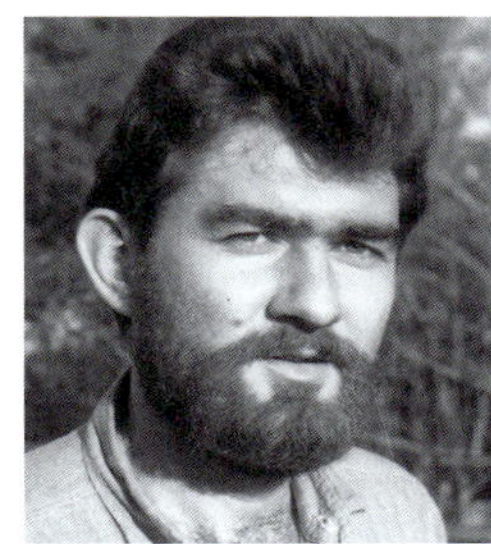

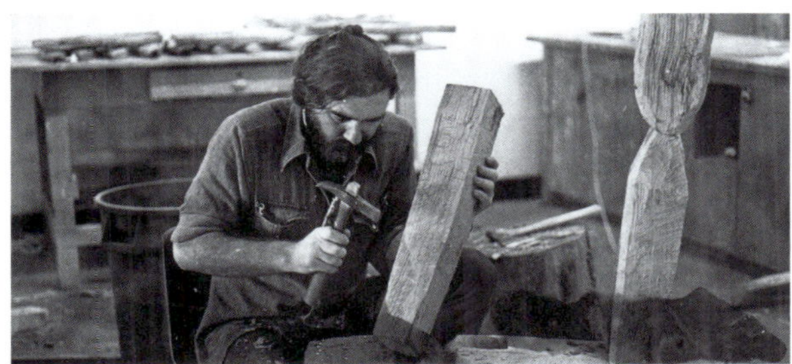

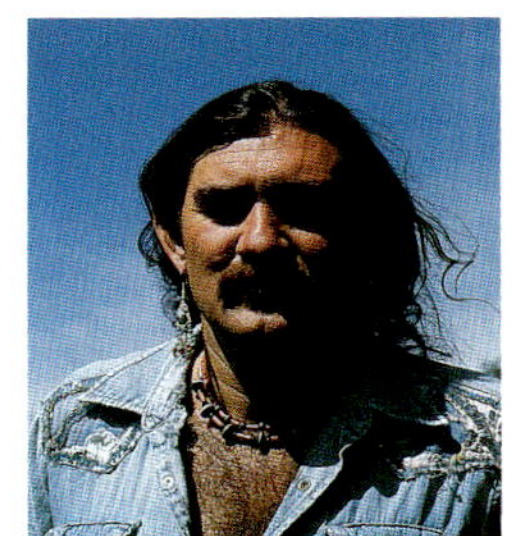

for students as well by being an active, productive artist and being involved in the art community in an even larger context by curating shows and events. This involvement grew to fulfillment at the Lawndale Art Annex of the University of Houston and events that were held at our studio in Splendora throughout the 1980s and early 1990s.

At the time I met James, I was studying psychology and sociology, reflecting on human motivation and behavior, and the structure and development of cities and cultures. Branching out into art history and the studio classes of the art department added another dimension to my education. The capacity to translate knowledge through physical forms and materials, the object becoming a vehicle to communicate feelings and ideas and perceptions of the universe, became increasingly fascinating to me. Over time psychology and art meshed in my sculpture.

When James and I met again, there was the instant flash of recognition of a soul mate, a person who would be in my life for the duration. We launched into an intense adventure of personal exploration and a quest to see our shared visions realized. We searched and found The Place where we could accomplish all these things and invest it with our beings. We sketched and drew plans for architectural structures, some fantasy, some real; made models and eventually built structures of all kinds to fill needs and formed the land to fit our picture; grew gardens and landscaped; walked the woods over and over to discover and enjoy its variety, its lushness, its sense of life in excess, its "wildness" as described by Gary Snyder (in *The Practice of the Wild*), in other words, its sense of freedom. James had grown up primarily in the country and after some years of life in the city was thrilled to return to a place with room to roam with few constraints, a place that could expand to encompass family members and even employees, could be totally formed to fulfill the big picture. I believe that the most important thing that Splendora gave both of us—but particularly James—was a sense of unlimited potential, of unfettered ability to form our environment to our liking and to build and focus on producing art.

There is no overemphasizing the impact of that landscape on our lives and our art. James, of course, could actually sift the woods for materials for sculpture. Ideas flowed from that source or a preconceived idea would be seen in physical form in a treetop or a branch. For me it was an internalizing space under the canopy, a temple-like space, not the dark,

PAGES 16-17
FIGURE 1
James and Charmaine in the woods, Splendora, Texas, 1976

PAGE 18
FIGURE 2
Surls in Splendora house studio, 1980

ABOVE, LEFT TO RIGHT
FIGURE 3
Surls at Sam Houston State College, Huntsville, Texas, 1965

FIGURE 4
Surls at University of Houston sculpture studio working on *Burning Dog*, 1976 (see **FIG. 29**)

FIGURE 5
Surls at Wind River, Taos, New Mexico

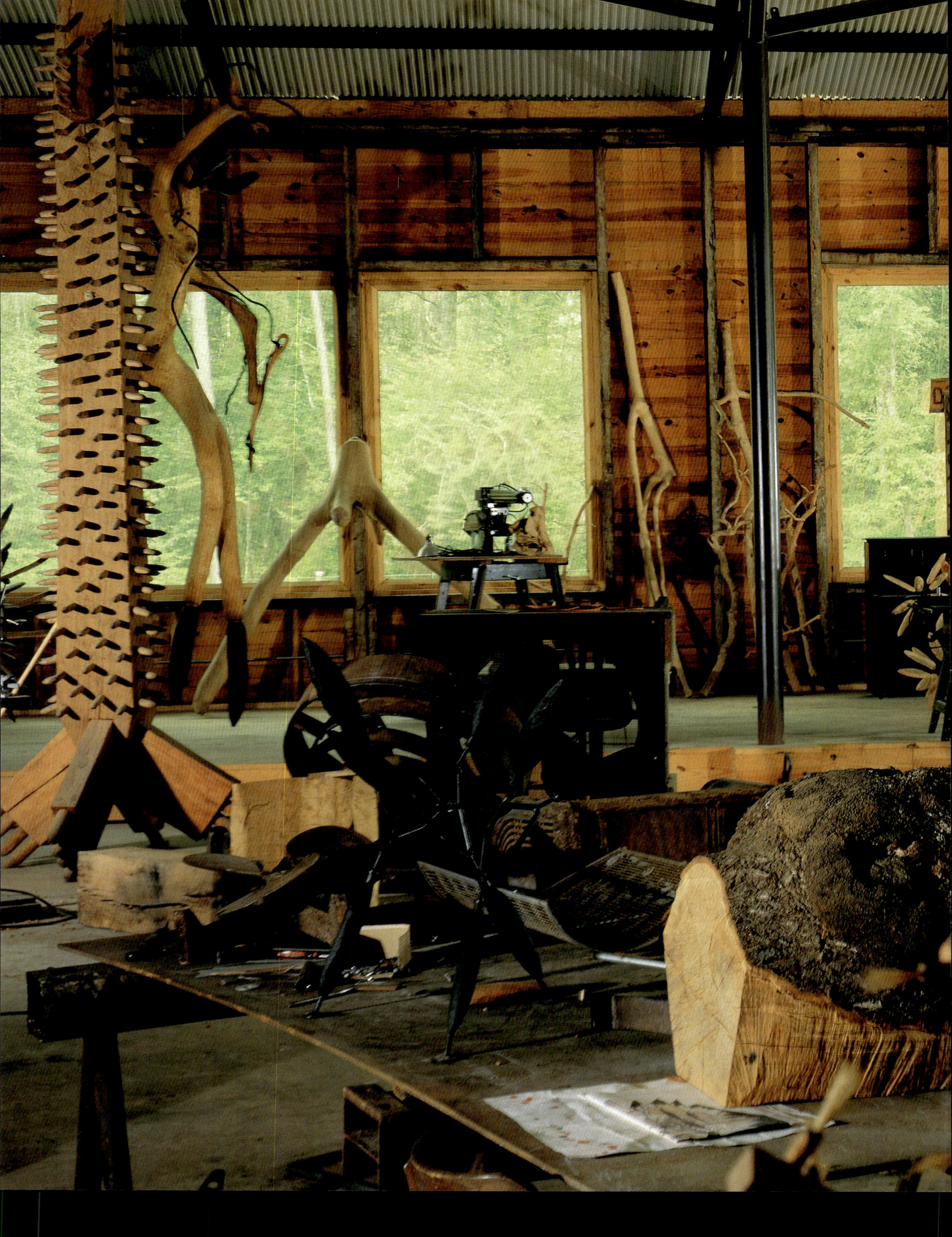

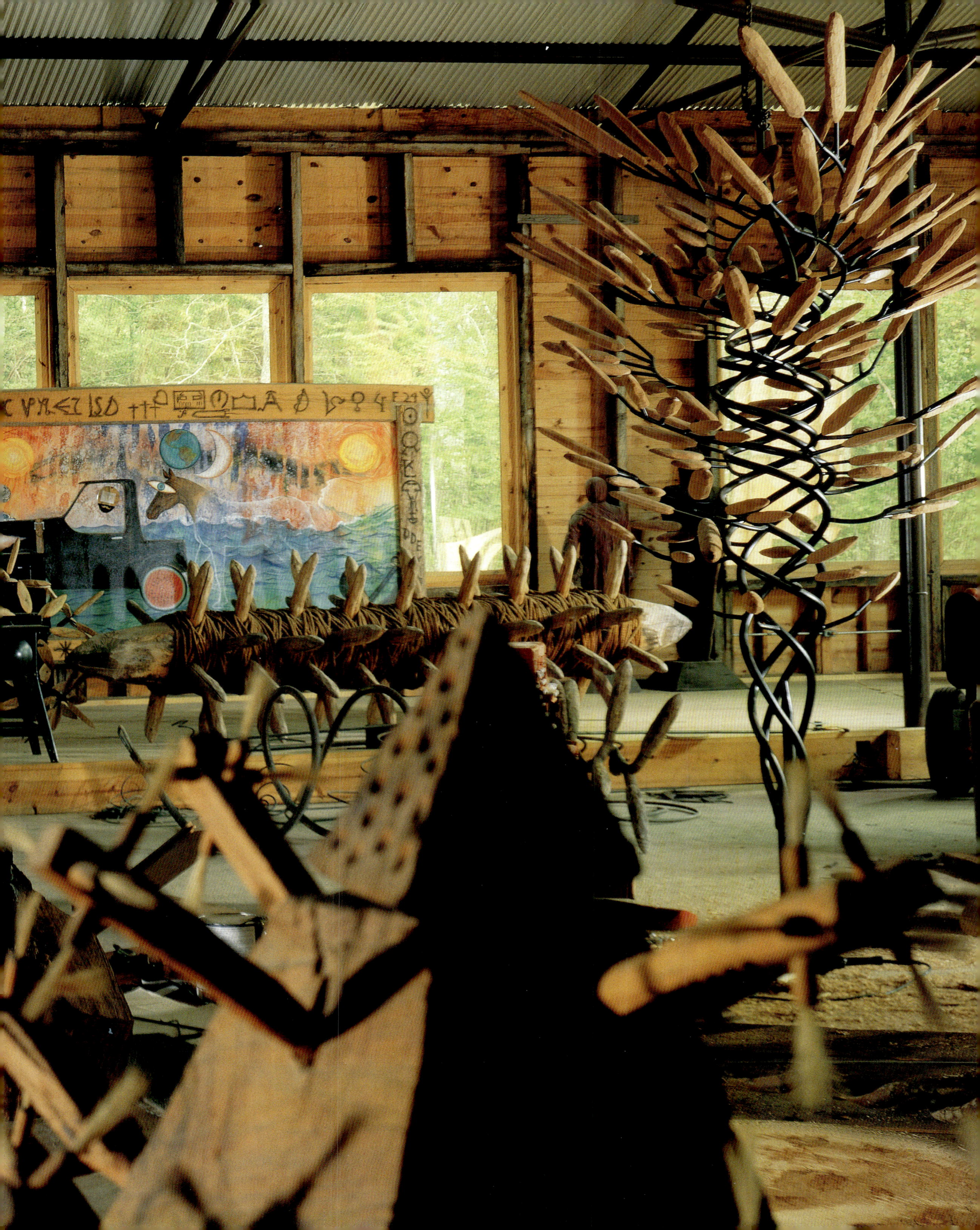

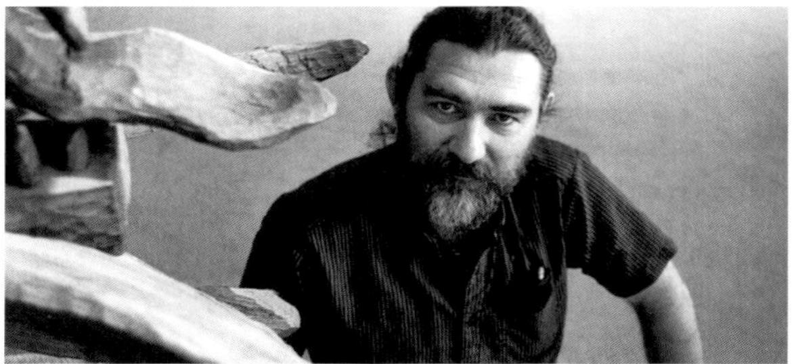

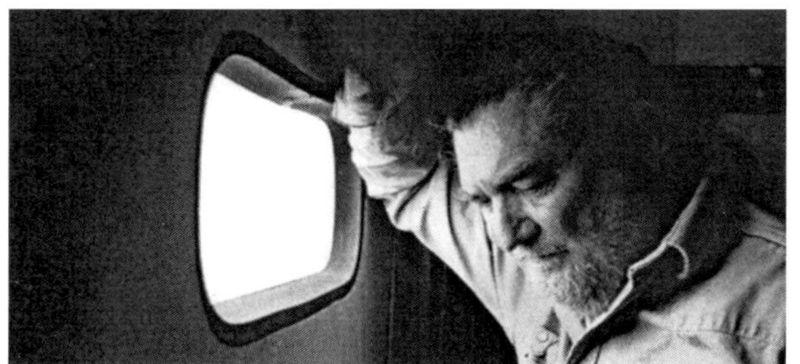

forbidding forest that many see. The hardwood bottomlands of the Big Thicket are one of the discarded jewels of our environment and, like so many other jewels, are simply being trashed. The awareness of life in that almost jungle-like world is tangible: the decay and rot giving way to fruition, to sprouting organic forms, the odors and sounds of different species, the tangles of vines and branches piling up and over into masses that hid and gave shelter to other types of organisms. The profusion and rampant growth were a mirror of James's predilection for abundance and generosity, his more-is-better, full-to-overflowing life philosophy. This geographic area, which is very similar to the native, untrampled lands that were here for the settlers to find, lends itself to a frontiersman style of independent self-sufficiency.

Every summer we built another structure or part of the studio. The studio was a hands-on labor of love, a five-year project for which James and an assistant welded each seam of the twelve-thousand-square-foot structure. The first studio at the house was later demolished to make way for more living space; the second shed studio overflowed with art; and by the time the new studio was complete, it was quickly filled with pieces of enormous scale. A building was constructed to house a print facility, and many, often large-scale, prints emerged. However, the complex man of paradox felt the lure of the city.

Landscape (terrain) and proximity to a cultural center have been the two most important factors in our choices of places to live. In 1976, when we moved from Dallas to Houston, Houston was on the brink of a twenty-year period of boomtown expansion. With the oil and banking industries flourishing and NASA and the implications of the space age huge, there was a sense that anything was possible. What a place for James Surls, who again found this freedom to be the key to unleash his incredible energies and imagination. Not content to teach and build and produce art at a prodigious rate, he launched into a major curatorial effort for the Contemporary Arts Museum in Houston in the interim after Jim Harithas's departure. He reached all across Texas for artists to include in the exhibition *FIRE!* and produced the catalogue.

Support for the arts in Houston grew. Venues for exhibiting, including alternative spaces, and galleries promoting local artists increased, as did the number of artists coming to live in Houston. Artists created alternative places to live and work, exhibit, and perform. It was an incredibly dynamic environment to be in, and it fueled the fires of those involved in creative

PRECEDING PAGES

FIGURE 6
View of artist's studio in Splendora, 1988

LEFT TO RIGHT

FIGURE 7
James Surls with *Burning Dog*, 1984

FIGURE 8
Surls in Silt, Colorado, studio, 2003

FIGURE 9
View of artist's studio in Silt, 2003

endeavors. Lawndale Art Annex became James Surls's next major avenue of exploration. Nothing deterred him in his pursuit of giving students insight into the making and exhibiting of art on a "real" level, of providing opportunities that wouldn't have existed elsewhere. They started off by rebuilding the spaces designated as galleries, repainted, built pedestals, found donors for lighting and materials, and had shows of student work. It progressed to inviting artists from other places in the state, and later around the country, to show work. When this was expanded to include performances of major avant-garde music, theater, dance, lectures, and symposia, sometimes involving construction of massive elements or sets, constantly changing gallery spaces, it was nearing the level of a full-time job. This was a three-year period of extensive involvement, constant activity, and it had taken on a life of its own. A formal entity was formed that continues the life of Lawndale into the future.

James returned to full-time sculpture production, finished the studio, and set out to fill it to capacity, soon adding another work space and entertaining spaces. There were many beautiful and transformative moments and evenings in the studio when people and art came together. There were wonderful musical and dance performances, food extravaganzas, and quiet Sunday mornings of conversation with friends and family.

Family. A hugely important component in James Surls's life and psychological makeup.

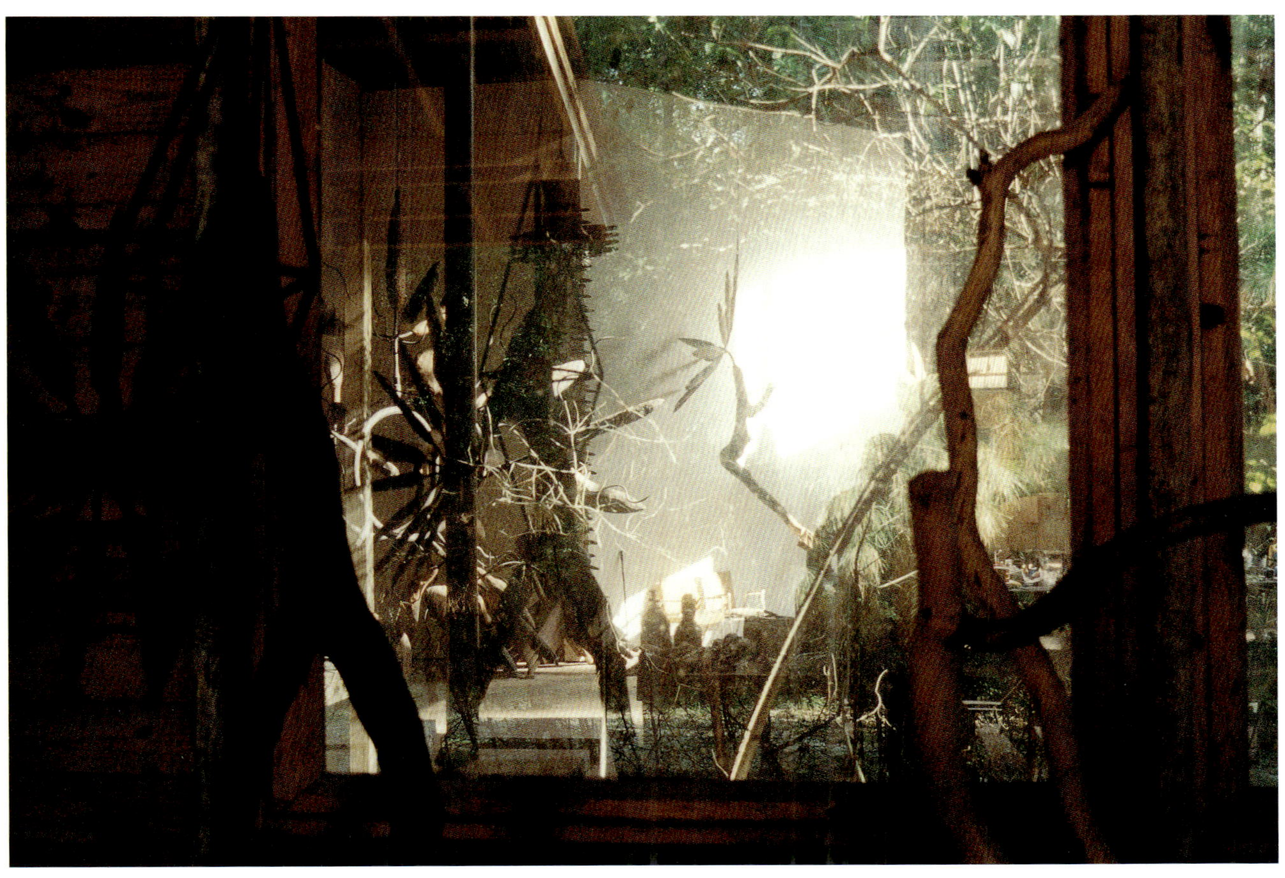

Always primary, always at the top of the list. He has consistently gone to great lengths to secure the well-being of what he calls his "core"—his seven daughters, extended family members, and me.

The move to Colorado in 1997 was earthshaking. Colorado was the only other location we had ever "seen" ourselves as functioning in—and that on a very hypothetical level. We were both teaching at Anderson Ranch in July and after doing some research in the area decided that it was something that could work. The Aspen Valley is antithetical to the area northeast of Houston in every way except that in both places nature is predominant. In Colorado, however, the landscape is preeminent and inspiring in quite a different way. The clarity and distance of the visual field are invigorating. After all the adjustments and resettling, the move has proven very positive and beneficial for all the family. How this translates into changes in visual style or content is not clear. But certainly you would expect to see this new environment reflected in the work.

One other aspect of James Surls and his work that would be essential to integrate into this essay is his boundless imagination. In the best tradition of storyteller and mythmaker, he aggrandizes and adds an amount of fiction to fact to draw us in, tantalize, and absorb us into the weaving of his tales: "Once I saw a spotted woman whose belly was round like a ball" is the title of an early work that seems to be the beginning of a story. Whether the titles are explanatory or just a hint, the sculptures lay out a scenario of adventures and encounters, as well as pilgrimages of the mind onto turf that only the mind can tread. In this, James ventures into areas that some of his favorite artists, the Surrealists, René Magritte in particular, favored. As when Magritte paints a boulder in midair or men with briefcases lifting off into the sky, there are Surls pieces that defy gravity, that appear to be floating in opposition to natural laws. When disparate images or objects are placed where they don't seem to belong, when a gun looks like a wall or a flower is black and emerging from an ominous black being, this is unfamiliar territory and disturbs preconceptions. Suspension of disbelief is asked for, frequently one is taken by surprise, sometimes we look in awe. Occasionally there is a lyrical piece that flows smoothly and in harmony, or in symmetry. The drawings go even further into this "mind zone" where the unexpected is to be expected, where skeletons walk, eyes emerge from hands, diamonds and crystals are as large as heads and fly through the atmosphere. It's an internal space where anything goes, all is possible, so of course James Surls is there.

FIGURE 10, OPPOSITE
James Surls in Silt, Colorado, studio, 2003

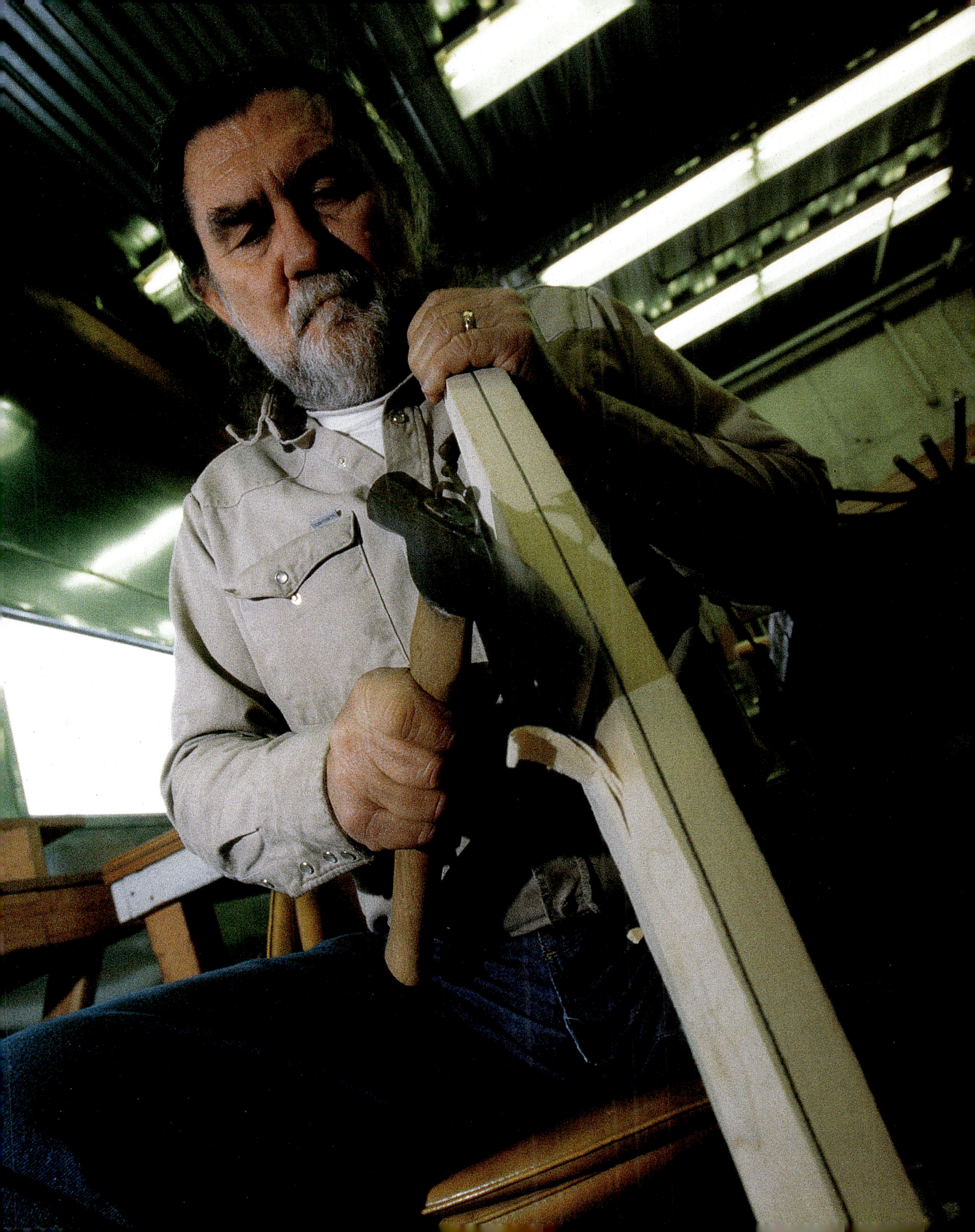

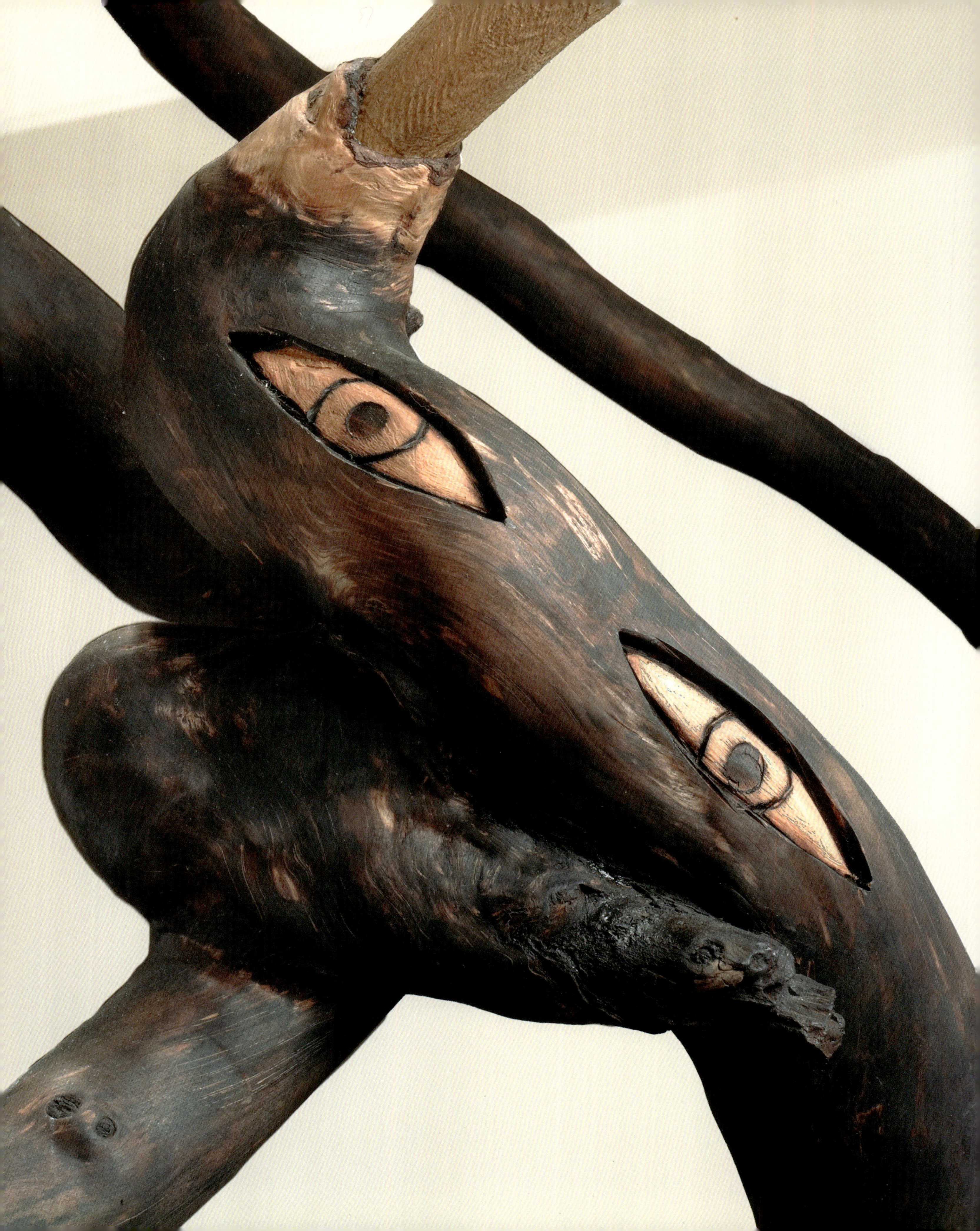

MARK THISTLETHWAITE

An Art of the Eye and the I

For more than thirty years, James Surls has been carving—literally and figuratively—a niche for himself in the history of American art. He has embodied the modernist ideals of originality and invention, and of pushing his art continually forward. His art is uniquely and recognizably his own; a Surls is a Surls, and no one else's. His art has been described as ritualistic, totemic, animistic, surrealistic, primitivistic, romantic, and mystic. He has been called a shaman, magician, poet with an axe, and "Lone Star Michelangelo."[1] He creates art that is intensely personal but that seeks universality. He sees with his eye; he looks into his I (self). He brings fields of flowers into being by hacking, peeling, chiseling, carving, rasping, burning, oiling, and rubbing pieces of wood. He strives to be avant-garde yet subscribes to the belief that art tells a story. His art is accessible and engaging, complex and paradoxical, not unlike the artist himself. James Surls, in sum, is an American original.

James Surls and his art loomed large in the Texas art world of the last quarter of the twentieth century. Without exaggeration, it is safe to say that anyone—inside and outside the state—reflecting on contemporary Texas art would immediately think of the work of James Surls. In 1991 he was celebrated as "Texas Artist of the Year" and was elevated to the status of legend in 1993. Ever since 1984, when an exhibition at the Dallas Museum of Art surveyed ten years of his work, art writers have unanimously hailed him as the state's preeminent living artist. He and his wife, the artist Charmaine Locke, became the First Couple of Texas art, as they not only created and exhibited art but also actively advocated and promoted the importance of the arts in a variety of ways and venues. Their home, with its extraordinary twelve-thousand-square-foot studio spaces in the East Texas Piney Woods town of Splendora (FIG. 12), attained mythic dimensions as the idyllic physical, psychological, and creative epicenter of their lives and art, and, consequently, of the Texas

FIGURE 11, OPPOSITE
All in the Wind (detail), 1999 (PL. 3).

art world. For years, Surls personified Texas art and defiantly proved an artist could make a career outside New York City. He was so rooted in Texas that it came as a shock in 1998 to learn that he, in his words, "had gone over the mountain" to settle in Aspen Valley, Colorado.[2] Despite the move, Surls still regards himself as a Texas artist as part of his birthright, and many people in the state and across the nation, not realizing he resides in Colorado, still consider him "the" contemporary Texas artist. However, he does live in Colorado, and his environment, which has always been an essential source for conjuring his art, has changed significantly.

The opportunity to engage with his new Colorado-produced artwork and to evaluate how (or if) it differs from the art of his Texas years presented itself in early 2003, with the opening of the exhibition *In the Meadows* at Southern Methodist University's Meadows Museum in Dallas (FIG. 13). Intended to feature works executed during the five years since Surls settled in Colorado, the exhibition inspired the artist to create several large pieces specifically for the museum's galleries and plaza. Surls, who has always had a penchant for working large—"I love to make big art"—took advantage of the museum's grand, open spaces to realize this ambition. Besides fulfilling his innate desire to work on a large scale, the monumental sculptures he specially fabricated for the exhibition were clearly meant to stun viewers. From the exhibition's inception, Surls had planned to offer museum visitors a "jaw-dropping experience" that would induce a state of "bewildered wonderment." Through a thoughtful installation of a wide range of works (sculptures, maquettes, drawings, and prints), Surls achieved his goal.

In the Meadows not only provided the occasion to view recent works by the artist but was also a homecoming of sorts for him. He was back in Texas and back at SMU, where he had taught in the early 1970s. The exhibition also was the impetus for this essay, which chronicles the arc of the artist's career to this point, by offering an overview of his art, its critical reception, and a consideration of the impact the move to Colorado has had on his work.

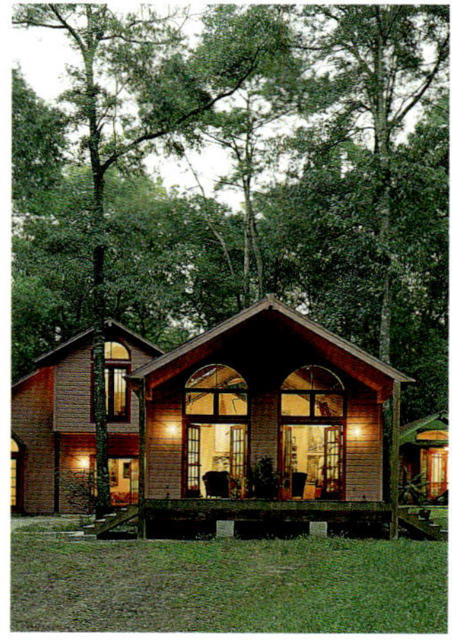

FIGURE 12
View of Charmaine and James's home, Splendora, Texas

A Being of the Woods Goes over the Mountain

James Surls's awareness of history, family, and place has fundamentally conditioned his art and his sense of himself. Thus, Surls's art must be identified with his life. Because Surls believes art is "a slice of you," he has continually characterized his art as self-portraiture. Given this stance, it is neither surprising nor a sign of artistic egotism to discover that the titles of more than forty of Surls's artworks begin with the word "Me." To separate Surls from his art, which he sees as embodying a search for the self, simply cannot be done.

James Surls was born in Terrell, Texas, in 1943, and grew up in and around Malakoff, in the northeast wooded region of the state. This forested land proved essential to his identity and, ultimately, to his art. Years later, he would look back on his happy childhood and refer to himself as "a Being of the Woods."[3] Tramping in the forests around his family's farm

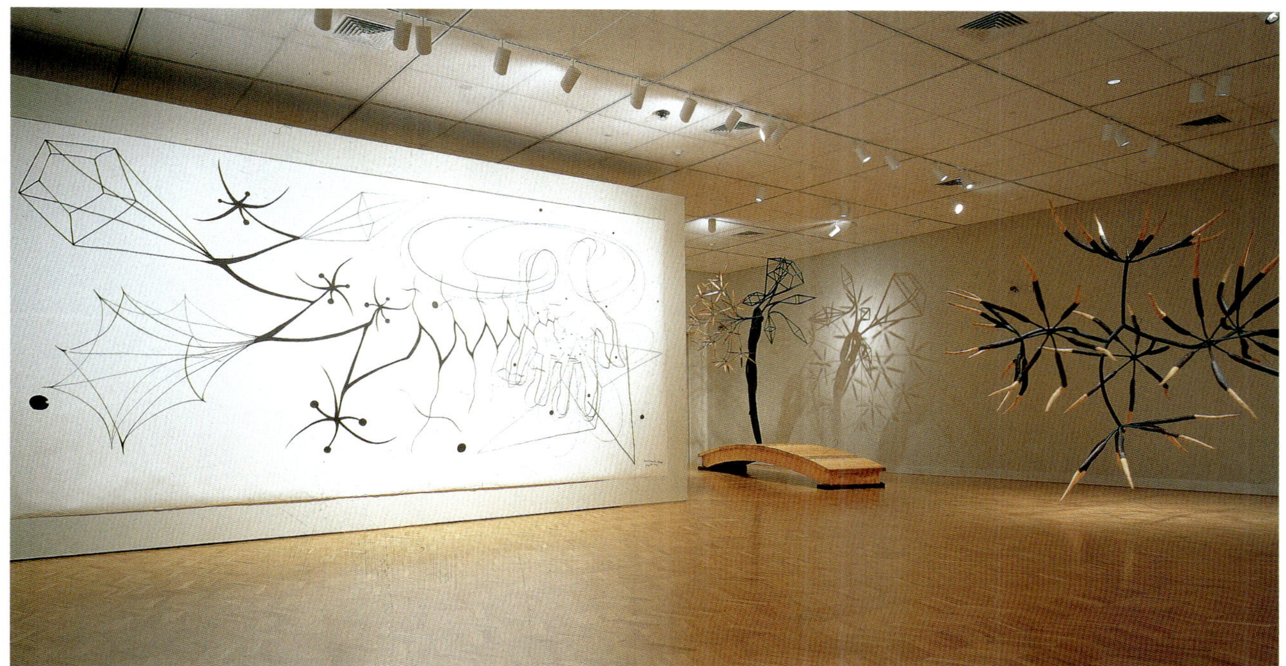

and hacking away at trees prompted him and his older brother Larry to inscribe proudly on the gate to their house: "Home of the Bushwhackers." Their father, Joe, a carpenter, built the house in which the boys grew up. Joe's strong work ethic and skills in construction led his sons to believe that there was no kind of structure that their father could not figure out how to build. This admiration for his father shaped the mature artist's own can-do attitude: "I operate under the premise that all things are possible. . . . I believe if you can think of it to do, then you can do it."[4] While his father instilled in his son the virtues of hard work and good craft, and provided an environment of freedom in which anything seemed possible, Surls's mother, Martha Sebastian, who is an artist and writer, engendered in him a sense of creativity. She allowed him the opportunity to "exercise his imagination." When not chopping wood, splitting fence posts, and building corrals, barns, and bridges, the boy constructed imaginative wooden toys, little wagons, and tree houses. As a child, James Surls grew up in a place literally shaped by wood.

After graduating from Malakoff High School in 1961, Surls enrolled in Henderson County Junior College in Athens, Texas. He left the school in 1963, traveled to California, sold cars, and attended San Diego State University. Soon, however, he returned to Texas to take classes at Sam Houston State University in Huntsville. To this point in his college career, most of his courses had been in physical education, history, and anthropology; he had never taken an art course. When enrolling at SHSU he learned that he needed to declare a major. As Surls has often recounted, he picked up the course catalogue, turned

FIGURE 13
Interior installation view of the 2003 exhibition *In the Meadows*. Shown left to right: *Me, God, Evolution, Love, Relationship and you* (**PL. 48**), *Bridge & Needle* (**PL. 9**), *Seven and Seven Flower* (**PL. 1**)

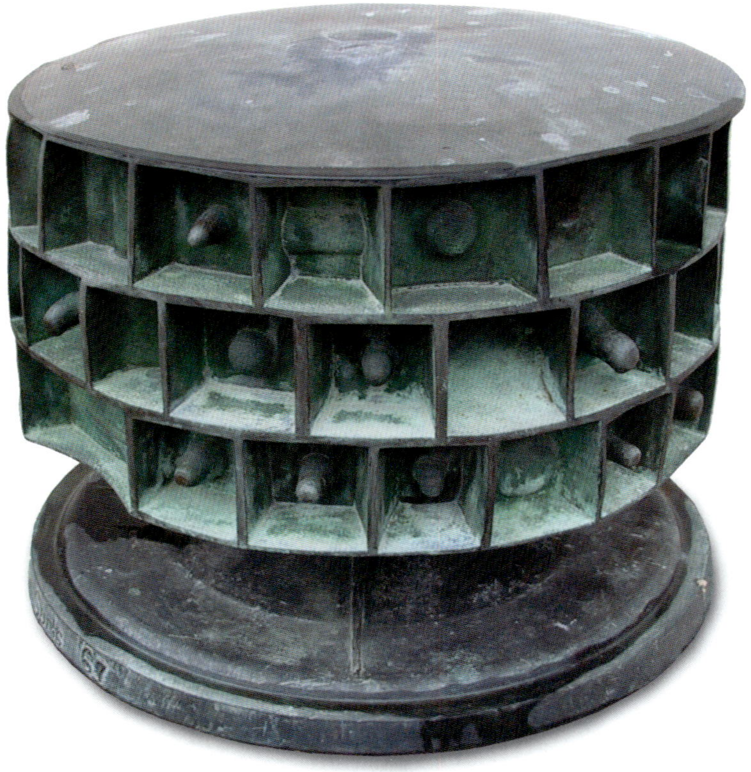

to the first page, looked under "A," saw the art listings, and signed up. As he walked to the art department, he came across the sculptor Charles Pebworth carving an image out of a log. Seeing this "rekindled childhood freedom and an exhilarating force of self-expression."[5] This was a Eureka! moment for Surls and the beginning of his life in art.

In addition to studying sculpture, Surls enrolled in painting classes. His abstract paintings showed the ongoing influence of Abstract Expressionism, which, despite the advent of Pop art and Minimalism, was still the dominant force on young artists outside New York and Los Angeles. However, Surls's colorful, expressionistic manner was initially informed more by Mexican art than by the New York School. One summer Surls attended a painting class in Mexico. While there, he saw José Clemente Orozco's 1938–39 man of fire fresco in the dome of the Hospicio Cabañas, Guadalajara. The powerful swirling, almost spiraling forms greatly affected him, and he began to emulate Orozco's style by including figurative elements in his compositions. While he admired the heroic vitality of the Abstract Expressionists, especially the action paintings of Willem de Kooning, Surls maintains that he knew of Orozco's expressionism before he was acquainted with that of de Kooning.

In 1967, a year after graduating from Sam Houston State University, Surls enrolled in the prestigious graduate program of the Cranbrook Academy of Art in Bloomfield Hills, Michigan. This was an artistic environment a world apart from that of Huntsville. Concentrating on sculpture, Surls produced abstract works in bronze, cast steel, and cast aluminum,

FIGURE 14
Untitled, 1967
Bronze
18 x 23 ½ x 23 ½
University Art Collection, Southern Methodist University, Dallas, Texas.

FIGURE 15
Art, 1971
Elm
37 ½ x 19 x 18
Arkansas Arts Center Foundation. Purchase: 14th Annual Delta Art Exhibition, 1971.

including the largest single-casting sculpture produced at the school to that time (FIG. 14). These sculptures were more formally complex than the reductive mode of Minimalist art, and sometimes Surls incorporated elements suggestive of figures. Overall, his pieces were more abstract than representational. Like that of many students, Surls's art reflected the stylistic qualities and artistic concerns of his teachers. Much of the art he produced at Cranbrook followed the modernist, machinelike aesthetic of his primary professor, Julius Schmidt, who headed the school's sculpture department. Schmidt's work had received national recognition, especially after it appeared in the historically significant *Sixteen Americans* exhibition at the Museum of Modern Art in New York (1959), a show that also featured works by Jasper Johns, Ellsworth Kelly, Alfred Leslie, Louise Nevelson, Robert Rauschenberg, and Frank Stella. Schmidt, whose work ethic matched that of Surls's father, was committed to the technique of casting metal, and, consequently, Surls found himself enthralled with process more than with concept or subject matter. The action of making art commanded attention, rather than questioning why the art was being made and what it meant.

By the time he received his master of fine arts degree in 1969, however, Surls's attitude had altered dramatically and he now questioned the validity and purpose of his work, and even what it meant to be an artist. "I was just making art that sat there and looked good. . . . It's a stark thing when all of a sudden you don't believe in what you've been doing for years."[6] His change in attitude coincided with a shift occurring in contemporary sculpture: artists were reacting to the impersonal formalism, factory-fabrication of Minimal art by producing work more obviously personal, more visceral in engaging the materiality of sculpture, and seemingly more casual in technique. Sculptures by Louise Bourgeois, Lynda Benglis, and Eva Hesse, in particular, challenged the dominance of Minimalism. For Surls, however, doubts about his work and himself as an artist were so strong that he stopped making art.

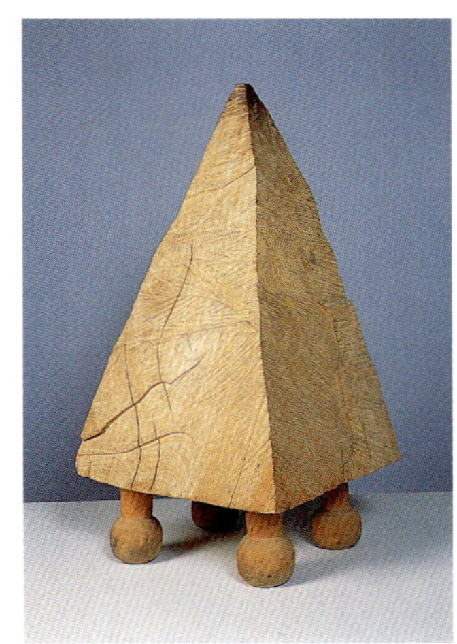

During this two-year hiatus, Surls worked in a foundry in Buffalo, on pipelines in Louisiana, and in a welding shop in Dallas. He also became an instructor at Southern Methodist University, where he was to teach until 1975. At SMU, he tentatively returned to making sculpture and moved from manipulating metal to working in wood. In 1971 he produced a "beaten, banged and hammered" piece titled *Art* (FIG. 15). He also used a chain saw for the first time. Slightly over three feet high, the rough-hewn elongated pyramidal sculpture, elevated by four small, relatively delicate ball feet, seems a crude, randomly found object rather than an example of fine art. However, its title announces boldly, and humorously, that this object is indeed "art." In a significant way, *Art* also announced Surls's renewed and reconceived commitment to making sculpture.

Surls regards *Art* as "the beginning of it"—"it" being his own visual alphabet. The sculpture, he says, could have just as easily been titled *A*, because it served as the initial component in his goal of developing a visual alphabet. He needed this system to build a language to convey what he came to regard as a fundamental attribute of a work of art: its message. "Art with no message is not art," declared the artist at the end of the 1970s.[7] One consistent message conveyed in Surls's art is his steadfast belief in paradox—"everything having its other side"—as the basic condition of life.[8]

Art's form refers, paradoxically, to both the human-made and the natural. Its shape suggests ancient pyramids with their religious-ritual associations, and *Art* is the genesis for the house, which will become an integral symbol in Surls's visual alphabet. *Art* refers to the natural, by approximating a crystal. This form and its permutations as a diamond and prism, like the house, will become essential elements in Surls's visual alphabet and appear in great numbers in *In the Meadows*. Each of *Art*'s four triangular sides can be regarded as a delta, which also signifies both the natural—a river delta, as well as a position in the structure of an organic molecule—and the human-made—the fourth letter of the Greek alphabet. In addition, the triangular shape occurs in numerous cultures throughout history as carrying symbolic meanings, including divinity and the sacredness of the number three. Surls has long been fascinated by the power of numbers; for example, he describes "three" as "a very heavy-duty number" and speaks of the "connection of three" to centering, balancing, and building things.

The triangle-delta configuration that delineates each of *Art*'s facets may be the ancient source, as Surls well knew, for the alphabet letter A. *Art* is, once again, the A of Surls's visual alphabet. But if *Art* represents A, what is B? This question proved difficult for the artist to answer, and while *Art* signaled the end to his hiatus from art making, Surls's renewed art production did not begin in earnest for another year. Three events occurred in 1972 that contributed to pushing him forward. One was Buckminster Fuller's visit to the SMU campus. Surls found Fuller's intellectual breadth and his "amazing level of consciousness" to be exhilarating and inspiring. Through his profound insights, Fuller personified the Romantic poet-artist William Blake's dictum: talent thinks, genius sees. Another event affecting Surls was viewing a Lucas Samaras exhibition at the Whitney Museum of American Art in New York. Samaras exploited a variety of materials in his sculptural works, including yarn, and he often encrusted his forms (sometimes books and boxes) with sharp objects like pencils, pins, nails, and razor blades. Combining the personal, the eccentric, the beautiful, and the disturbing, Samaras's art has never fit comfortably into any stylistic category. The rugged, raw, and violent qualities of his art appealed to Surls, as did Samaras's ability to make such tough work "look so easy." But what really struck Surls about Samaras's art was the importance of concept that he felt each piece conveyed. This awareness of concept was important for Surls at the time he was abandoning his earlier emphasis on process and technique. A third, and ultimately the most significant, event of 1972 was his becoming acquainted with Charmaine Locke, an SMU student with a major in psychology and a minor in art who was enrolled in one of his courses. Surls refers to their meeting as the catalyst for setting in motion a huge transition in his life and art by revealing to him a realm of new possibilities through introspective analysis. To this self-described macho guy and product of the "Texas patriarchal system," Locke brought an entirely "different way of looking at things." He tapped into, and began to express in his art, unexplored aspects of his feelings and experiences. Rejuvenated by this relationship and alternative way of thinking, Surls made the final break from fixating on the process of art making to concerning himself with art's content. The question "What does the work of art mean?" now assumed primary importance for him. To answer the question of a work's meaning, Surls realized that he needed a deeper sense of himself. This led him to engage in what might be called memory work.

Surls delved into memories of his East Texas childhood, trying to go as far back as he could. One of his earliest recollections—concerning an experience that occurred when he was five and his older brother was seven—has been recounted in so many interviews with the artist and writings about his art that it has taken on the character of an origin myth. Deciding one day to chop down a tree, the two boys took a hatchet from their father's toolbox and set out to find among the many trees on the family's property an appropriate one to cut. They came across an oak that was about as big around as the two of them together could reach. The boys spent the day taking turns hacking away at what seemed to them to be "the biggest tree on the planet." After finally felling the tree, the young "bushwhackers" returned home, where they encountered their father. Rather than being angry at them for taking something from his toolbox or putting themselves in harm's way or destroying a tree, Joe Surls praised their enterprise and appreciated the wood for its potential as a corner post for a turkey pen. It is hard not to perceive this event as a twentieth-century version of Parson Weems's fable of the six-year-old George Washington being confronted by his father after cutting down a cherry tree. In both stories, a foundational attribute of the child's character—telling the truth, for Washington; creating something out of the environment, for Surls—received recognition and praise. For Surls, the memory of the incident reminded him of the freedom he had enjoyed as a child playing and working in the woods.

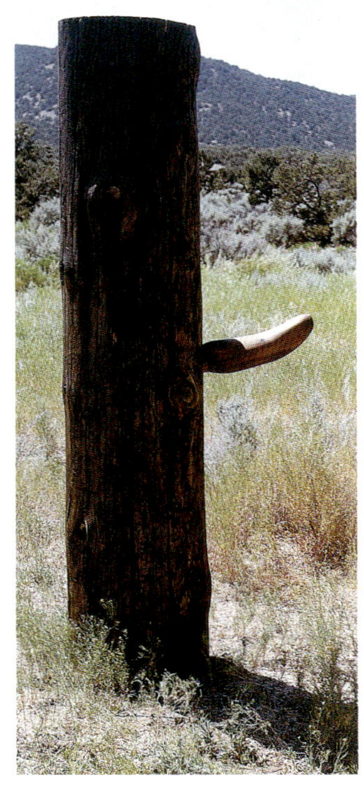

FIGURE 16
Julian's Dream, 1973
Pine, bois d' arc
90 x 18 x 36

The positive nature of this memory, along with the impact of seeing Lucas Samaras's art, beholding the genius of Buckminster Fuller, and being transformed by his relationship with Charmaine Locke, reenergized Surls's interest in making sculpture. Picking up where he left off with *Art*, Surls began carving wood with a chain saw to produce art that was figural, narrative, and personal. Examples of his efforts first emerged in the summer of 1973, when he was in Taos teaching an art class. Fueled by what he calls his first "imbued moment," Surls quickly produced a half dozen wooden sculptures, including a seminal work, *Julian's Dream* (FIG. 16).

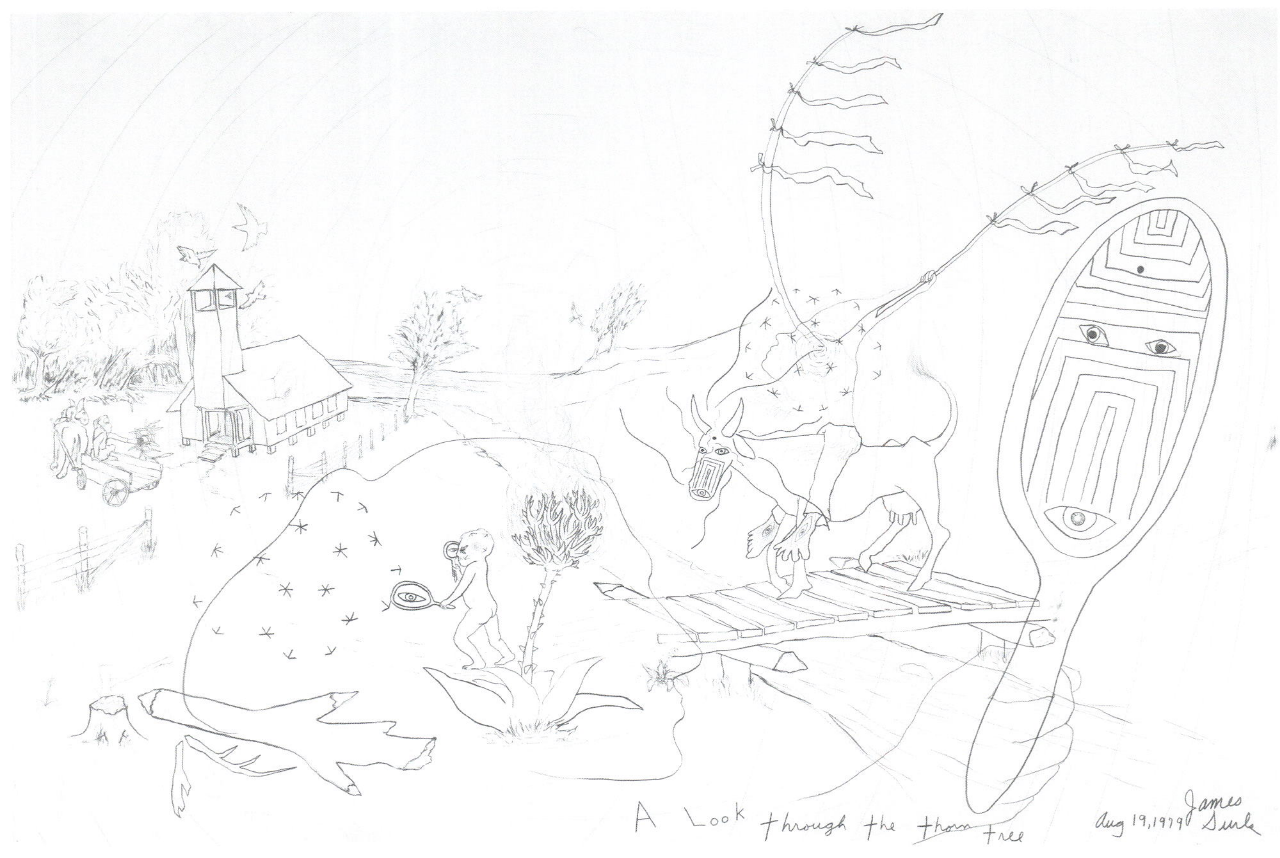

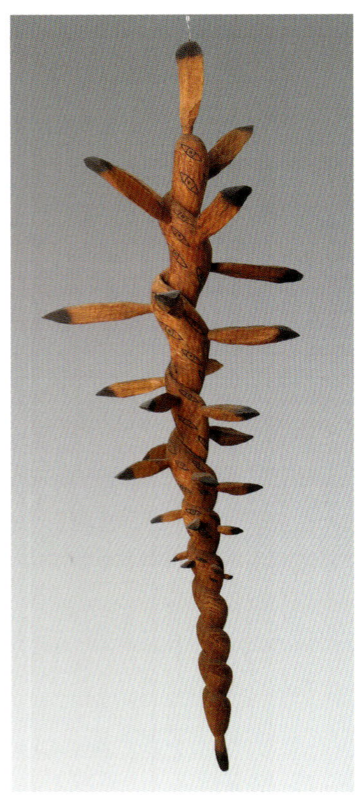

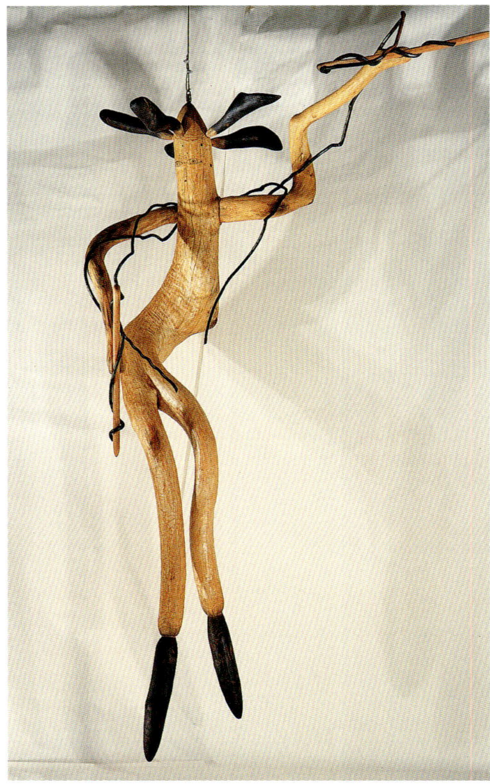

TOP LEFT COUNTER CLOCKWISE

FIGURE 17
A Look through the Thorn Tree, 1979
Graphite on paper
29 x 42

FIGURE 18
A Look through the Thorn Tree, 1979
Pine, oak
98 x 31 x 31

FIGURE 19
Woods Angel, 1984
Pine, rattan
175 x 98 x 48
South Texas Institute for the Arts.
Purchase funded by Sondra and Celso Gonzales-Falla and Harris A. Kaffie.

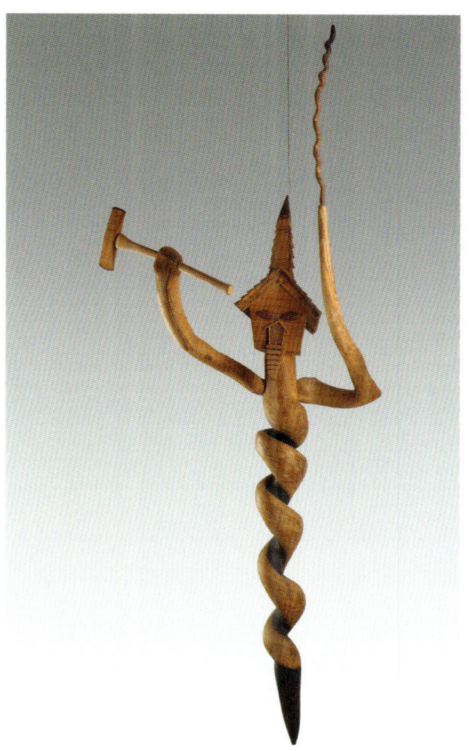

The seven-and-a-half-foot-tall log with its erect phallic form expresses what the artist felt to be the life of the log. *Julian's Dream* is the first of Surls's works to convey an animistic sensibility, a quality that art critics and writers have continually associated with his art, especially that of the later 1970s and throughout the 1980s **(FIGS. 17-19)**. Surls was able to pull sculptural forms from the inner life of a tree, infusing them with a distinctive vitality. The resulting sculptures resembled spirits—sometimes whimsical, at other times malevolent—that had been lodged in the wood's natural configurations. Surls seemed to possess an almost magical ability to see into nature and bring what he saw to life. This vision-insight, as exemplified first in *Julian's Dream*, centers on the "eroticism of conjuring."

To conjure is to cast a spell and to summon or produce by magic. The word describes the heightened, stimulating, sensuous process by which Surls mines his memory and imagination and "pulls" from his environment, in order to bring something into tangible reality. Surls embraces the magical and visionary aspects of conjuring while recognizing the distance between the immediacy and clarity of conjuring and the labor needed to transform the vision into a real, palpable object without losing any of the magic. "It's the puff I'm after. The hocus-pocus the Merlin types used to produce. I love it that they could wave a wand and from a flash of light and a puff of smoke would appear an object. I make objects. It takes so long. It would take me a lifetime just to build what I can dream in one day."[9] A later work, *Me, the Axe and the Wand* **(FIG. 20)**, specifically symbolizes Surls's

FIGURE 20
Me the Axe and the Wand, 1982
Pine, mahogany, oak
125 ½ x 44 x 26

desire to be Merlin, with the axe representing the physicality of the process and the wand, the conjuring part. The squiggly wood of the wand resembles a spark of energy (like a lightning bolt) and, in its blackened state (from having been burned), smoke. Like much of his art, *Me, the Axe and the Wand* is ingrained with humor and playfulness: a church ironically forms the head of the conjurer, with the steeple as the magician's pointed hat and its steps as his beard.

Conjuring for Surls is filled with feeling, and though it is obviously allied to rituals and ceremonies involving shamans and magicians, conjuring can also be thought of as a part of the Romantic movement of the late eighteenth and early nineteenth centuries. For William Wordsworth (a poet Surls holds in high regard), a distinguishing feature of the poet was the ability to conjure up in himself passions.[10] Surls's juxtaposition of the immediate "puff" of conjuring to the time required to make actual objects recalls, in a general way, Wordsworth's definition of poetry as the spontaneous overflowing of powerful feelings based on emotion recollected in tranquility. Surls, who writes poetry and has collaborated with poets, might be called a Romantic modernist, because of his focus on the self, nature, feeling, and imagination.

Another word for conjuring may be dreaming. The title *Julian's Dream* refers to Surls's young friend at the time, Julian Schnabel, who impressed Surls with his enthusiasm for dreaming large. The title also suits the sculpture's place of origin—New Mexico, Land of Enchantment. Surls returned to the state the following summer (1974), and the openness of the landscape inspired him to create a work of performance art. Following the Happenings and Fluxus actions of the 1960s, with the artists' efforts to redefine art by incorporating time, movement, and space and their own bodies into the artwork, performance art often took on ritualistic dimensions. In *Five Minutes of Blue in Wind River* (see FRONTISPIECE 1), Surls assumed the attitude of a shaman as he danced through the Kit Carson State Park while holding two long aspen poles embellished with fluttering strips of blue and yellow cloth.

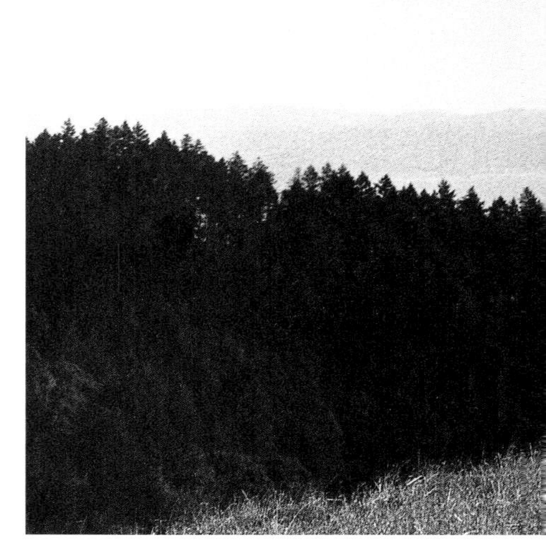

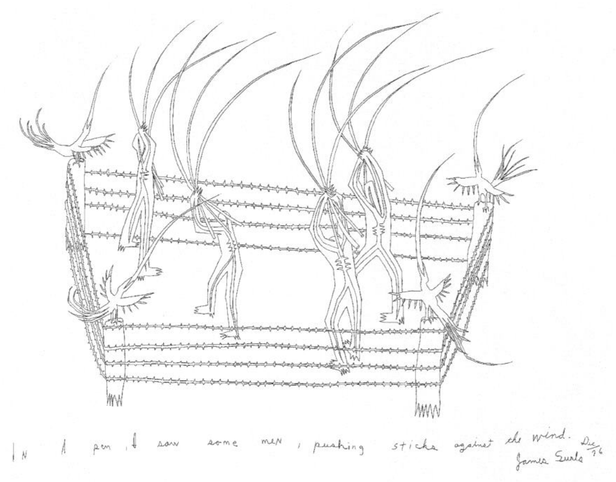

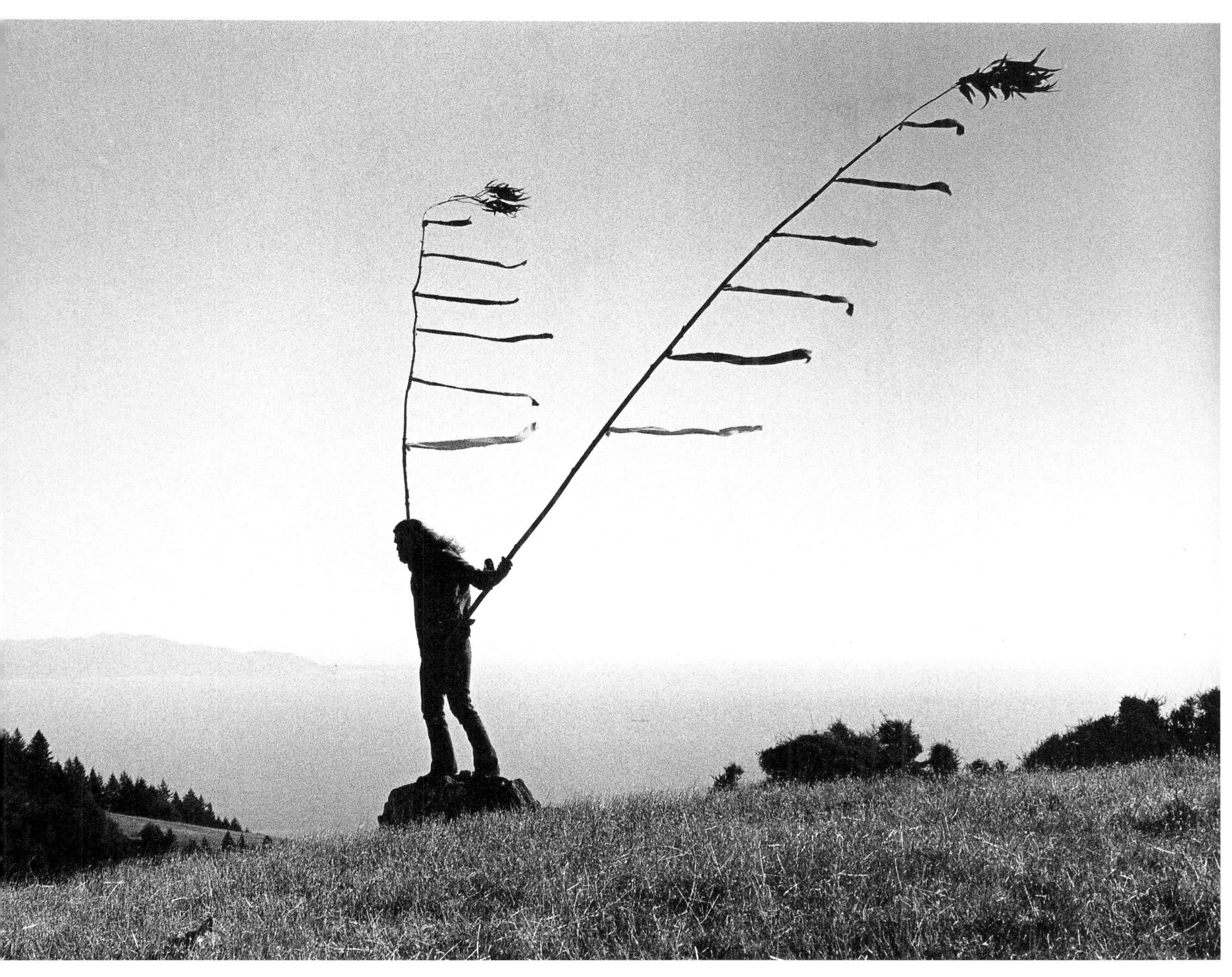

FIGURE 21
In a Pen, I saw some men pushing sticks against the wind, 1976
Graphite on paper
22 x 30
Collection of Susanne Ghez

FIGURE 22
California Dance, 1976

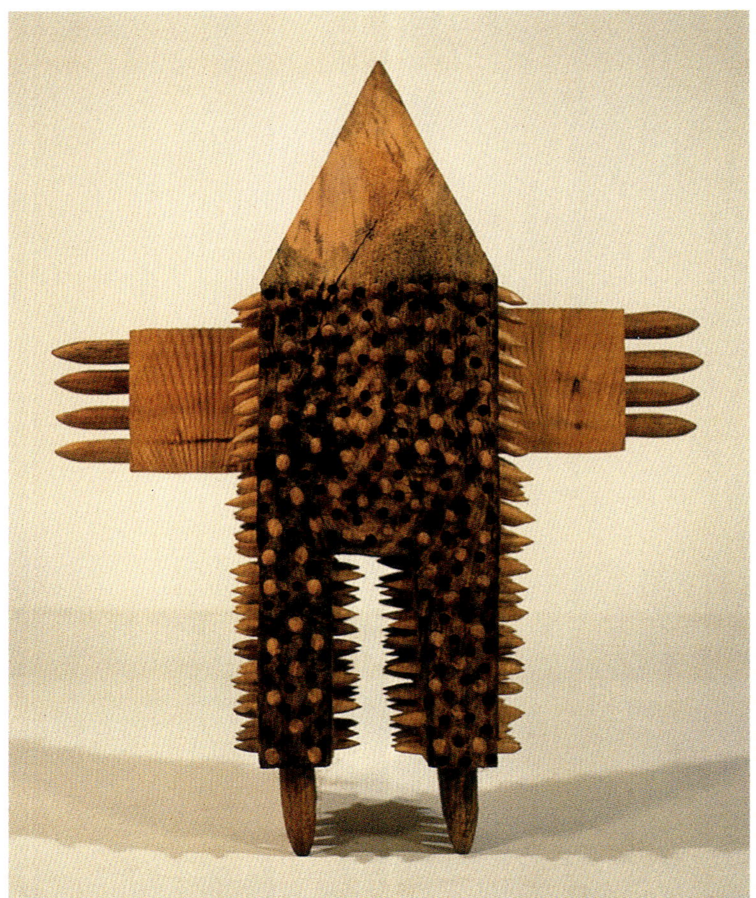

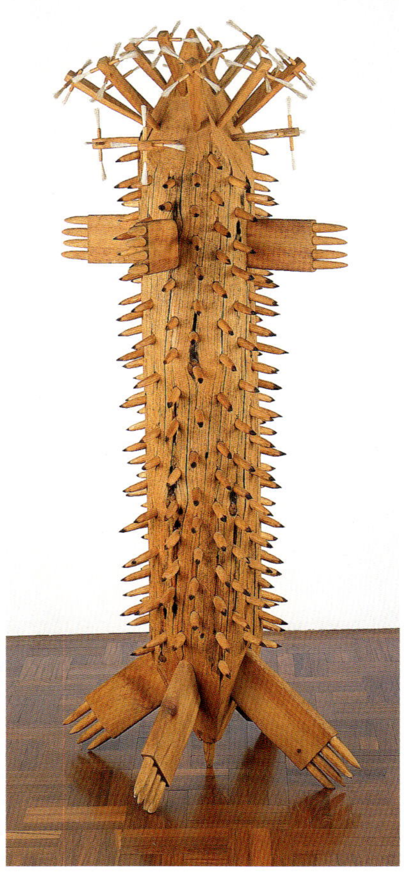

He embodied and expressed the dynamics of a bird in flight. The Wind River piece, like all of Surls's work, contained a personal dimension. As a boy living on a farm, Surls had herded turkeys into their pen by prodding and guiding them with long sticks. He produced a drawing in 1976 titled *In a Pen, I saw some men, pushing sticks against the wind* (FIG. 21), which referenced both his childhood memory and the New Mexico performance piece.

Five Minutes of Blue in Wind River and a similar action, *California Dance* of 1976 (FIG. 22), which Surls performed in Northern California overlooking the Pacific Ocean, dramatically attest to his desire to work directly and personally in and with nature. This passionate immersion in nature, first manifested in *Julian's Dream*, has informed Surls's art throughout his career. "I belong, front-and-center, to the American landscape," the artist affirmed in 1997.[11] This declaration of attachment to the land echoes Romantic sentiments expressed by American artists from the nineteenth-century landscapist Thomas Cole ("We are still in Eden") to the twentieth-century modernist Jackson Pollock ("I am nature").

Surls's second trip to New Mexico particularly energized him, and the year 1974 became

LEFT TO RIGHT

FIGURE 23
Eagle Man, 1974
Pine, maple
36 x 30 x 12
Collection of Gisela-Heidi and Juergen Strunck, Southlake, Texas.

FIGURE 24
High Flying Man, 1974
Pine, hog hair, oak
79 ½ x 34 x 33
Collection of the Modern Art Museum of Fort Worth. Museum purchase, The Benjamin J. Tillar Memorial Trust.

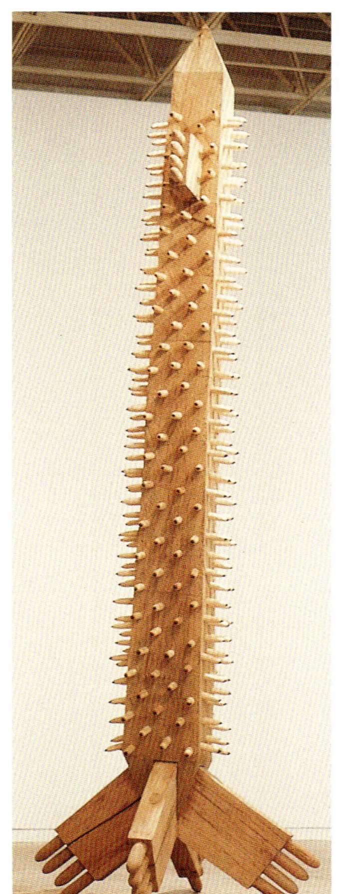

FIGURE 25
High Man Coming to See, 1974
Oak, maple
204 x 48 x 48

a "high-powered year," as he produced a great deal of work, including *Eagle Man* **(FIG. 23)**, *Eagle Woman*, *High Flying Man* **(FIG. 24)**, and *High Man Coming to See* **(FIG. 25)**. Using a chain saw, Surls sculpted numerous symmetrical figures, their arms tautly extended. Bristles of hog hair and pointed sticks radiate out of (or are pierced into) the forms. These add a dynamic energy and sense of violence to the pieces; either way, the attraction to touch, and the danger of touching, the sculptures is compelling. The figures' outstretched gesture provokes many readings, including flight, reaching out to gather in, proffering an embrace, signaling a warning, proclaiming innocence through openness, and symbolizing religion, through the cross-crucifixion-like configuration. The figures are geometric, their heads derived from the pyramidal form first seen in *Art*; Surls employs his A to expand his visual language with the 1974 figures. The sculptures are abstract, but this is not a description that Surls cares for. He regards the notion of abstraction as fundamentally problematic and declares he does not believe in abstraction because it implies that if something is not recognizable it is not real. He finds it impossible to conceive of anything not being real. Because he grounds his art in the reality of his life and environment, he perceives his work as absolutely tied to reality and in no way an exercise in or example of abstraction.

In the fall of 1974 Surls's first solo exhibitions took place, back-to-back, at the Tyler (Texas) Museum of Art and the Delahunty Gallery in Dallas. A review of the Delahunty show, which included several pieces from the Tyler exhibition, appeared in *Art in America*, bringing his art to national and international attention for the first time. The reviewer, Jozanne Rabyor, linked Surls's art to "primitive" art as well as to the works of Samaras, Eva Hesse, and Jackie Winsor. She also noted a paradoxical quality in his art: "Surls' sculptures seem physically to constrain great quantities of intense, perhaps violent potency. He also conveys a subtle, gently mocking sense of humor."[12] Variations of her comments would repeatedly characterize the later literature on Surls's art.

Labeling Surls's sculpture as "primitive" derives from a perception of the pieces' totemic and animistic qualities, and the rough handling of the wood through chain-sawing, chopping, hacking, rasping, and cutting. Surls's work did not display, nor did he intend it to, the more refined handling of wood of artists as diverse as, for instance, H. C. Westermann and Raoul Hague. Art writers would frequently associate Surls's "primitivism" with folk art. Of course, as a recipient of a master of fine arts degree from a leading art school and an artist savvy in the ways of the art world, James Surls could never be a folk or "primitive" artist. He admires folk art and perceives a connection between his work and it, but one that is less about a shared raw, direct, and naïve aesthetic and one more about being endowed with what he calls "the power of the singular belief." He understands folk artists to possess a powerful, intuitive belief in themselves. Surls views folk artists as having "psychologically come to terms with themselves, and they like themselves. Consequently, it gives them a weird kind of power of singular belief," which empowers them to create "a system of order which is what art is. I [too] have a power of singular belief in that respect."[13]

High Man Coming to See exemplifies the early sculpture that attracted the "primitive" and "folk" labels. The seventeen-foot-tall *High Man Coming to See* literally stood out from the other sculptures when it was installed in Surls's one-person exhibition at the Houston Contemporary Arts Museum in 1975. The show was conceived by Jim Harithas, the museum's dynamic director, whom Surls would come to regard as a mentor. *High Man Coming to See*'s elongated shaft reads as a soaring body, an ancient Egyptian obelisk, and a modern rocket. The pointed sticks, porcupine-spine-like, with their darkened tips, cover the shaft-body. The sticks suggest eyes, and Surls has spoken of them as symbolizing his looking at Charmaine Locke, as well as the sculpture looking back at the viewer. The notion of eyes looking back at you came, in part, from Surls seeing the "eyes" on the trunks of aspen trees in New Mexico. Having the sculpture gaze at the spectator is one way that Surls imbues his work with a sense of vitality and life force. The shape of the eyes in Surls's sculptures will become more eyelike over time. The eye, as a signifier of life, will enter the visual alphabet. References to eyes and their activities occur early on in Surls's titles and continue to the present; examples include *The Eyes Have It* (1974) **(FIG. 26)**, *Seeing in the Wind* (1987) **(FIG. 27)**, *Looking Across the Way* (1993) **(FIG. 28)**, and *eye See the Workhorse down* (2002) **(PL. 36)**.

Surls considers a title an integral part of each work of art. He believes designating a work of art as "Untitled" (as he did with his abstract sculptures at Cranbrook) implies that the artist does not truly know what the work is about. "Untitled" also frustrates the spectator trying to discern meaning. A title triggers a response from the viewer, offers an entry into the work of art, and provides a way of getting hold of it. Likening a title to a skillet handle, Surls observes that you can fry with a skillet that lacks a handle, but it's a whole

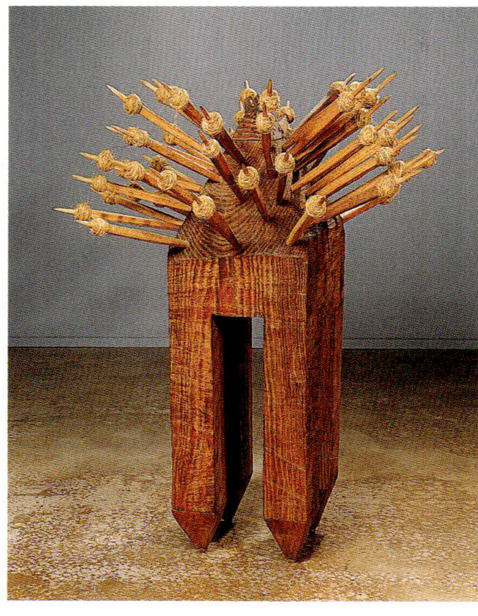

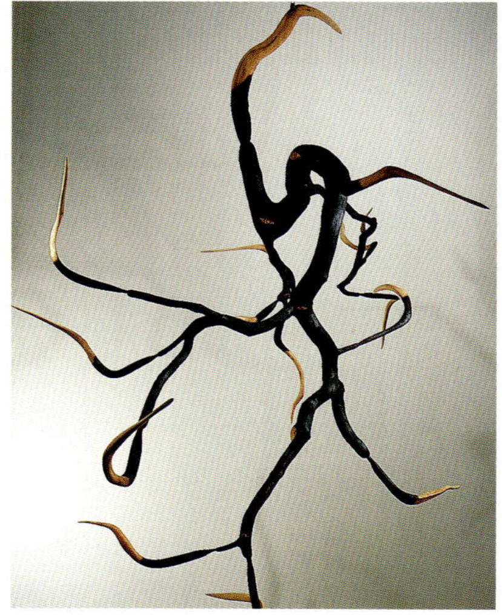

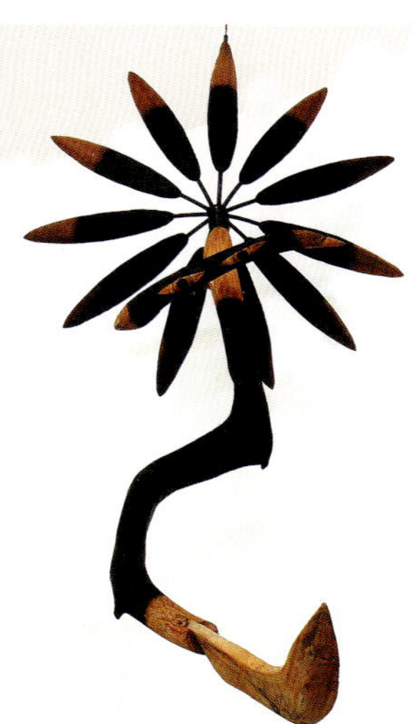

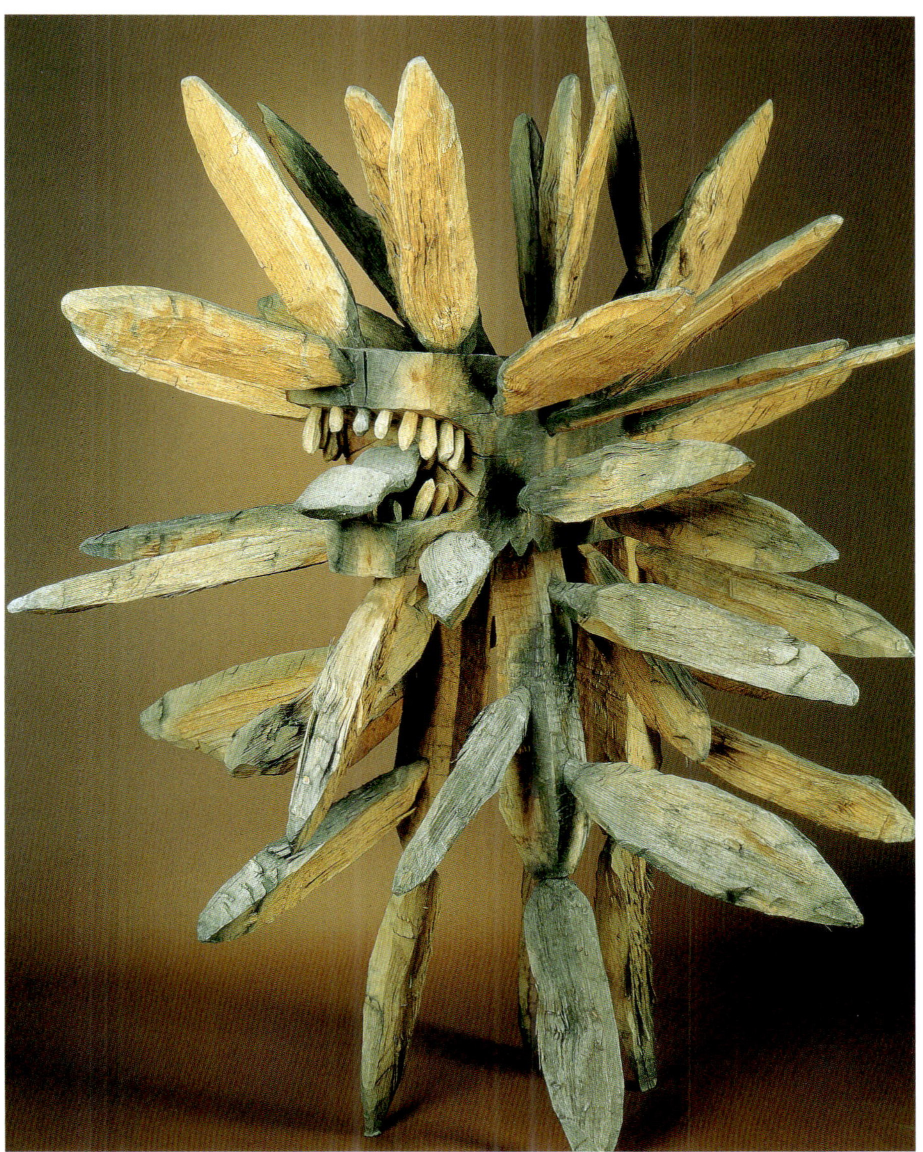

LEFT TO RIGHT

FIGURE 26
The Eyes Have It, 1974
Pine, maple, glass, twine
54 x 38 x 38
San Antonio Museum of Art. Gift of Mrs. Nancy B. Negley.

FIGURE 27
Seeing in the Wind, 1987
Oak
119 x 70 x 129
High Museum of Art, Atlanta, Georgia. Gift of Martin Sklar, 1992.74.

FIGURE 28
Looking Across the Way, 1995
Oak, redwood, pine, steel
120 x 80 x 70

FIGURE 29
Burning Dog, 1976
Oak
74 x 47 x 65
Collection of Gerald Peters.

lot eas er if you have something to hold onto.[14] Because he regards a work of art as a form of communication, a title plays an essential role in opening its visual language to the spectator. Sometimes Surls's titles are clearly descriptive, but more often they are poetically evocative. In most cases, titles precede the actual work of art and derive from the artist's poems or words he has jotted down.

A work that is disturbing in title and image is *Burning Dog* (**FIG. 29**). The spikes—pointed sticks projecting out of—impaled in his sculptures are in this piece weighty and broad. Surls had already created several sculptures related to animals, including *Turtle* (1974) and *Dragon Lady* (1975) (**FIG. 30**). The idea of *Burning Dog* originated in a popular exhibition Surls and the poet Bob Trammell had organized at SMU's University Gallery in 1975,

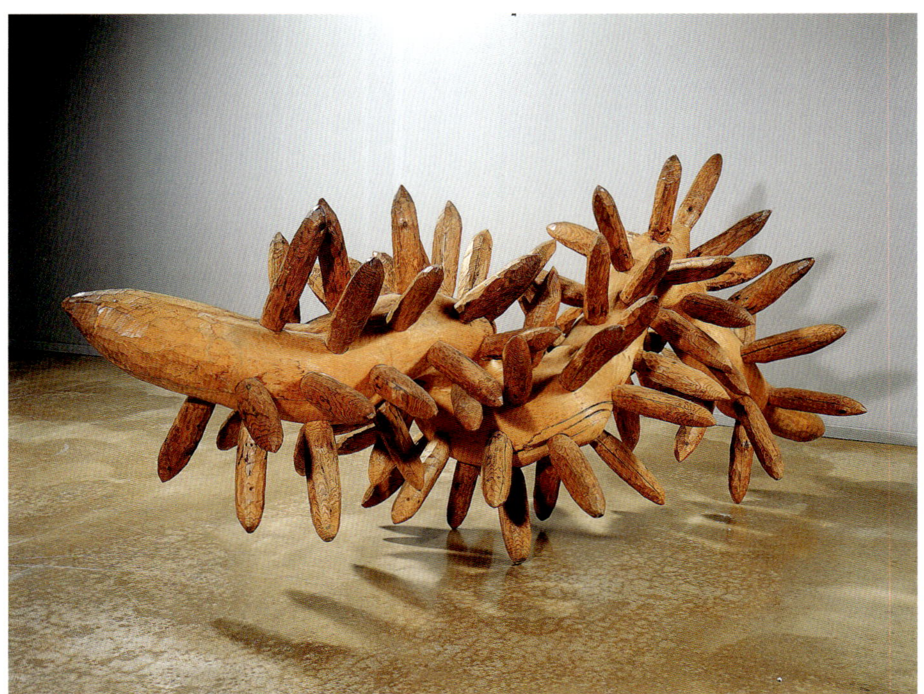

called *The Dog Show*. Even though he had executed a piece titled *Screaming Dog*, nothing in his work quite prepared the viewer for the searing intensity of *Burning Dog*. The exploding log of a sculpture conveys the agony of the animal through its grotesque, anguished open mouth and its extraordinary protruding tongue. Chaotic flames of hacked, chopped, and axed wood encircle the canine's body. The wild form and alarming content of *Burning Dog* contrast strikingly with the more orderly and benign nature of his previous work. As an image of suffering and pain being inflicted, *Burning Dog* acknowledges and addresses the inhumanity that is an undeniable and paradoxical aspect of humankind. From this point on, Surls's work will move back and forth between the affirmative and the negative, the voluptuous and the dark.

Burning Dog was created at the University of Houston, where Surls began teaching in 1976. He and Locke had moved to Houston, then settled forty miles north in the community of Splendora, in the heart of the Piney Woods in the Big Thicket. They lived in a tiny one-room house set in a twenty-two-acre plot. Over the next twenty years, their house, acreage, and family would grow substantially. Surls quickly established himself in the Houston area. *Sticker Woman* (**FIG. 31**), a forty-foot-long spiky piece of creosote-soaked pine logs held in place with steel and resembling a World War II anti-landing barrier, received a top prize in Houston's 1976 Main Street Festival. He was one of the Houston artists invited to represent the city in an exhibition at the Institute of Contemporary Art in

FIGURE 30
Dragon Lady, 1975
Pine
49 x 108 x 49
San Antonio Museum of Art. Purchased with funds from the National Endowment for the Arts and contributions in memory of Nelda Cordts.

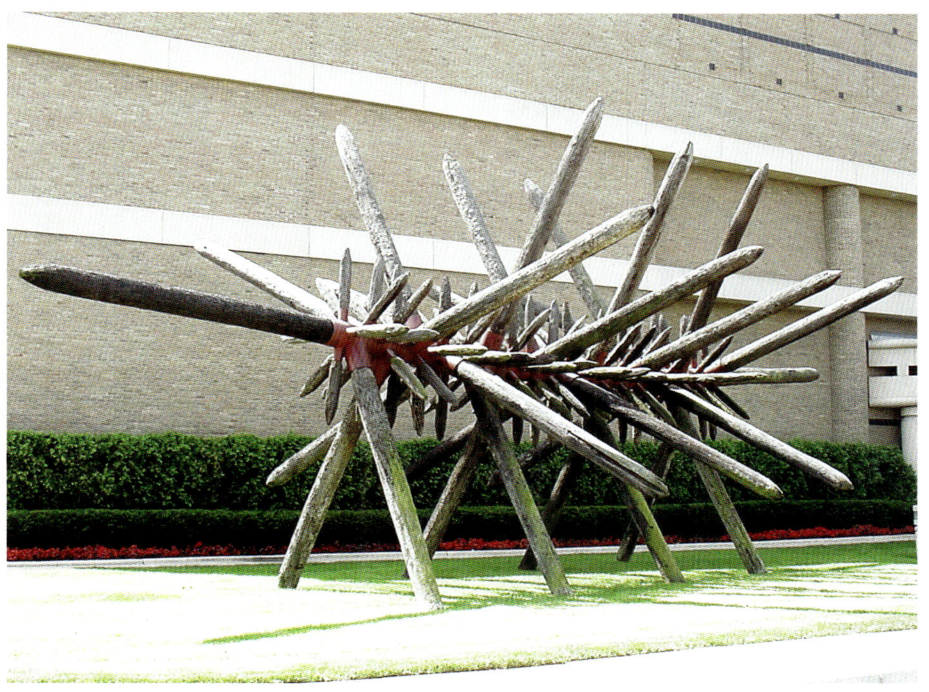

Philadelphia. Surls was also attracting national attention, as his sculpture appeared in exhibitions in Los Angeles and Artpark, in Lewiston, New York. The most impressive indication of his rising prominence was his work's inclusion in the exhibition of emerging artists in 1977 at the Solomon R. Guggenheim Museum, New York, *Nine Artists: Theodoron Awards*.

When John Russell's review of this show appeared in the *New York Times*, the only artwork reproduced from any of the nine artists—who included, notably, Mary Miss and Dennis Oppenheim—was Surls's 1974 *I Saw a Man with Shovels in His Hands Scooping Fire from the Sky* (**FIG. 32**). (Coincidentally appearing on the same page, just a column away, was a photograph of Eva Hesse, an artist whose work, like Surls's, challenged the hegemony of Minimal art. Hesse is pictured with her arms raised in a manner resembling Surls's sculpture.) Russell likened Surls's work to "primitive" art but qualified the reference by noting that "the directness, the vivid imagination, the power of ideas and the sense of superabundant and well-directed physical effort add up to an invigorating idiom." The title *I Saw a Man with Shovels in His Hands Scooping Fire from the Sky* captivated Russell: "If you think that that sounds like something from the Book of Revelations you're absolutely right." The reviewer continued, "He is carved from a block of pine wood that radiates strength and well-being. But the two blackened shapes that stand for shovels strike a sinister note, as if fire had come down from the sky, and been kept at bay for this first time only."[15] Finding the sculpture to be simultaneously benign and sinister, Russell falls in

FIGURE 31
Sticker Woman, 1976
Cresote-soaked pine
240 x 648 x 240
Courtesy of the Neiman Marcus Collection, Troy, Michigan.

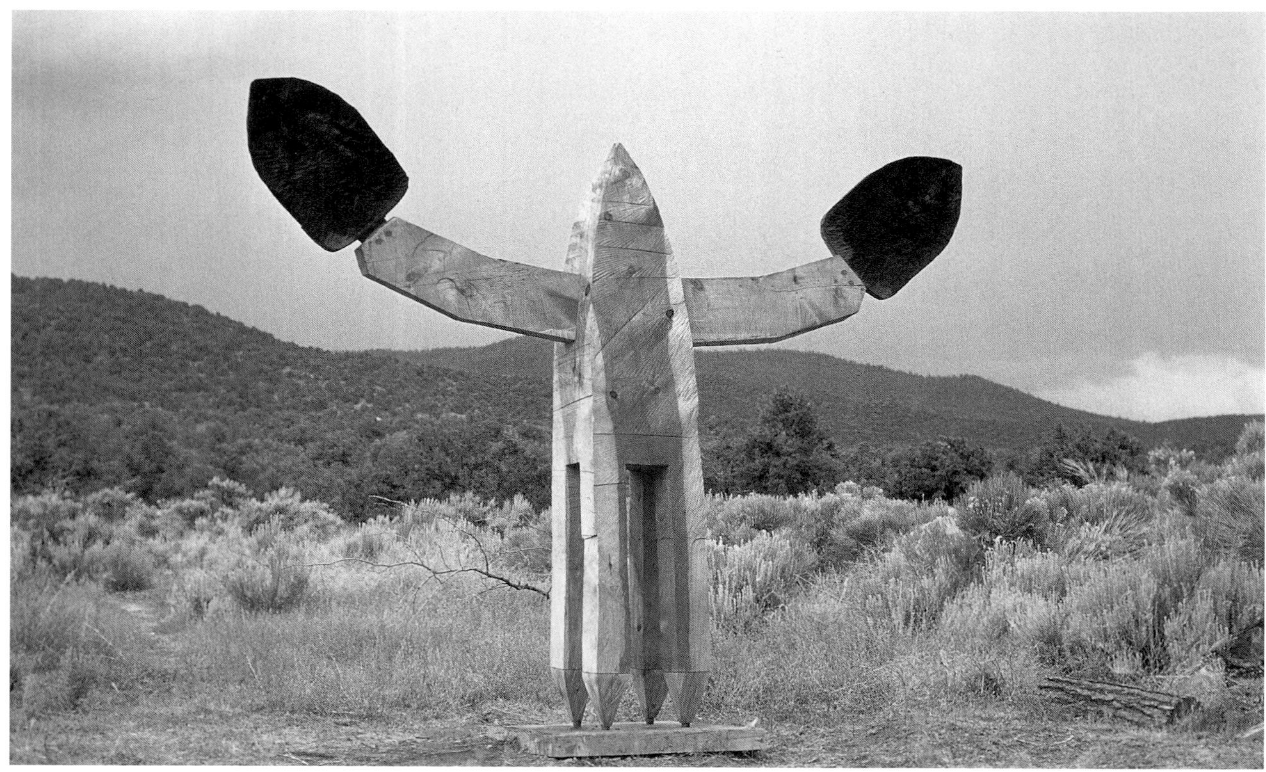

line with other writers in recognizing the element of paradox underlying Surls's art.

Two years after the Guggenheim show, Surls gained further national recognition when his work was included in the Whitney Biennial Exhibition. In addition, he received a National Endowment for the Arts fellowship and organized and curated *FIRE!*, a much-discussed exhibition of one hundred Texas artists, held at the Houston Contemporary Arts Museum. Lucy Lippard, reviewing this exhibition in *Art in America*, characterized it as "a regional show par excellence."[16] This high praise also carried with it an implicit put-down: a great show, but not a show of New York art. A problem with regionalism is that while the term draws attention to art that has been overlooked because it is produced and shown outside the art capital of New York, the term inherently reiterates the distance between the periphery and the center. Surls assigns regionalism to the confining "iron box" of labeling. "Being a 'Texas artist' doesn't bother me. . . . I *am* a Texas artist, but I don't want to be *just* a Texas artist, not just a 'regionalist artist.'"[17] Surls turned the regionalist designation on its head by asserting that New York art was just another example of regionalism. He declared that he "aspired to a bigger context" than that city. A bigger context presented itself when the vast readership of *Time* magazine had the opportunity to see and read of James Surls in a review of the 1979 Whitney Biennial Exhibition.

The review in *Time* reproduced five images from the biennial (of the 110 objects installed); one was Surls's *Tornado* (FIG. 33). Robert Hughes, the magazine's art critic, wrote

FIGURE 32
I Saw a Man with Shovels in His Hands Scooping Fire from the Sky, 1974
Ponderosa pine
114 x 133 x 24
Private Collection

FIGURE 33
Tornado, 1977
Sweet gum, oak, pine
103 x 29 x 39 ½
Private Collection

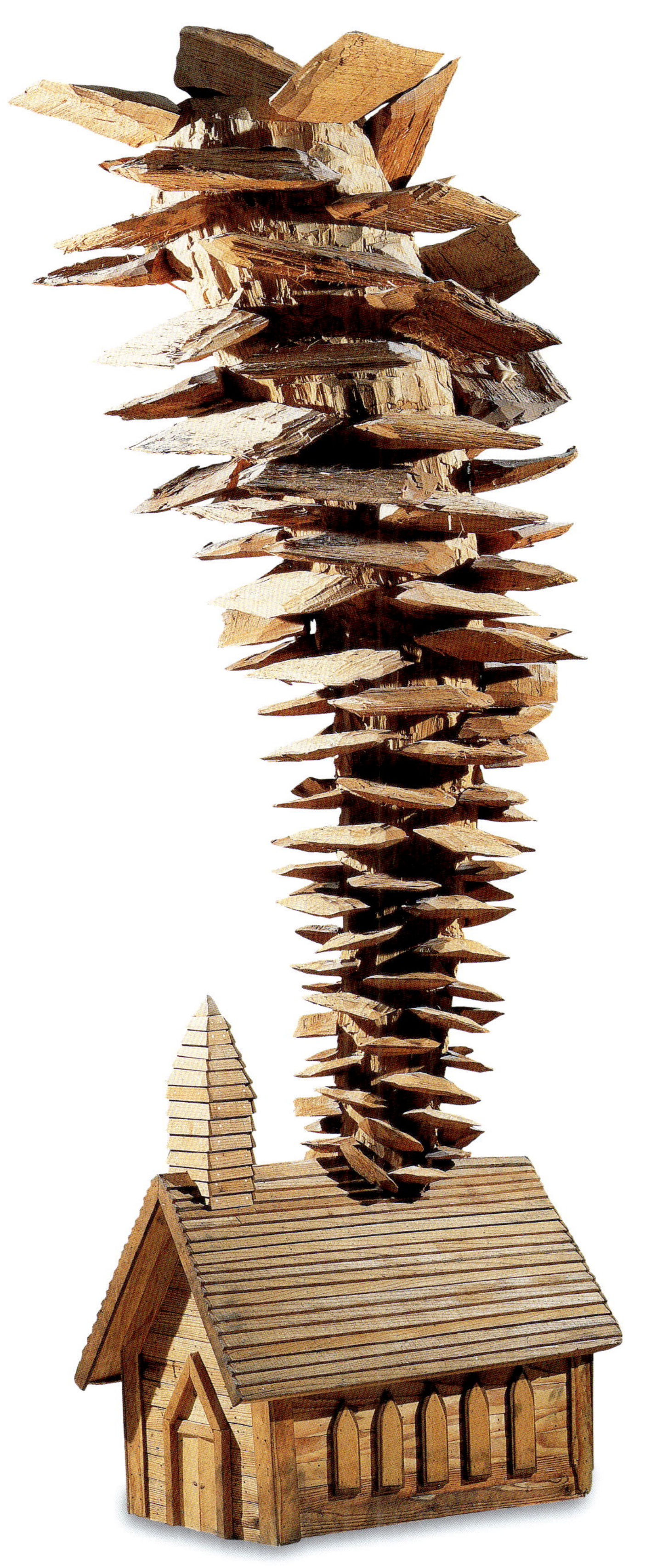

of the sculpture: "There is also a hilarious piece of funkiness by a Texas sculptor, James Surls, representing a tornado chewing its way through the roof of a church; Surls' debt to that master of buckeye surrealism, H. C. Westermann, is obvious enough, but the image has a wobbly comic-strip blatancy about it that carries conviction."[18] Unlike Hughes, Surls does not consider *Tornado* or any other of his artworks to exemplify "funkiness." Surls adamantly argues that his art is neither funky nor part of the Funk art movement of the 1960s and 1970s. *Tornado*'s hallucinatory violence justifies the reference to Surrealism, and the sculpture does exhibit a humorous aspect: the tornado's cartoonish chaotic funnel nails the pristine church to the ground. Paradoxically, the tornado appears to be growing up from the roof as much as it is nailing it down or chewing through it. *Tornado*'s church is the first inclusion of a specific architectural type in Surls's art; churches and, especially, houses will frequently be important motifs in his work.

In his review, Hughes cited H. C. Westermann as an obvious influence on Surls's art, yet Westermann, who did work in wood and incorporated houses into his art, is not an artist whom Surls considers as having affected him. The artists he most admires include John Alexander, Louise Bourgeois, Bert Long, and René Magritte. Surls does not identify with Westermann, although he likes the art of the Hairy Who, a group of Chicago artists of the later 1960s whom Westermann certainly influenced. An artist whose work greatly appeals to Surls is Alexander Calder. Surls praises the huge Calder mobile hanging in the East Building of the National Gallery of Art in Washington, D.C., as "the most voluptuous thing I've seen." But it took years for him to grow fond of Calder's art. By contrast, Surls was immediately awestruck by the Louisiana bayou–influenced work of Clyde Connell. "She is one who looks and listens and sees and hears and knows. She is one who gifts our world with the purity of truth."[19] He was so impressed with her art that he organized an exhibition in 1981 that marked the first appearance of her work in Houston. Among the artists he admires, two stand far above the others. Joseph Cornell—"one of the greatest artists who ever lived on earth"—is "the No. 1 guy" for Surls, while the artist he acknowledges as having the widest and deepest influence on him is Charmaine Locke. Throughout his career, Surls has repeatedly acknowledged her impact on his art. Just as he is "in" each of his works, Locke's presence, he says, is also everywhere in his art.

The year in which he showed in the Whitney Biennial for the first time, 1979 (his work would also be included in 1985), and organized the *FIRE!* show also saw the hyperactive artist founding the Lawndale Annex of the University of Houston. Surls felt empowered to launch Lawndale—the city's first alternative art space—because of the influence ("the psychological jump") of Jim Harithas, who left his post as director of the Houston Contemporary Arts Museum in 1979. Surls served as director (until 1984) and created an extraordinarily lively arts and community center, where "permission was given to do all sorts of things." The Lawndale Annex contributed immensely to the burgeoning Houston

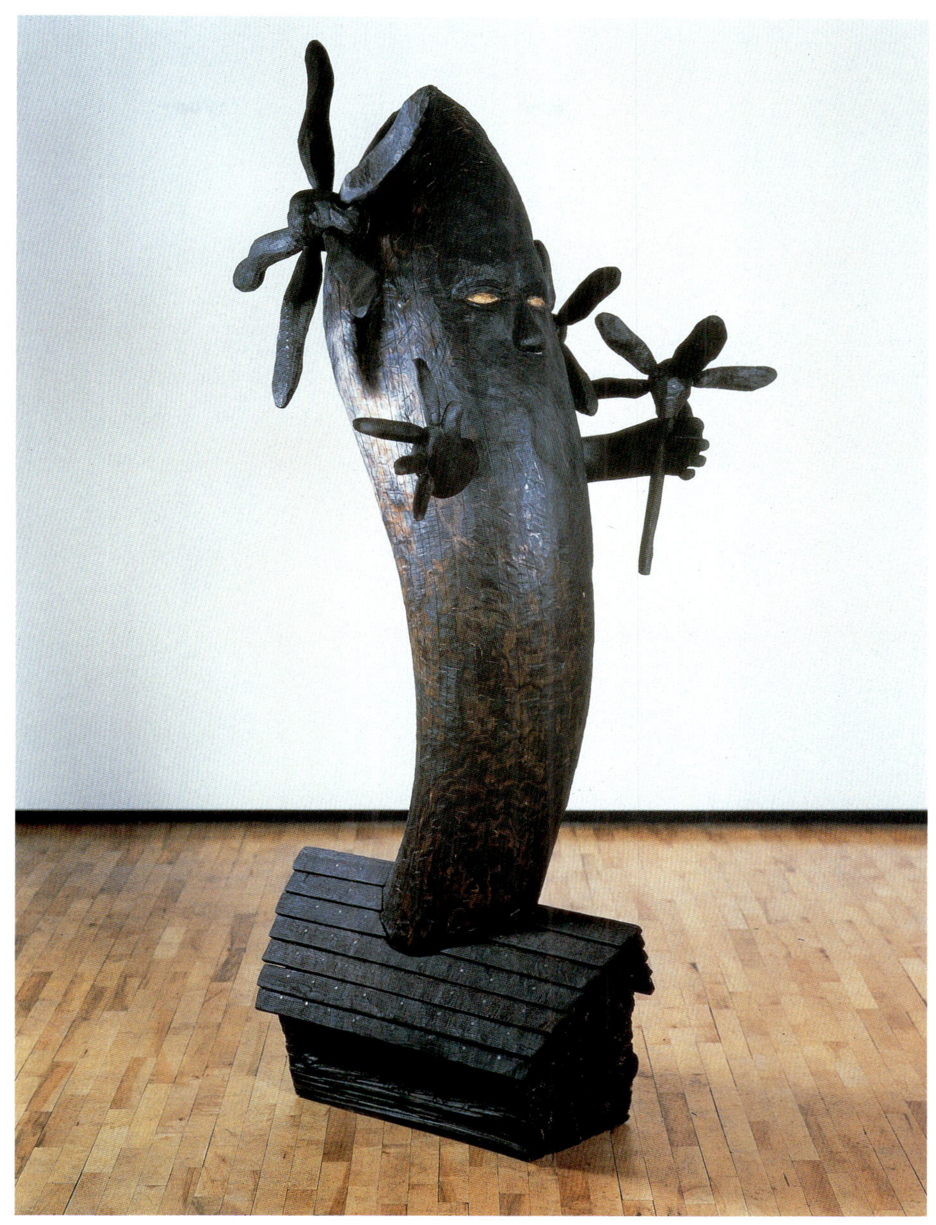

arts scene and solidified Surls's reputation as the impresario of Texas contemporary art.

In May 1980 James Surls's first one-person exhibition in New York opened at the Allan Frumkin Gallery. Hilton Kramer, then the art critic for the *New York Times*, reviewed the show favorably, stating "it straightway establishes [Surls] as a sculptor with large ambitions and a very individual point of view." The critic singled out *Night Vision* **(FIG. 34)** for its suggestive affinities with Easter Island carvings and Surrealism. The minimal carving of the seven-foot-high form likely triggered Kramer's association of it with Easter Island

FIGURE 34
Night Vision, 1980
Pine, oak, sweet gum root, alder
91 x 48 x 42
Private Collection

heads. The nightmarish, charred figure rising out of the similarly blackened house recalls Surrealist dream imagery. Like writers before him and after, Kramer was quick to qualify the "primitive" and Surrealist affinities to Surls's art, by emphasizing that "the sheer energy and invention of the work place it well beyond the sources that nourish it. This is a sculpture devoted to conjuring up magical personages and strange rites." The *Times* critic concluded by citing *Night Vision* as representing "an attitude toward sculpture that fell toward disfavor during the reign of Minimalism, but that now shows signs of making a significant come-back."[20] A similar recognition of this transition from reductive, austere Minimal art to work that embraced allusion and narrative motivated the Albright-Knox Art Gallery's 1987 exhibition *Structure to Resemblance: Work by Eight American Sculptors*. This show highlighted works of art by Surls and other major artists, including Lynda Benglis, John Chamberlain,

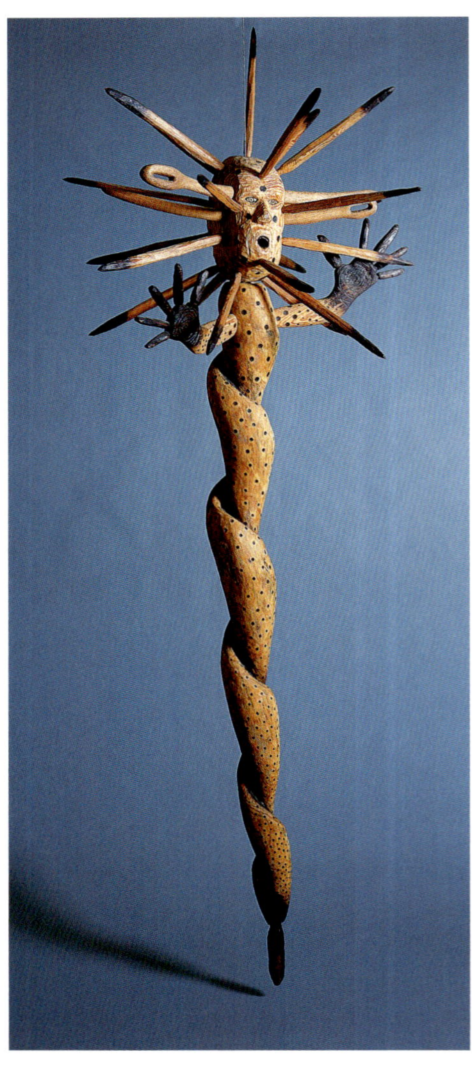

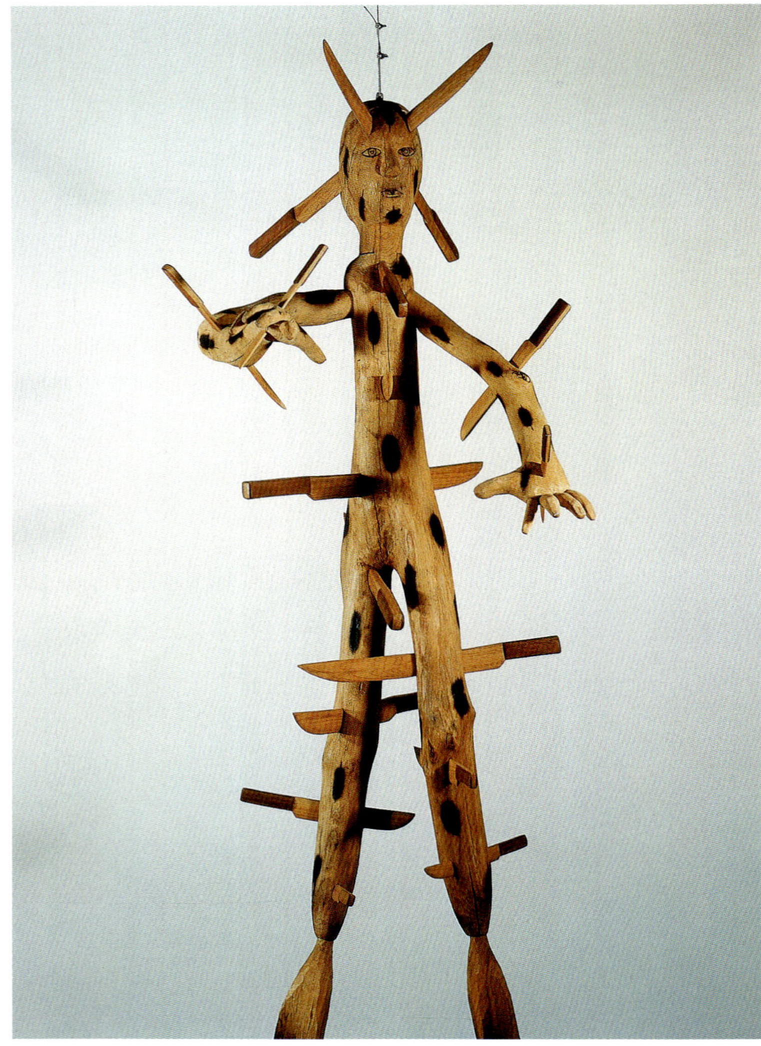

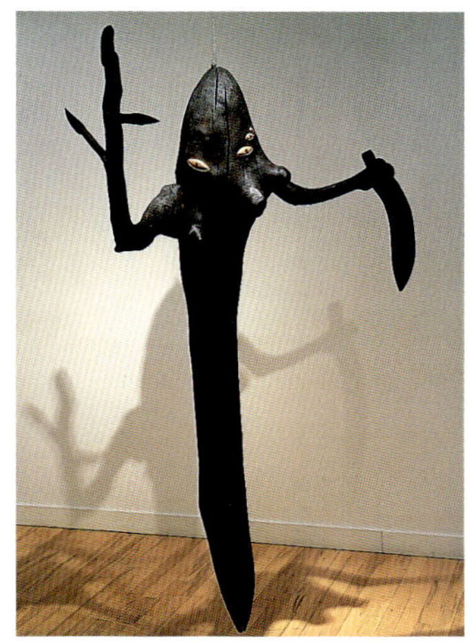

Nancy Graves, and Martin Puryear, to exemplify the turn to an art that was more subjective and symbolic in form and content.

The burnt, ghostly presence of *Night Vision* rising out of the house (which, compositionally, resembles *Tornado*) is unsettling in part because it originates out of and dominates the house, a traditional site of comfort and security. To see a house in jeopardy, at the mercy of a malevolent creature, emphasizes the nightmarish violence of *Night Vision*. In addressing the "dark side," the sculpture is by no means unusual in Surls's artistic output; in the 1980s a number of pieces gave violence free rein.

Atop the corkscrew body of *Needle Man* (FIG. 35) appears a head impaled with pointed sticks, burnt on their ends, and two needles. This may be the first time Surls incorporated needles into one of his sculptures. In his visual alphabet, needles signify the feminine element that binds humanity together. In *Needle Man*, what initially appears to be a figure in excruciating pain may be instead (or simultaneously) a figure radiating intense energy. *Me and the Butcher Knives* (FIG. 36) is a particularly disturbing work in which knives pierce almost every part of the figure's body. Burn marks all over the figure add to the violence that has been done. Surls sees this piece as being about the pain people inflict on themselves—each person being his or her own worst enemy. On a personal level, the artist speaks of the piece as also addressing his deteriorating relationship with the University of Houston; he was to leave the school in 1984. "How do you represent greed?" is the question that prompted *Greedman* (FIG. 37). This "nasty ass character" is armed with a knife and possesses a body that echoes the sharpness of the blade. Works like these led the critic David Bourbon to assess Surls, in 1984, as "one of the most forceful, original, and disconcerting artists to have emerged in the last decade."[21] Surls was, in fact, working with symbolism, narrative, and nature in powerfully evocative and creative ways that were unmatched in the art of any other American sculptor of the day.

During the 1980s Surls's artistic reputation continued to grow, with seven more solo exhibitions: a second one at the Allan Frumkin Gallery (1982) and a ten-year retrospective at the Dallas Museum of Art (1984), as well as shows at the Akron Art Museum (1982), St. Louis Art Museum (1982), Honolulu Academy of Art (1984), Delahunty Gallery, New York (1984), and Pittsburgh Center for the Arts (1987). Surls's show at Delahunty in Soho caught Robert Hughes's eye, and he wrote an article reviewing Surls's work alongside that of Nancy Graves. It was an appropriate pairing because both sculptors' art involved organic imagery and incorporated accretions of nature directly into their works. Although her bronze sculptures rarely display the figural qualities of Surls's work, Graves's art, from the early 1980s until her death in 1995, is closer in spirit to his work than that of any of his contemporaries. However, as Hughes suggests, Graves's focus on spatial construction differentiates her art from Surls's concern with storytelling—"Clearly, Surls is turning into a fabulist of the most engaging kind." The critic also represents Surls vis-à-vis Graves

LEFT TO RIGHT

FIGURE 35
Needle Man, 1980
Pine, oak
115 x 40 x 43
Private Collection

FIGURE 36
Me and the Butcher Knives, 1982
Oak, mahogany
101 x 37 x 39
Whitney Museum of American Art, New York. Purchased with funds from an anonymous donor, 82.14.

FIGURE 37
Greedman, 1984
Oak, sycamore
70 ½ x 36 x 26
Private Collection

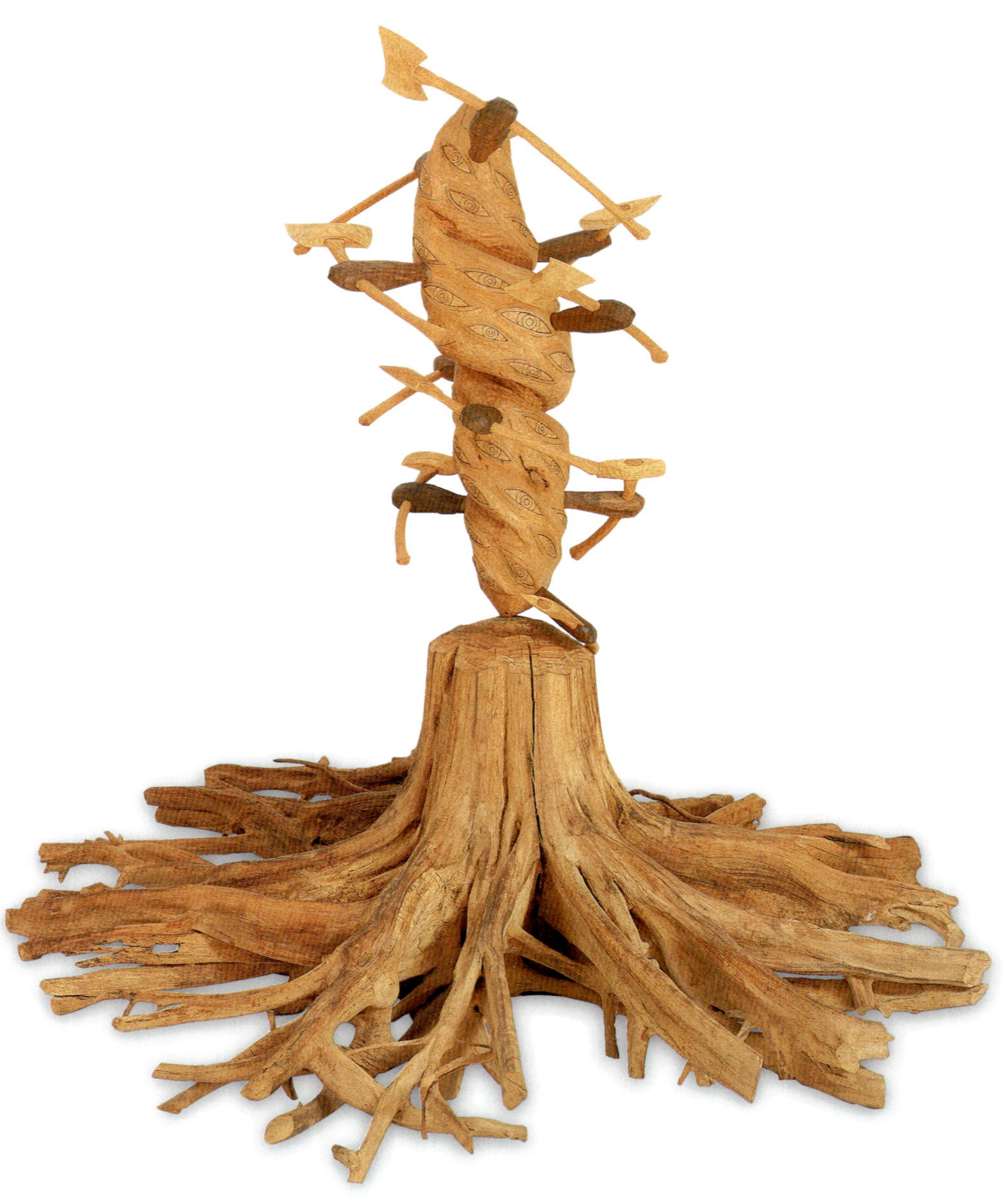

as an "outsider" artist, describing him as "a muscular farm dweller from Splendora, Texas, who is sometimes mistaken for Willie Nelson." Hughes praises the artist's skill in pegging and joining branches and roots to maintain their "straight-from-the-ground" look even as they are transformed into figures. Surls's "sense of the demonic" particularly appealed to Hughes, who said of the artist's work: "It is infused, at the start, with a real sense of fright: the noonday demon, as it were, lurking in the woodpile. Surls' huge wraiths posture and writhe on point with a sort of evilly humorous grace; they summon up nursery horrors, tree demons, swamp critters. . . . You can laugh at the devil, but not too hard or long." In citing precedents for Surls's artistic sensibility, Hughes names Joan Miró and, again, H. C.

FIGURE 38
Working in the Garden, 1981
Oak, elm, poplar
98 x 104 x 97
Dallas Museum of Art, gift of Laura Carpenter, the Mary Margaret Munson Wilcox Fund, the Jolesch Acquisition Fund, Museum League Purchase Fund, and the Texas Artists Fund.

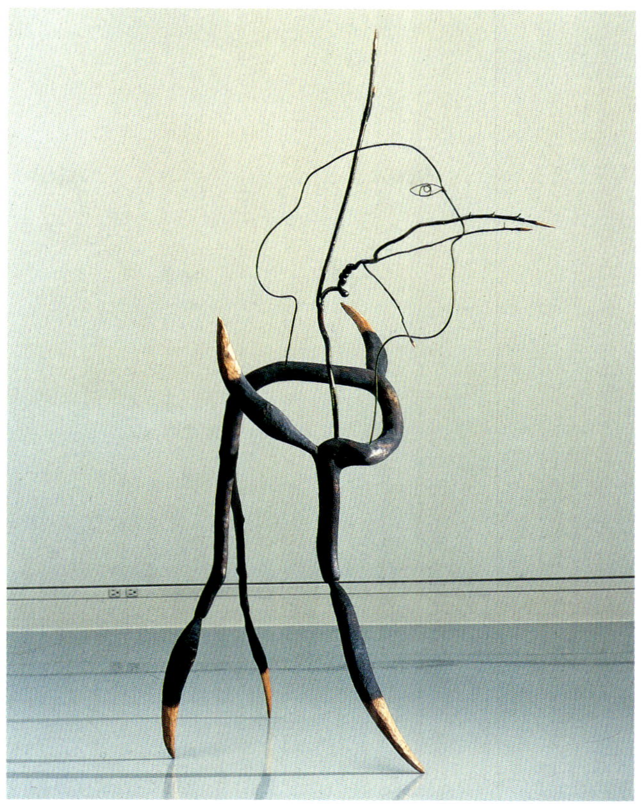

Westermann. Hughes deems the sculpture reproduced in the article—*Working in the Garden* (FIG. 38)—"a masterpiece of the special American genre of buckeye surrealism."

The eight-foot-high *Working in the Garden* is a stunning piece, which, as Hughes aptly writes, "manages to be funny, menacing, otherworldly, and stridently physical all at the same time."[22] On top of a massive tree root is poised what appears to be a swirling creature covered with eyes and having multiple hands, each wielding an axe or hatchet. The sculpture expresses the relentless spiraling energy of a whirling dervish. It is an image that is as much about destruction as it is about construction and brings to mind the images of Shiva, the many-armed Hindu god of destruction and regeneration. The violence of this cutting creature belies the benign activity suggested by the sculpture's title, but it does remind us that a garden grows from cleared land.

The critic Grace Glueck, in her *New York Times* review of the same Delahunty show, found the "furiously" axe-flailing *Working in the Garden* to be "marvelous." She did worry about the potential for "anthropomorphic cuteness" in Surls's work, but she felt he usually managed to avoid it. She thought that in a couple of pieces he was "unwilling to leave well enough alone, he incorporates the outlines of human figures 'drawn' in steel, which add nothing."[23] Surls had begun to include the wire-steel image of a human profile (usually

FIGURE 39
Walking in Heaven, 1983
Pine, oak, vine, wire
56 x 26 x 30
Private Collection

his, sometimes Locke's) in his work beginning in 1983, with a sculpture such as *Walking in Heaven* (FIG. 39). This would continue to be an important feature of his work, as seen in a much later, even larger work, such as *Me, the Flower and the Pistil* (PL. 7). Since the 1990s drawing in steel has become an integral element in his art, but other writers have not echoed Glueck's concerns.

Besides appearing in solo exhibitions during the 1980s, Surls's art was seen in many group shows, including particularly significant ones at the International Sculpture Center (Washington, D.C., 1980), San Francisco Museum of Modern Art (1982), Whitney Museum of American Art (1983, 1984, and the 1985 Whitney Biennial Exhibition), Cincinnati Contemporary Arts Center (1985), Art Gallery of Western Australia (1986), Groningen Museum (the Netherlands, 1988), and Renwick Gallery, Smithsonian Institution (1989).

His exhibition activity continued unabated in the 1990s, and he produced work at a prodigious rate. His art appeared in more than fifty group shows and six solo exhibitions, with venues including the Contemporary Art Museum in Honolulu (1991), Marlborough Gallery (New York, 1994), Savannah College of Art and Design (1996), and the University of Texas at Tyler (1997). His status as "the" Texas artist was confirmed when he received the Texas Artist of the Year Award from the Houston Area Art League in 1991 and was further solidified by his being named first recipient of the Dallas Visual Art Center's Legend Award (1993). The latter honored his multiple contributions to developing and enhancing the visual arts within the state. He expanded his commitment to promoting arts in the community when he and Locke founded Amazing Space, in the small community of Cleveland, Texas, in 1993. This alternative art space was intended to fill a void in the public school program and to interact with the community by providing a place where art, philosophy, and science could be integrated. On the home front, his Splendora house had grown substantially—"expanded like a patchwork quilt"—and his huge studio not only allowed him to produce increasingly monumental works but also served as the site for an array of art exhibitions, receptions, lectures, readings, and music and dance performances. Surls has always spoken of the positive impact that moving to Splendora had on his life and art. Here he felt "an absolute sense of permanence . . . an absolute sense of belonging. I sort of screwed myself to the earth right here."[24] With his claiming that this is where he would live forever, and with his often-stated commitment to work as an artist in Texas, it was hard to believe that in the summer of 1998 he had moved to the Aspen Valley in Colorado.

Surls had gone to Colorado in the mid-1980s to work with the printmaker Chip Elwell at the Anderson Ranch Arts Center in Snowmass, as well as to offer workshops there. He and his family returned each summer. In 1997, after Locke talked of the Aspen Valley as a wonderful place to live and raise the younger of the couple's seven daughters, the decision was made to move. Despite Splendora's being for Surls a "very contained, very secure, very happy place and time," he acknowledges that it was time to leave (see FIG. 6 and FIG. 40). Not

FIGURE 40
View of Surls's studio in Splendora, Texas, 1988

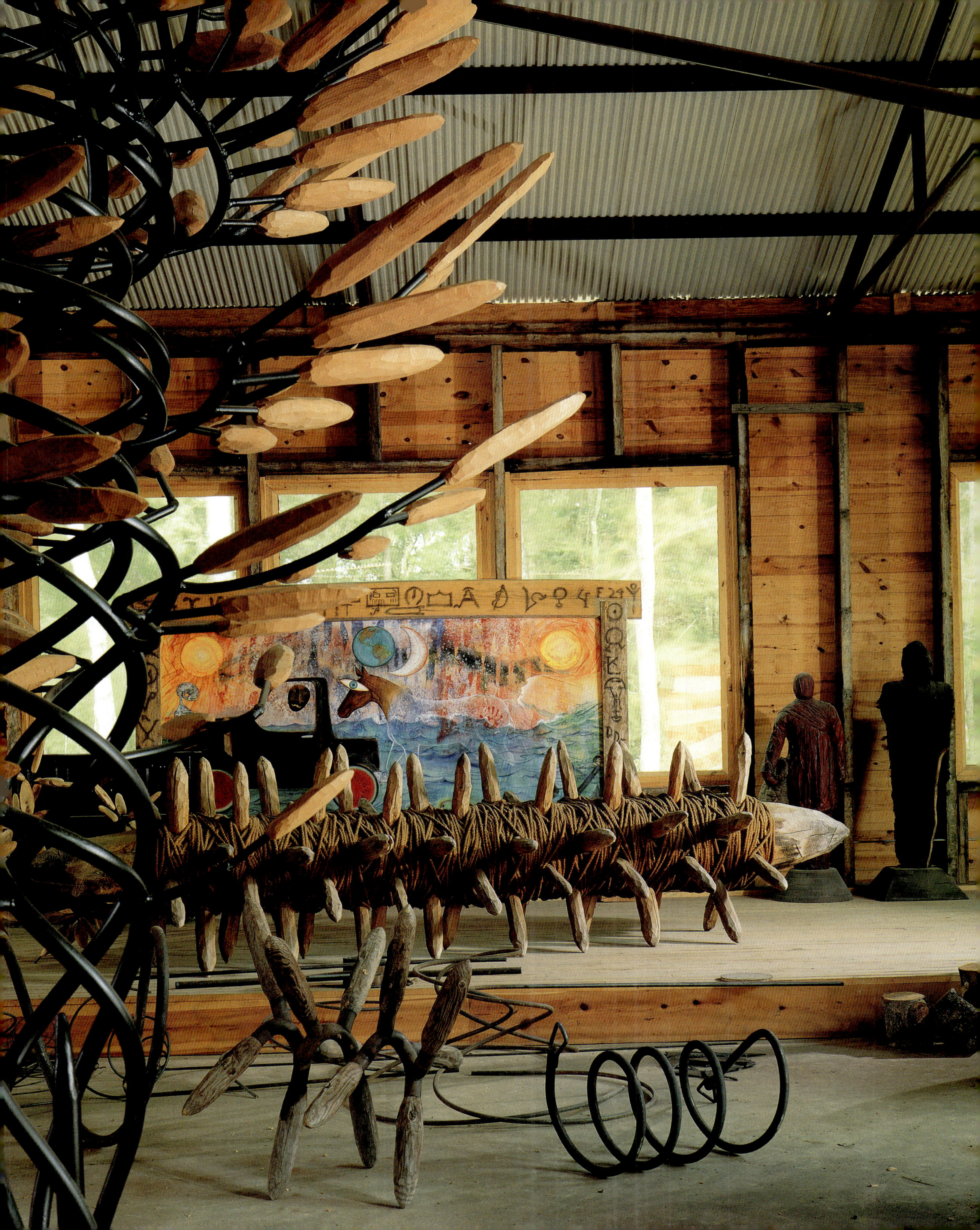

only was he affected by seeing the surrounding land being "butchered" by land developers and loggers, but he also felt that a "psychological demise" had been reached. He had everything he had ever dreamed of—beautiful house, gigantic studio, lots of wooded acreage—it was the ideal environment (it was even featured in *Architectural Digest*), but it had also become so consuming that there was a feeling of being devoured by "too much stuff." It was time to leave what Surls calls the jungle and "go over the mountain to live in the meadows." Nevertheless, the move was difficult, and when Locke and the girls moved to Colorado a year before he did (he had to fulfill a teaching commitment), the artist likened his mood to that of a state of mourning. To make matters worse, he fell off a log while crossing a creek and broke his arm, limiting his ability to make art for most of a year.

In the Meadows

When he arrived in Colorado in the summer of 1998, Surls—a self-styled "creative-minded go-getter"[25]—hit the ground running, in spite of not having a studio. He accepted the idea that art can, in fact, be made anywhere and was reminded of his situation of being without a studio in New Mexico in the early 1970s and in Splendora when they had first moved there. Fortunately, the Anderson Ranch Arts Center awarded him a two-year residency, making its facilities and equipment available to him. Although studios were cramped (for example, he was not able to assemble and complete some of his large pieces) and used by several others, he found it an invigorating, high-energy place. By the end of 2002 Surls and his family were able to move into a new mountaintop home, complete with a studio.

Since settling in Colorado, Surls has had his work shown in solo exhibitions in galleries in Aspen (1998), Dallas (1999, 2002), Houston (1999), New York (1999), and the El Paso Museum of Art (2000). The last show led to his being asked to participate, along with Louise Bourgeois, Jonathan Borofsky, Claes Oldenburg, Frank Stella, and other internationally known artists, in an outdoor sculpture exhibition in Monaco (2000).

Although he has been in Colorado for several years, the specific influence the move has had on his art is still evolving; even Surls thinks it is perhaps too soon to assess the full impact. Nevertheless, it is clear that his art features a greater expansiveness, which directly relates to his surroundings. In describing his new environment he could very well be characterizing his recent art: "Now, it is open, now it's vistas, now it's clearer, and now it's much cleaner—it's a whole different world." His 1999 sculpture *Forever Gone* (PL. 4), made not long after the move to Colorado, addresses the geographic and psychological changes in his life and begs the question: What is forever gone? Certainly, he is gone from Splendora. Yet, for an artist for whom memory has been an essential part of his artistic imagination and production, Splendora will never be truly gone. The house, a frequent Surls motif, in *Forever Gone* signifies both Splendora-as-home and the artist—"I am a house"[26]—with memories dwelling within him. *Forever Gone* represents Surls coming to grips with a major transition in his life and straddling his Texas memories and his new Colorado reality.

Surls knew well before his major exhibition of work "basically made in Colorado" opened at the Meadows Museum in early 2003 that *Forever Gone* would be situated on the landing at the top of the stairs near the exhibition's entry. He thought the sculpture was the perfect piece to symbolize his move from Texas to Colorado, because its top part—the branches coming out of the roof—came from wood he found in Splendora, while the roof was cut from dead trees he came across in Colorado. Though taken from different locales, both forms come from pine trees. With its boarded windows, the house signifies the closure of one era, while the sweeping, Art Nouveau–like arabesque of the limbs points to the future. The stability of the house is overwhelmed by windswept tendrils, which lead the spectator's eye to the vistas and away from the security of the home. On its own, but especially in the context of Surls's life, *Forever Gone* is an extraordinarily poignant and evocative work of art. Surls was absolutely right in seeing it as the ideal piece to begin the exhibition.

In planning for the Meadows Museum exhibition, Surls paid particular attention to the building's spaces. This is not an unusual practice for Surls, who has always attended to how his work is displayed. However, the spaciousness of the museum and his new experience of living in the vast landscape of Colorado caused him to focus with heightened intensity on the installation of his work. Attracted to the museum's large, open galleries and the monumental plaza in front of the building's main entrance, he conceived the idea of creating several site-specific works. Within less than a year, Surls had produced, with the unflagging help of studio assistant Tai Pomara, an amazing number of sculptures, including three thirty-foot-high steel sculptures for the plaza, a twenty-foot hanging-wood-and-steel sculpture for the staircase, a thirteen-by-twenty-eight-foot wall sculpture, and two seventeen-foot sculptures for the main gallery. During the installation of the exhibition, he also created two wall drawings, one measuring fifteen by twenty-nine feet. Surls has long stated that he loves to work big, and he has produced some monumental pieces, but for *In the Meadows* he outdid himself in terms of grand ambitions and achievements.

The Meadows Museum exhibition was not intended to be a retrospective of Surls's art, since it focused on works executed since 1998. However, because the show featured a profusion of sculptures, maquettes for large sculptures, drawings, and prints, it did present a comprehensive survey of the range of media in which Surls has worked and the motifs—his visual alphabet—he employs. Symbols that Surls has used for nearly twenty-five years appeared in abundance: eyes (life), diamonds (intellect/rationality), needles (female/fertility/binding), knives (weapon/tool/utensil), flowers (emotion/life/beauty), spirals (life force/aspiration), bridges (transition), and houses (security). These "big picture symbols" come together in *From the Pitcher* (PL. 11). Specifically created for *In the Meadows* (and, because of its great size, not seen complete by the artist until the exhibition's installation), this immense piece features a massive table, representing his studio worktable (the "operating table"), on which stands a pitcher. "Poured" from the pitcher (essentially a steel drawing in space) onto the table is the artist's visual alphabet—needles, diamonds/crystals, houses, axes, knives, pins. The artist is laying his cards on the table, so to speak. Out of this jumble of forms, art will emerge. *From the Pitcher* is a huge, carnivalesque three-dimensional still-life composition, which, with its scattering of his signature motifs, is also a portrait of the artist.

From the Pitcher is not Surls's first representation of his worktable; his 1993 *Table*, and in 1994, *Me and the Mixing Bowl* (FIG. 41), for example, include a knife, a bowl with objects, and a linear steel profile of the artist set in a vase. However, the Brobdingnagian scale of *From the Pitcher* sets it apart from earlier work and aligns it with the expansiveness that has characterized his work since the move to Colorado. Similarly, the motifs of *Bridge & Needle* (PL. 9) are found throughout Surls's art since the late 1970s but are now rendered in gargantuan size: the seventeen-foot-high steel needle nearly scraped the Meadows gallery's ceiling, while its twenty-one-foot wooden bridge spread across the floor. The bridge's weighty horizontality contrasts powerfully with the dynamic verticality of the needle. Each form symbolizes transformation and change: the needle's threads spinning out floral and gem shapes, the bridge signifying a crossing over to new terrain. When bridges had appeared earlier in Surls's art, they stood as general metaphors for mental change and moving ahead to imaginative new worlds. However, since Surls has likened moving over a mountain to crossing a bridge, the motif in *Bridge & Needle* specifically stands for the artist's passage to Colorado. Its massive size communicates the immensity of the move for Surls. *Bridge & Needle* also expresses a transformation occurring in Surls's art, from the wooden sculptures of his Texas years to his increasing interest since moving to Colorado in producing works in steel. The bridge (his past art) literally and metaphorically supports the needle (his new art). Surls purposely drew attention to the steel needle by the manner in which he installed *Bridge & Needle* in the Meadows Museum: by carefully adjusting the lighting on the piece, the artist caused the work to cast eye-catching shadows on the wall behind it. These shadows, resembling marks on the wall, gave the needle an even greater physical expansiveness, while emphasizing its character as a drawing-in-space.

In the Meadows also included many drawings and prints. Most of Surls's prints (twenty-five to thirty in number) date from the late 1980s or early 1990s.[27] However, Surls also produced a suite of lithographs at Anderson Ranch in 1998. These visually energetic compositions (which include pieces titled, significantly, *Bridge Crossing* (PL. 62) and *Two Bridges* (PL. 65)) differ from the artist's previous prints in being highly abstracted. Variations of his signature motifs are evident in these prints, but only in suggestive and

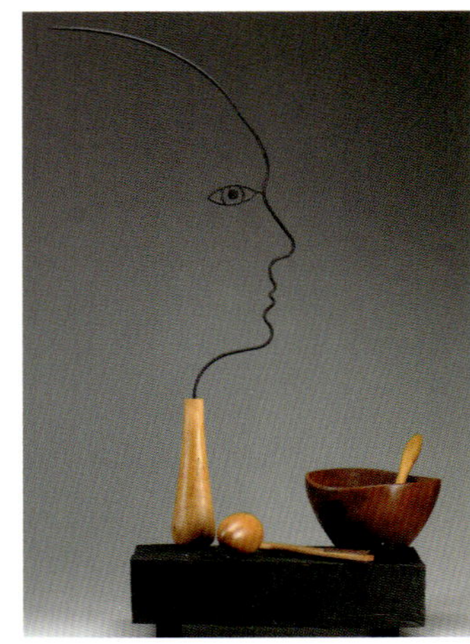

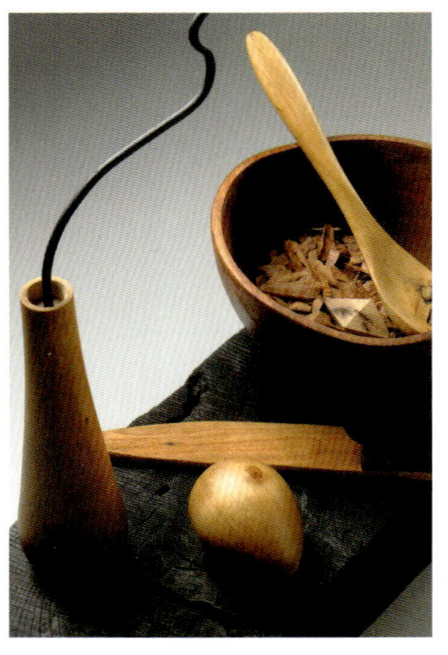

TOP

FIGURE 41
Me and the Mixing Bowl, 1994
Oak, sycamore, pine, mahogany, walnut
53 ½ x 32 x 13
The Barrett Collection, Dallas, Texas

BOTTOM

Me and the Mixing Bowl (detail), 1994
Oak, sycamore, pine, mahogany, walnut
53 ½ x 32 x 13
The Barrett Collection, Dallas, Texas

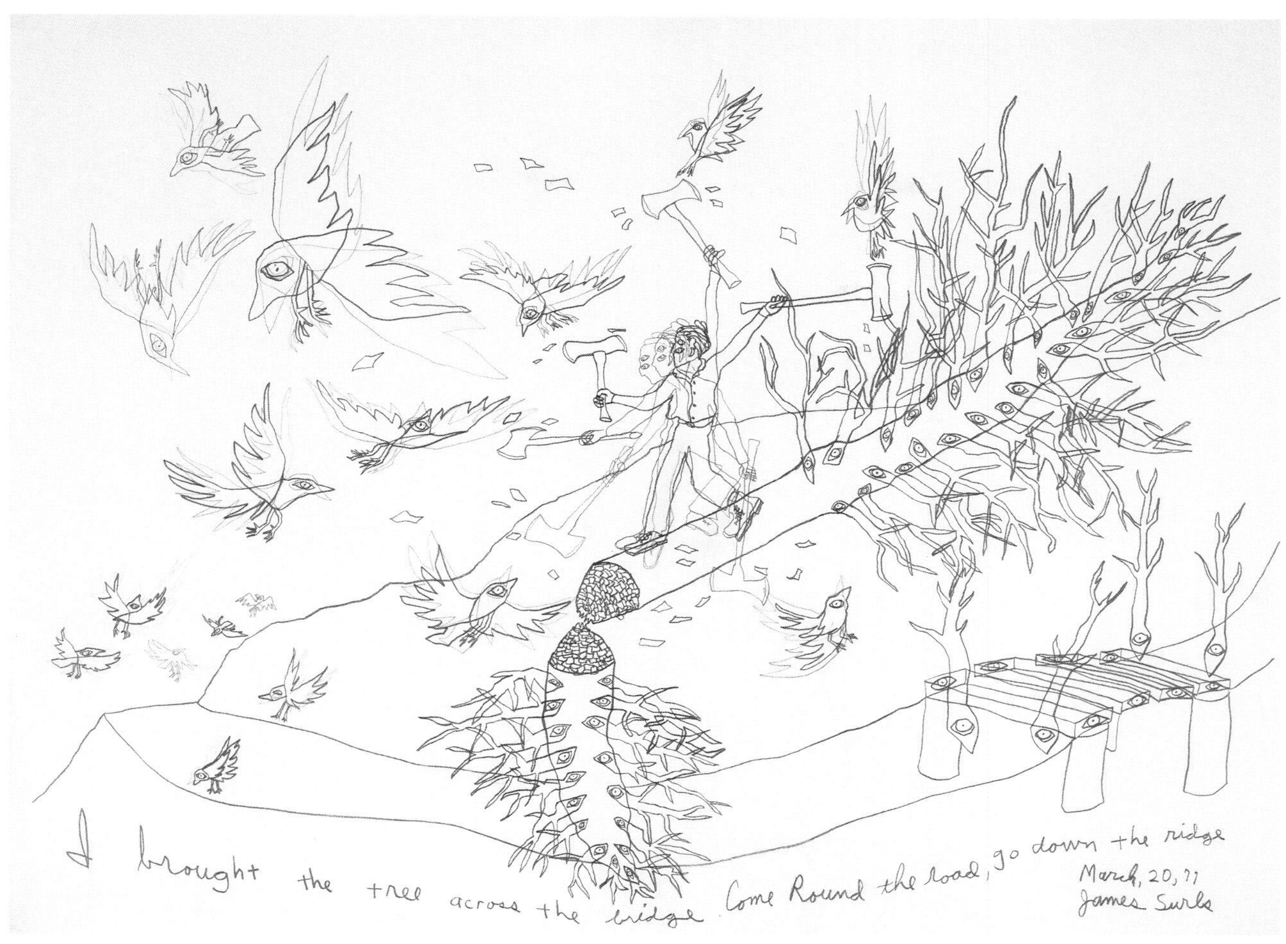

subtle ways. While his prints were produced during a fairly concentrated period, Surls's drawings, by contrast, have been more constant in and essential to his art since 1977. Some drawings relate to specific sculptures and essentially serve as blueprints. More numerous, and of greater visual interest and virtuosity, are his graphite contour drawings that express his stream of consciousness **(FIG. 42)**. Initially, Surls started drawing in the mid-1970s to pin down his childhood memories (he did not draw much either as a child or as an art student). He adopted an approach to which he still adheres: no correcting, erasing, or smudging. Surls operates under a sense of complete freedom that assumes there truly are no mistakes. An impressive example of the artist's approach to drawing is his *Into the Snow* **(PL. 40)**.

Working graphite on a large sheet of paper, Surls produced a composition of such extraordinary energy that it appears as if it cannot be contained by the paper's edges. Combining slashing strokes with variations of his signature flower motif, the drawing offers an image that is simultaneously airy and dense. The composition relates to the wall sculptures of 2002, *Into the Flowers* **(PL. 13)** and *Into the Flowers Too* **(PL. 12)**. Like these sculptural fields of flowers, *Into the Snow*'s overall-ness and fluidity recall the organic

FIGURE 42
I brought the tree across the bridge, Come round the road, go down the ridge, 1977
Graphite on paper
30 x 40

vitality of Jackson Pollock's classic drip paintings of the late 1940s and early 1950s. The drawing's title suggests that the flowers be read as snowflakes, which may signify a new Colorado-influenced motif and artistic direction. The composition's flurry of graphite marks conveys in heightened fashion the immediacy of drawing that Surls finds so appealing.

Surls likens the directness of drawing to the concentrated intensity ("close to the bone") that he associates with poetry. He has, in fact, created drawings in collaborations with poets, including Robert Creeley and Cynthia Macdonald, and made drawings related to his own poetry. The colossal wall drawing in the exhibition (PL. 48), which by engulfing the spectator's peripheral vision absorbs the viewer into its field (again, bringing Pollock's paintings to mind), bears the equally all-encompassing title from one of his poems, "Me, God, Evolution, Love, Relationship and you." Typical of his working process, the poem preceded the drawing.

Surls commenced this drawing by delineating an immense outline of his hand. This was an intriguing beginning: the artist's hand rendering the artist's hand. To gain some measure of the huge blank space he faced, Surls inserted himself (his hand) directly into that vast emptiness to establish his human presence. By claiming the space with the rendering of his hand, Surls reaffirmed the universal human impulse to make marks to confirm one's identity and existence, a practice that traces back eons to hands painted on Paleolithic cave walls. Surls personalized the universal hand by placing on it a ring consisting of seven eyes, representing his seven daughters. With the immense, almost flowering, crystal on the left and the tiny, orbiting dot-worlds on the right coexisting in the same space, the drawing conflates the microscopic and macroscopic, the personal and universal. In merging the small and the large, the composition recalls the opening lines of "Auguries of Innocence" (c. 1803) by William Blake, a Romantic poet much admired by Surls:

To see a World in a Grain of Sand
And a Heaven in a Wild Flower
Hold Infinity in the palm of your hand
And Eternity in an hour

The breadth and focus of the drawing are also akin to the spirit expressed in a Creeley poem that is one of Surls's favorites:

So simply vast
placed
in this space—
everywhere

This drawing and several of the sculptures display the physical expansiveness that increasingly informs Surls's visual alphabet. *Into the Flowers*, a wall sculpture thirteen feet across, is a whirl/world/swirl of life, and *Fourteen Flowers* **(PL. 10)** hung in the midst of the museum's staircase, bridging two floors. Although Surls was making large sculpture of great breadth before moving to Colorado, he is now more than ever engaged in producing large-scale works.

The grand plaza fronting the Meadows Museum offered Surls the opportunity to install four large steel sculptures, with three of them—*Reaching Out* **(PL. 18)**, *Again in the Meadows* **(PL. 17)**, and *Stairway to Heaven* **(PL. 19)**—specifically created for the site; the fourth work—*Walking See Flower* **(PL. 16)**—dates from 2001. Producing outdoor sculpture is not new for Surls. Throughout his career, several of his wooden sculptures have been placed in outdoor locations, including, intriguingly, a piece in Aspen. As part of its 1986 exhibition *Sculpture/Aspen*, the Aspen Art Museum selected Surls, along with Alan Saret, Jackie Ferrara, Michael Singer, and John Torreano, to install work on the museum's grounds. Surls described his contribution, the wood-and-steel sculpture *From the Center* **(FIG. 43)**, as "a natural geometric growth pattern."[28] In 1992 his *Points of View* **(FIG. 44)**, a piece that also features wooden planks spinning out of a spiraling steel core, was installed at the center of redesigned Market Square Park in downtown Houston. The concentrated vertical spirals of both of these, and other, earlier outdoor works, differ from the openness distinguishing Surls's recent steel sculptures.

Walking See Flower, *Reaching Out*, *Again the Meadows*, and *Stairway to Heaven* are essentially dynamic drawings-in-space. Linearity and openness are their primary characteristics. The lines of steel define the forms as large flowerlike configurations that are simultaneously organic and geometric. For example, *Walking See Flower* takes a circular form, with its petals-with-eyes seemingly propelling the flower-creature forward. Each of the three thirty-foot-high sculptures sets an elongated vertical diamond as its stem-stalk, from which sprouts, depending on the sculpture, flowers, gems, tendrils, or a stylized stairway. The tendrils in *Reaching Out* may be read as hair, which gives the work, as do the stairway in *Stairway to Heaven* and the walking in *Walking See Flower*, an anthropomorphic dimension. This abstract-human association contributes to the uniqueness of these works within the field of contemporary sculpture, while placing them within the modernist tradition of works such as iron sculptures by Pablo Picasso and Julio González of the late 1920s and early 1930s, Picasso's painting *Flower Woman* of 1946, and Fernand Léger's large ceramic sculpture *Walking Flower* (1951).

Again in the Meadows, *Reaching Out*, and *Stairway to Heaven* all convey a sense of growth upward and then outward. In form more open than massive, the works frame and incorporate their surroundings into their visual realm; being in the round, the sculptures and their environments change as the viewer moves from one angle of vision to another.

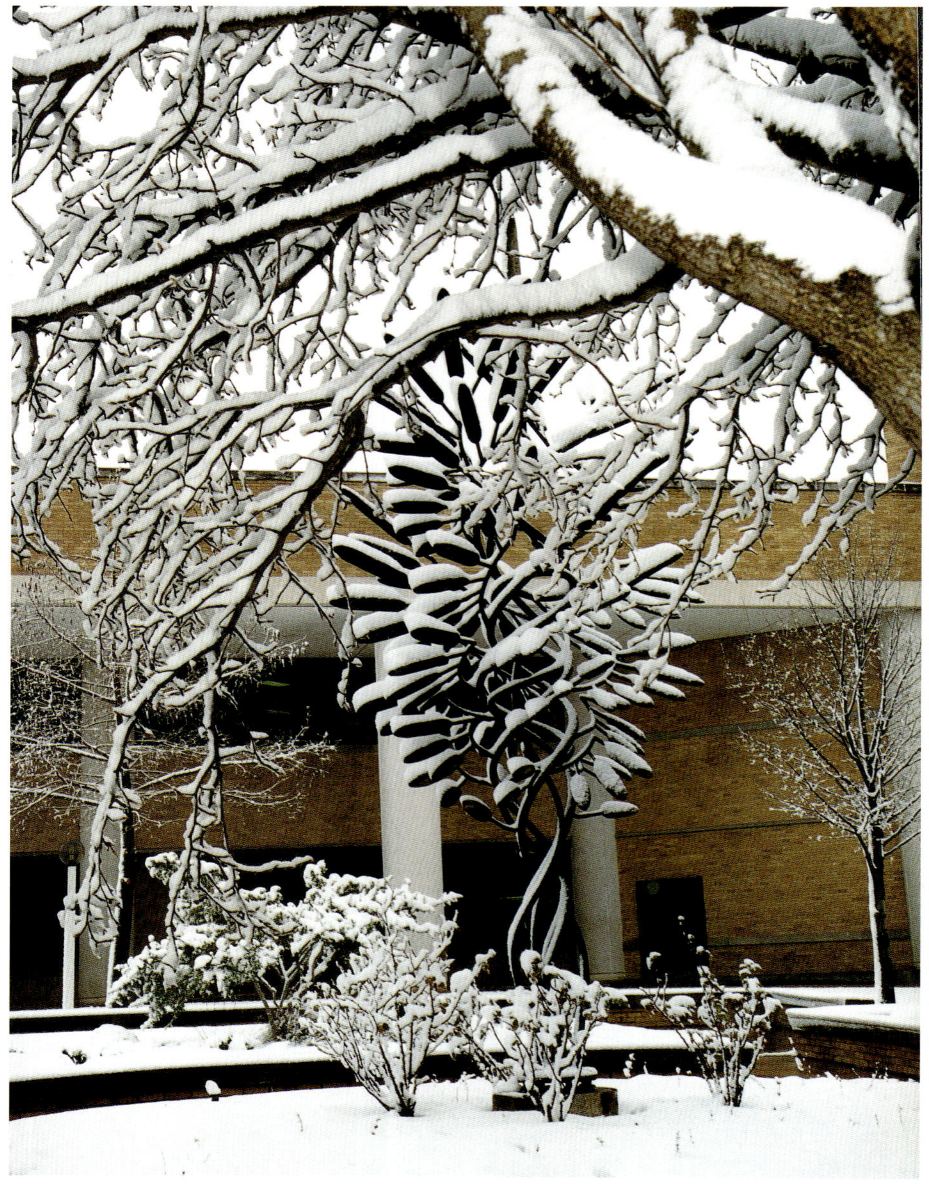

The placement of the works on the Meadows Museum's entrance plaza showed how well they work as public art. Surls's current artistic inclinations align with the widespread interest in public art (his works have been installed as part of art-in-public-places programs in Santa Barbara and Los Angeles). With more and more American cities initiating and expanding percent-for-the-arts programs, it would not be surprising to find Surls emerging as a major figure in the sphere of public art in the next few years.

Each of the tall sculptures produced for *In the Meadows* was sited to take advantage of the open sky as a canvas on which the work appeared to be drawn. This idea of sculpture drawn against, and into, the sky is a new area of artistic exploration for Surls and is a direct result of his living in Colorado. The artist has repeatedly described his astonishment

FIGURE 43
From the Center, 1986
Redwood, steel
191 x 87 x 86
Collection of Austin College, Sherman, Texas

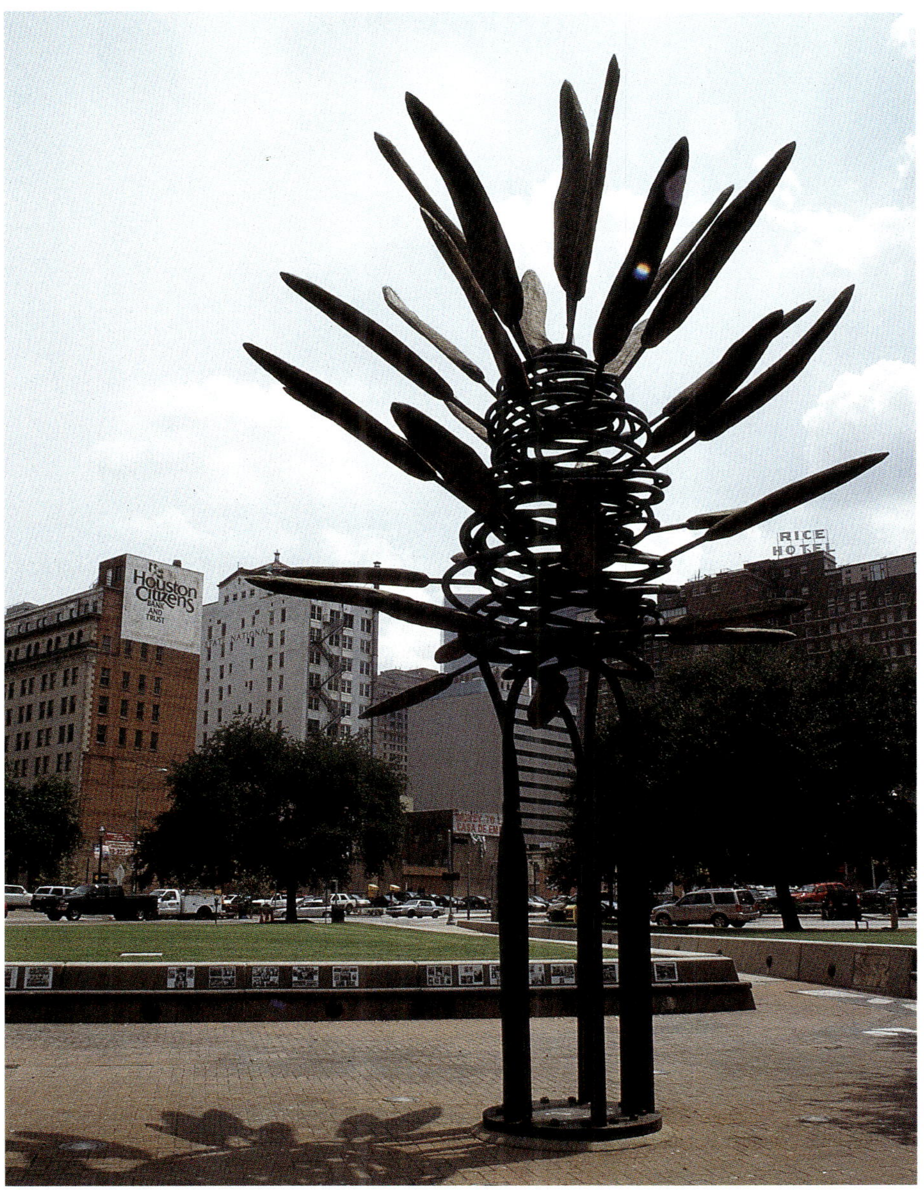

at the open vistas of Colorado, where "the sublime runs rampant"; his wonderful description reminds us of Surls's fundamentally Romantic sensibility. Since moving to the mountains, he regards the sky as an active component in the perception of his large outdoor sculptures. And he feels the expansive Colorado space has caused his "head to open up." Surls has always believed in the fundamental importance of environment to art, since "everyone conjures from his environment."[29] Living and working in Colorado have opened for him the possibilities of expanding his art, literally, to incorporate the surroundings. This is the direction that his art now has taken. Whether this manifests the true impact of the move to Colorado remains to be seen. What is clear is that James Surls, conjurer extraordinaire, will continue to look deeply with his eye and into his I.

FIGURE 44
Points of View, 1992
Pine, steel
336 x 156 x 156
Diverse Works. The Market Square Project (1985-1992), Houston, Texas.

NOTES

1. David Bourbon, "Whirled without End," *Vogue*, December 1984, 78.
2. Unless otherwise noted, all Surls quotations are taken from interviews conducted by the author in Glenwood Springs, Colorado, on August 9–11, 2002, and in Dallas on January 17, 2003.
3. Quoted in James Surls, *Swimming in Forever* (Tyler: Meadows Gallery, University of Texas at Tyler, 1997), n.p.
4. Quoted in Susan Freudenheim, "James Surls: The Power of the Singular Belief," *Artspace*, Spring 1985, 11.
5. Quoted in James Surls, *Swimming in Forever.*
6. Quoted in Suzanne Muchnic, "Artist Plants His Style with Roots in East Texas," *Los Angeles Times*, October 12, 1985, 3.
7. James Surls, *FIRE!* (Houston: Contemporary Arts Museum, 1979), n.p.
8. Quoted in Freudenheim, "James Surls: The Power of the Singular Belief," 12.
9. Quoted in Robert Creeley, *Looking Out: Drawings and Prints by James Surls* (Honolulu: The Contemporary Museum, 1991), n.p.
10. *The Norton Anthology of English Literature*, ed. M. H. Abrams, 6th ed., vol. 2 (New York and London: W. W. Norton and Company, 1993), 147.
11. Quoted in James Surls, *Swimming in Forever.*
12. Jozanne Rabyor, "Dallas—James Surls at Delahunty," *Art in America* 63 (March–April 1975): 107.
13. Quoted in Ed Wilson, "Interview with James Surls," *(Houston) Public News*, October 6, 1983, Art News, 7.
14. Janet Kutner, "James Surls Beats the Bushes for Art," *Dallas Morning News*, February 18, 1979, sec. C, 5.
15. John Russell, "Intimations of Catastrophe," *New York Times*, March 20, 1977, sec. D, 27.
16. Lucy R. Lippard, "Report from Houston: Texas Red Hots," *Art in America*, July–August 1979, 30.
17. Quoted in "James Surls Exhibits during May," *Allan Frumkin Gallery Newsletter*, Spring 1982, 3.
18. Robert Hughes, "Roundup at the Whitney Corral," *Time*, February 26, 1978, 73.
19. Quoted in James Surls, *Swimming in Forever.*
20. Hilton Kramer, "Art: 'Illustration & Allegory' on View," *New York Times*, May 23, 1980, sec. C, 27.
21. Bourbon, "Whirled without End," 78.
22. Robert Hughes, "Intensifications of Nature," *Time* 32 (April 2, 1984): 81.
23. Grace Glueck, "Art: Baziotes, a Rarely Seen Fantasist," *New York Times*, March 16, 1984, sec. C, 21.
24. Quoted in Sue Graze, *Visions: James Surls, 1974–1984* (Dallas: Dallas Museum of Art, 1984), 27.
25. Quoted in *Face to Face: Back to Back* (Fullerton: Main Art Gallery, California State University, 1984), 27.
26. *The Image of the House in Contemporary Art* (Houston: Lawndale Art and Performance Center, University of Houston, 1981), n.p.
27. Surls has produced one print after the Anderson Ranch suite: *Cut Hand, Hurt Eye II* (1999), which is the second edition of a woodcut first published in 1986. During the *In the Meadows* exhibition, a collector who owned a print from the first edition objected to the existence of a second edition (even though it was of different paper and ink). In response, Surls elected to "execute" the second edition by having artist and marksman David Bradshaw fire shots from a .45 automatic pistol at the prints. Both Surls and Bradshaw then signed the new body of work.
28. *Sculpture/Aspen*, curated by Linda Macklowe and Julie Augur (Aspen: Aspen Art Museum, 1986), n.p. Today, *From the Center* occupies an outdoor site at Austin College in Sherman, Texas.
29. Quoted in Elizabeth Heilman Brooke, "A Ranch in the Rockies for Famed Artists and Novices," *New York Times*, August 1, 2000, sec. E, 2.

FIGURE 45
From the Pitcher (detail), 2002 **(PL. 11)**

Sculpture Plates

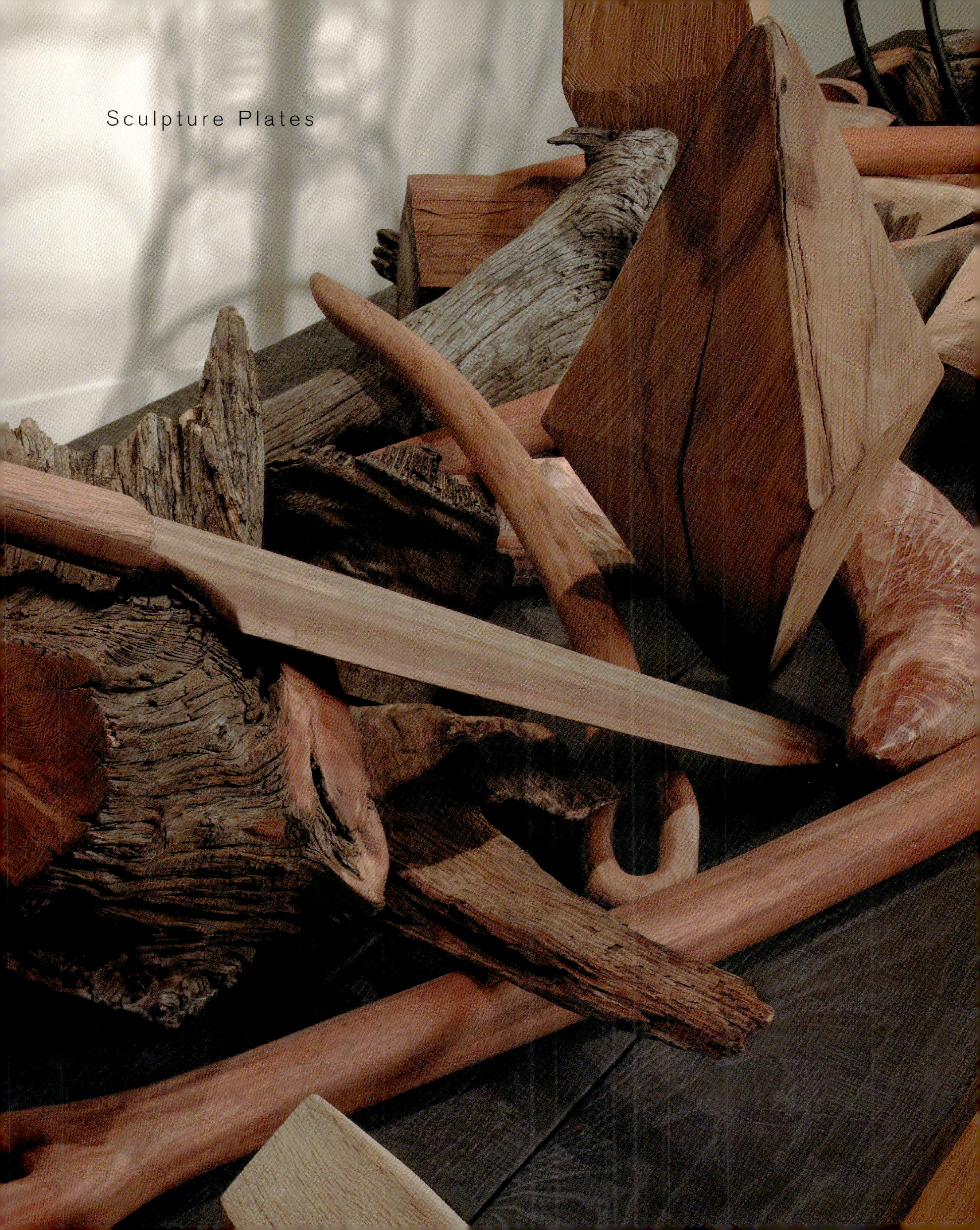

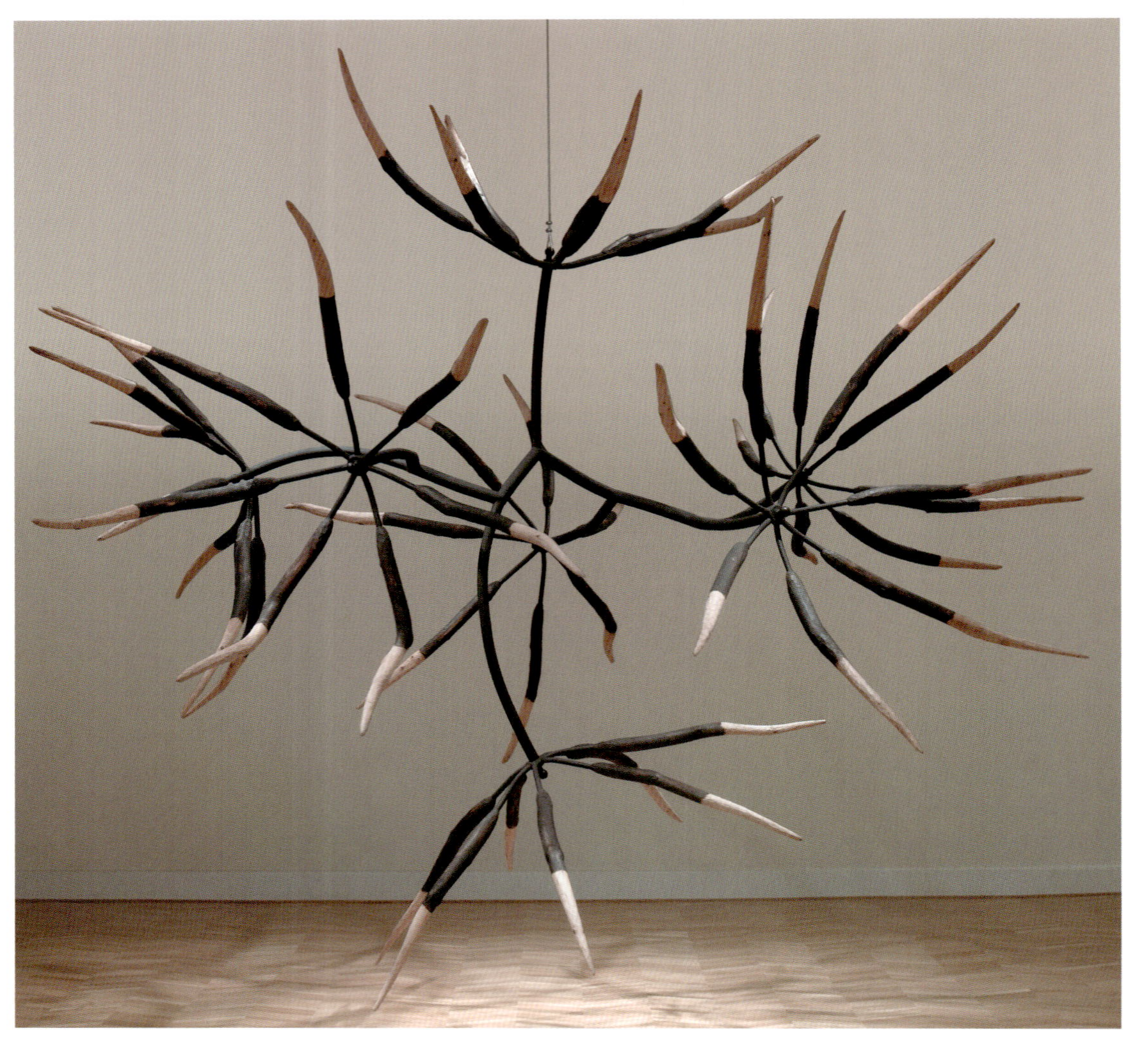

PLATE 1
Seven and Seven Flower, 1998
Pine, limbs, painted steel
185 x 180 x 198

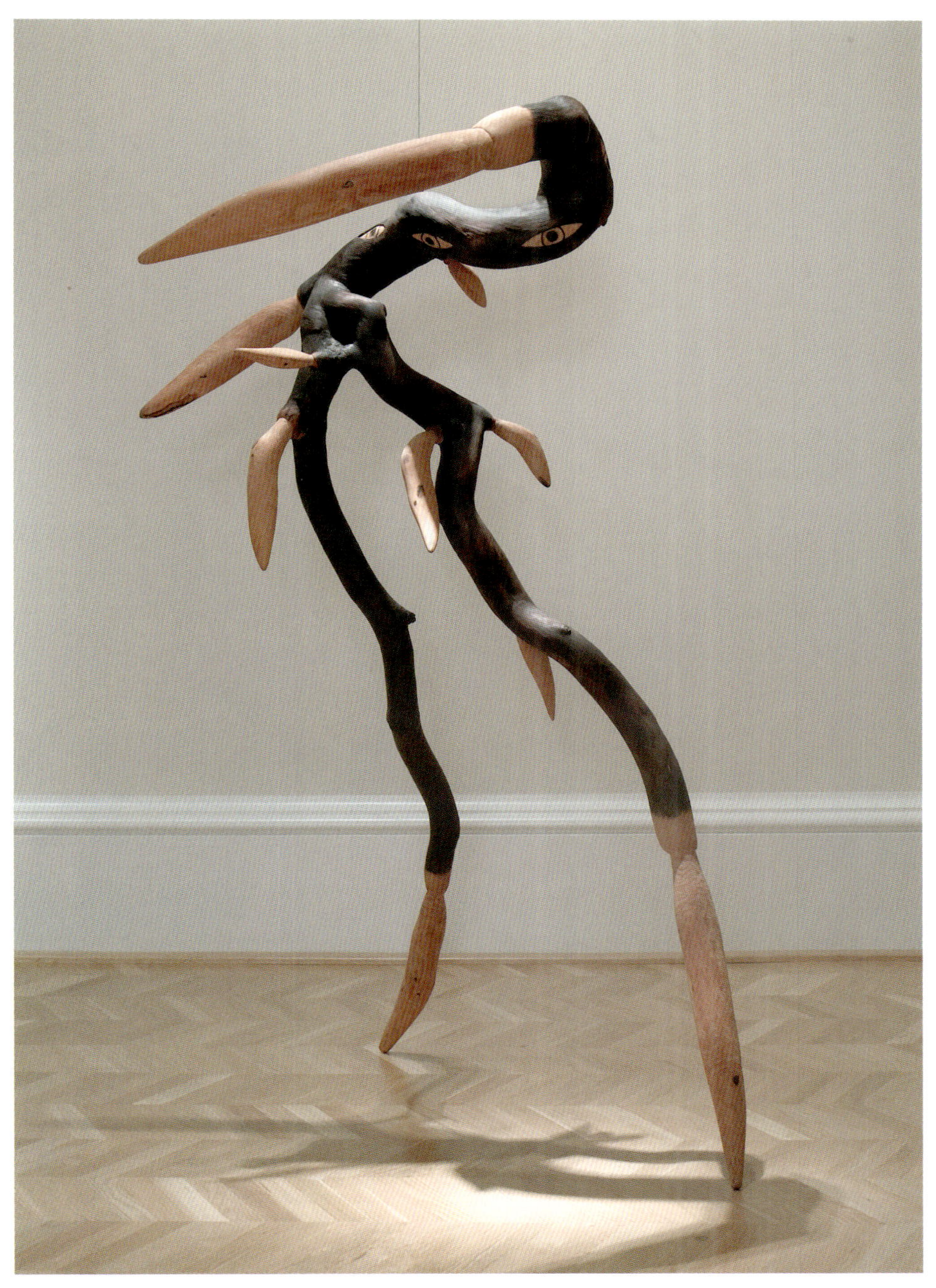

PLATE 2
Turning Around, 1998
Pine, oak
81 ½ x 57 ½ x 21

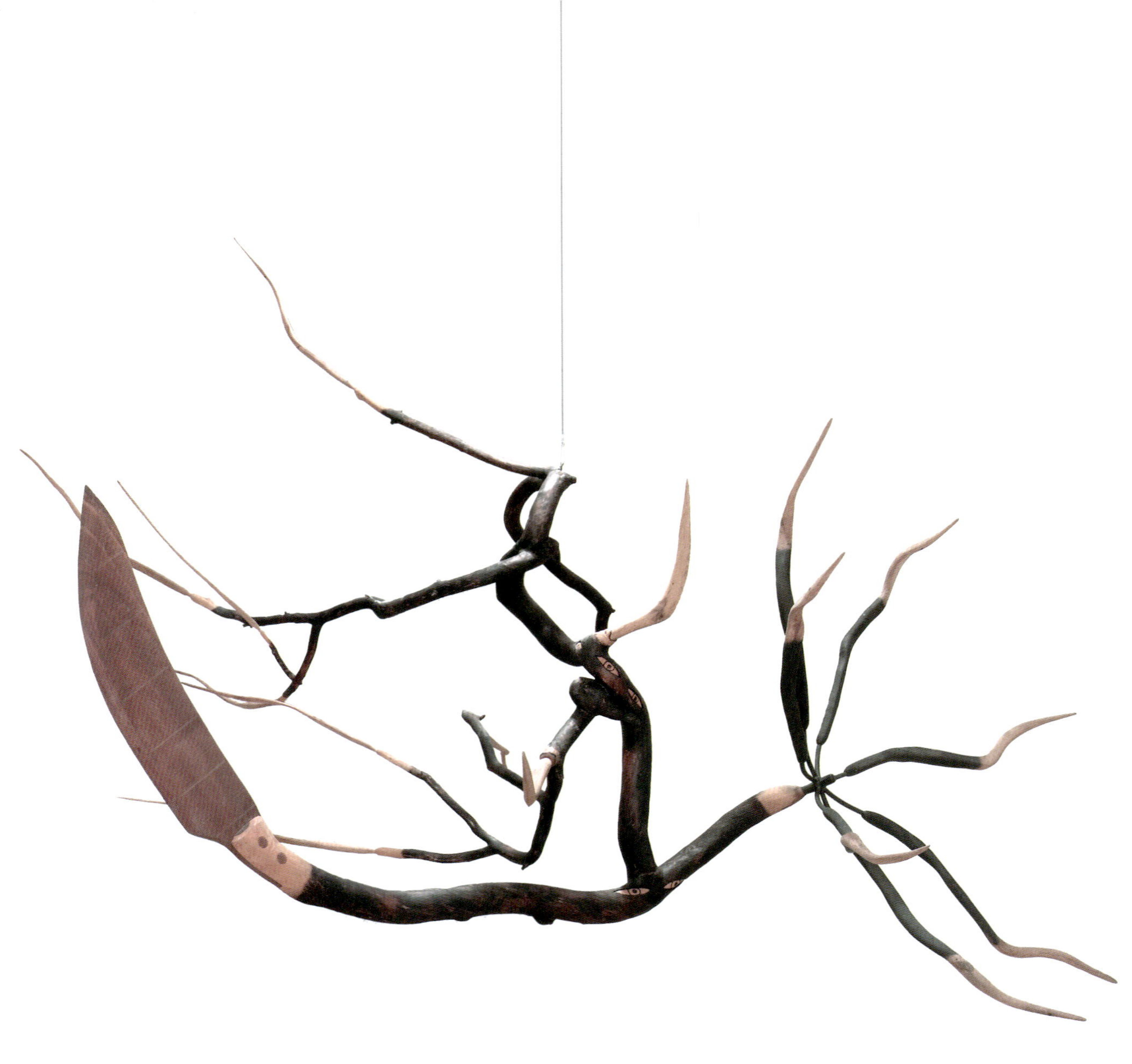

PLATE 3
All in the Wind, 1999
Pine, oak, walnut, painted steel
89 x 98 x 115

PLATE 4
Forever Gone, 1999
Oak, cherry, East Texas pine,
Basalt, Colorado pine
150 x 150 x 196

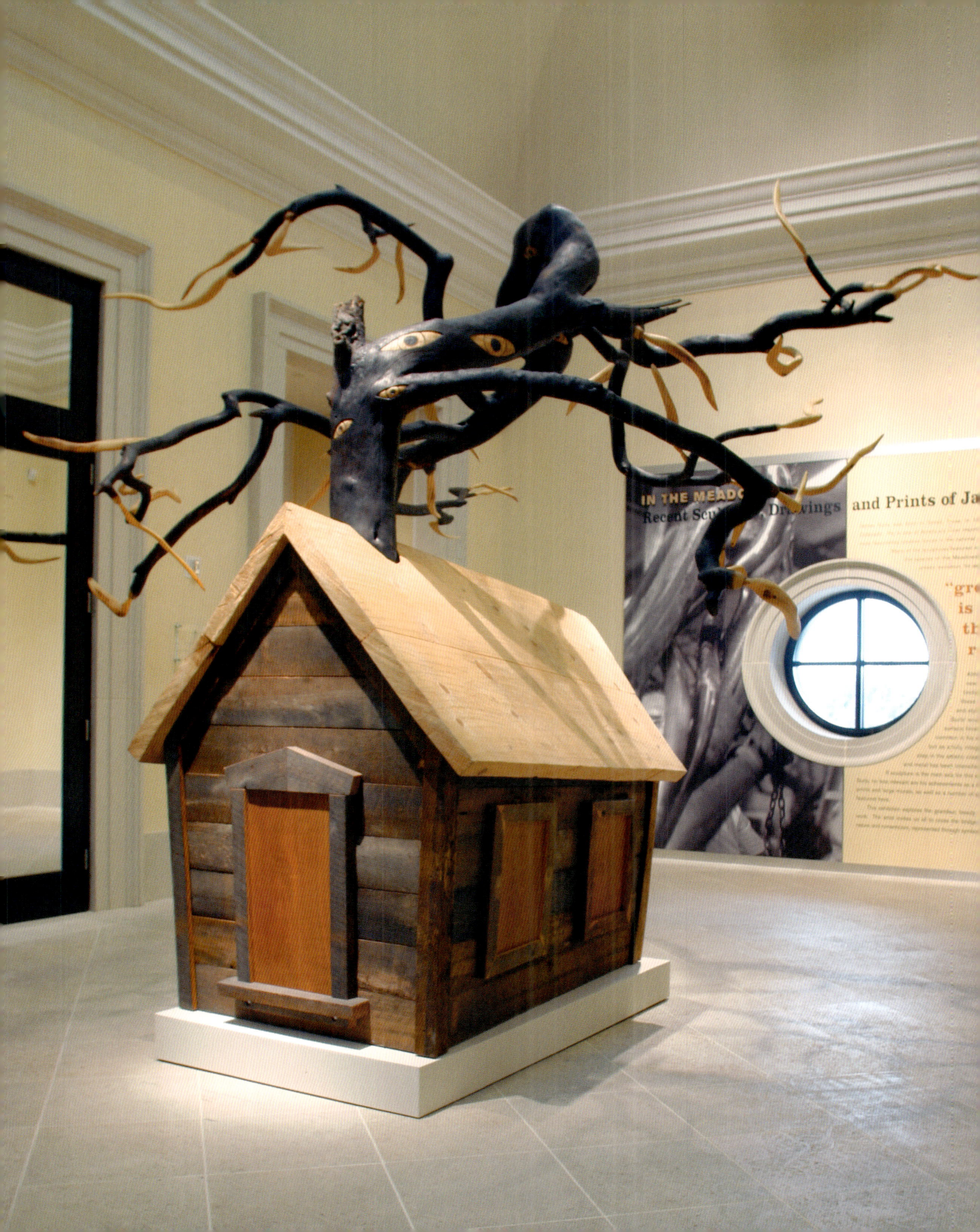
and Prints of

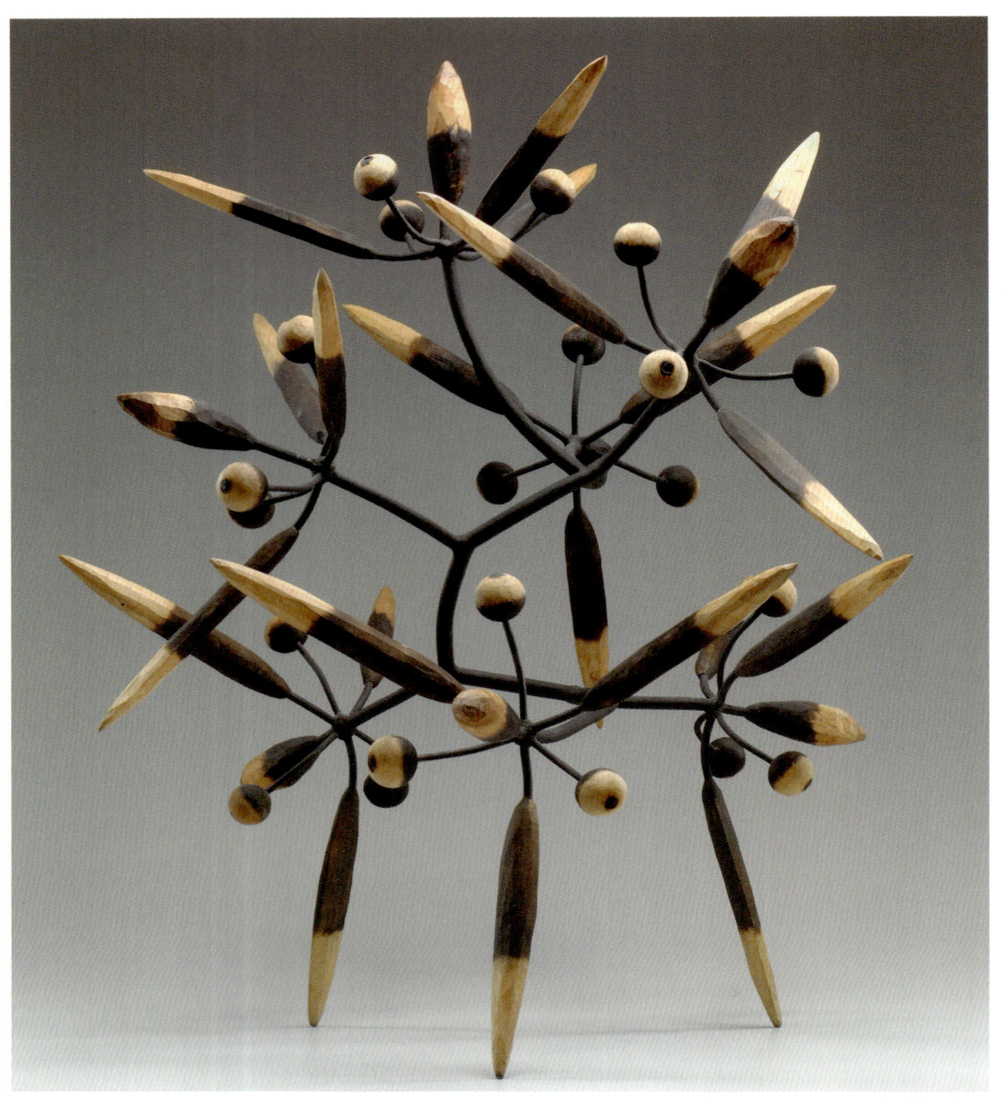

PLATE 5
Standing Three and Three and Seven Flower, 1999
Pine, poplar, painted steel
38 x 33 x 30

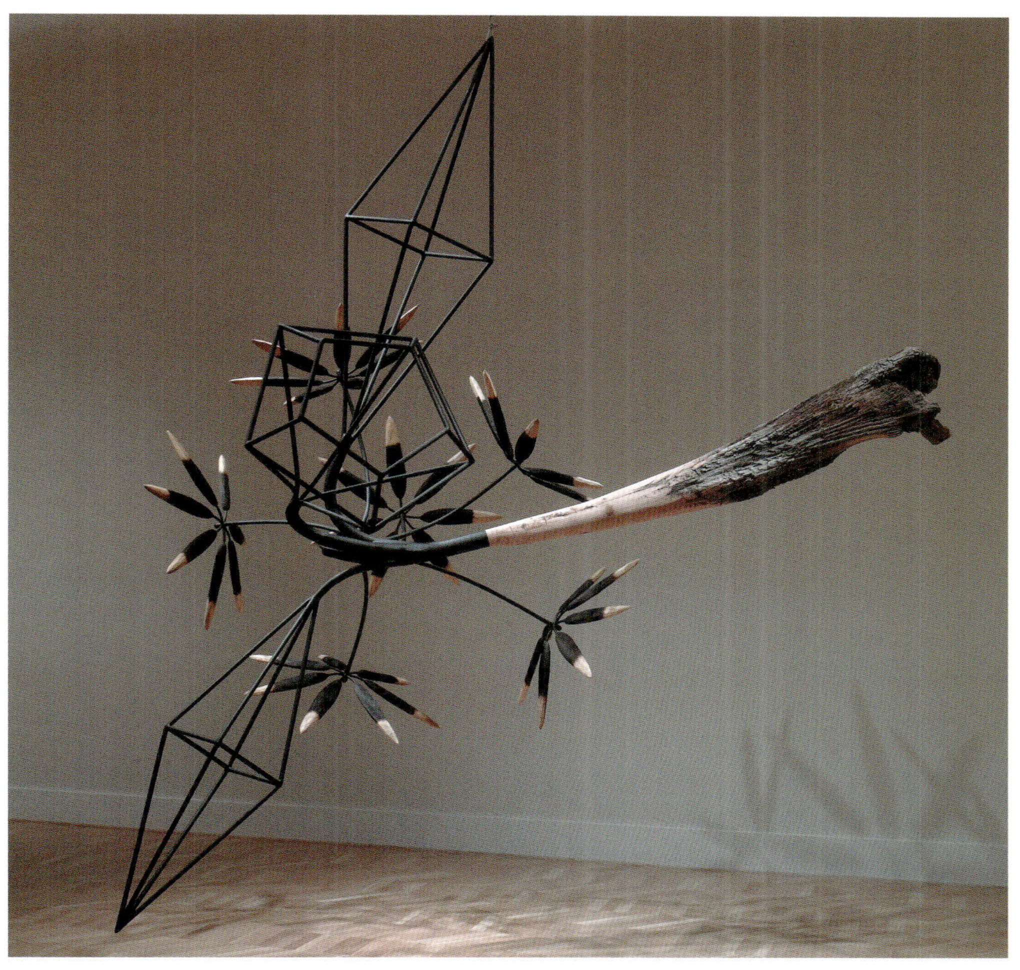

PLATE 6
It is Not About the Numbers, 2000
Pine, poplar, painted steel
120 x 132 x 108

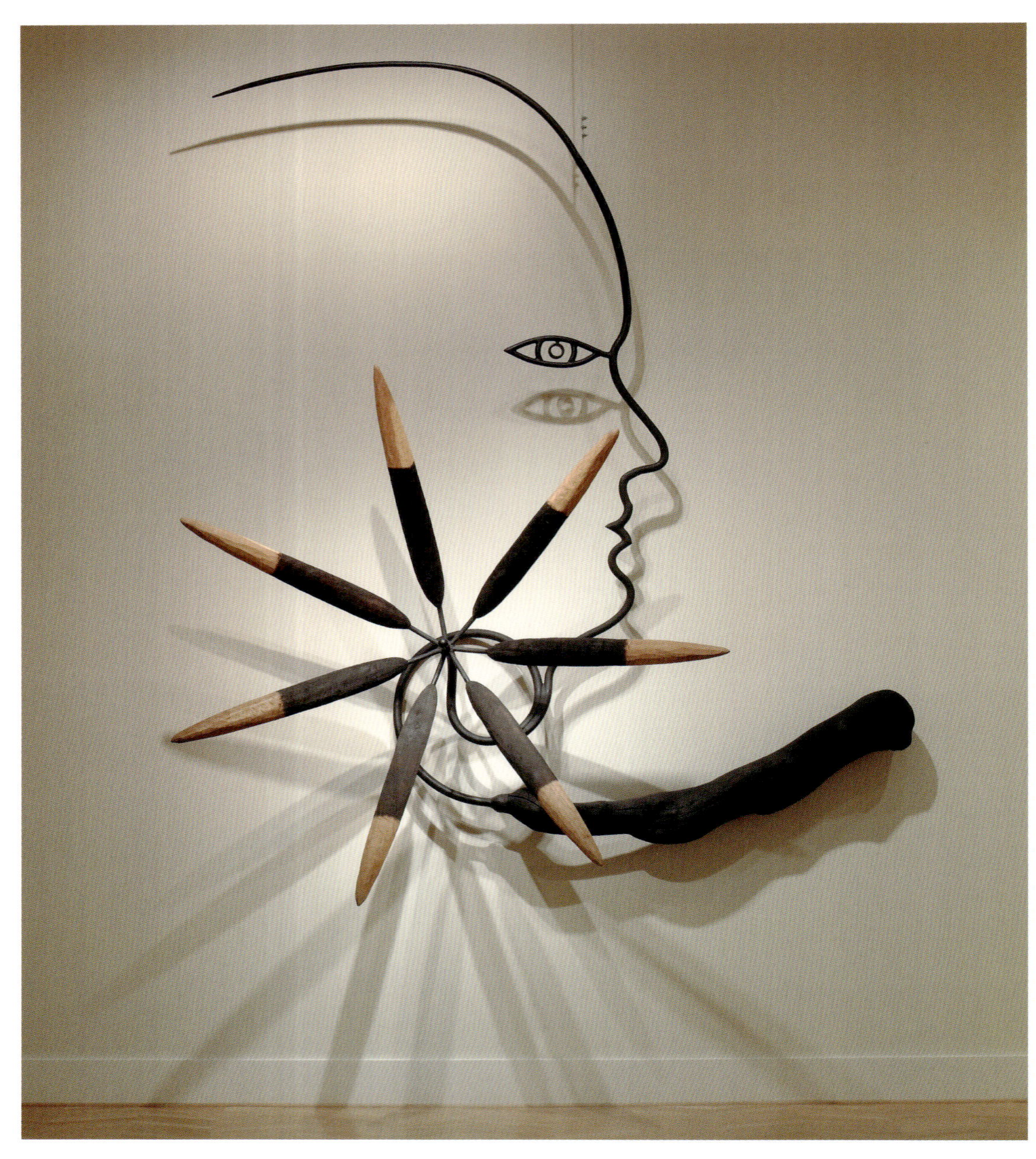

PLATE 7
Me, the Flower and the Pistil, 2000
Poplar, oak, painted steel
110 x 25 x 119

FIGURE 46
Me, the Flower and the Pistil (detail), 2000 **(PL. 7)**

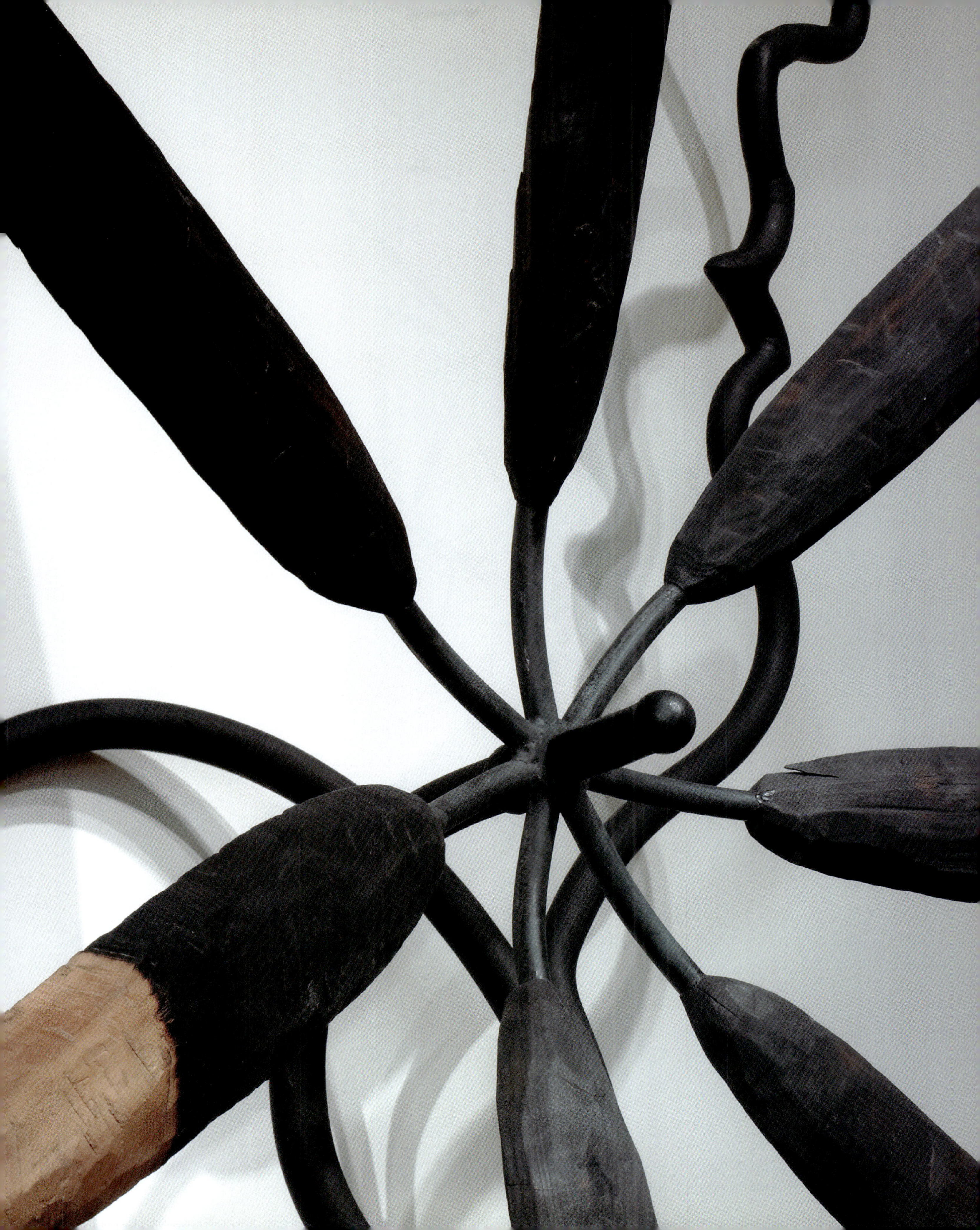

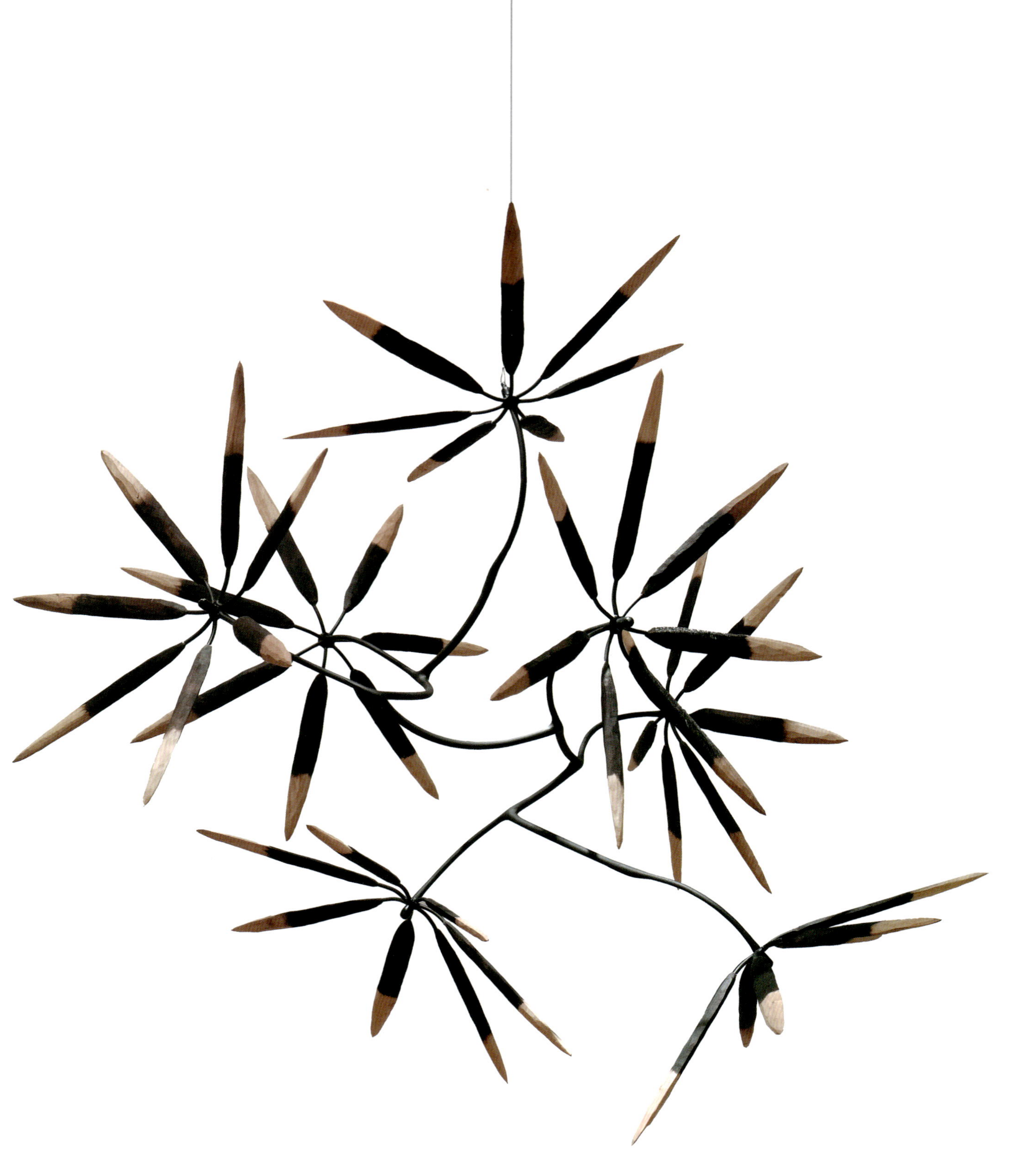

PLATE 8
Seven Flowers, 2001
Bronze, pewter patina
Edition 1 of 5
32 x 32 x 32

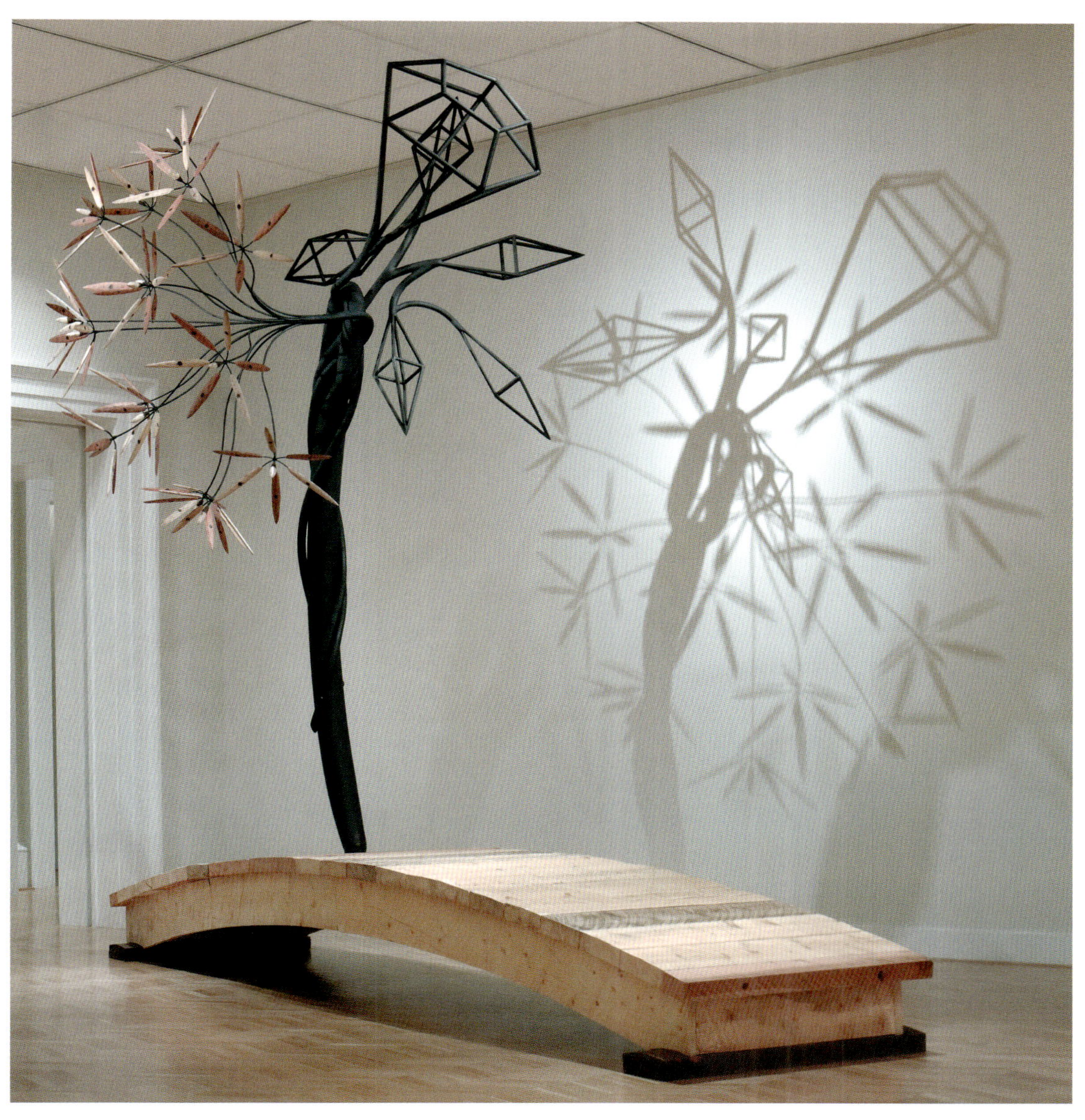

PLATE 9
Bridge & Needle, 2002
Pine, poplar, oak, redwood, painted steel
204 x 96 x 252

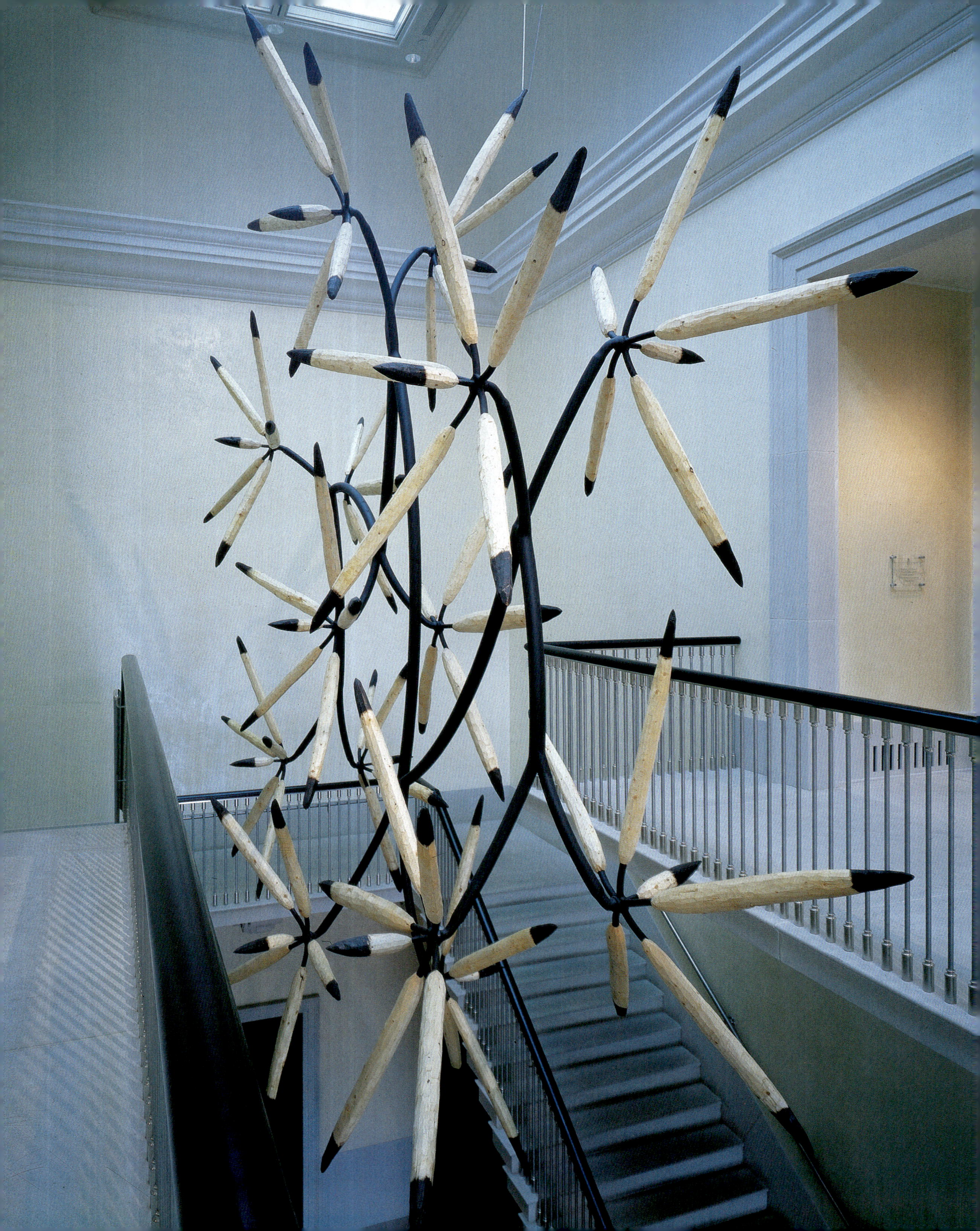

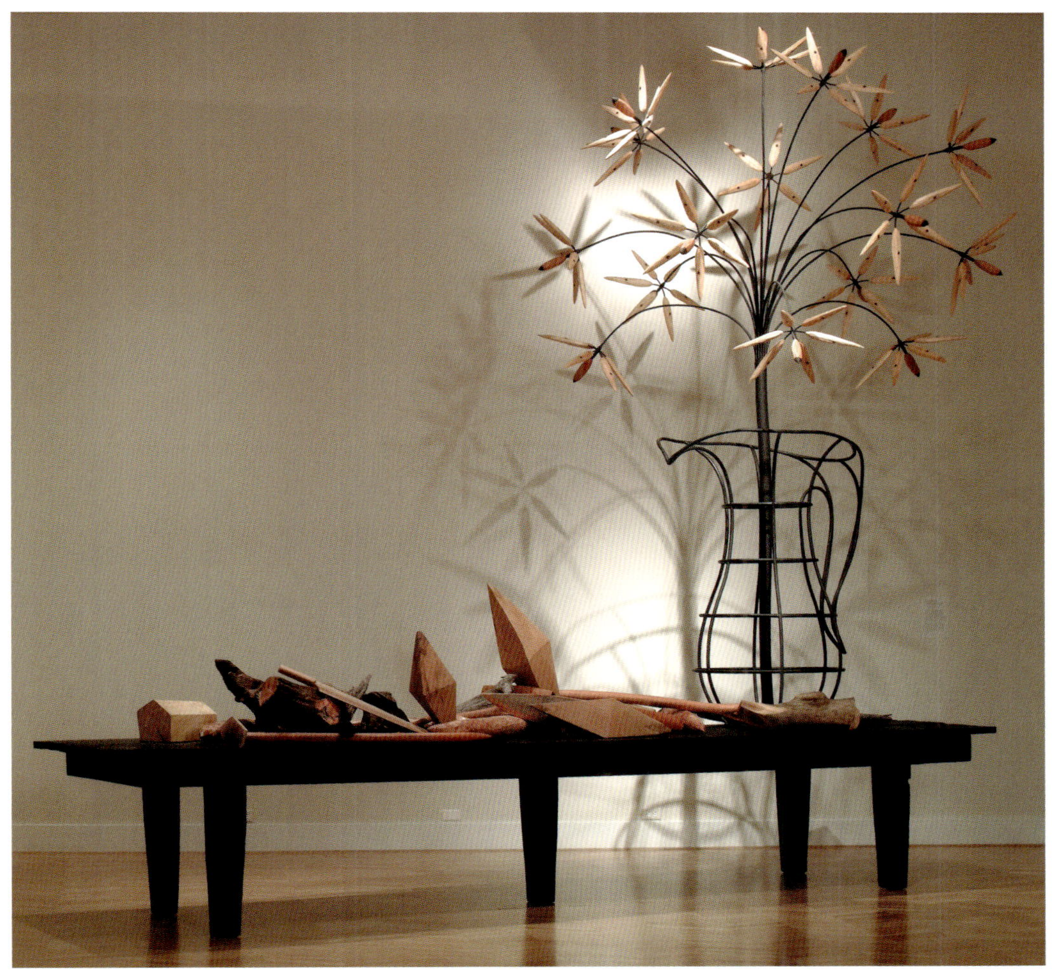

PLATE 10
Fourteen Flowers, 2002
Poplar, painted steel, pine
246 x 246 x 66

PLATE 11
From the Pitcher, 2002
Basswood, mahogany, pine, oak, gum, magnolia, bois d' arc, painted steel
204 x 108 x 192

OVERLEAF:

PLATE 12
Into the Flowers Too, 2002
Painted steel, basswood, mahogany
63 x 145 x 12
Collection of Ambassador Kathryn Hall and Mr. Craig Hall.

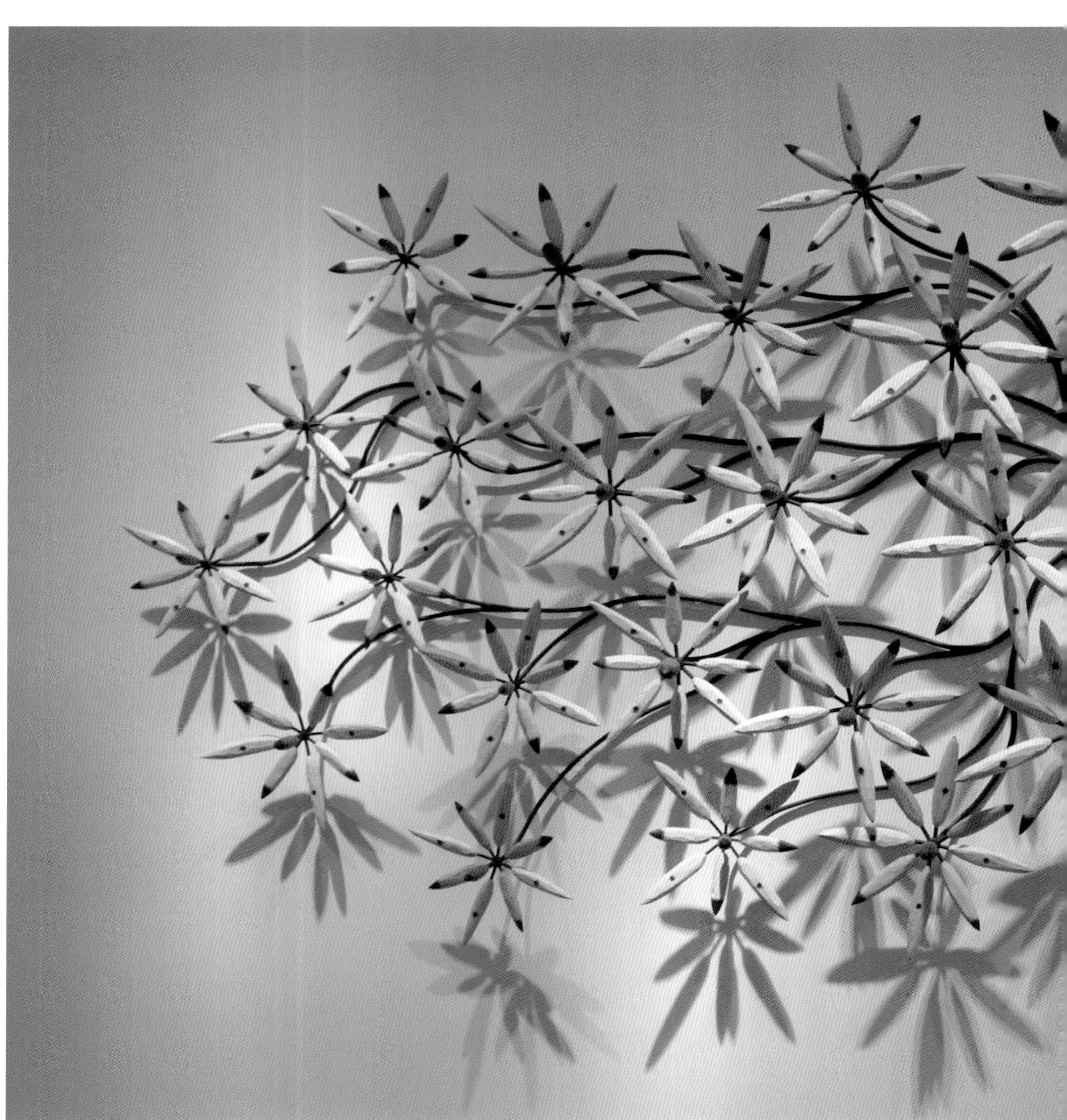

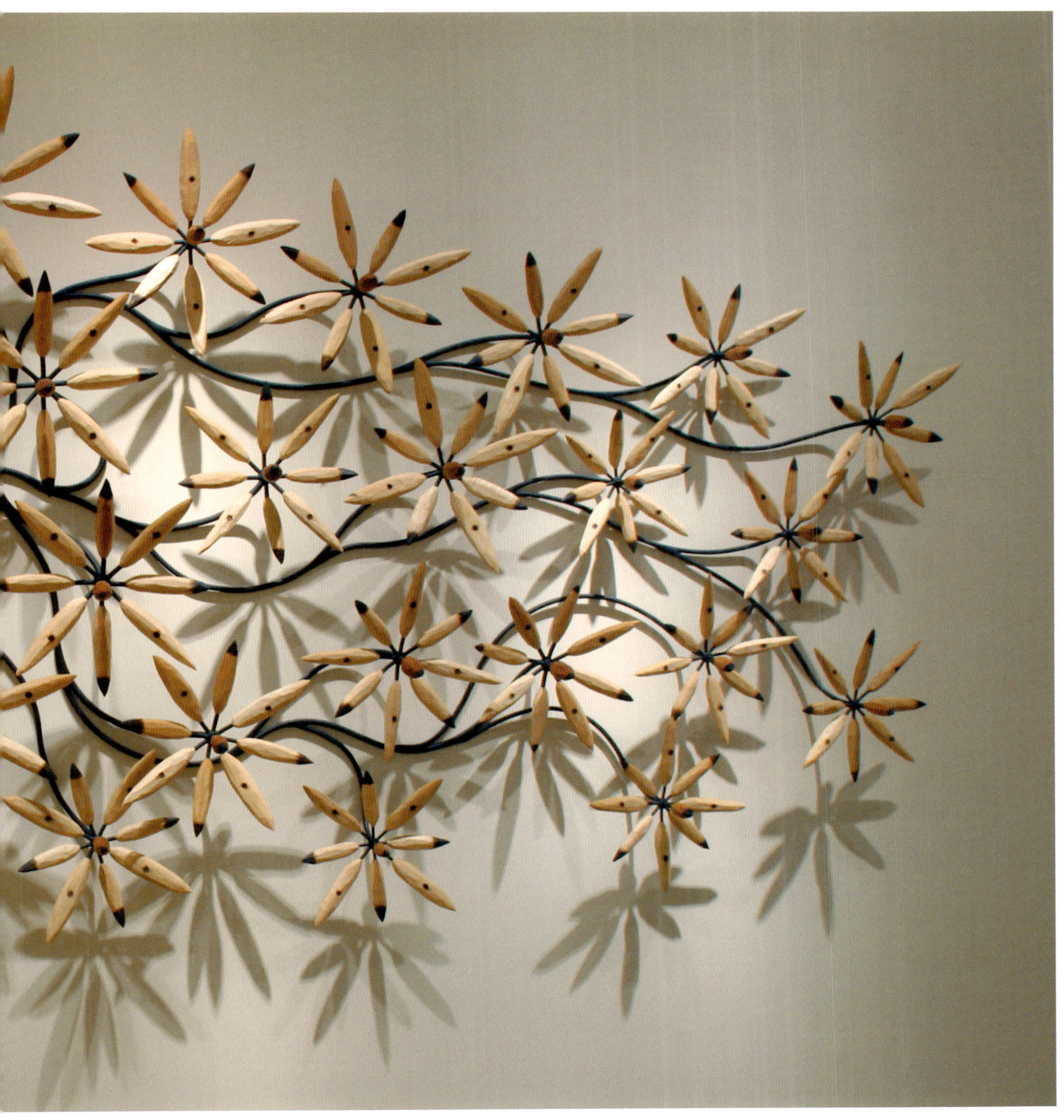

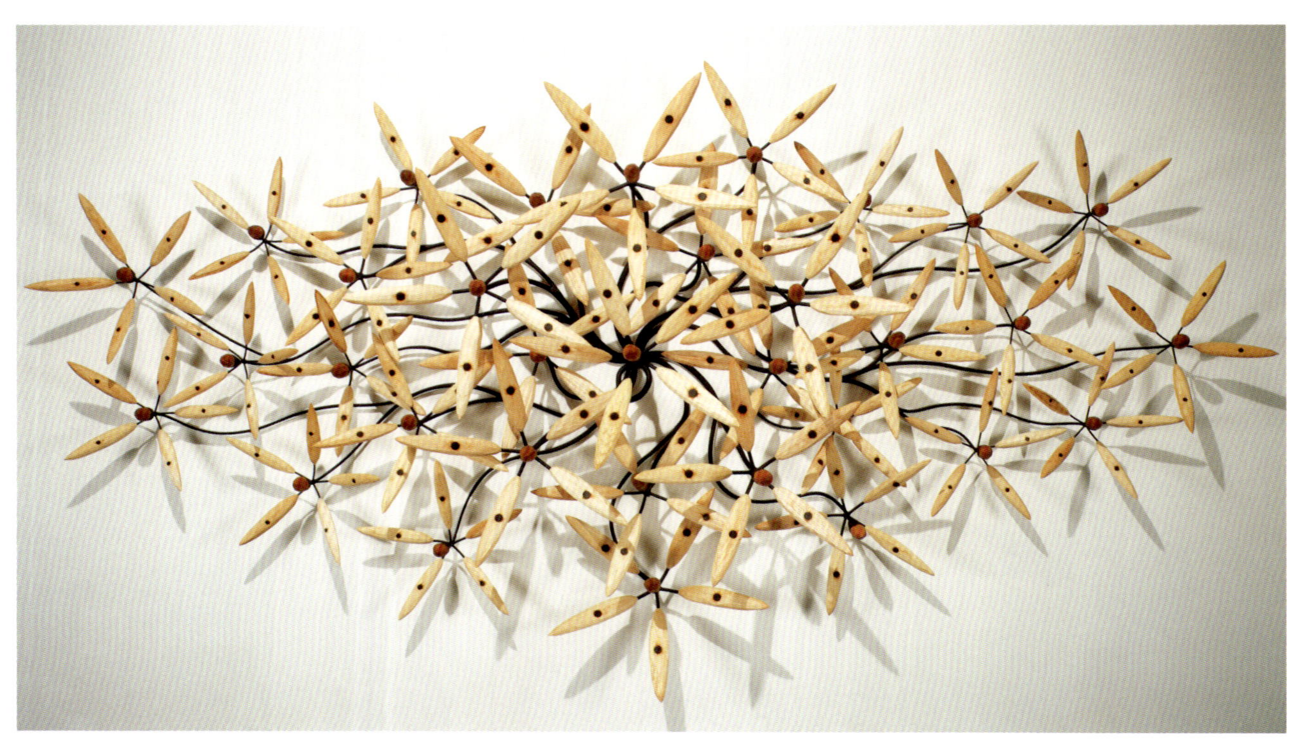

PLATE 13
Into the Flowers, 2002
Mahogany, basswood, painted steel
86 x 159 x 24
Collection of Bennett John and
Jo Ruby Wright.

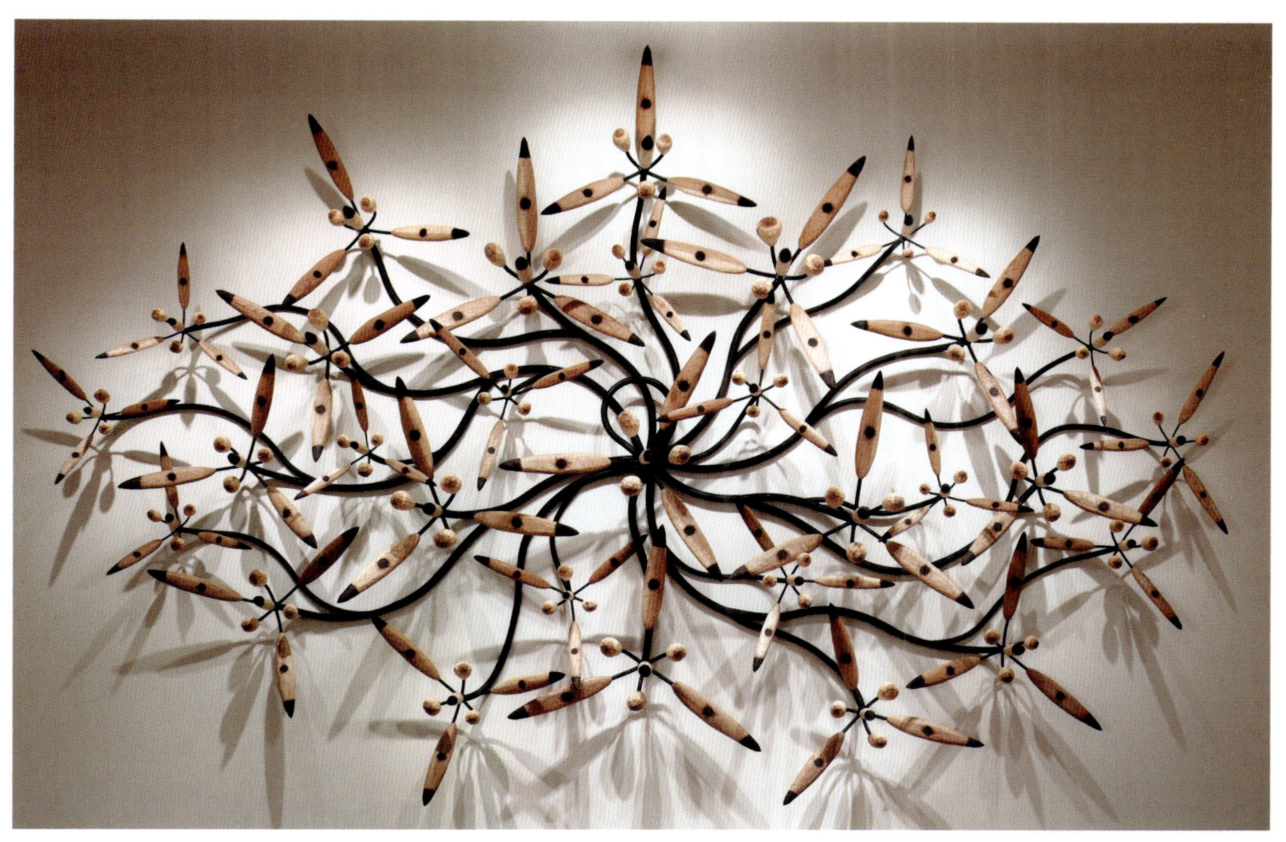

PLATE 14
Large Wall Flower, 2002
Poplar, pine, painted steel
156 x 282 x 30

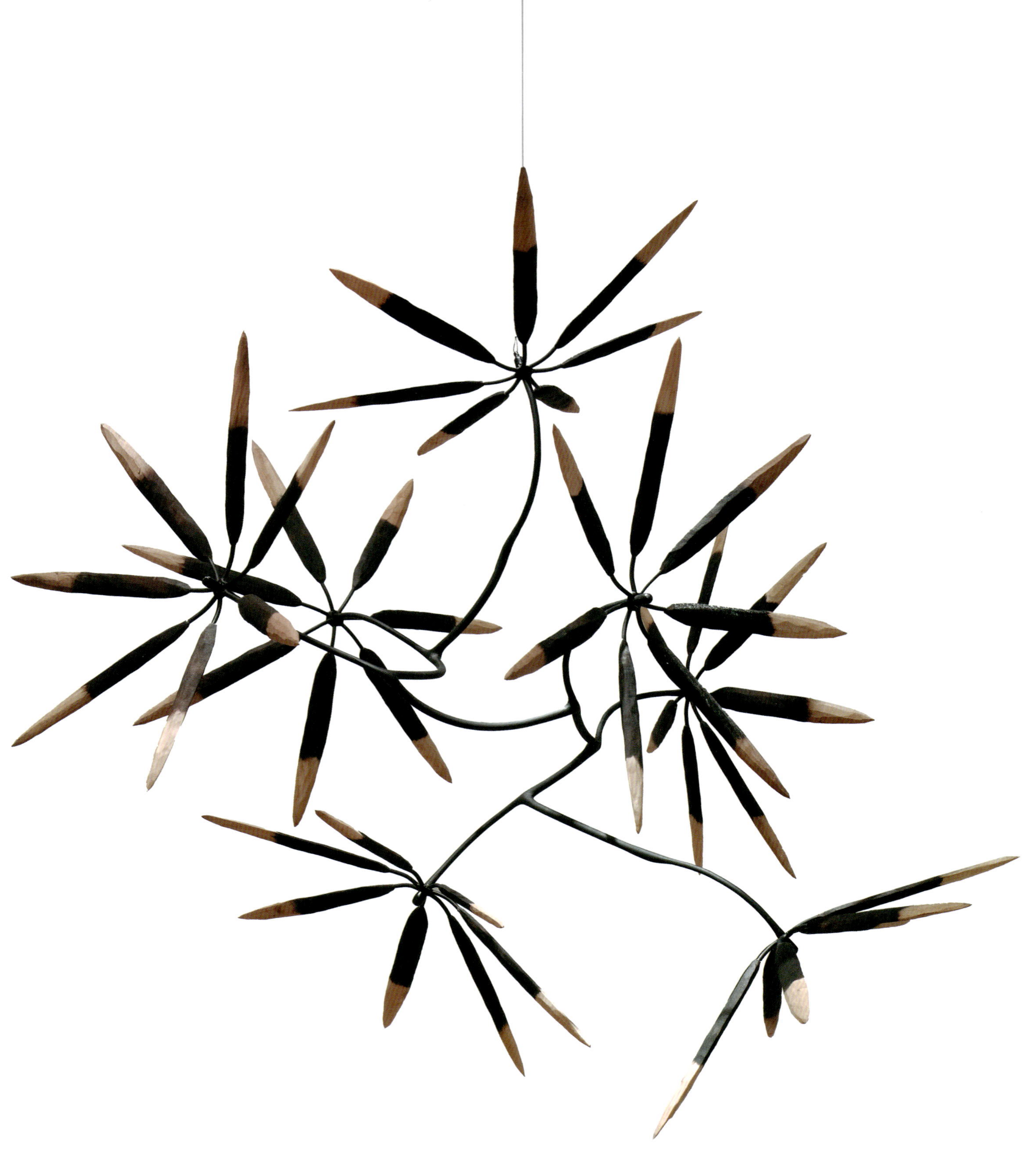

PLATE 15
Seven by Seven White Tipped Flower,
2002
Poplar, painted steel
53 x 48 x 47

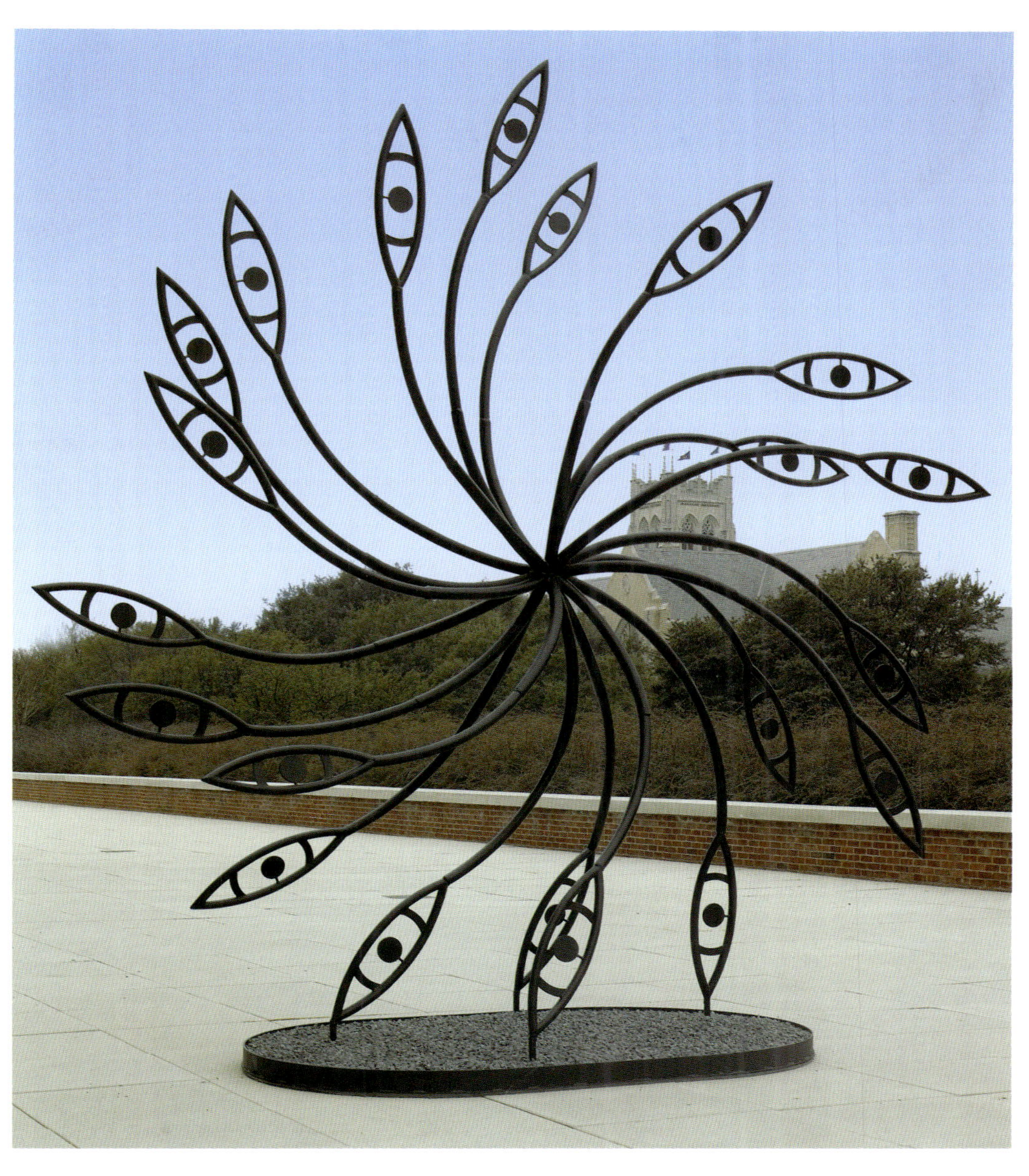

PLATE **16**
Walking See Flower, 2000-01
Painted steel
156 x 156 x 48

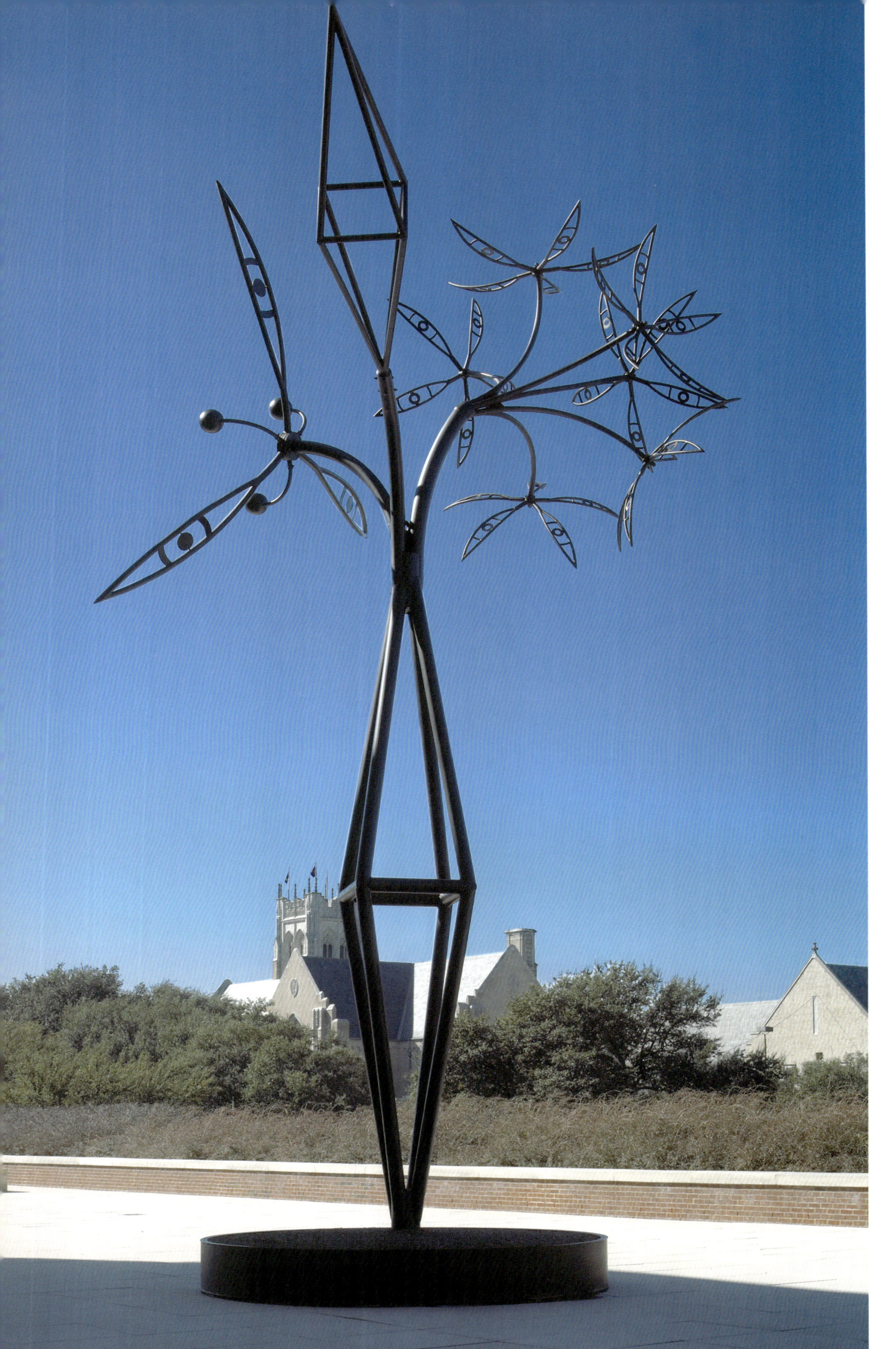

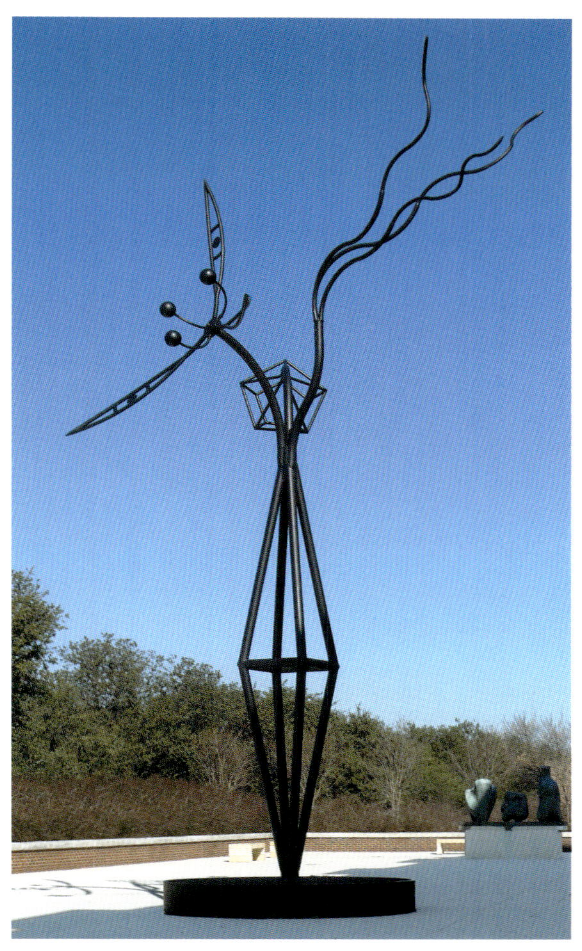

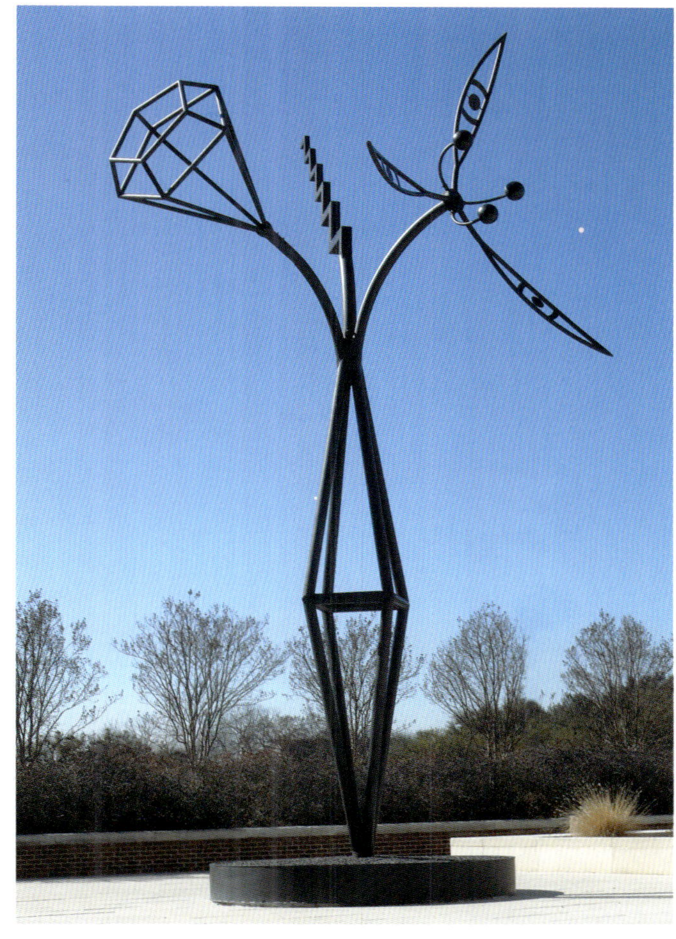

LEFT TO RIGHT:

PLATE 17
Again in the Meadows, 2002
Painted steel
360 x 216 x 228
Collection of Ambassador Kathryn Hall and Mr. Craig Hall.

PLATE 18
Reaching Out, 2002
Painted steel
366 x 168 x 252
Collection of Ambassador Kathryn Hall and Mr. Craig Hall.

PLATE 19
Stairway to Heaven, 2002
Painted steel
360 x 192 x 216
Collection of Ambassador Kathryn Hall and Mr. Craig Hall.

Maquette Plates

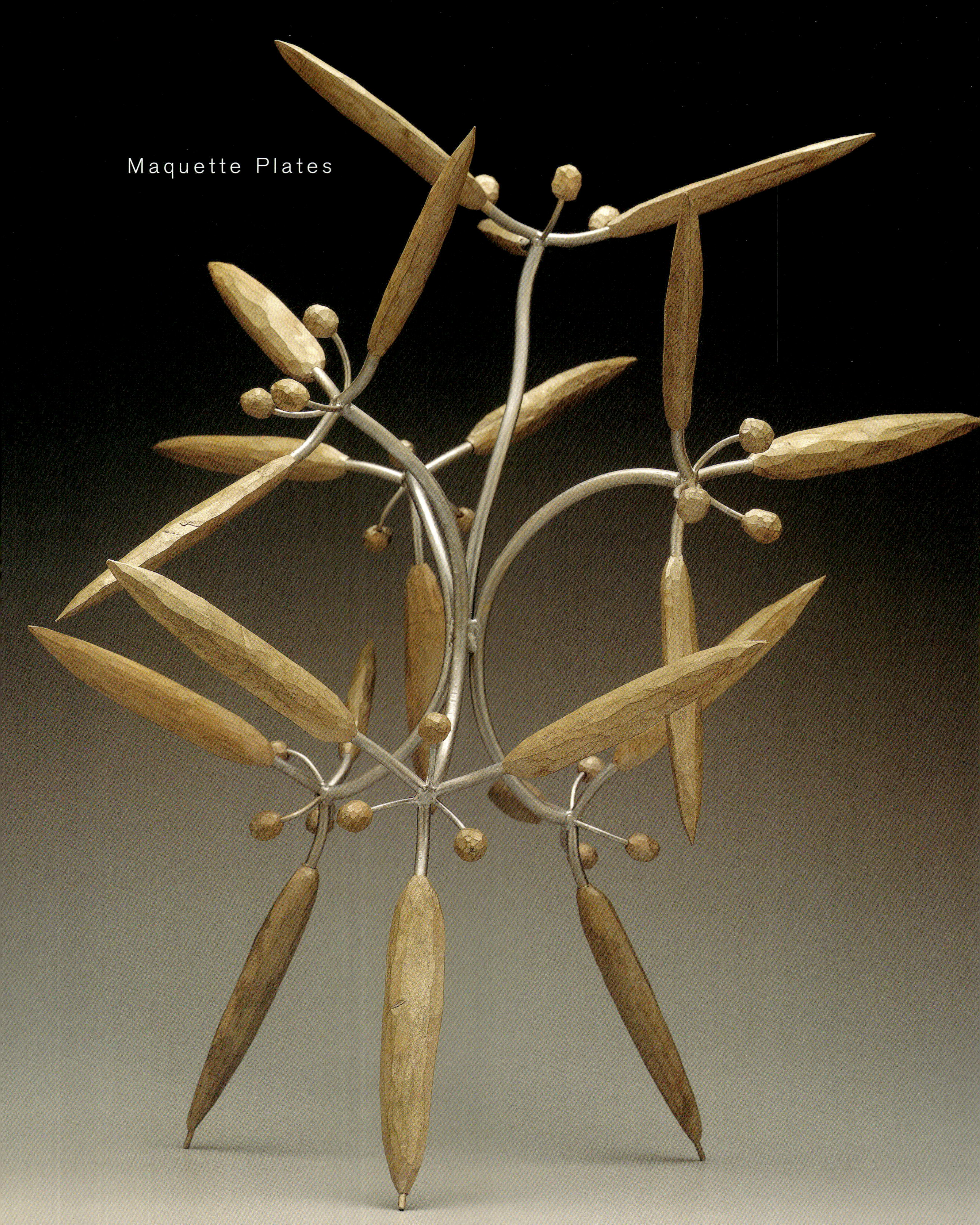

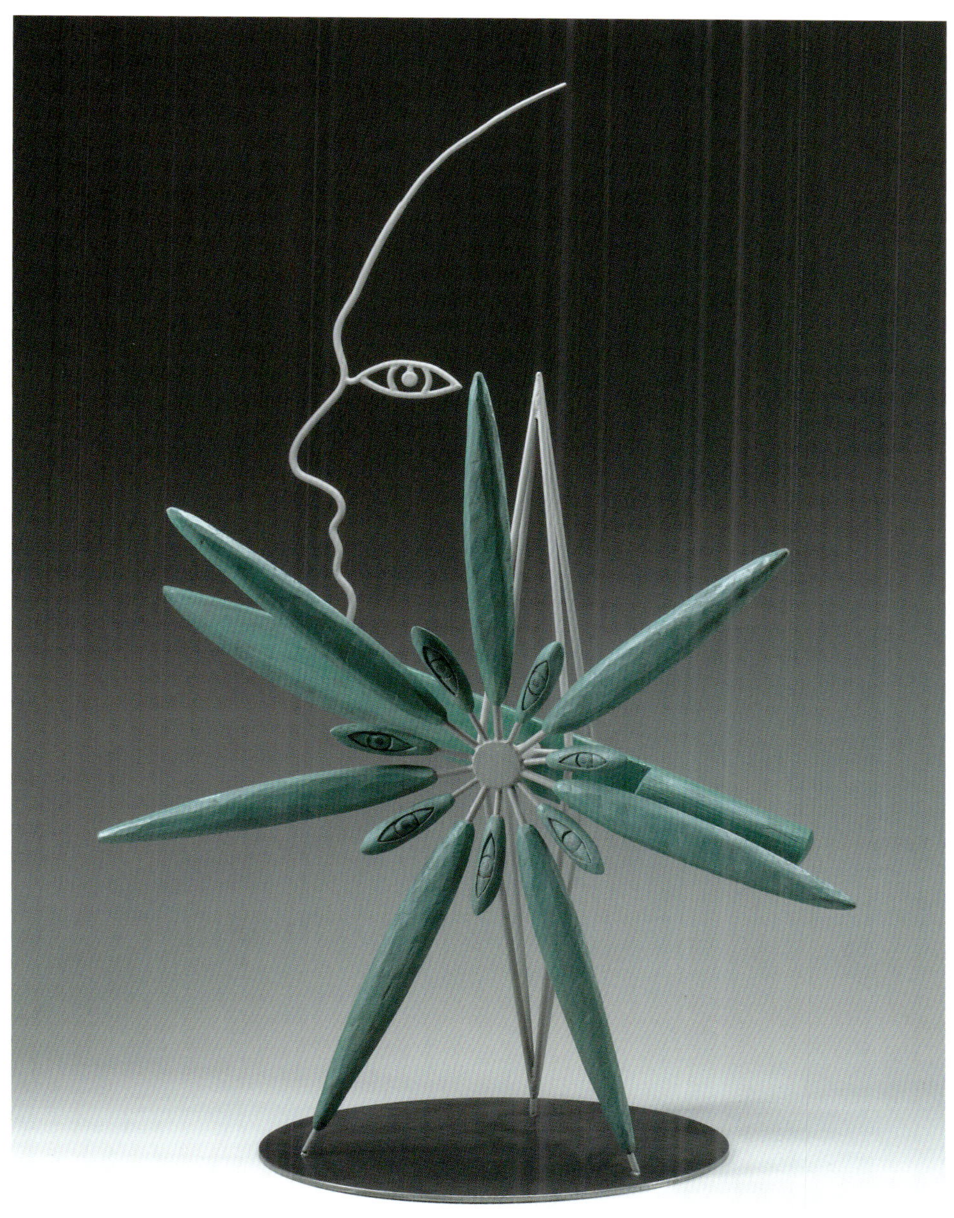

PLATE 20
Maquette for Three and Three and Seven Flower, 1998
Wood, painted steel
22 x 19 ½ x 18

PLATE 21
Maquette for Me, Knife, Diamond, and Flower, 1999
Painted steel, painted wood
42 ⅜ x 29 ¾ x 19

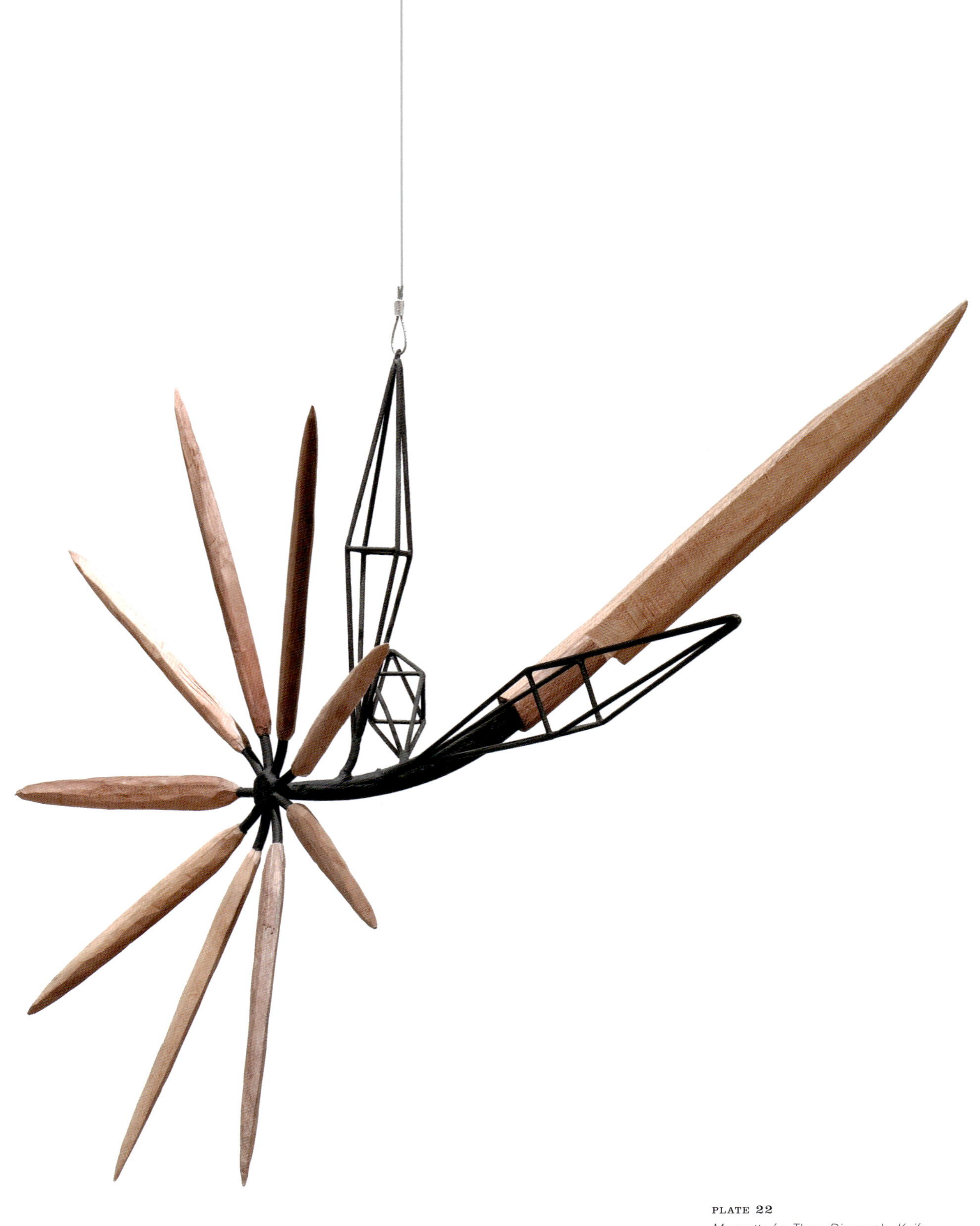

PLATE **22**
Maquette for Three Diamonds, Knife, and the Flower, 1999
Pine, poplar, painted steel
24 x 34 x 22
Collection of Tim and Nancy Hanley, Dallas, Texas.

FIGURE **47**
Maquette for Three Diamonds, Knife, and the Flower (detail), 1999 **(PL. 22)**

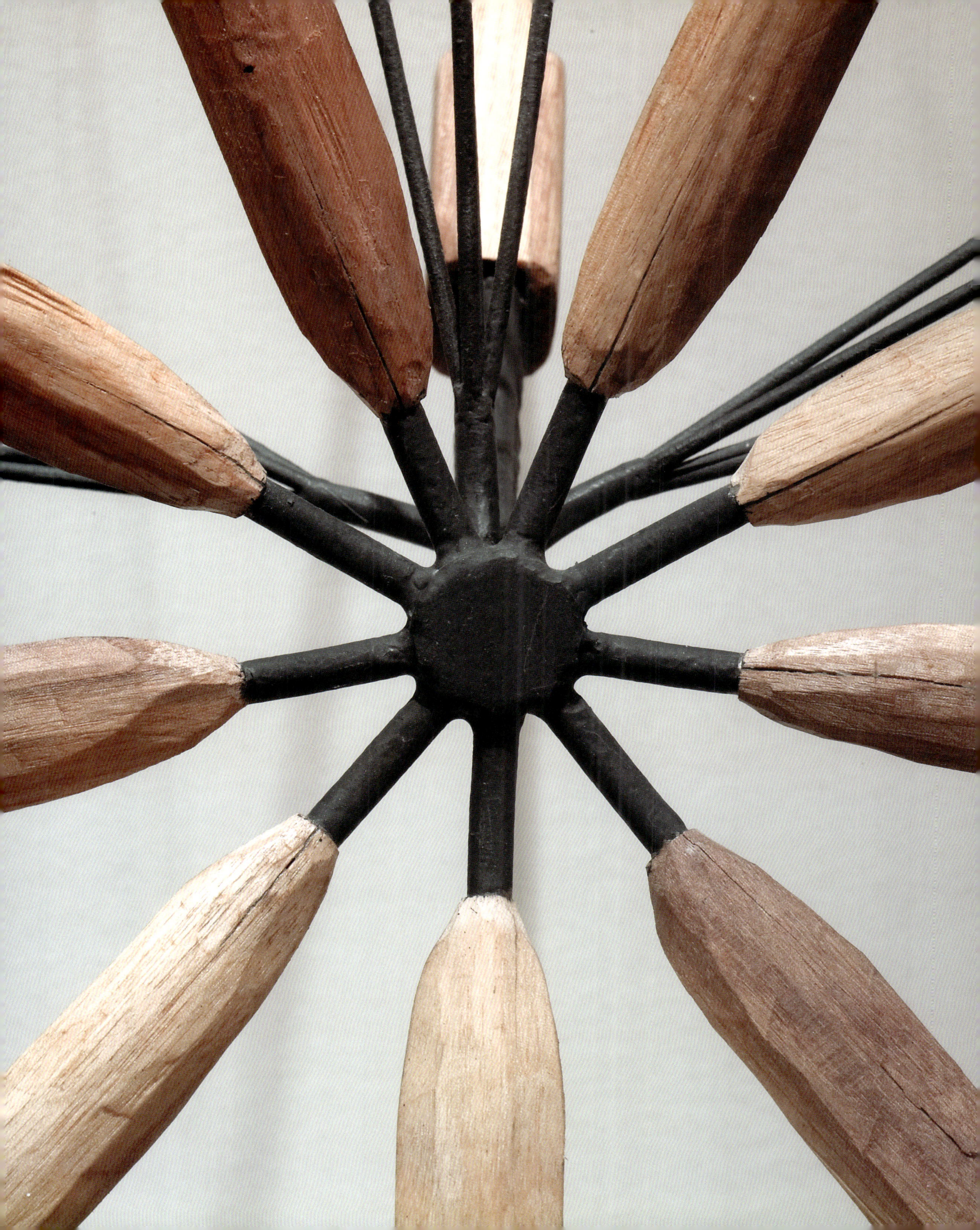

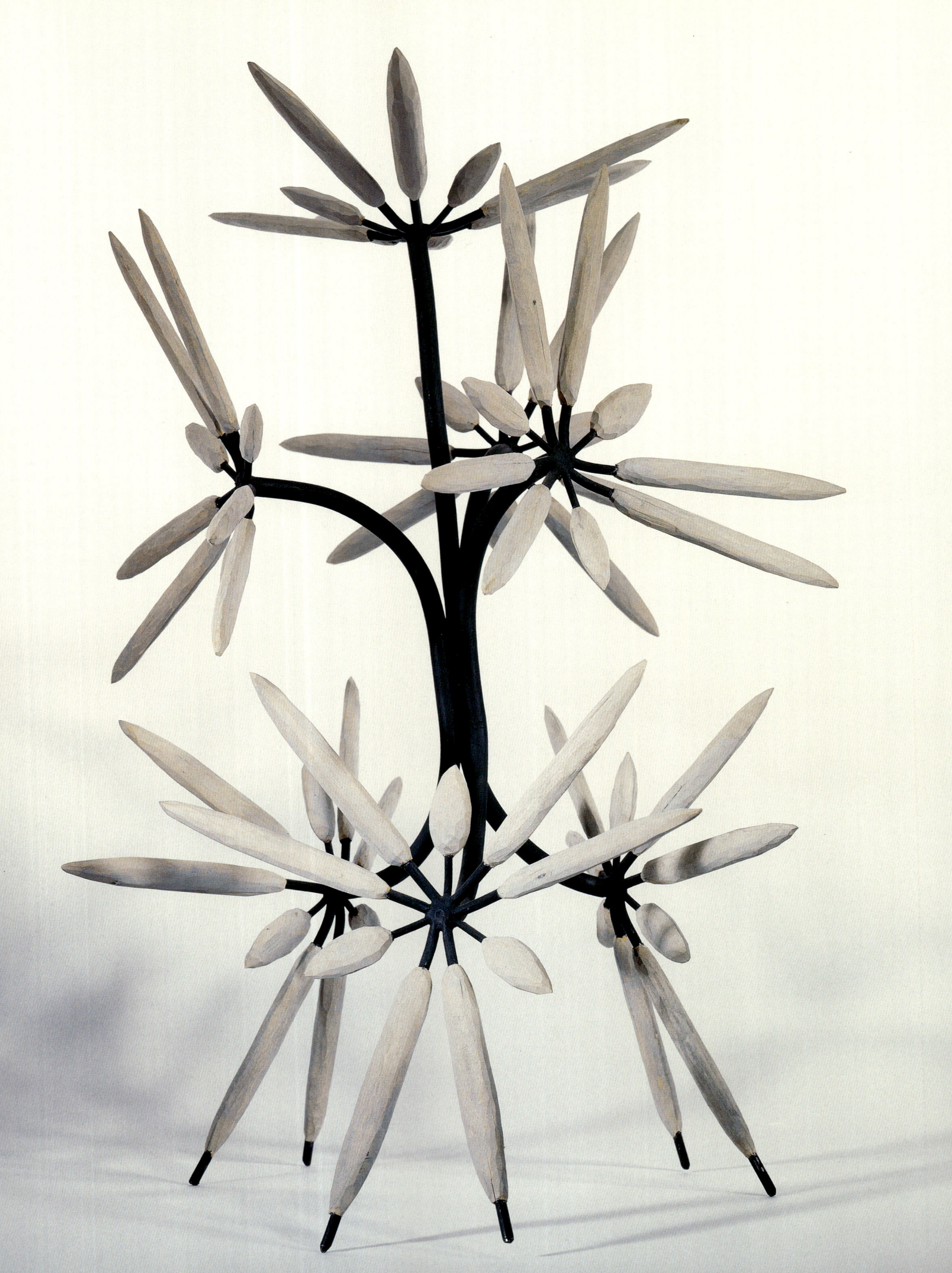

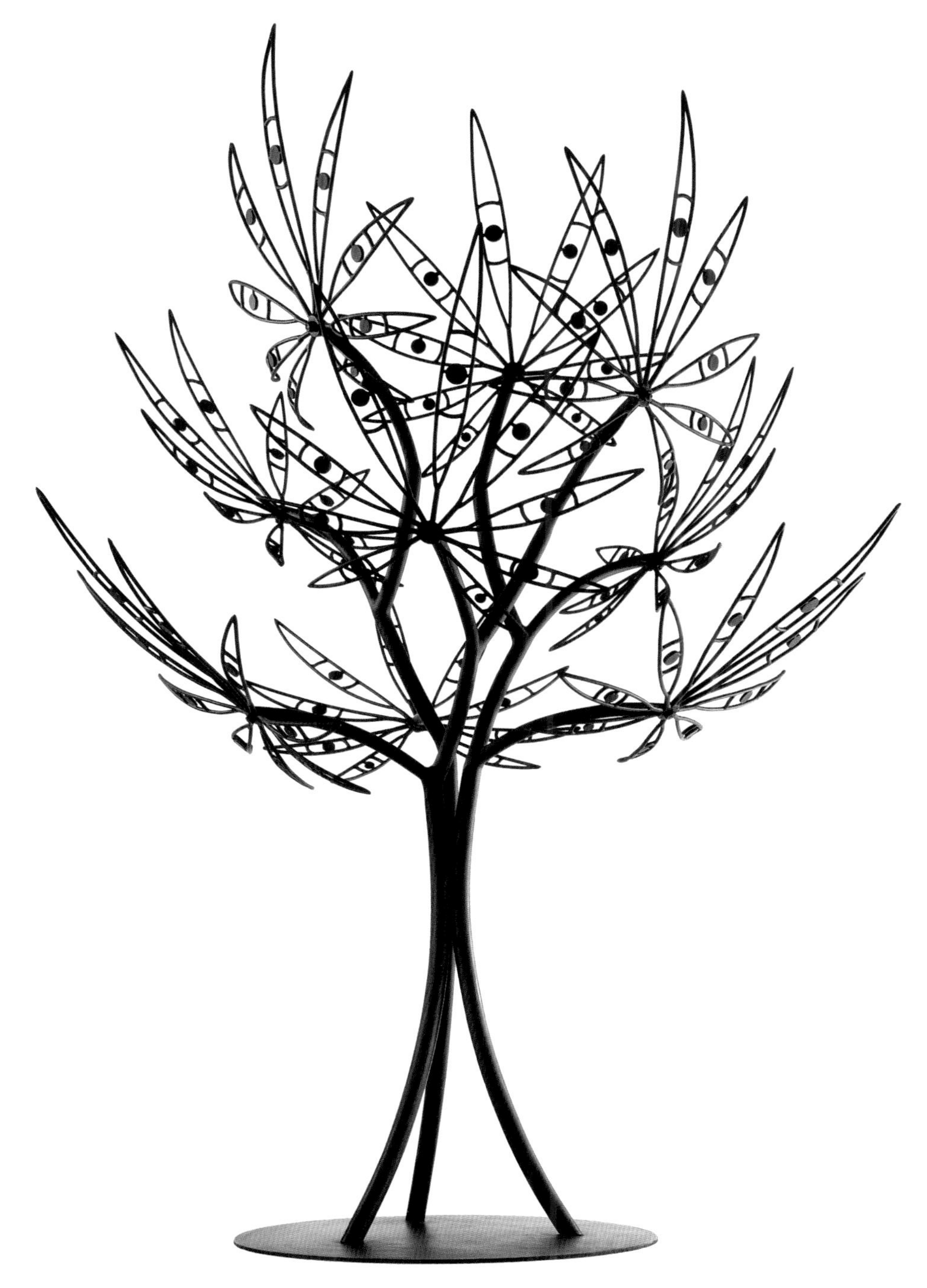

PLATE 23
Maquette for Two, Six, Nine & Seven, 2000
Painted steel, stained basswood
27 ½ x 20 x 20

PLATE 24
Maquette for Eye Flower, 2001
Painted steel
54 x 35 ½ x 36

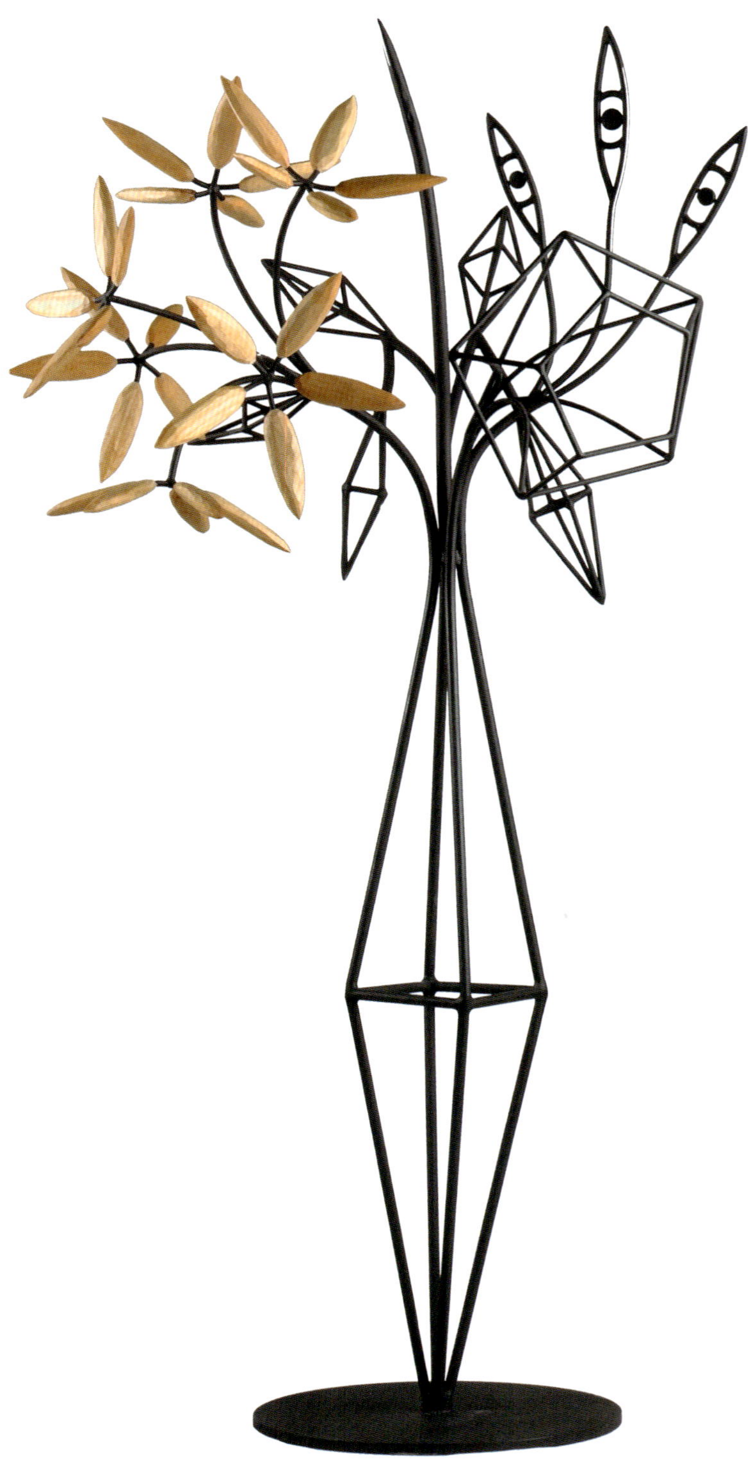

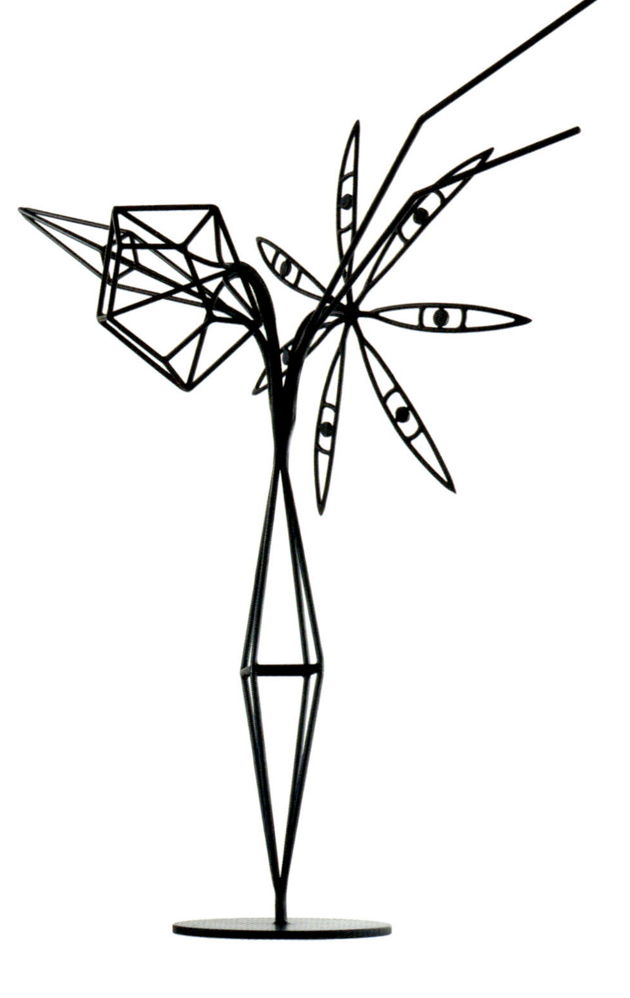

PLATE 25
Maquette for Diamond and Flower, 2002
Poplar, painted steel
46 ½ x 22 x 22

PLATE 26
Maquette for Drawing in Flower, Jewel, and Funnel, 2002
Painted steel
38 x 34 ¼ x 16

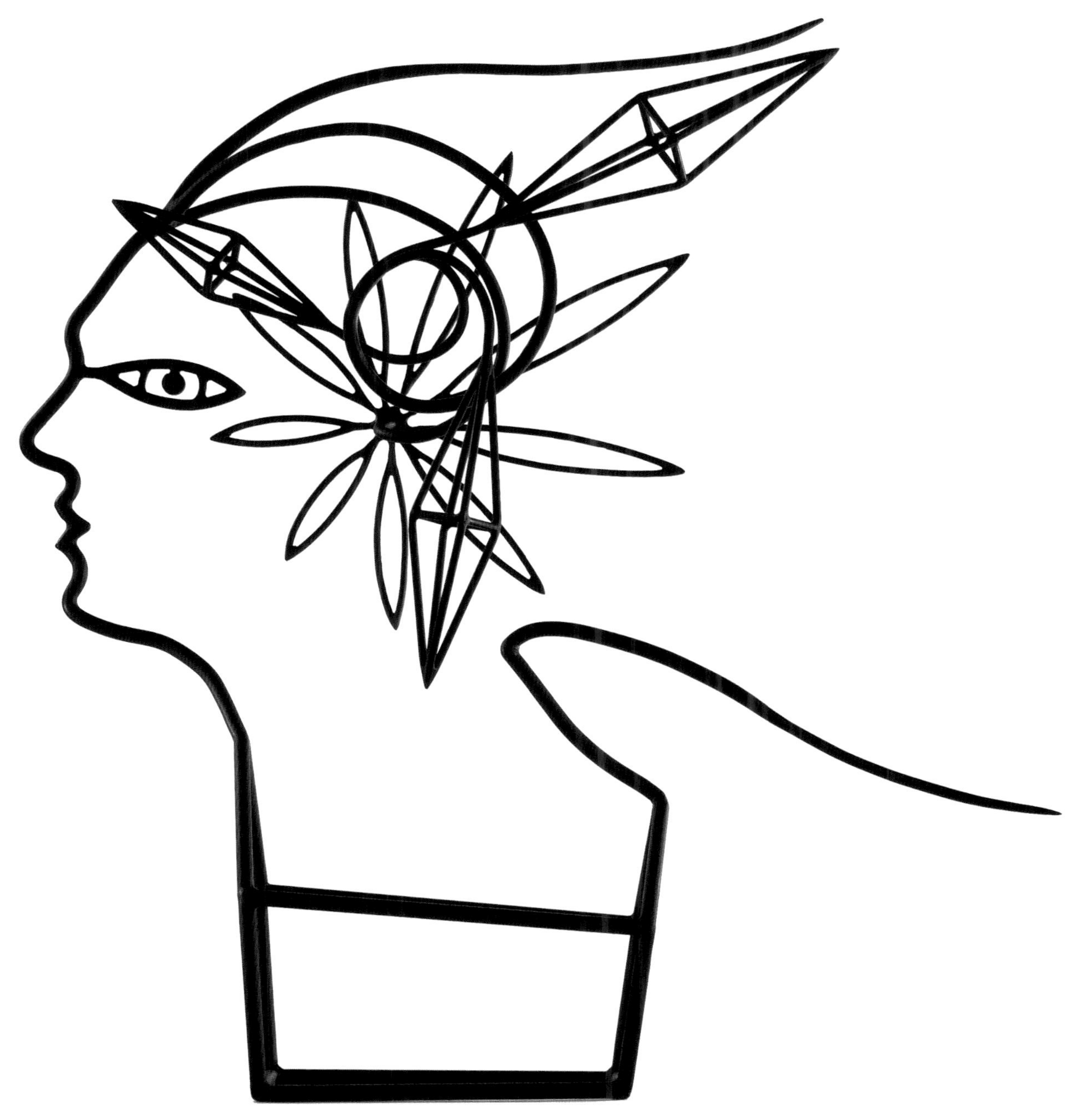

PLATE 27
Maquette for From the House, 2002
Painted steel
36 ¼ x 33 x 18 ¼

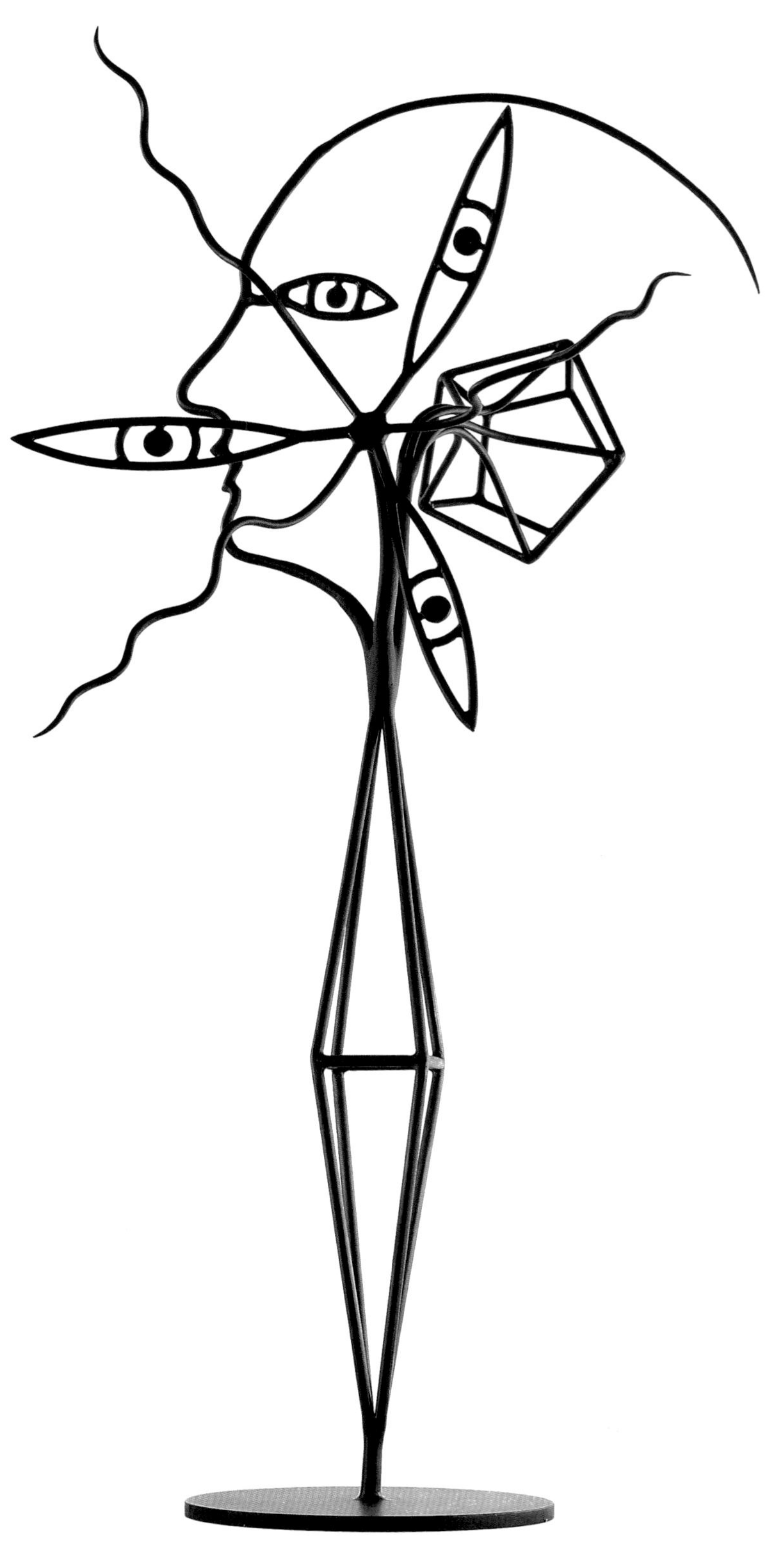

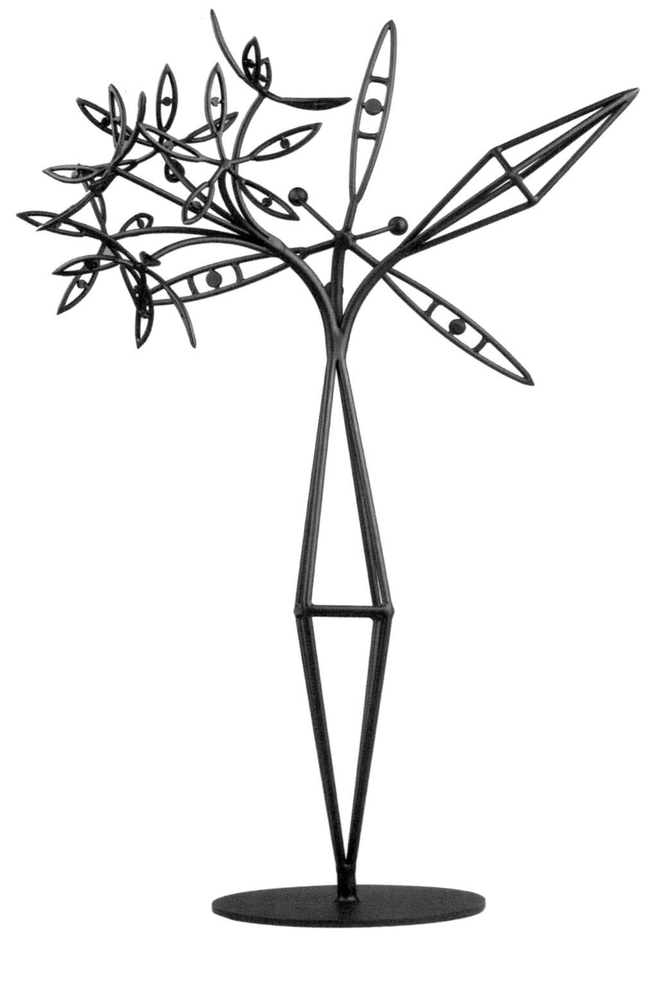

PLATE 28
Maquette for Me, Flower, and the Jewel, 2002
Painted steel
37 ¾ x 19 x 19

PLATE 29
Maquette for Again In the Meadows, 2002
Painted steel
38 ⅛ x 20 ½ x 19 ½

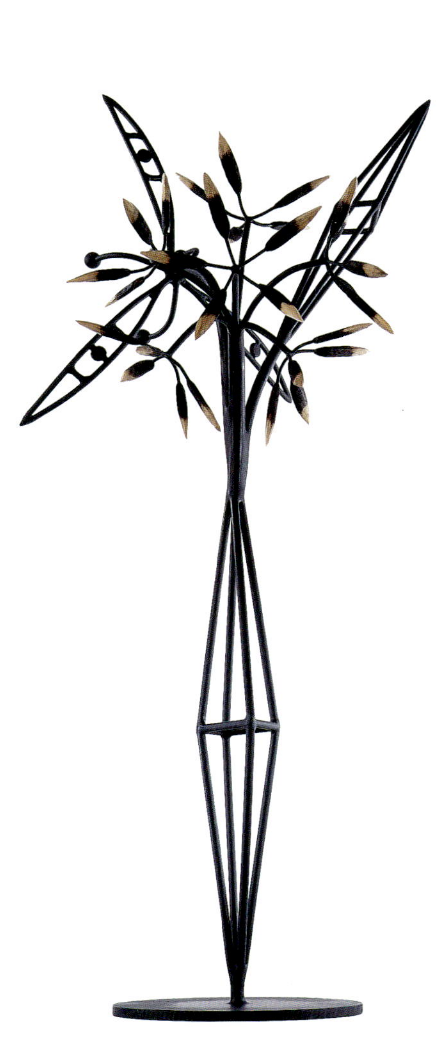

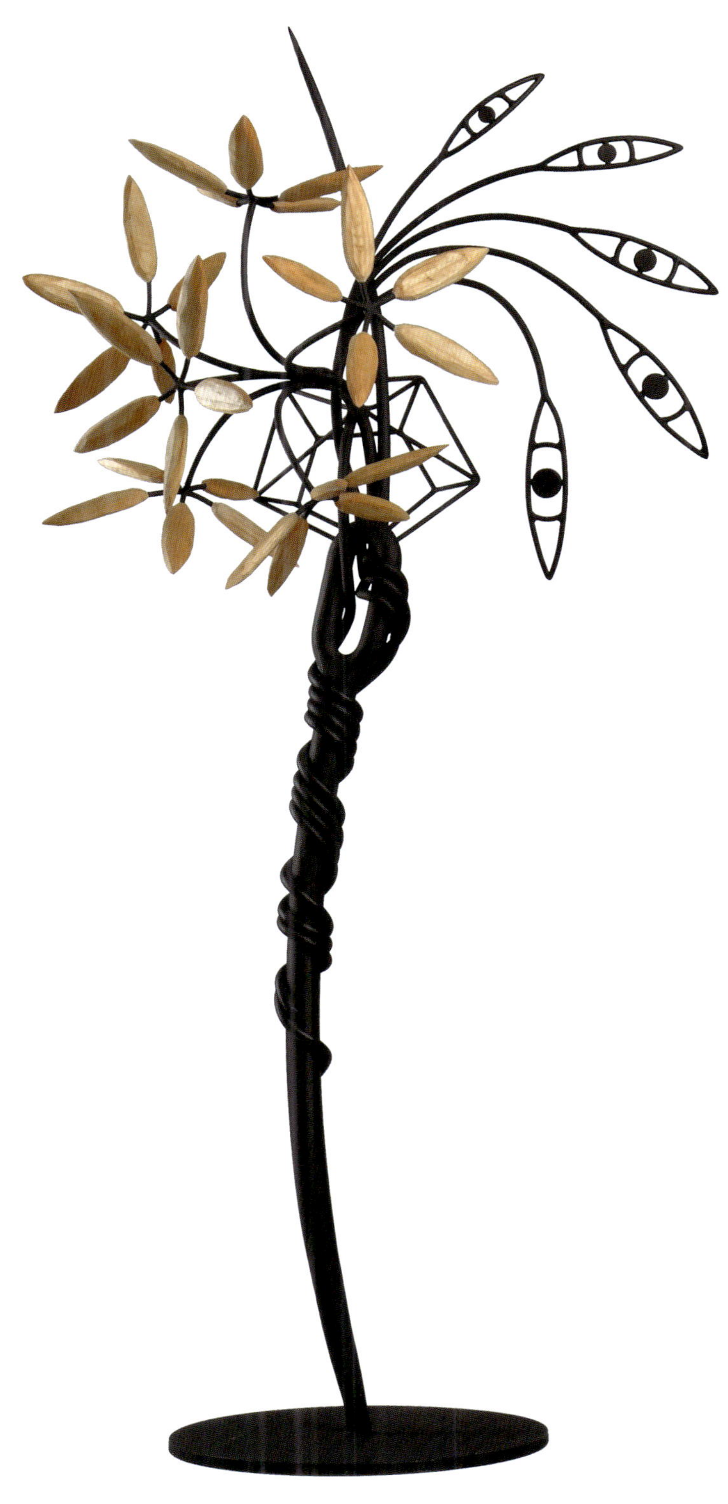

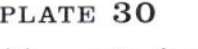

PLATE 30
Maquette for In the Meadows, 2002
Poplar, painted steel
37 ¼ x 19 x 17

PLATE 31
Maquette for Needle, Thread and Flower, 2002
Poplar, painted steel
47 ½ x 20 x 22

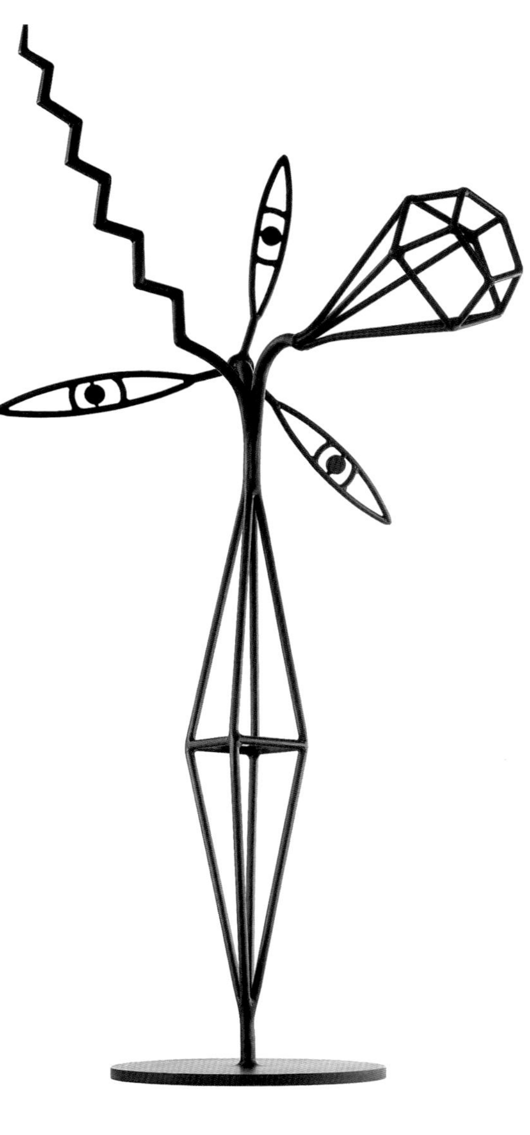

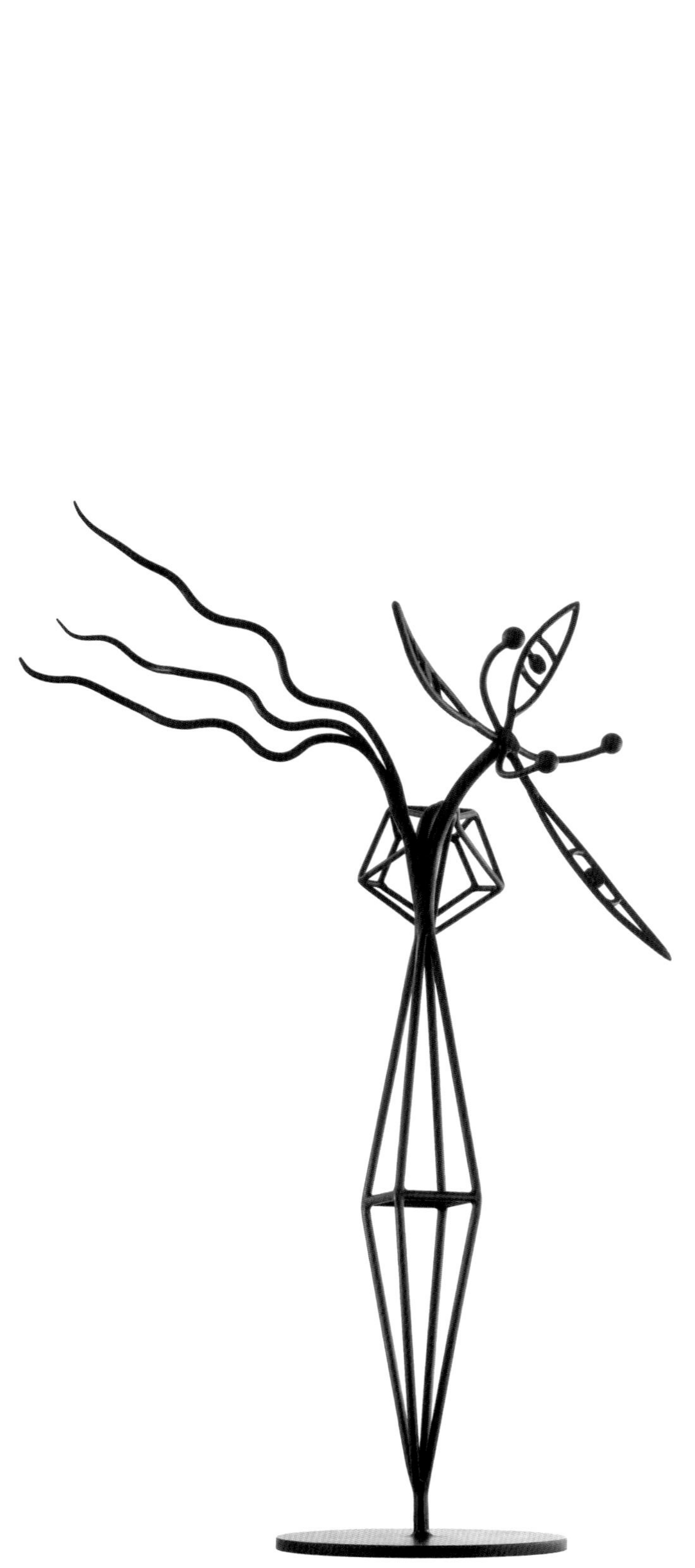

PLATE 32
Maquette for Reaching out—Flower and Jewel, 2002
Painted steel
34 x 21 ½ x 20

PLATE 33
Maquette for Stairway to Heaven, 2002
Painted steel
35 ¾ x 17 ¾ x 20

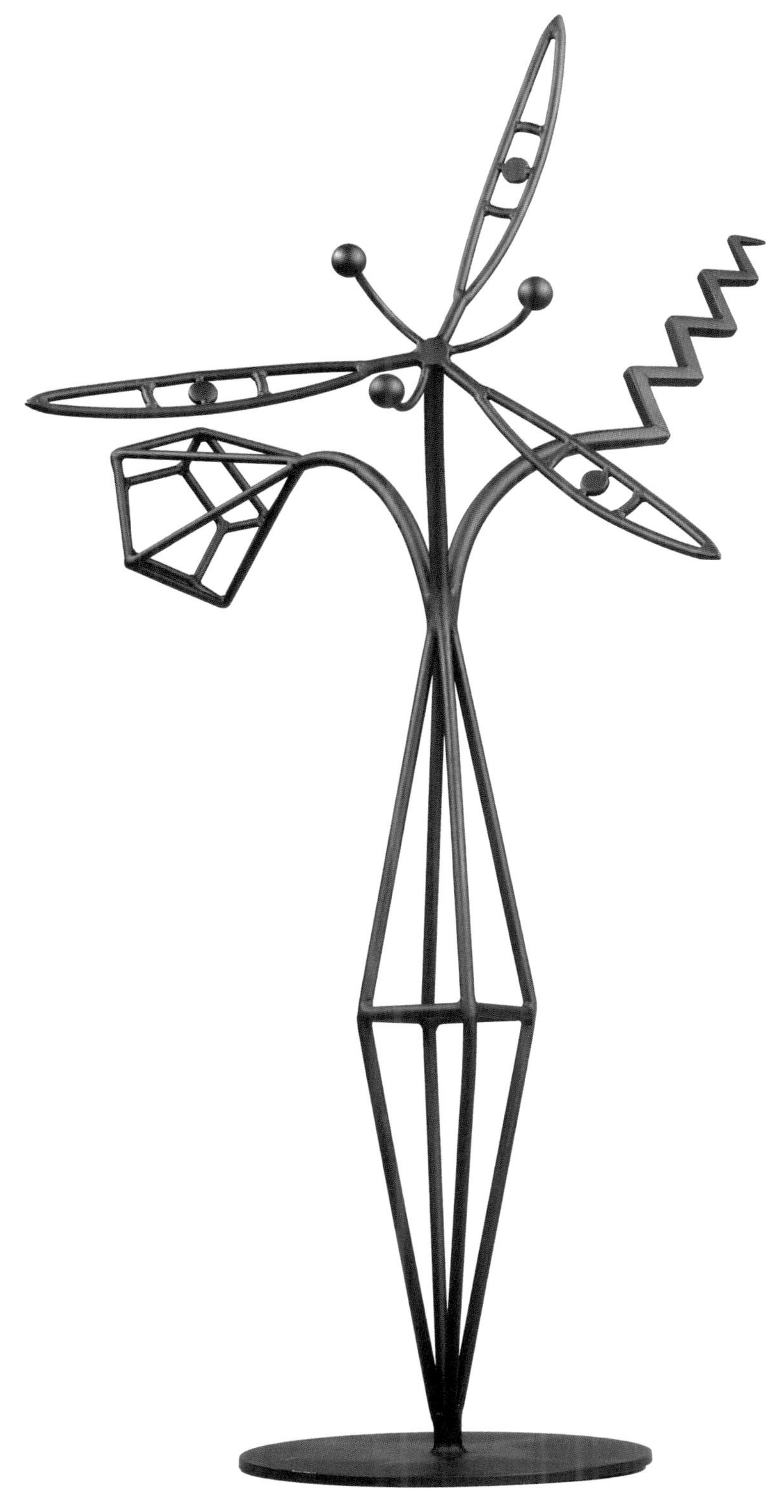

PLATE 34
Maquette for Stairway to Heaven II,
2002
Painted steel
38 ⅛ x 21 ½ x 19 ½

Drawing Plates

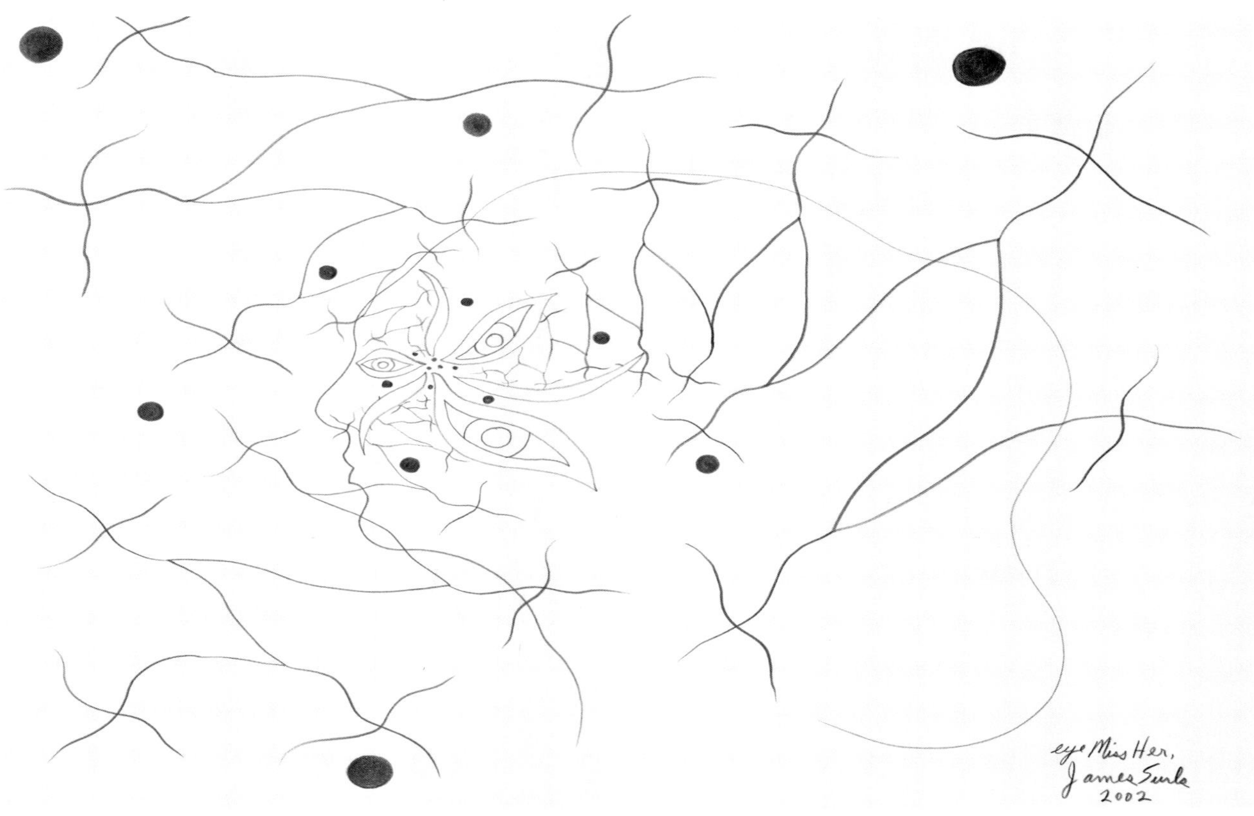

PLATE 35
eye Miss Her, 2002
Graphite on paper
18 x 22

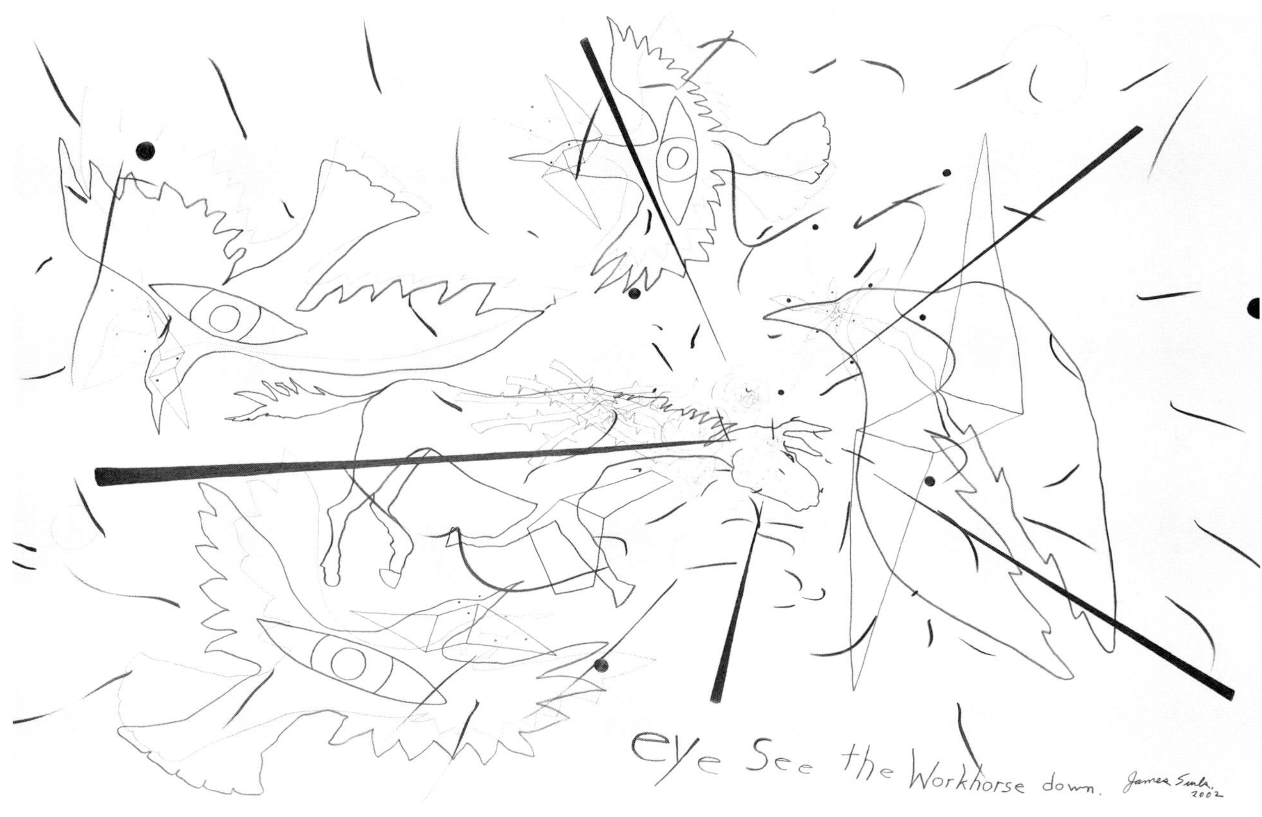

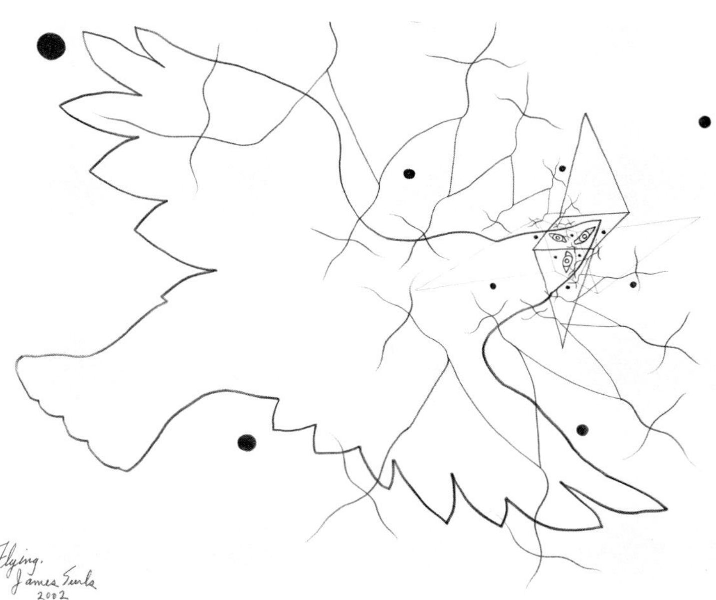

PLATE 36
eye See the Workhorse down, 2002
Graphite on paper
40 x 60

PLATE 37
Flying, 2002
Graphite on paper
18 x 22

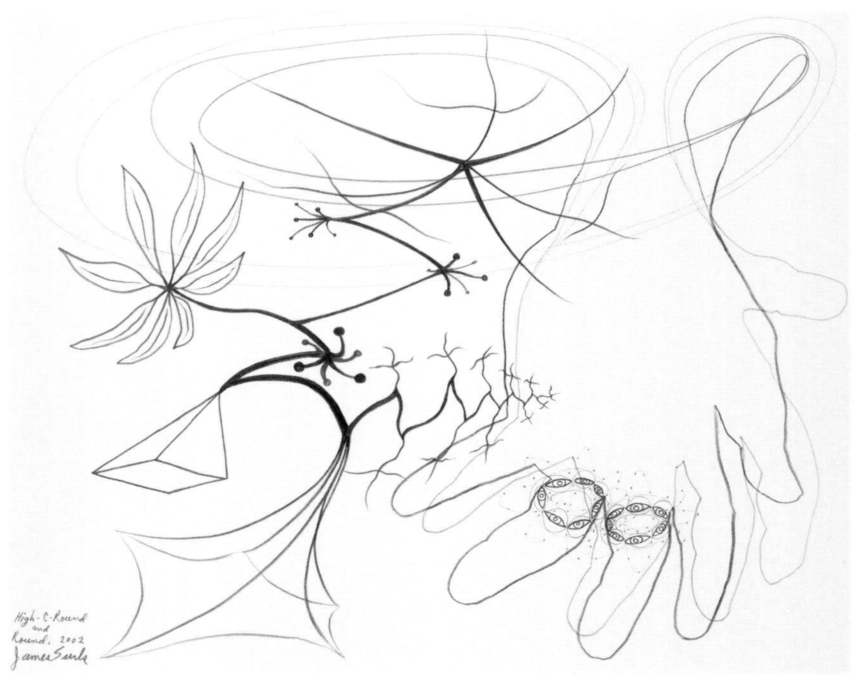
High-C-Round
and
Round, 2002
James Surls

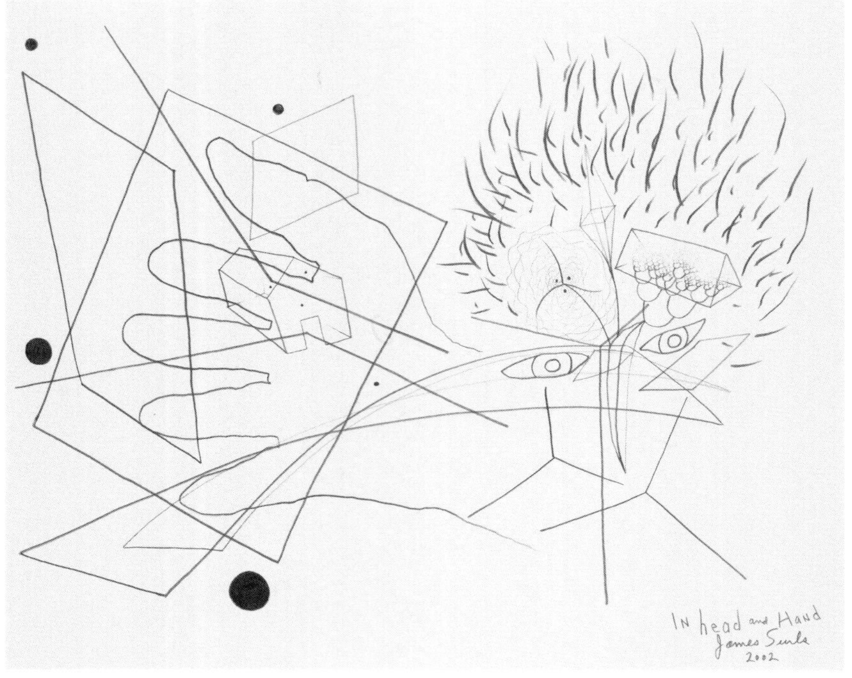
IN head and Hand
James Surls
2002

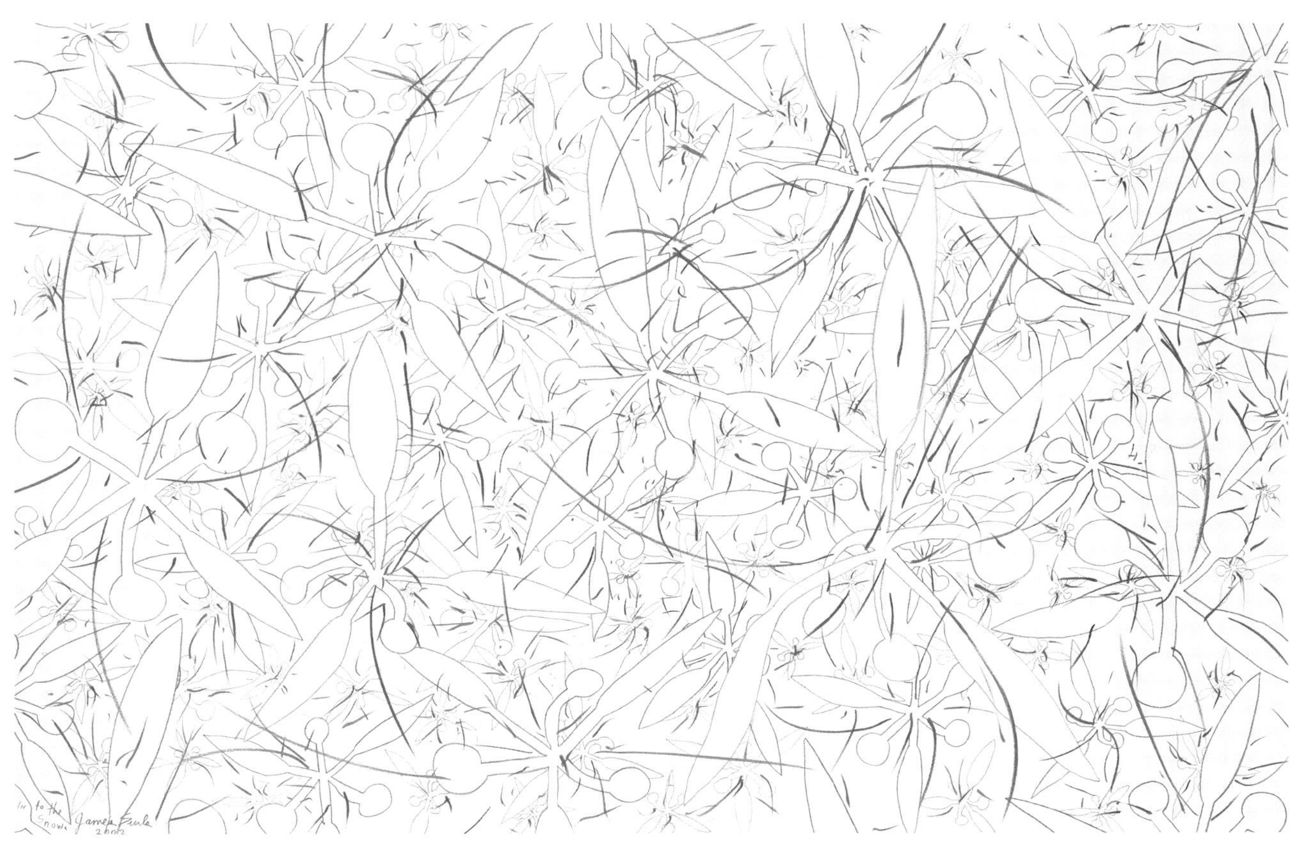

TOP LEFT TO RIGHT:

PLATE 38
High-C Round and Round, 2002
Graphite on paper
18 x 22

PLATE 39
In head and Hand, 2002
Graphite on paper
18 x 22

PLATE 40
Into the Snow, 2002
Graphite on paper
40 x 60

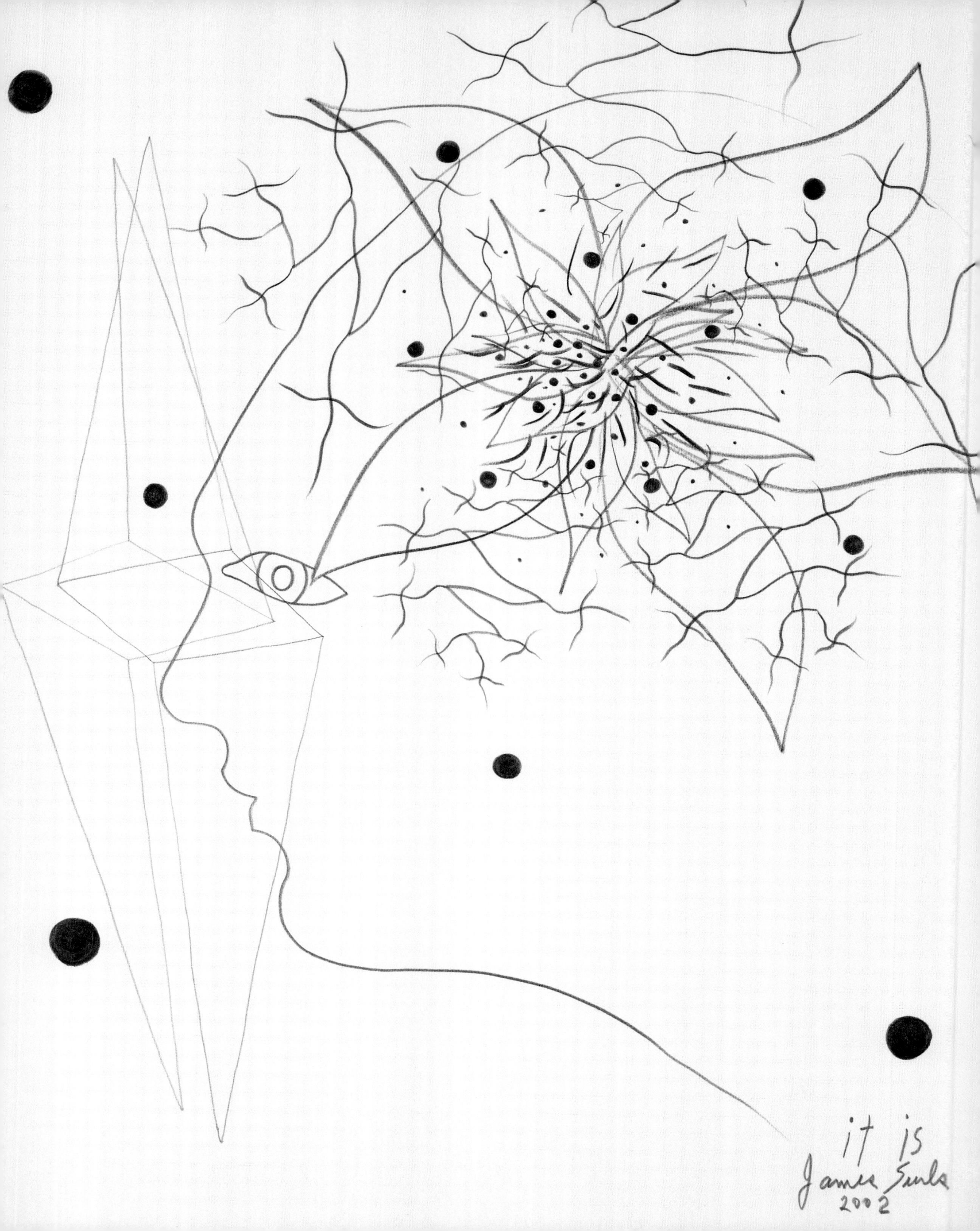
it is
James Sienk
2002

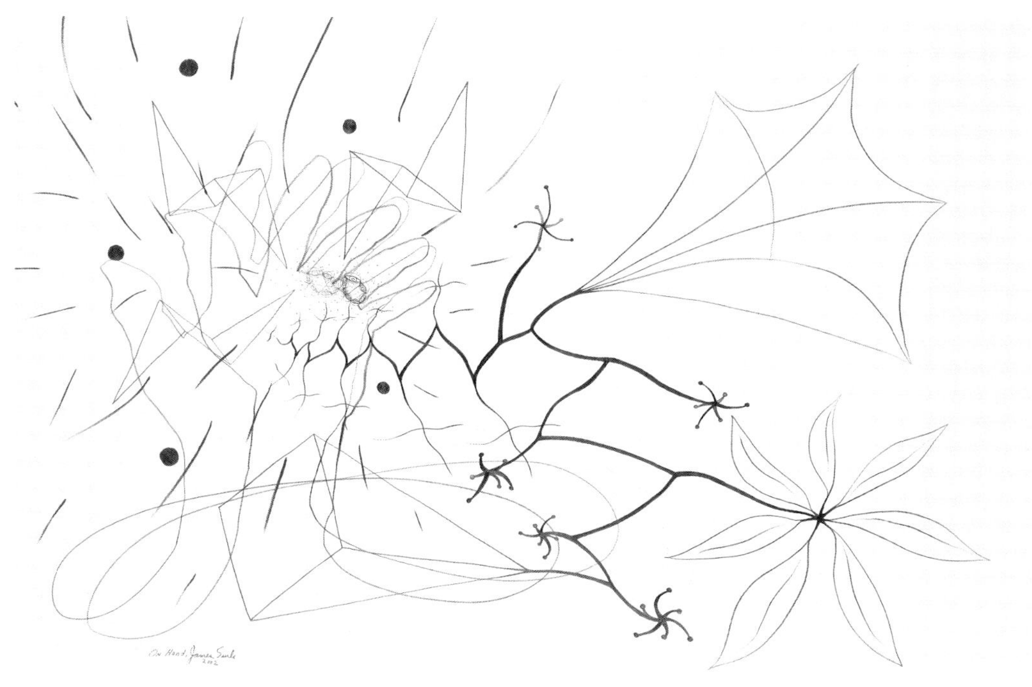

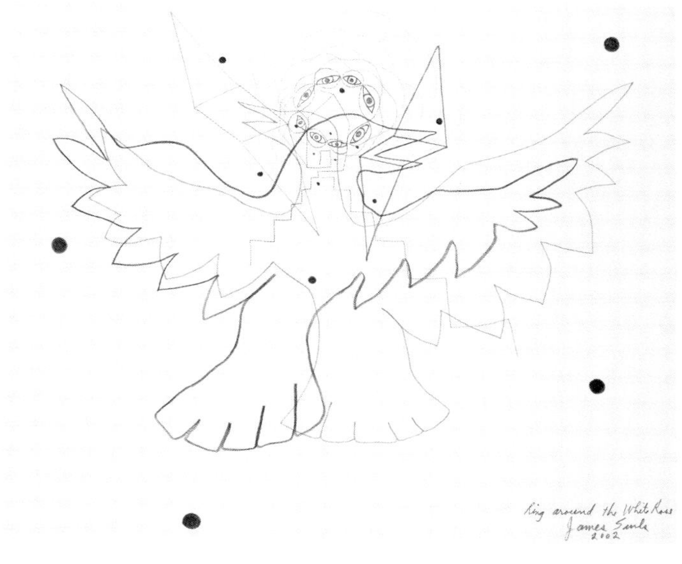

PLATE 41
it is, 2002
Graphite on paper
22 x 18
Collection of Dr. Robert Wright.

PLATE 42
On Hand, 2002
Graphite on paper
40 x 60

PLATE 43
Ring around the White Rose, 2002
Graphite on paper
18 x 22

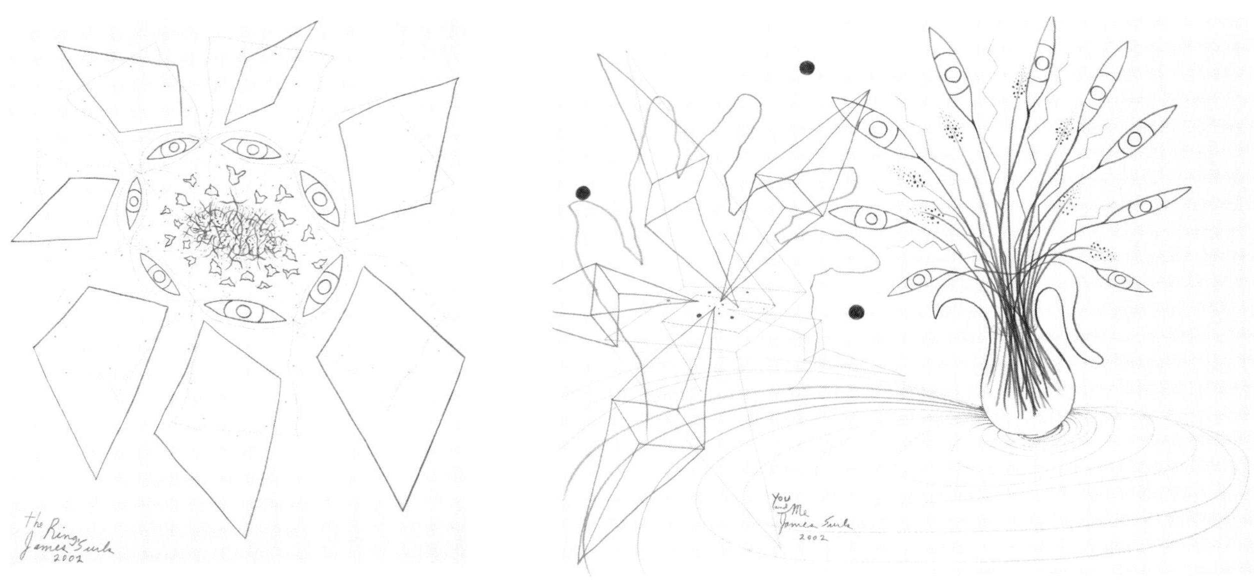

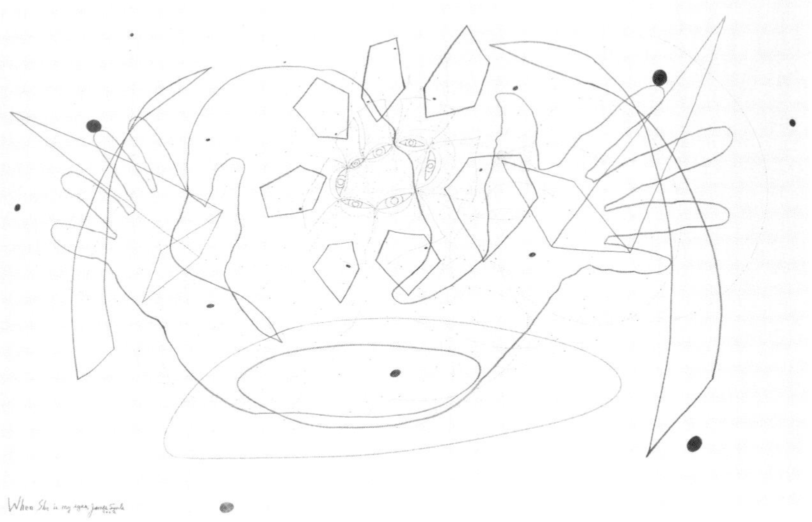

TOP LEFT CLOCKWISE:

PLATE 44
The Rings, 2002
Graphite on paper
22 x 18

PLATE 45
You and Me, 2002
Graphite on paper
18 x 22

PLATE 46
When She is my eyes, 2002
Graphite on paper
40 x 60

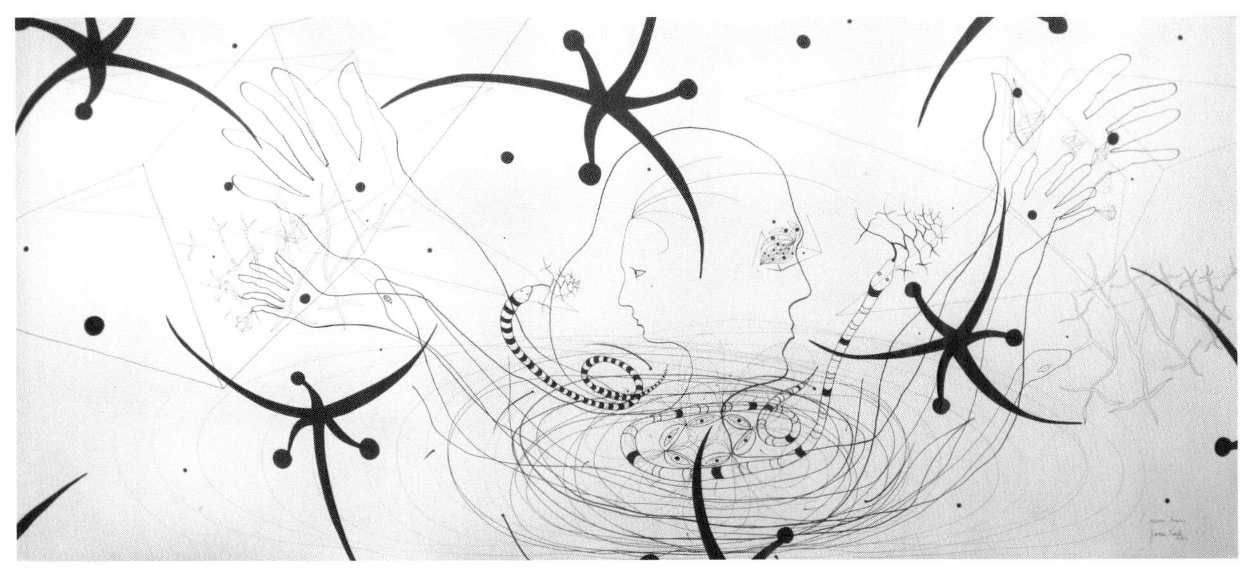

PLATE 47
I Never Knew, 2003
Ink on paper
80 x 174

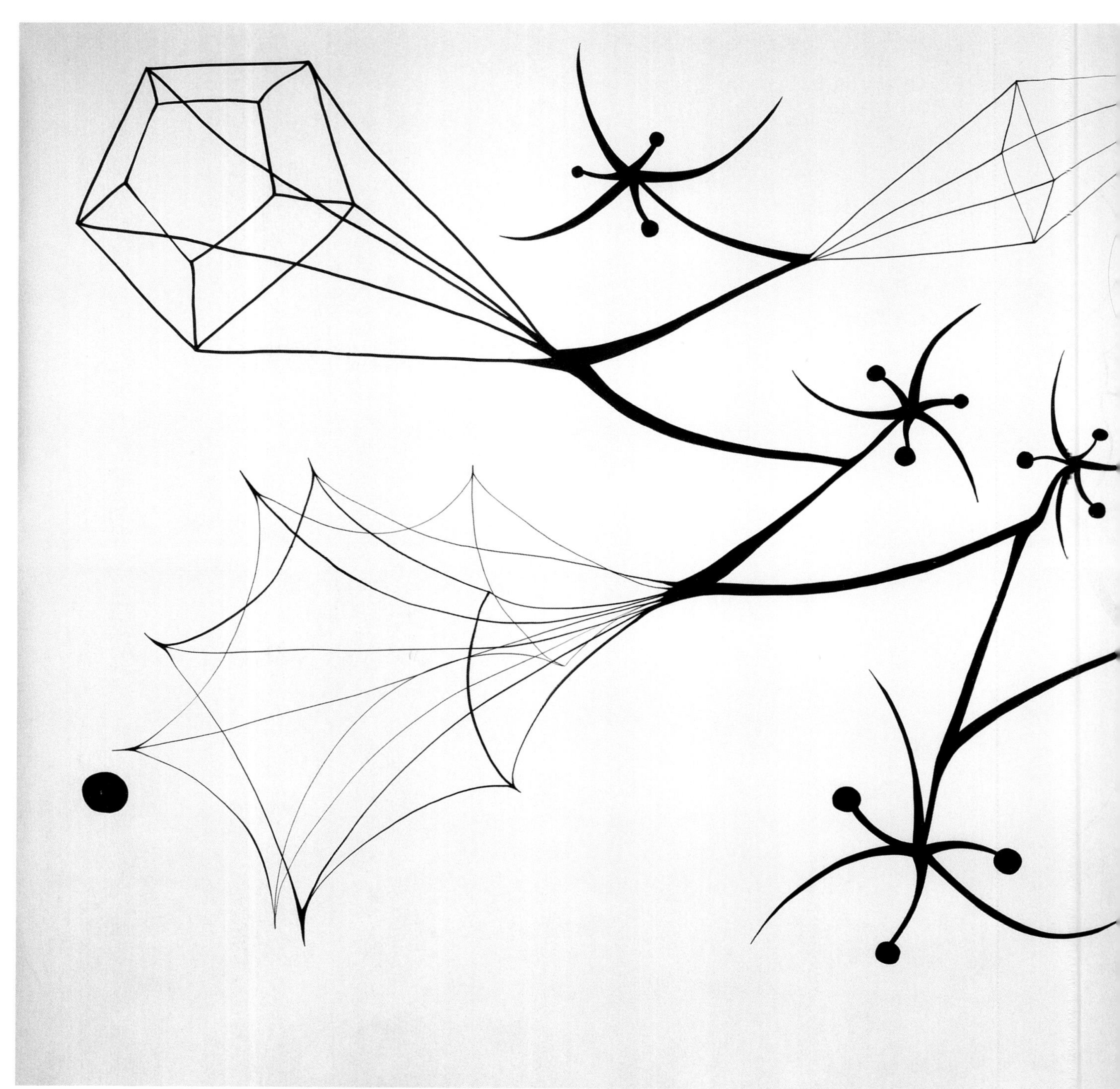

PLATE 48
Me, God, Evolution, Love, Relationship and you, 2003
Ink on paper
160 x 324

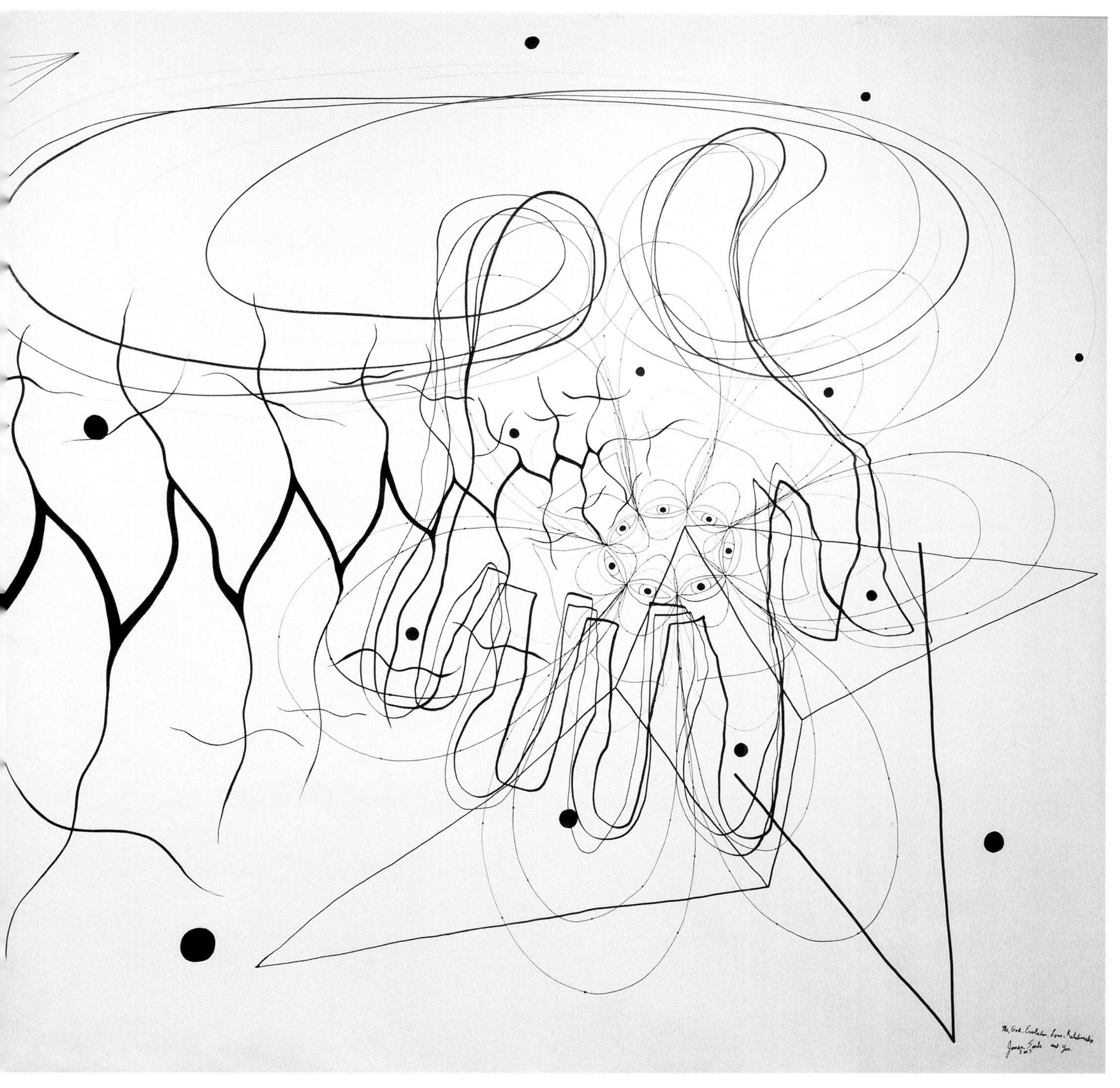

Sketch Plates

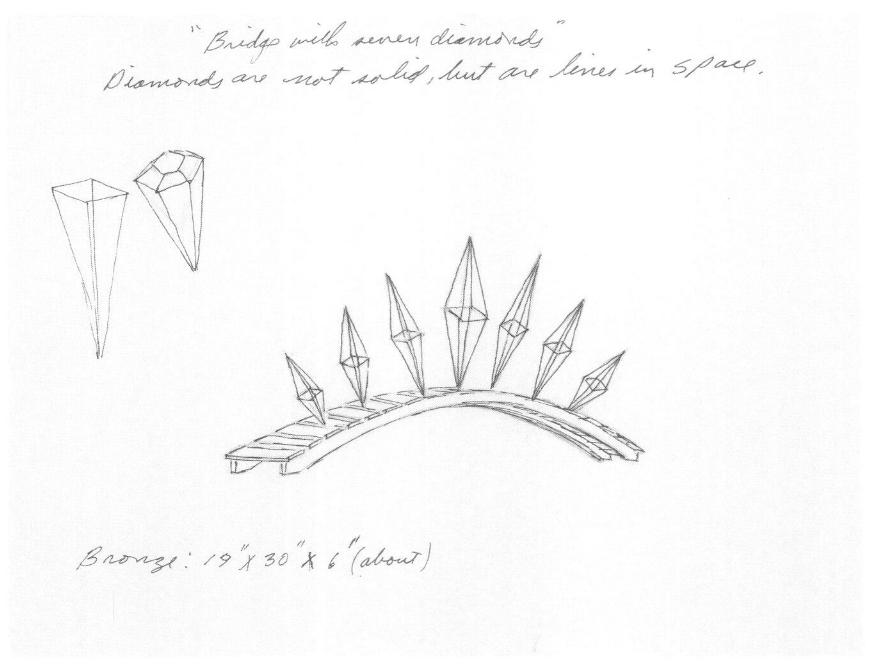

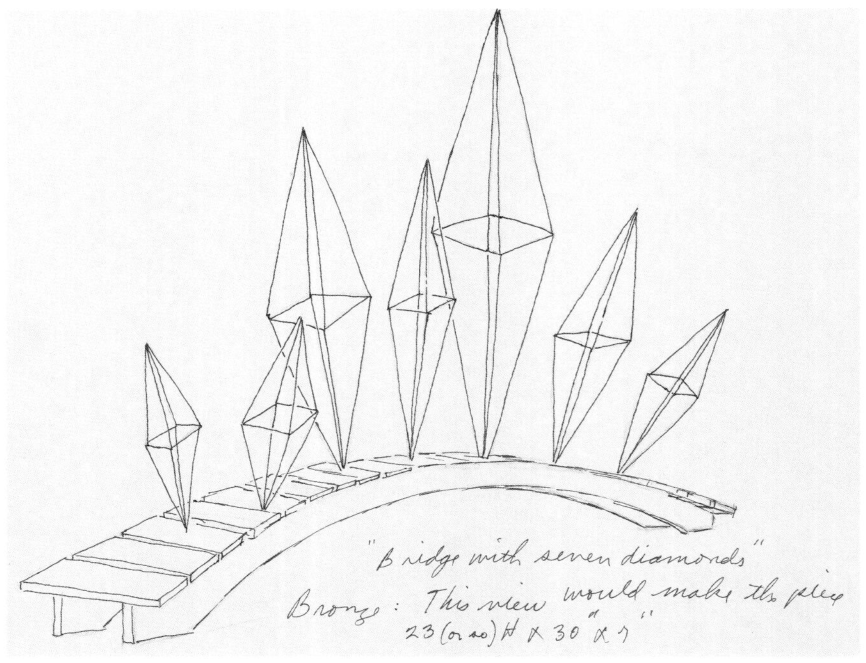

PLATE 49
Sketch for Bridge with Seven Diamonds I,
c.1993
Black ink, pencil on paper
8 ½ x 11
Collection of the Meadows Museum, gift of James Surls and Charmaine Locke.

PLATE 50
Sketch for Bridge with Seven Diamonds II,
c.1993
Black ink, pencil on paper
8 ½ x 11
Collection of the Meadows Museum, gift of James Surls and Charmaine Locke.

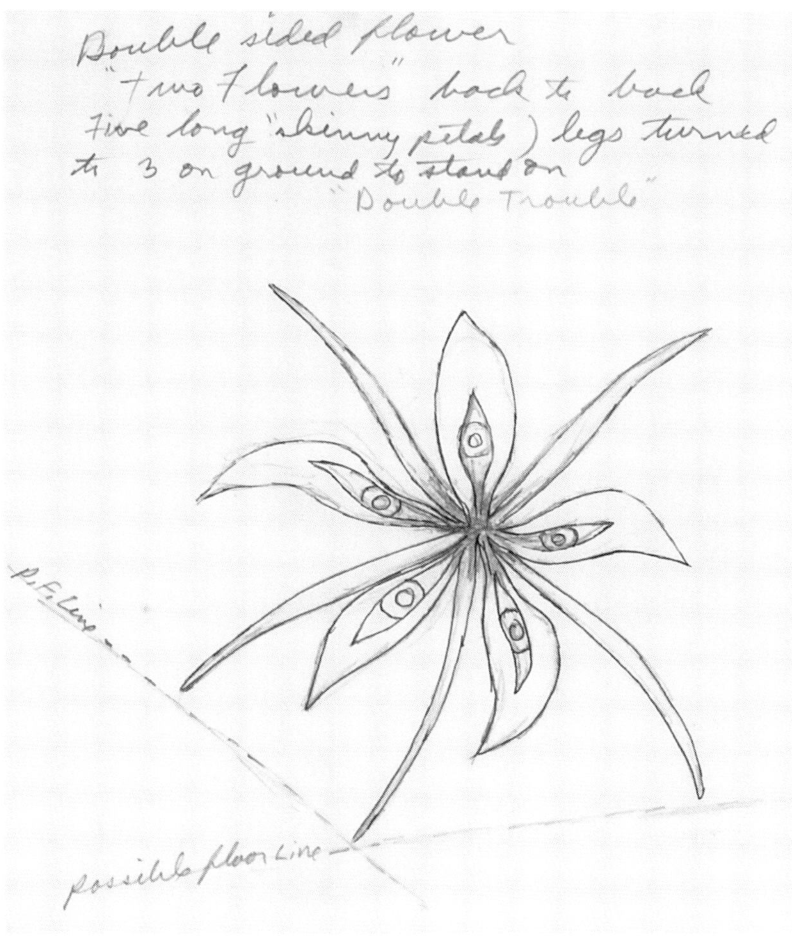

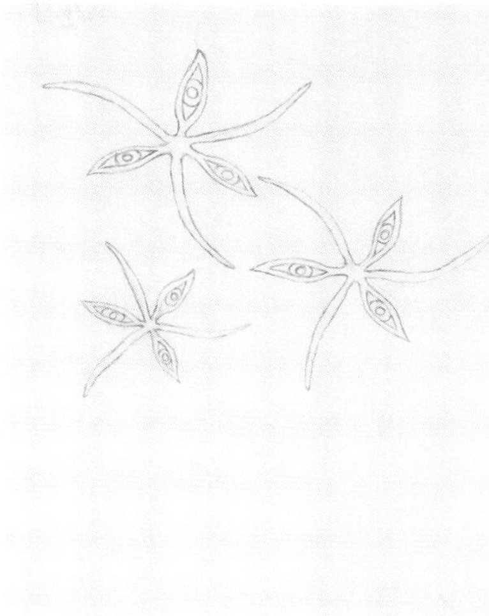

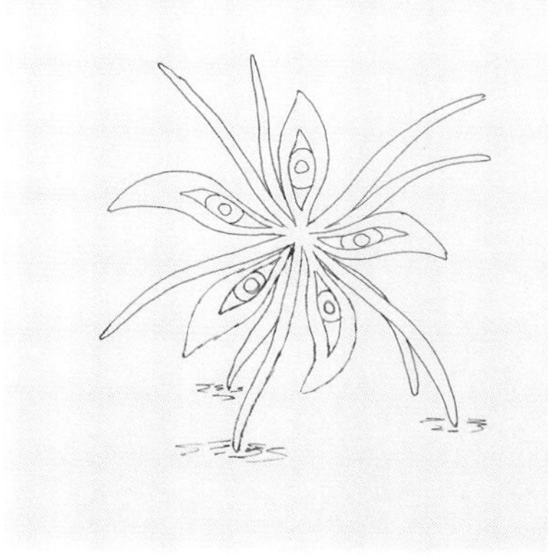

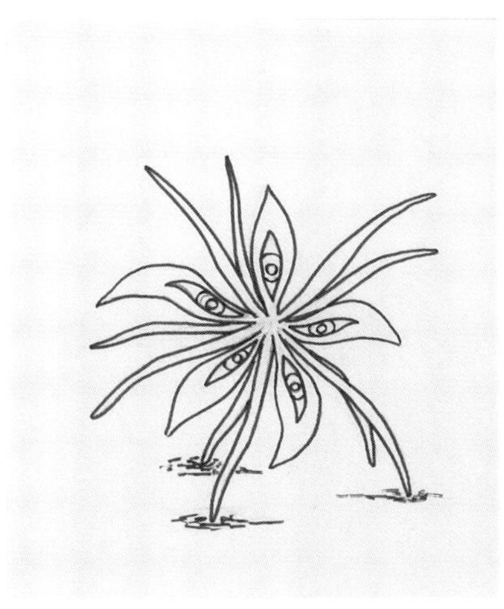

TOP LEFT CLOCKWISE

PLATE 51
Sketch for Walking Flower I, c.1993
Black ink, pencil on paper
11 x 8 ½
Collection of the Meadows Museum, gift of James Surls and Charmaine Locke.

PLATE 52
Sketch for Walking Flower II, c.1993
Black ink, pencil on paper
11 x 8 ½
Collection of the Meadows Museum, gift of James Surls and Charmaine Locke.

PLATE 53
Sketch for Walking Flower III, c.1993
Black ink, pencil on paper
11 x 8 ½
Collection of the Meadows Museum, gift of James Surls and Charmaine Locke.

PLATE 54
Sketch for Walking Flower IV, c.1993
Black ink, pencil on paper
11 x 8 ½
Collection of the Meadows Museum, gift of James Surls and Charmaine Locke.

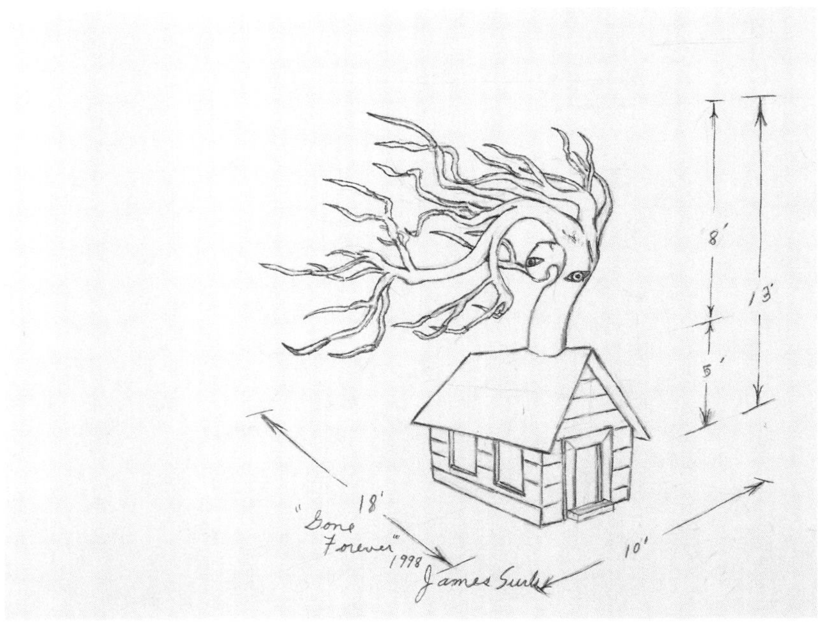

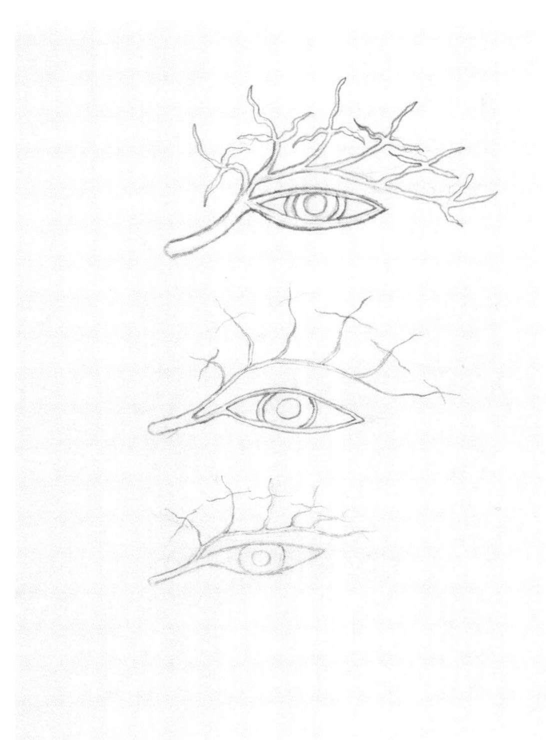

PLATE 55
Sketch for Gone Forever, 1998
Black ink, pencil on paper
8 ½ x 11
Collection of the Meadows Museum, gift of James Surls and Charmaine Locke.

PLATE 56
Sketch for Eyes, c.1997
Pencil on paper
11 x 8 ½
Collection of the Meadows Museum, gift of James Surls and Charmaine Locke.

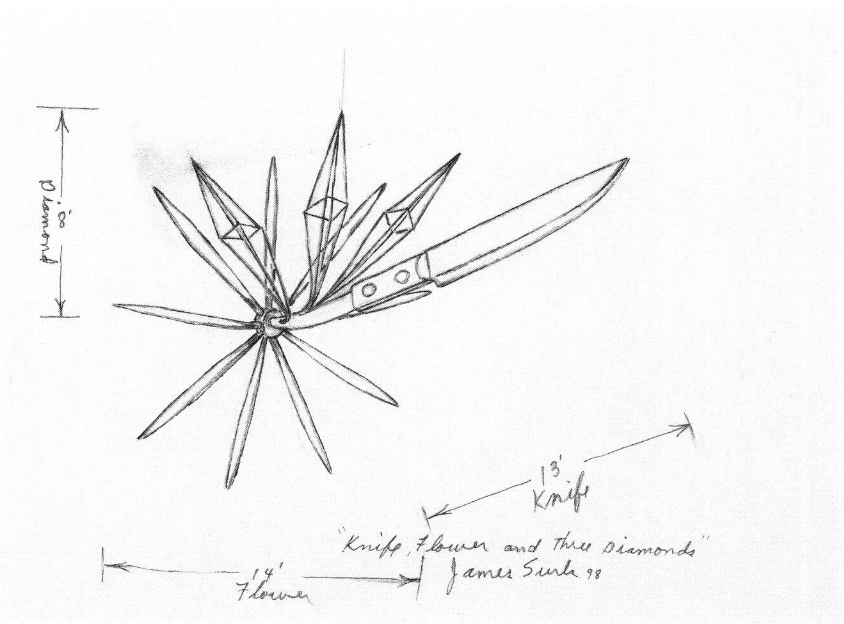

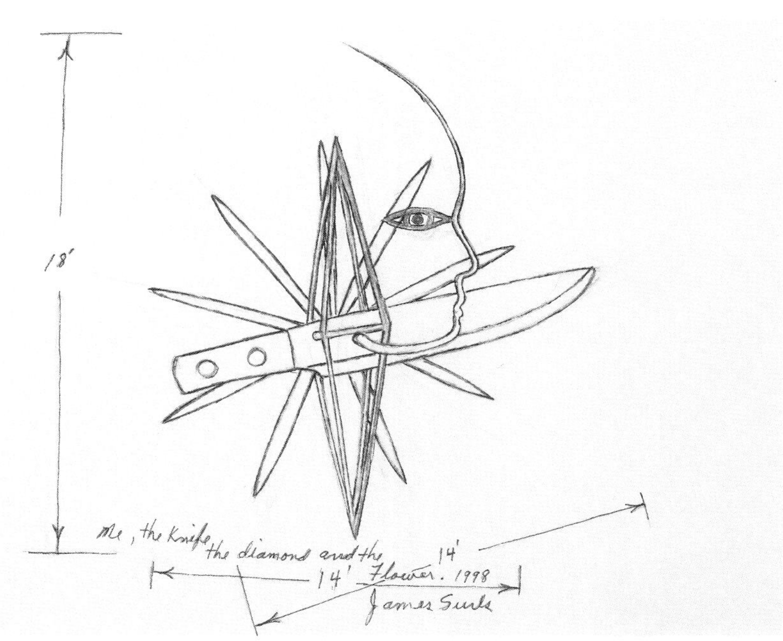

PLATE 57
Sketch for Knife, Flower and Three Diamonds, 1998
Black ink, pencil on paper
8 ½ x 11
Collection of the Meadows Museum, gift of James Surls and Charmaine Locke.

PLATE 58
Sketch for Me, the Knife, the Diamond and the Flower, 1998
Black ink, pencil on paper
8 ½ x 11
Collection of the Meadows Museum, gift of James Surls and Charmaine Locke.

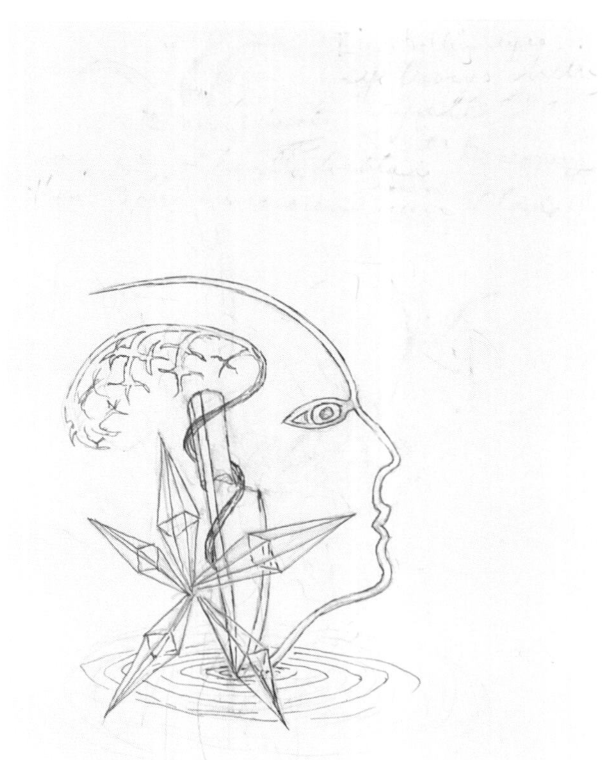

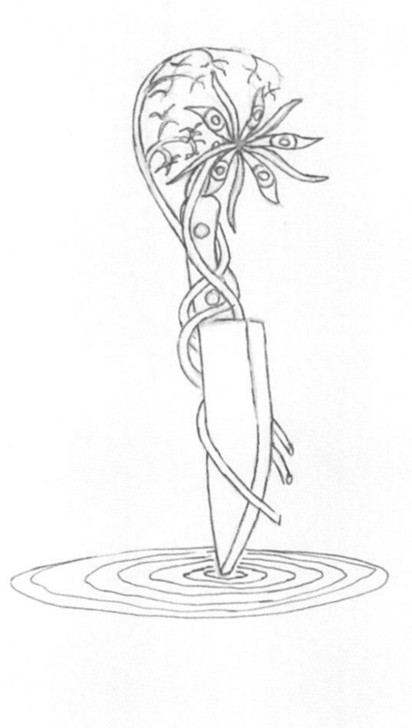

LEFT TO RIGHT:

PLATE 59
Sketch for Two Flowers and a Vine—male, c.1998
Black ink, pencil on paper
11 x 8 ½
Collection of the Meadows Museum, gift of James Surls and Charmaine Locke.

PLATE 60
Sketch for Two Flowers and a Vine—female, c.1998
Black ink, pencil on paper
11 x 8 ½
Collection of the Meadows Museum, gift of James Surls and Charmaine Locke.

PLATE 61
Sketch for Me, the Flower and the Pistil, 2000
Black ink, pencil on paper
11 x 8 ½
Collection of the Meadows Museum, gift of James Surls and Charmaine Locke.

"Me, the flower and the pistle"
about 10' X 9' X 3' – 2000
poplar, oak and steel
Hangs from cable
will weigh about
400 lbs.

10 ft

6 1/2 ft

5 1/2 ft

about 9 to 10 ft

Print Plates

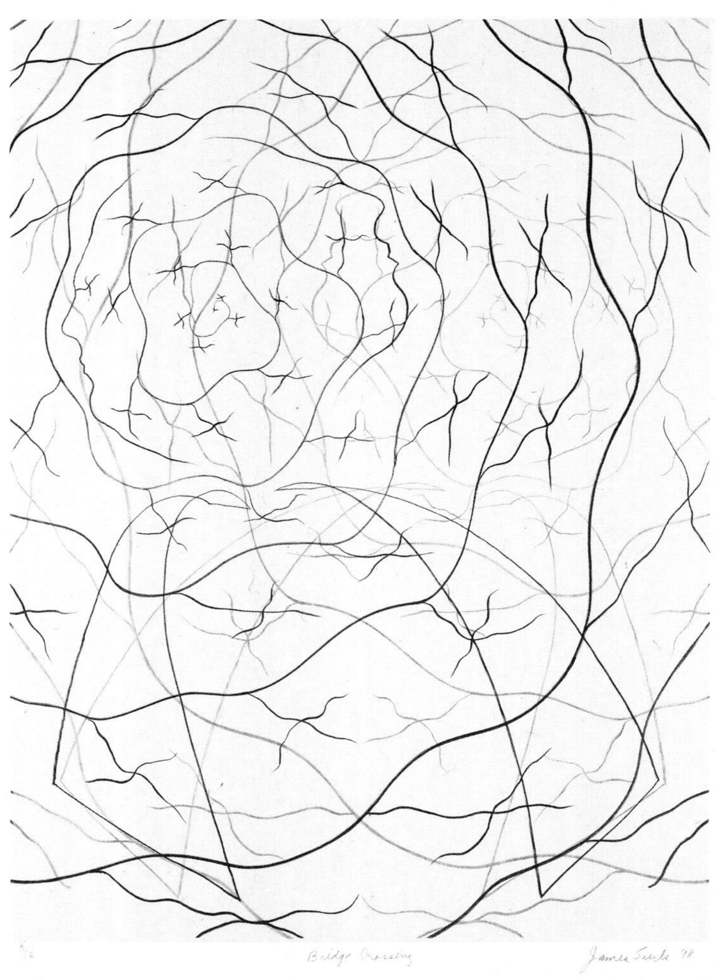

PLATE 62
Bridge Crossing, 1998
Lithograph
Edition 7/18
29 x 22

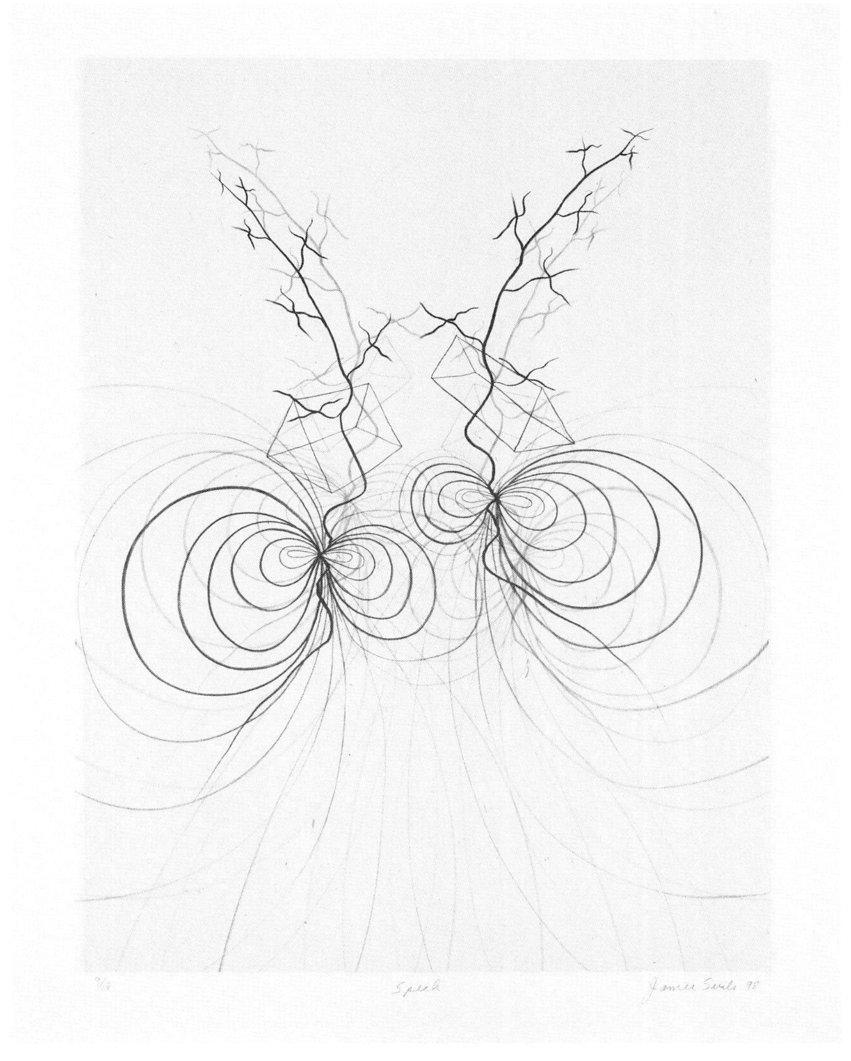

PLATE 63
Speak, 1998
Lithograph
Edition 7/18
29 x 22

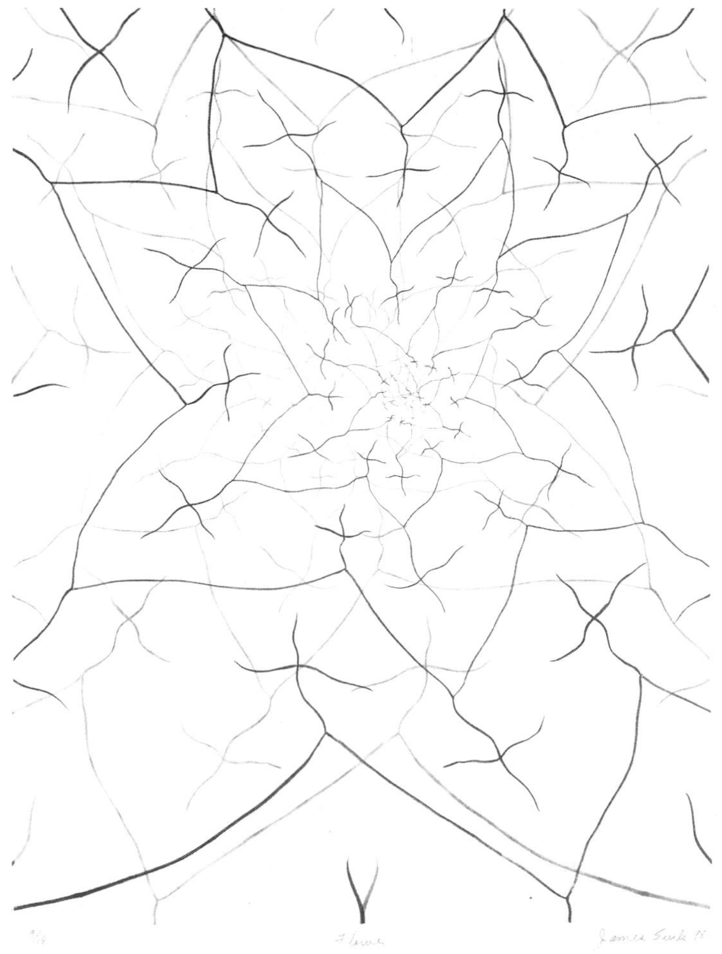

PLATE **64**
Flower, 1998
Lithograph
Edition 7/18
29 x 22

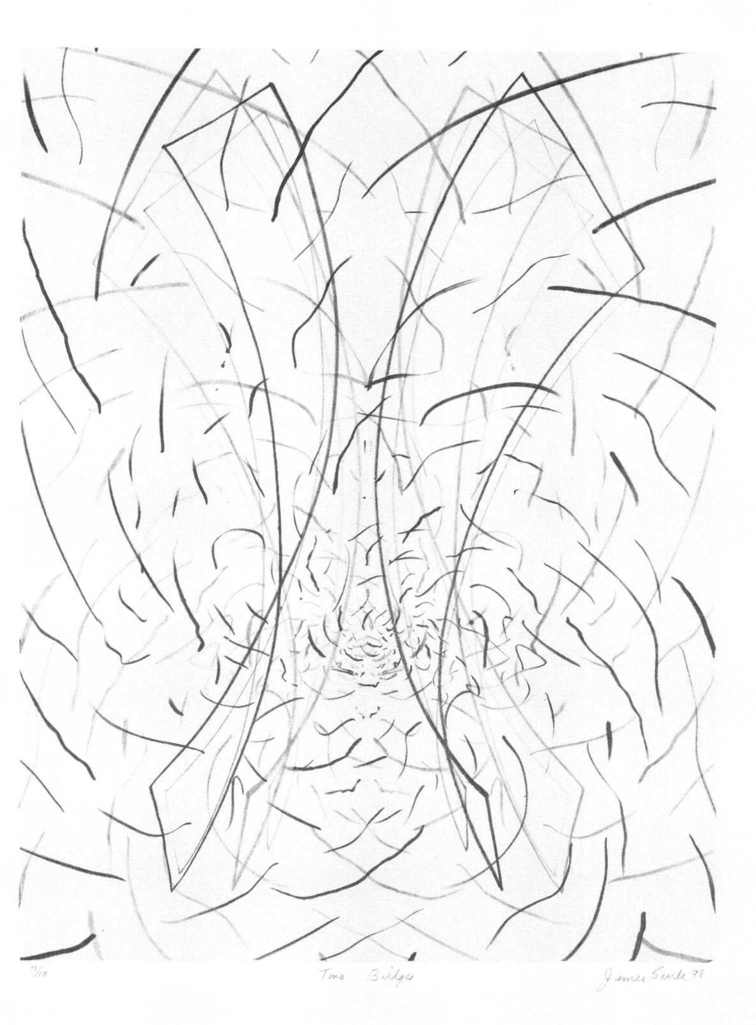

PLATE 65
Two Bridges, 1998
Lithograph
Edition 7/18
29 x 22

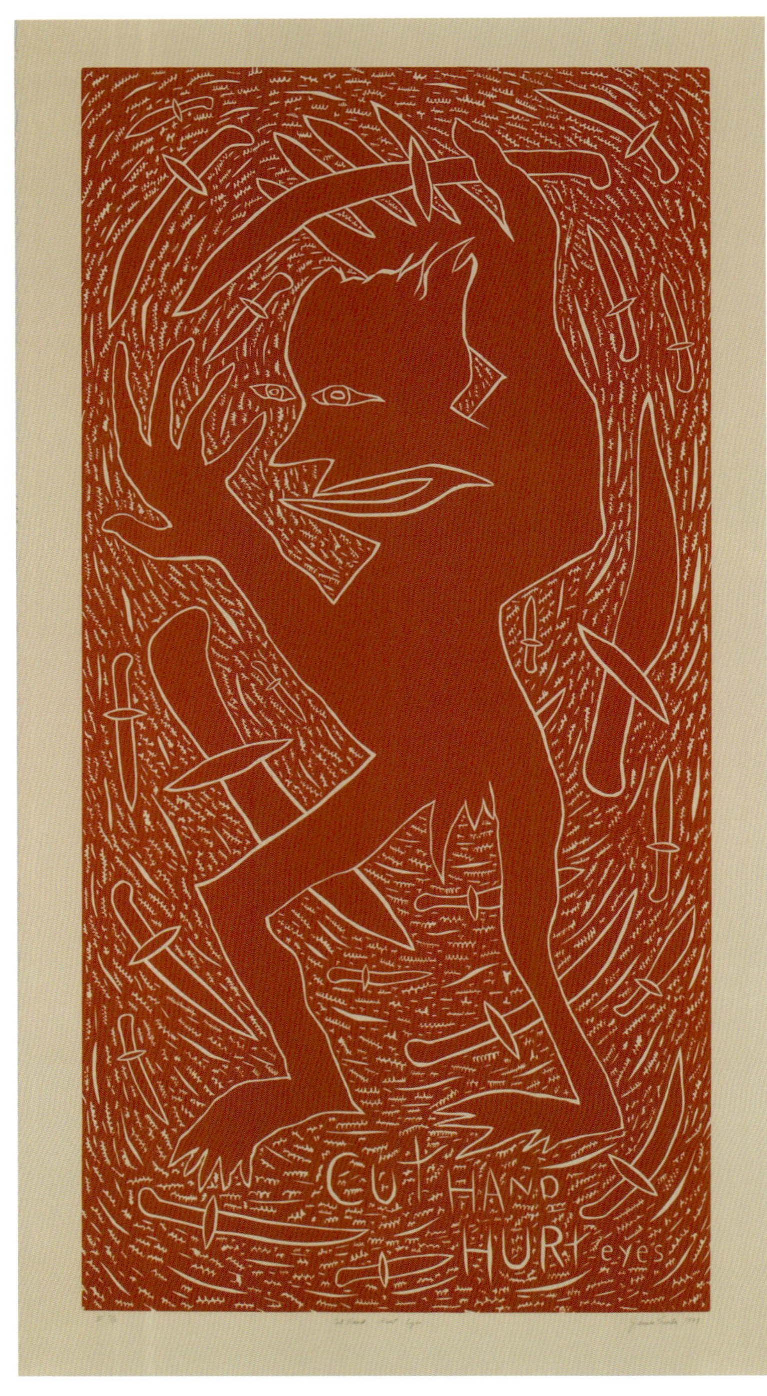

PLATE 66
Cut Hand, Hurt Eye II, 1999
Woodcut
Second edition 2/15
79 x 42 ½
Collection of the Meadows Museum, gift of James Surls and Charmaine Locke.

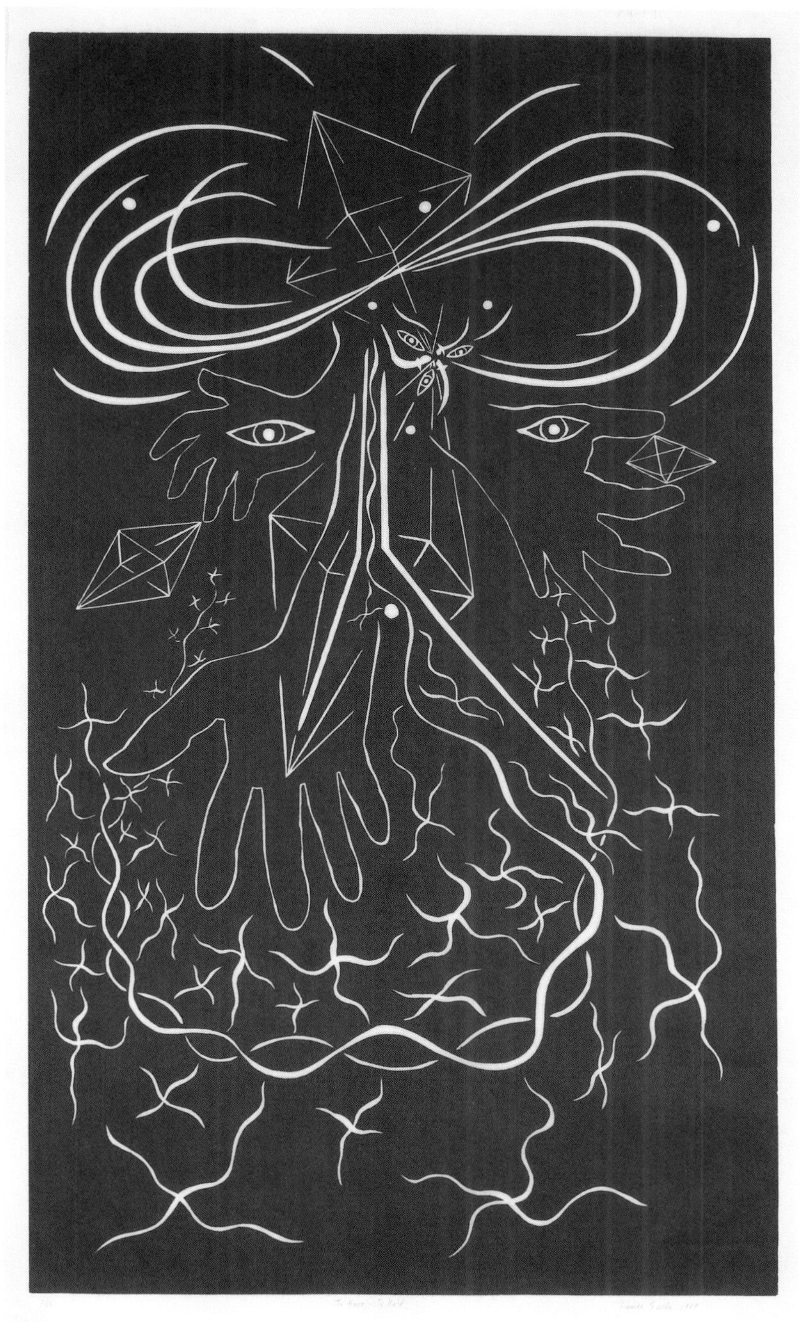

PLATE 67
To Have—To Hold, 1989
Woodcut
Edition 2/15
65 ½ x 37 ½

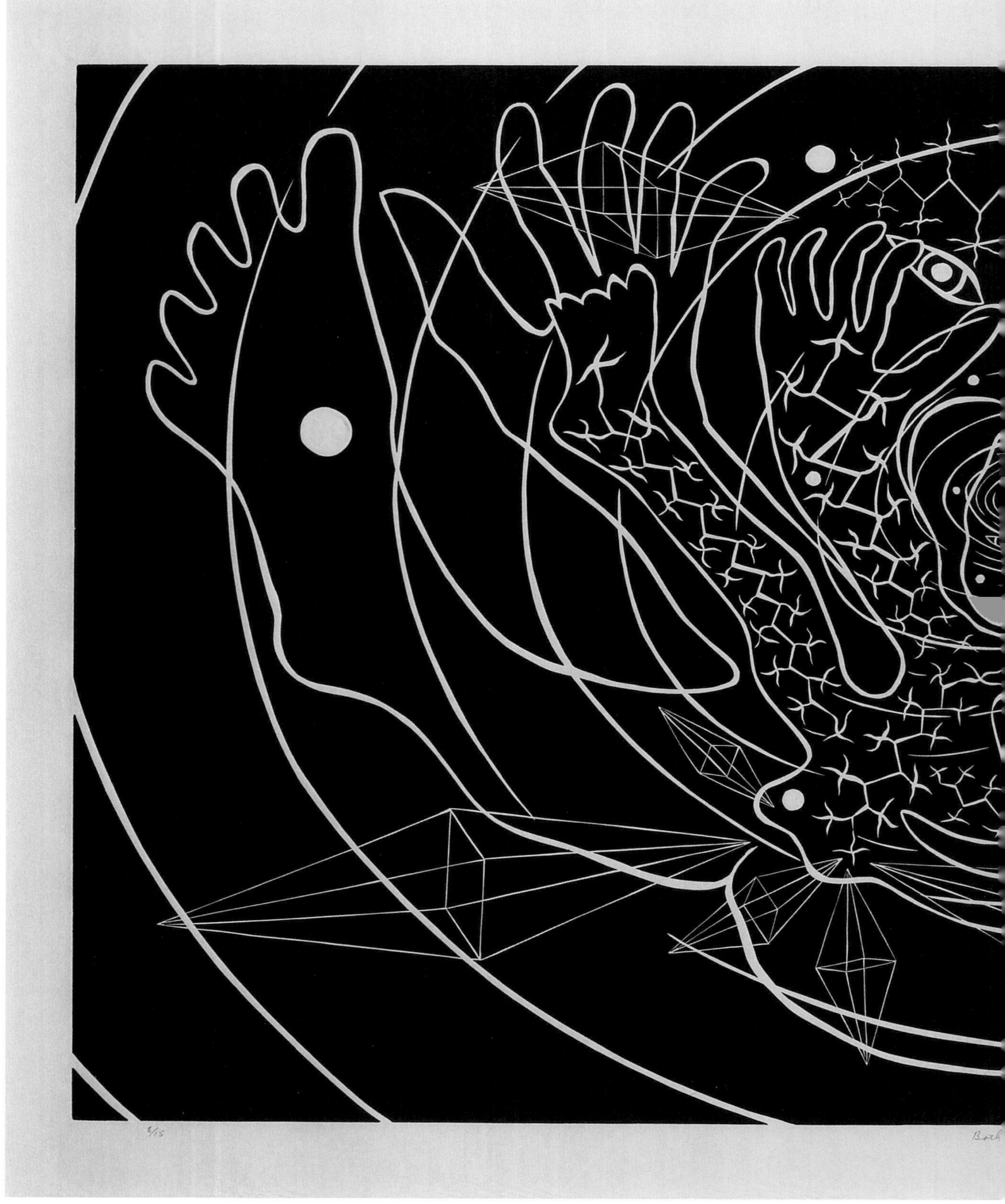

PLATE 68
Both of Us, 1990
Linocut
Edition 8/15
39 ½ x 66

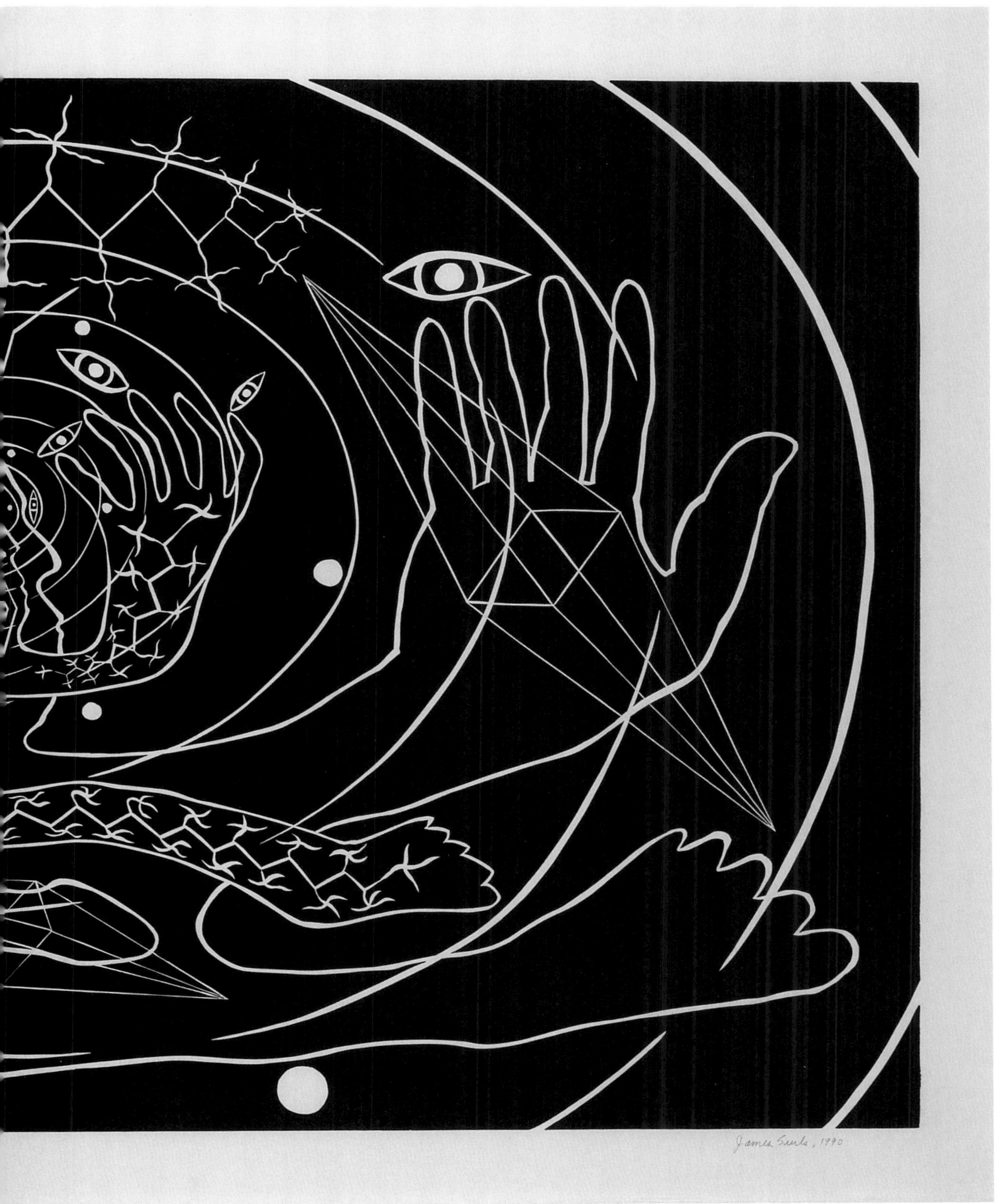

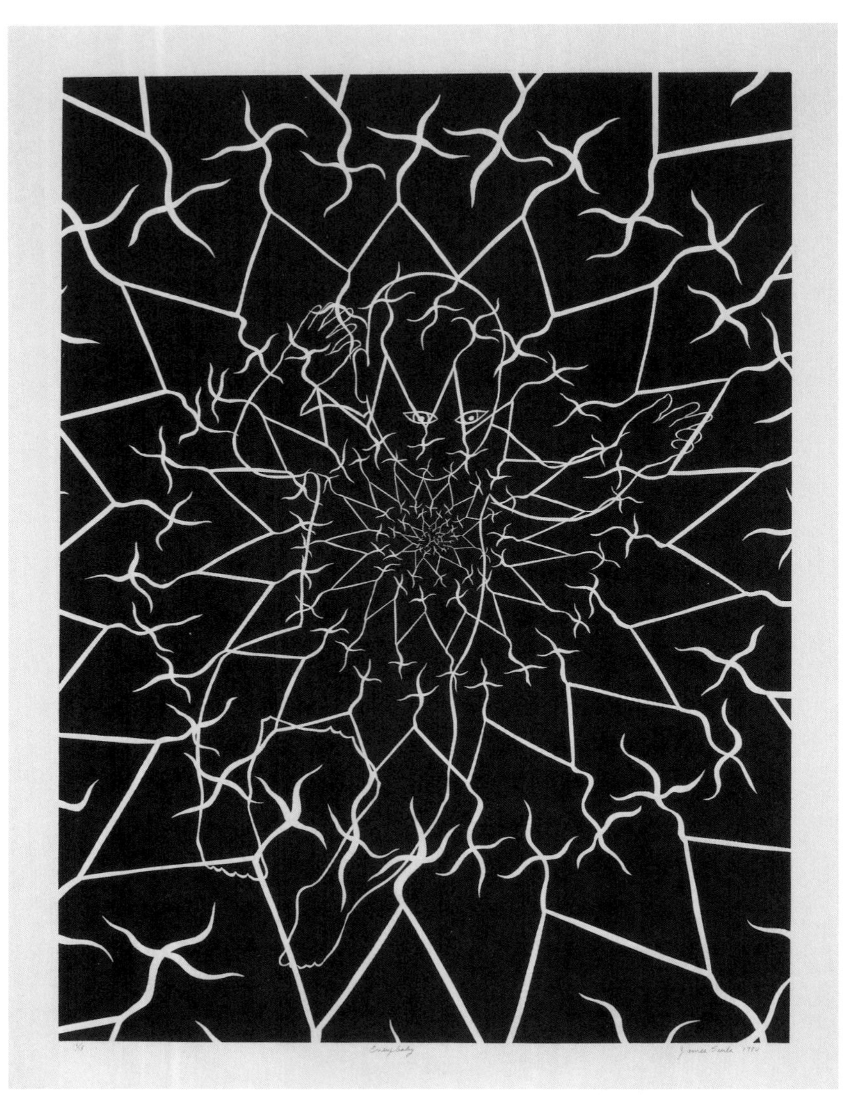

PLATE 69
Every Baby, 1990
Linocut
Edition 14/15
39 ½ x 53 ½

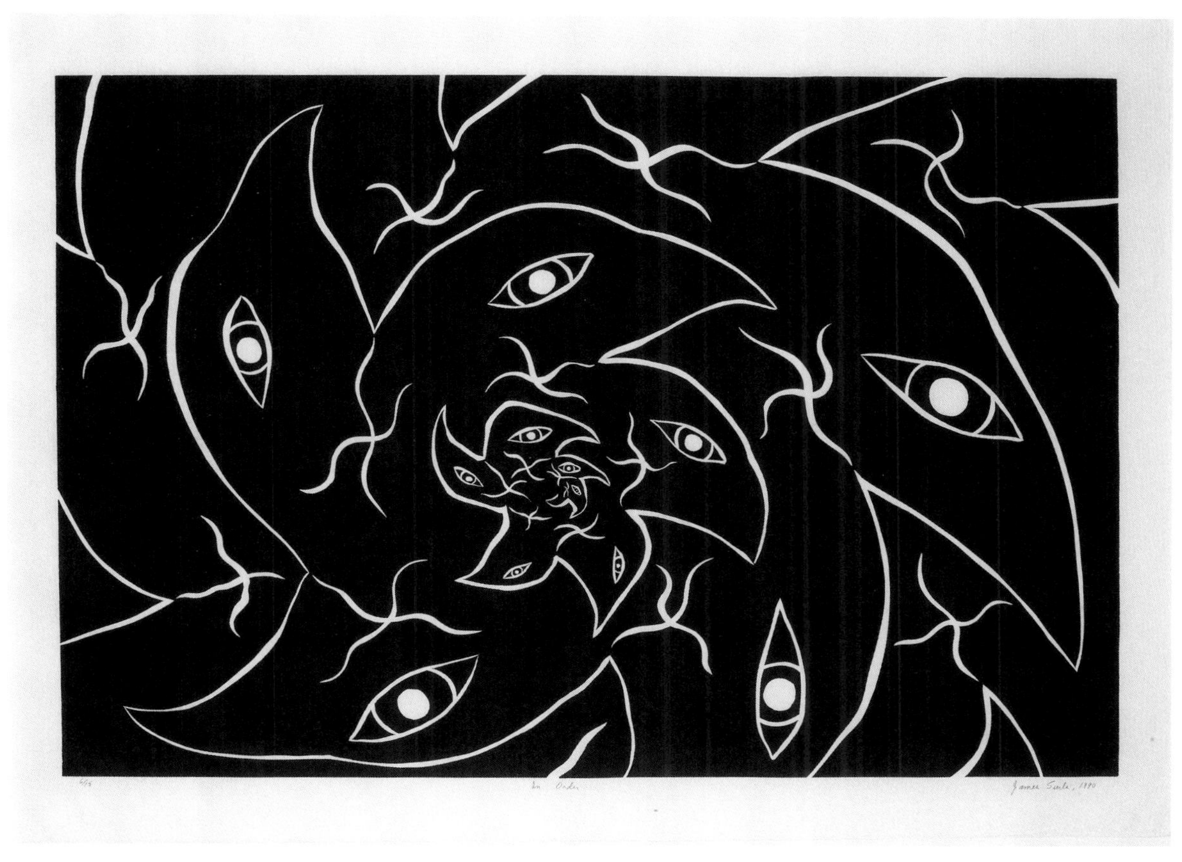

PLATE 70
In Order, 1990
Linocut
Edition 6/15
39 ½ x 53 ½

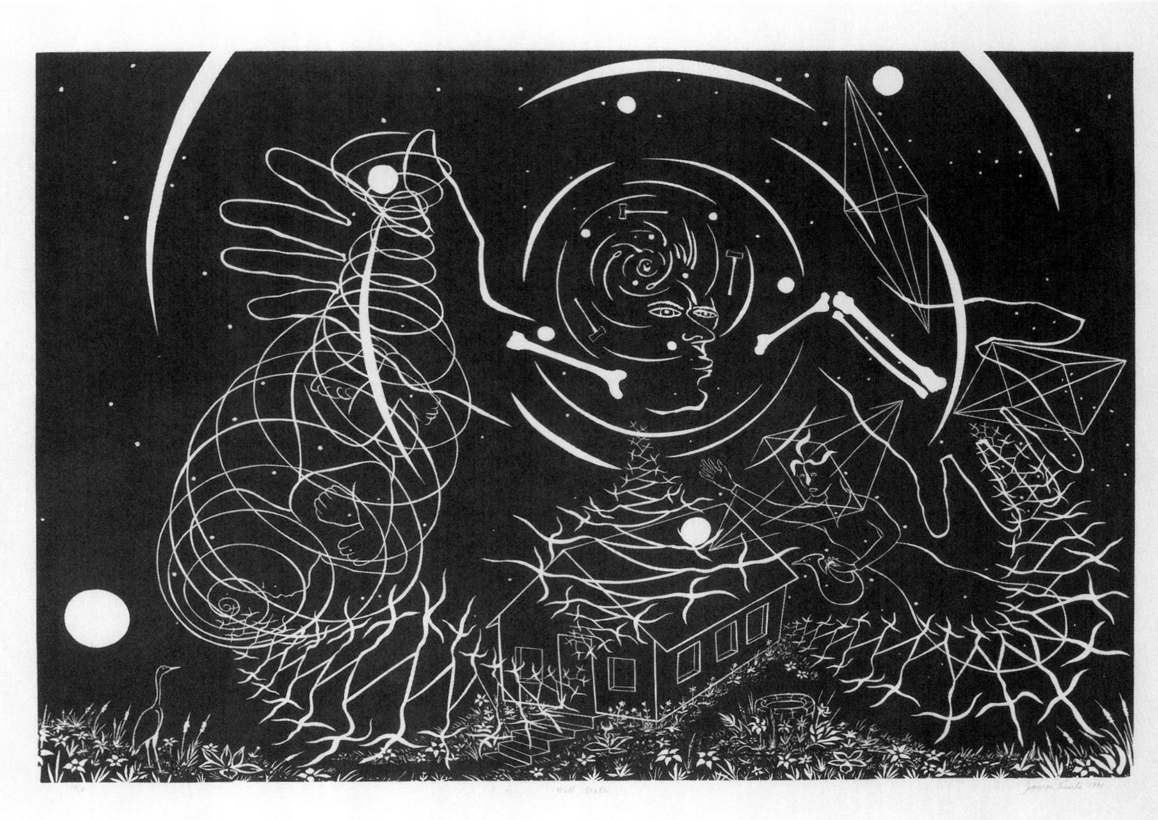

PLATE 71
Well Water, 1990
Linocut
Edition 13/15
39 ½ x 53

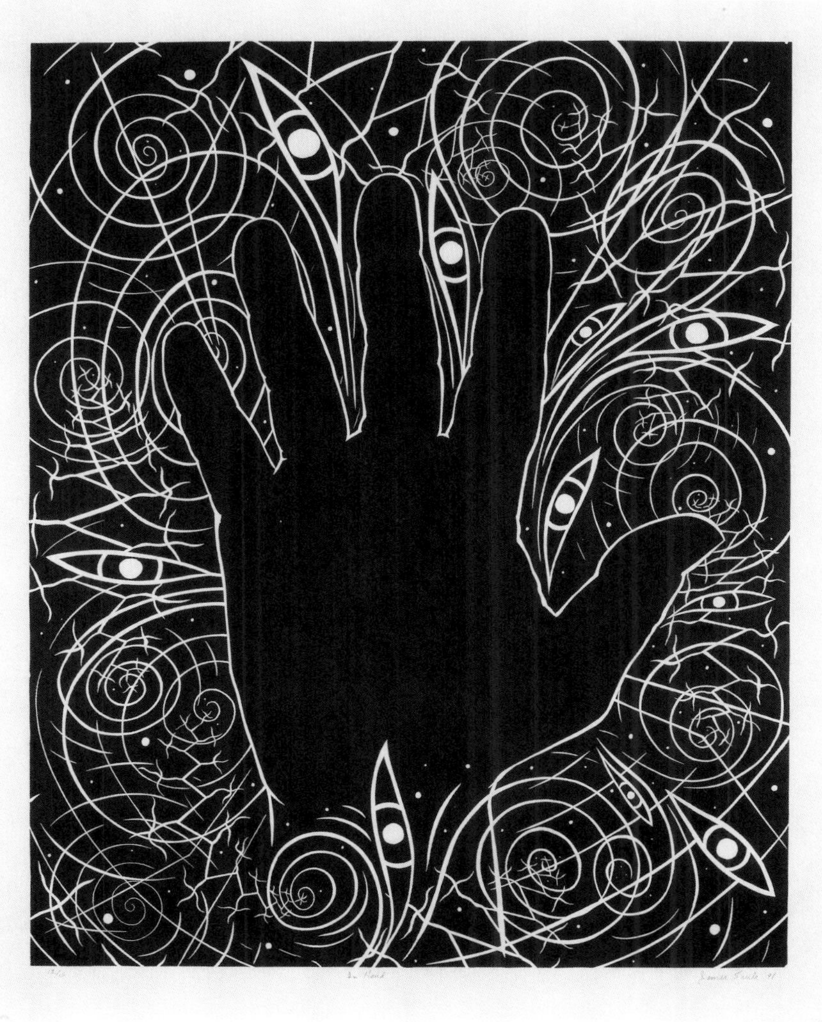

PLATE 72
In Hand, 1991
Linocut
Edition 12/15
49 ¾ x 39 ½

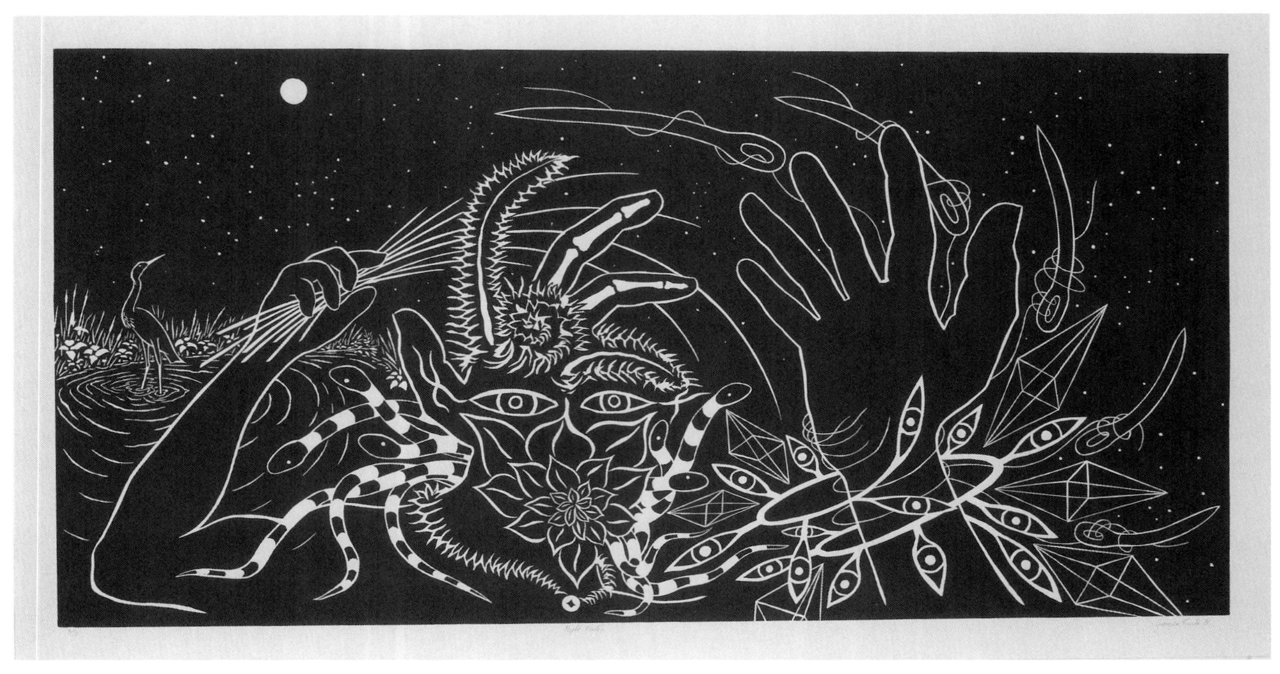

PLATE 73
Night Vision, 1991
Woodcut
Edition 10/15
40 ¼ x 66 ⅛

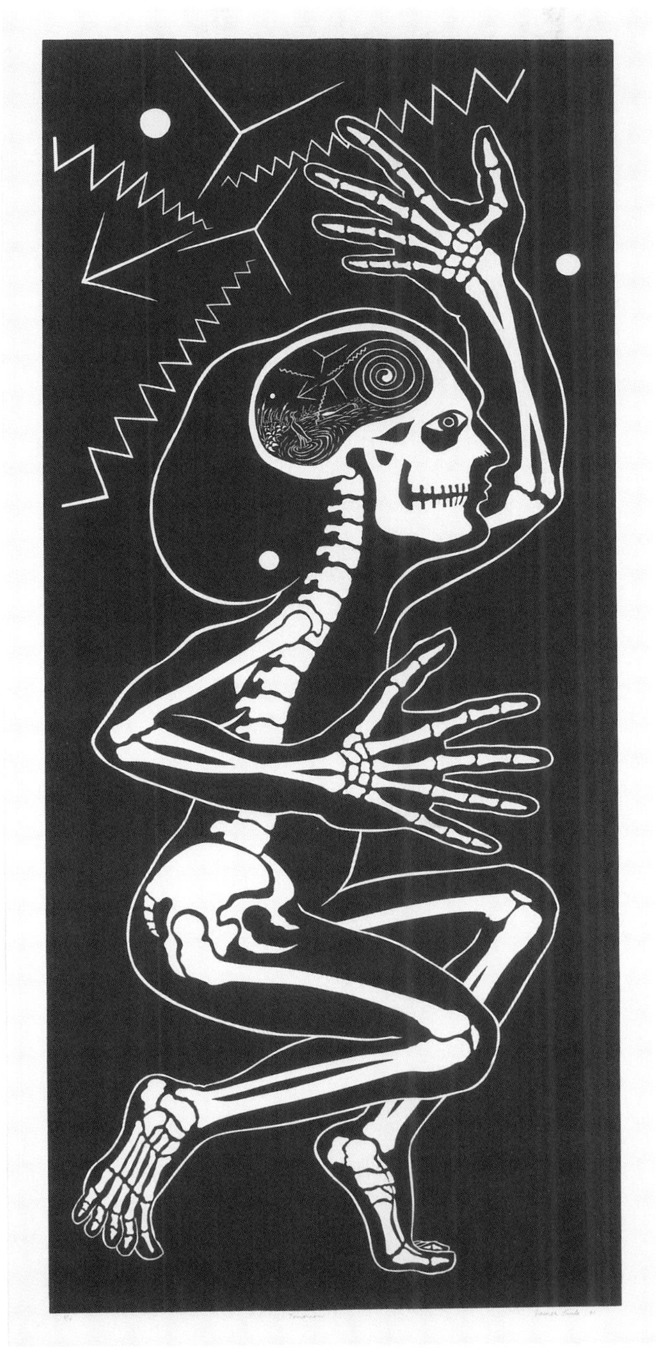

PLATE 74
Tomorrow, 1991
Linocut
Edition 8/15
88 ⅛ x 40 ⁷⁄₁₆
Collection of the Meadows Museum, gift of James Surls and Charmaine Locke.

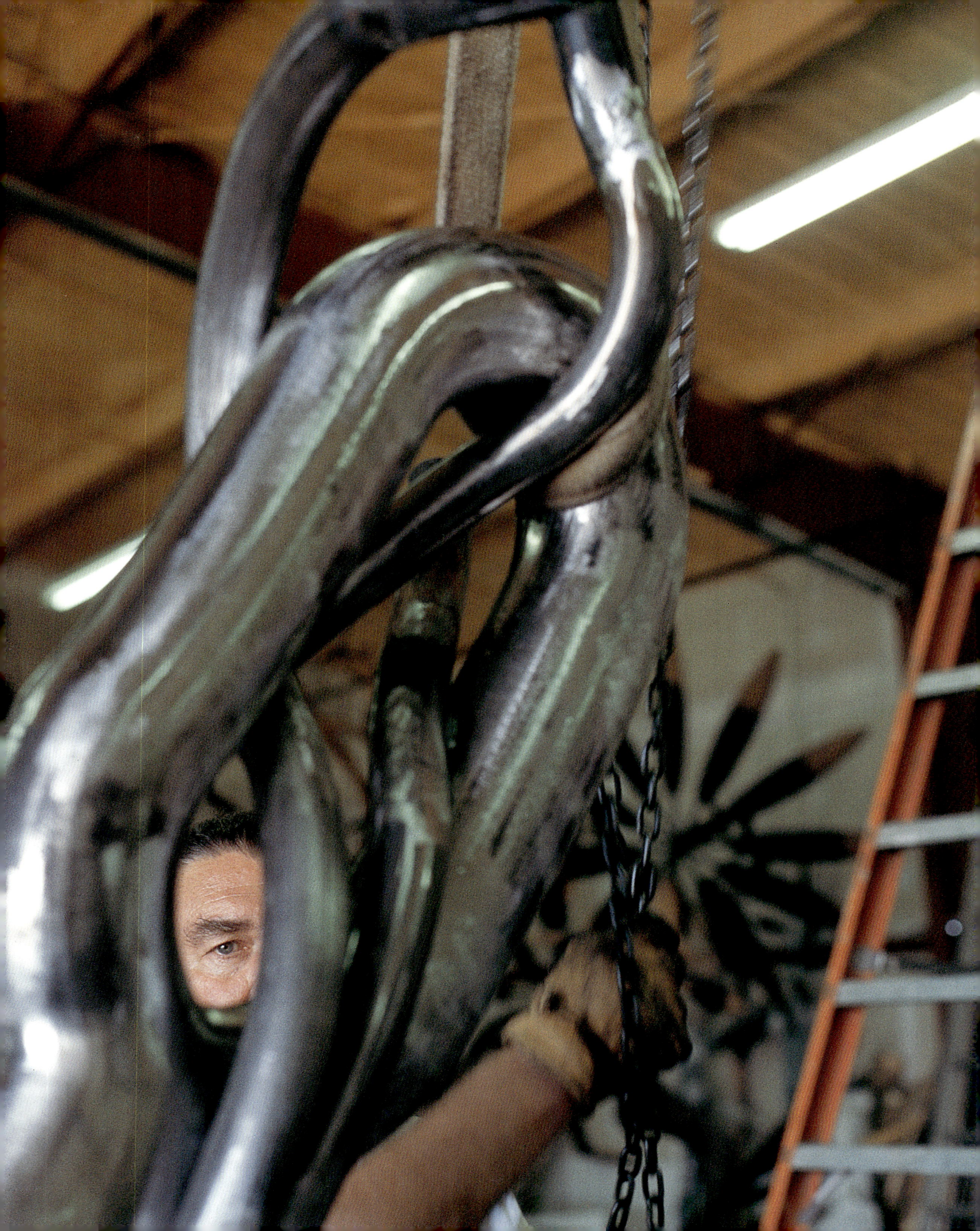

P. GREGORY WARDEN

In the Studio with James Surls

Part I: October 14, 2002. I met with James Surls in his studio in Silt, Colorado, to discuss his art and the upcoming exhibit at the Meadows Museum. The interview was recorded and filmed by James Brundage for an upcoming documentary on Surls by First Light Films. The following text has been edited from that interview.

Greg Warden: When did you move into this studio?

James Surls: About two years ago, but I really wanted to build a studio up at my land.

GW: Where do you live?

JS: Carbondale, you look out over the whole valley and, boy, it's totally amazing living where you can see and feel miles of mountains, valleys, rivers, having lived the first major chunk of my life in the east Texas piney woods, where, quite literally, you can't see a neighbor on the land next to you.

GW: Well, that was one of the questions I was going to ask you about, about the difference, but let's just start with *In the Meadows* and how that came about. What were you thinking as you prepared for the show?

JS: Well, there's always a lot of history that goes along with the show. I mean, people in museums—directors, curators, the museum proper, let's say—they don't really just do shows cold. They have to know who you are. There has to be some kind of prerequisite that brings you to that place at that time. Now, it makes total sense that this history has its focus point at the Meadows Museum, I mean, for any number of reasons. Obviously,

FIGURE 48
Surls in his Silt, Colorado, studio working on *Bridge & Needle, 2002* (**PL. 9**)

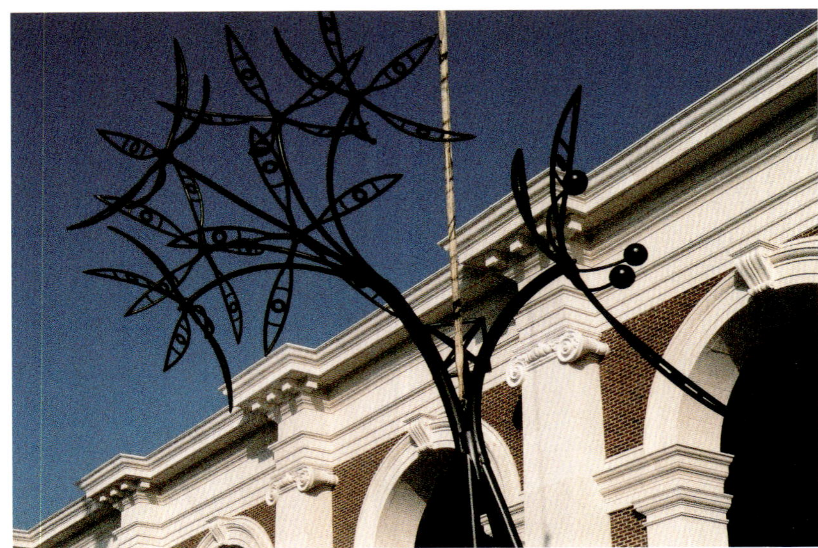

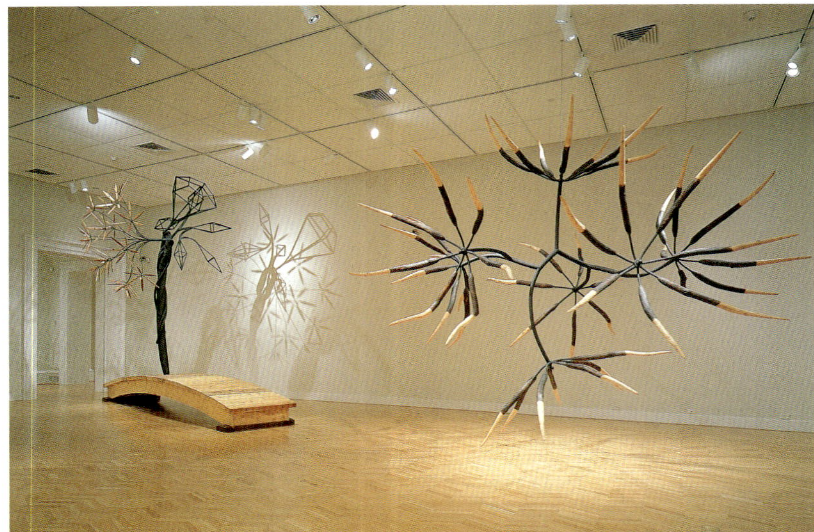

FIGURE 49
Exterior installation view of the exhibition *In the Meadows*. Shown: *Again in the Meadows* (detail) **(PL. 17)**

FIGURE 50
Interior installation view of the exhibition *In the Meadows*. Shown left to right: *Bridge & Needle* **(PL. 9)**, *Seven and Seven Flower* **(PL. 1)**

I taught at SMU. I have a history of being at SMU; the dance department at SMU had participated in one of the first exhibitions I had at a museum of consequence. So there's a history there.

GW: There were a couple of things that impressed me as we started to organize the exhibition. What is rather unusual is that you're paying attention to the museum as an institution, aware of its history, and fitting into that context. You are also reacting to both the spaces interior and exterior, and thinking about how your work fits into those spaces and might resonate with that very different building. That Neo-Georgian structure **(FIG. 49)** is quite a contrast to your sculpture, I think.

JS: Oh, absolutely. You know, it's like another era. It's not really my era, so you're actually taking something and melding it into an existing form. There were two things that impressed me about the building. The space is high, open, and clean **(FIG. 50)**.That's three big categories right there. In other words, if I couldn't put together a really beautiful and meaningful and elevating show in that space, I would have a real difficult time blaming the space. And spaces, a lot of times, particularly in galleries and commercial venues, are very dictatorial. In this one, I got to dictate the terms; I got to set the pace; I got to show what I wanted, and three of the interior pieces—the table, the bridge, and the big wall piece—four, actually, with the one going in the stairwell, were made specifically for that space. Outside, what I liked best is either when you're coming out of the building looking out over the terrace, or when you're walking up to the building, you get to the building, and you turn around. If you walk around out on that terrace, looking away from the building, what do you see? You see big, huge, fluffy, live-oak trees, green, very voluptuous, almost like those big clouds covering the landscape, and towering through that is the top of a church—a very specific and very beautiful structure that harkens to another era. You could very easily be in another time and another place. There is a certain timelessness to big, billowing, fluffy trees and church steeples. I really like that. I like the idea of having pieces that would be read against the open blue sky in the background. And having the church rise up out there through it, that's symbolic icing on the cake.

GW: Talking about that kind of space—and the trees and the steeple—brings to mind the contrast between the natural and the human-made. Do you think about that at all, as an element of your work?

JS: I think about the natural in the work or the human hand in the work. The work would not exist without the human hand. It is inherent. I argued once, to no avail, I might add, that a bulldozer was natural, and everyone in the room said, That is the most ludicrous thing I've ever heard. How can you say that? And I said, because it is natural for humans to make things and to create, and that's part of our creation. We made the bulldozer, so the bulldozer is then just in the chain of natural events. Now, that's stretching what constitutes natural. It is pretty amazing when psychology really entered into art, not just subliminally or from below the level of consciousness but when consciousness came into art. Boy, that's a huge step, so the truth of it is that you have to have those two elements mixed. I wonder how Walt Whitman would answer that. He looked at a locomotive as part of nature. There's an argument about abstraction. I don't necessarily even really believe in the term; I don't really use the term; I don't look at the term as having any kind of application anymore. I mean, to me, abstract is natural. That's part of what we inherently have the ability to do, and there's a lot of things in my art that fall within that genre of thought, like the diamonds. The diamonds are very clean, calculated, systematic, and very rational and very man-made, in a way **(FIG. 51)**. You certainly could argue the point that you find the tetrahedron in nature. It's the molecular structure of

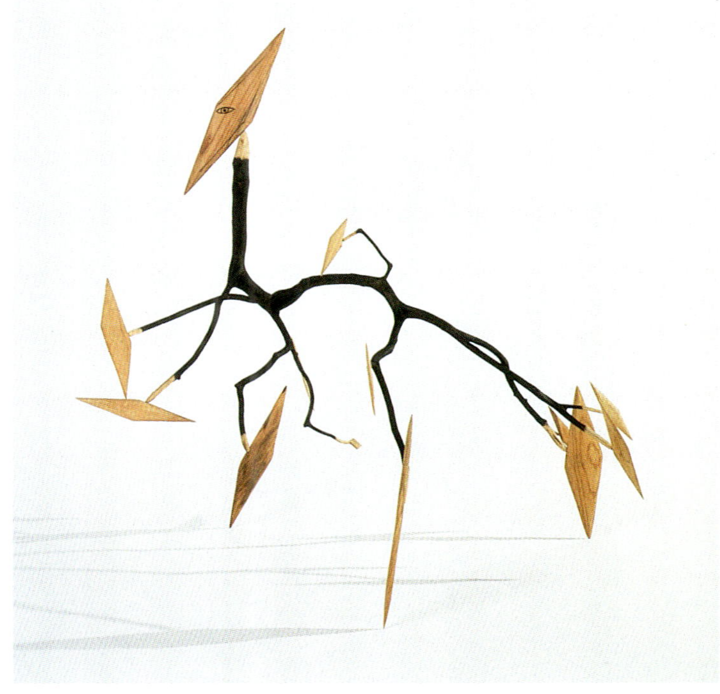

FIGURE 51
Diamond Head Man II, 1993
Oak
45 x 45 ¾ x 30 ¼

gold, you know; it's found in crystals. I mean, there's all kind of forms in nature that have that very clean and calculated and human-made look. I don't necessarily think of myself as making crystals as such, although I look at the prism. The prism shows up in my art a lot as this man-made thing. I think it's the combination between what you would call the natural and the human. It is human nature, too, and it's really pretty amazing to me that when psychology, the psychoanalysis kind of thing, the pre-Freudian era of the Romantic poets. . . . It was all inherent in there for Freud to pick up on, the conjuring from memory—your own personal memory—bringing your memory into a futuristic presence—now and for the future, but you took it out of your past, your personal past.

GW: Psychology makes us aware of those dualities. The natural and the human-made is one of those dualities, but your art has an even greater range of contrasts that, to me, give it a special interest and tension. Some people who have written about you have said that it's the contrast of male and female, the contrast of a number of different kinds of emotional elements (FIG. 52). It strikes me that this contrast, this ambiguity, is connected to a term that you have used yourself, a term that you're using a great deal now, Romanticism. You say that you are interested in a Romantic point of view. So, I wondered if we could talk about that. What are you thinking, what are you envisioning when you say that something is Romantic or when you say that your work is moving toward that kind of Romantic sensibility?

JS: I think Romantic absolutely has as part of its source a little magic, a little mystery, maybe even some wizardry, and there's a tough line between philosophy and religion and romance. All romance is not about glory and flowers, and sweet and wonderful, and full, voluptuous, and festive things. There's another side of romance, and I think that it inherently comes out. For instance, if you name something *Night Vision* (PL. 73), just the name, just the title has a certain dark side. "Night," you know, if you use the word "midnight," the term, just saying that will inherently strike a certain chord with a listener. Why? Because they have a preconceived kind of mystery that goes with it, and I think that Romantic art is filled with what some people call a dark side. Now, how dark

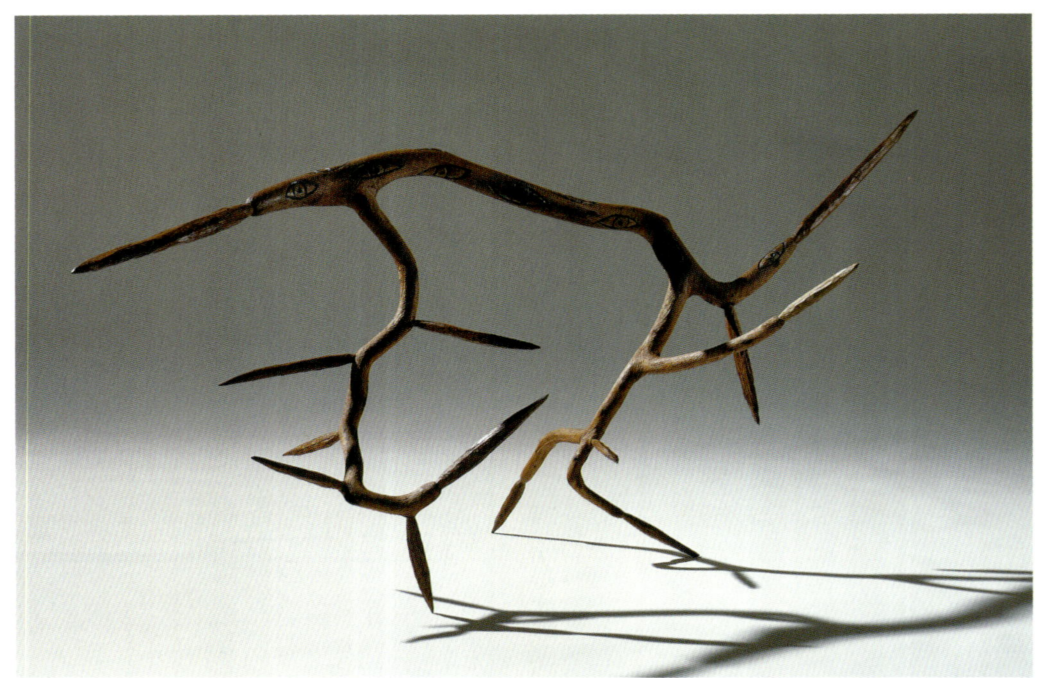

FIGURE 52
Two People Dancing and Singing, 1978
Pine, oak
20 ½ x 46 ½ x 22
Private Collection

is dark? I mean, how? Is it personally dark? Is it collectively dark? And that really does have to do with male and female and paradox, and with opposites. I ask this question, facetiously to some extent. Would you rather be charged by a female rhinoceros or a male rhinoceros? Well, who cares, either one you're dead. You can't say that females are only about the vessel and giving and that they're only about nurturing. They did, by the way, bring all of us over on this side into the world. So, we are half-and-half whether we like it or not; you can't negate that sort of genetic existence there. I think that paradox exists in male and female. I mean, I don't remember too many women armies. History is littered with male armies and males who would cut and slash and rape and pillage and burn, and it still goes on. You know it's amazing that 9/11 struck such horror in us as a country, us as a people, us as a culture. It was genuinely horrible—there's no question about that—just as dark as humanity can get. But do you know how many babies in the last ten years have had their arms cut off in Rwanda? You start scattering this whole business out across the globe, 9/11 was a drop in the bucket. You're talking about over two million people a year, you know we lost three thousand? I beg your pardon, it's a dark world out there, and I think that the so-called Romantics don't necessarily negate that. They dealt with that as part of our psyche, and it is a paradox, and I think that artists inherently live in paradox. I think that the real world tries not to. They don't really want to deal with negatives. I don't know who really gets to avoid it. Whether you're rich or poor you still have to deal with it. Whether you're sharp or dull, you still have to deal with it. I mean, it's just part of humanity and we do have to deal with it.

GW: You said that you're moving towards a different sensibility, that a more Romantic side of you will come out in this show, *In the Meadows*. Is the art itself changing? Is there stylistic change?

JS: Well, yes and no. If you ask the question, Is it now more Romantic than that, or is this changed from that, I would say a scary thing for an artist is to plagiarize. I mean, that's something that maybe at one time was not an issue. In today's world it is an issue. We don't want to plagiarize. Well, we don't want to plagiarize ourselves either. You don't write a poem and you then write the same poem over and over and over, and they ask you why you're doing it, and you say, what was wrong with it in the first place? You say it was a good poem then, it's a good poem now, so I'm just going to do the same one over and over and over. You want your art to grow, you want it to elevate. You want to personally grow and to personally elevate, and you certainly want that to be part of the perception that an audience gets, that if they are students of this particular strand of work, they know the history and would be able to look at it and say, it's different now. The feel is different. I think the difference is very important for this exhibition. This is the exhibition that basically is made in Colorado. Well, what's so big about that? Terrain, place, space, you know, that encircling kind of atmosphere that's around you, I think absolutely will help dictate the terms of your thinking. It will. It'll have an effect. If it doesn't, then you really are not looking. You're really not feeling. You're really not seeing it, and this show has a bridge in it—a huge bridge with a needle on the bridge [*Bridge & Needle* (**PL. 9**)]. There are threads. There are

FIGURE 53
Surls, at left, and assistant Tai Pomara installing *Bridge & Needle* (**PL. 9**).

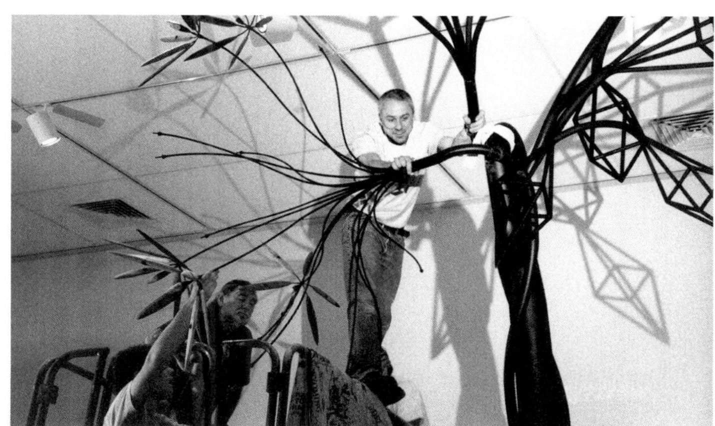

three threads that are wrapped around the needle, that go up through the eye of the needle and then turn into something (see FIG. 48). Each thread turns into its own thing. One of the threads turns into a big kind of starburst-flower, almost like an extended dandelion with a daisy out on the end of each stem, so it pops out (see FIG. 53 and TITLE PG.). Well, as a spectator you could ask, What does that mean? What's that? Why did he put a flower there? Why did he use the "flower" that way? One of the other threads turns into five diamonds or tetrahedron shapes that are arranged in a very explosive kind of pattern. The third one turns into a five-sided—I'm going to call it a gem; we could call it a crystal or we could call it a geometric shape; certainly the facets are cut like a jewel. So you ask yourself the question, What is the bridge? Why did he make a bridge? I've made bridges before. I made bridges when I lived in the jungle, and now I'm out here making a bridge. What does a bridge do? A bridge will take you from one place to somewhere else. What do you do here? Boy, it is open vision. This terrain is very, very open. I mean, my God, you can see a mile, ten miles, fifty miles. In some cases you can see a hundred miles. The only thing that gets in your way is the atmosphere. It's very open-headed. I've always lived in my head. You know, Blake, the poet William Blake, they say he lived in his head. Well, I think artists do. I think that's part of what artists do. You know, how could a composer compose music after he'd already gone deaf? It's in his head.

GW: You have lived in your head, but you have also been very open to what is around you. You're incredibly in tune with the woods, or now the vistas and the open space...

JS: Well, it's still the woods. There are woods here in Colorado. The woods here play a role as well. It's much more pocketed. It's just not as pervasive in the way of southeastern Texas, south Louisiana—what I call the old gulf, the old South, the sugar pines and the magnolias, and boy, the vines, the vines, the soft earth and the water. We lived in a marshy jungle, and now I live on a high plateau, with a great vista, two very paradoxical places.

GW: You have called the show *In the Meadows.* The pun is that you are now drawing inspiration from these open spaces rather than from the enclosed spaces that inspired you earlier.

JS: Well, why call the show *In the Meadows*? First, the museum is called the Meadows. That's natural, but why would I call it *In the Meadows*? Why didn't I call it *James Surls' New Work* or something else? Well, "the meadows" is a metaphor for Eden, if you will. You know, the whole history of the garden. The garden is where there is moisture and warmth, where the apple trees grow. That is something we depend on psychologically, almost like Linus's blanket. It's our hold on nature. It's where the early guys built their homes. It's where the villages started to pop up—there's water, there's growth, there's green—all the things you need to sustain life are there, physically but certainly psychologically, as well. *In the Meadows* to me is the perfect name. I didn't live in the meadows before; I lived in the jungle. The gulf coast may be one big, giant meadow in a sense, but you're too surrounded to be aware of it, but in Colorado you are absolutely aware of the meadows. Even if you hike and go over the mountain, where do you ultimately kind of land? You know, the place to stop, the place you go to eat your sack lunch? There is a certain psychological security, in the meadows. It's almost like a room; it's a natural kind of room.

GW: One of the things that strikes me very much is that when you talk about your art, what you're thinking about is this underlying sense of a real belief system, of nature and the natural. You are responding to that. You've referred to Blake, and in a sense the Romantics as well, whose belief system was in this kind of natural wonder, this sense of the spiritual in nature, and I think that's always been there in your art. Has it changed at all, or is it still the same set of principles that guides you now? Have things changed as you've gotten a little older?

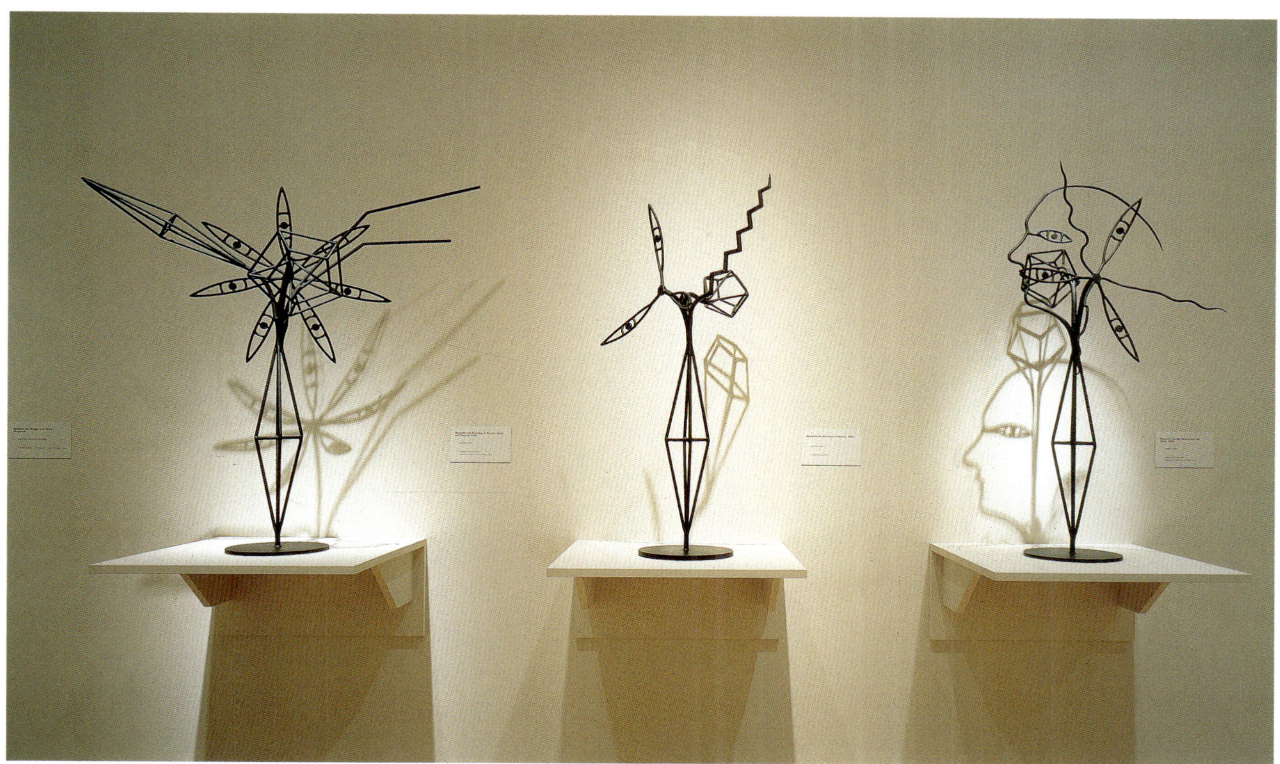

FIGURE 54
Installation view of maquettes. Shown left to right: *Maquette for Drawing in Flower, Jewel, and Funnel*, 2002, (**PL. 26**); *Maquette for Stairway to Heaven*, 2002, (**PL. 33**); *Maquette for Me, Flower, and the Jewel*, 2002, (**PL. 28**)

JS: The paradox is there as well. I would point out that Blake was a city boy. Blake liked London; he loved London. He liked the hustle, the bustle, the social, the activity, the action. He was an action junkie, in a sense, but he lived in a very kind of high-minded, Romantic place in his head, whereas Wordsworth rowed out into the lake and wrote about the mountains rising, and he hiked over and talked about the city down by the sea, and talked about the city as having this kind of female personality and being draped and wardrobed, and he really used the sublime of nature. It was a muse; it was an inspiration; it was a source that the Romantics drew on. I don't know that Blake liked the country, just to be honest with you, whereas I do. But now there's a paradox there, and this is the point I'm getting to. As Charmaine and I moved to the country, we moved way out in an idyllic sense—you could verbalize it in a very idyllic way—it was down a dirt road, across a bridge, a creek, around a bend, on the hill, in the woods, it's kind of a little too good to be true. That's the sort of ideal thing that people shoot for. Both Charmaine and I are action junkies. We love social events; we love to go where there are people. We love the dialogue. We love to be in the mix. Now, you can't do that and not have that influence you as well. I think that in making commentary—visual, artistic, creative commentary—you inherently put that personal piece of your private world in there. But then you also—and this may be where the paradox comes in—put into that piece that bigger picture, the communal, and maybe the world at large. We can speak of the world at large because we are cognizant of a world at large. It's debatable what the reach of any given community is. The modern-day artists, maybe all artists, aspired to reach as far as they could; they really spoke of humanity in a big-picture sort of world, but they inevitably put that stuff together in that real private, personal sort of world. Joseph Cornell is the perfect example. My God, man, this guy could take you to the edge of the universe; he could push you out by dropping a marble in a shot glass; he can literally take you out in outer space. That is an unbelievable artistic stroke, to be able to do that. Yet he worked in hatboxes. He worked in this small scale, like this. I like big. I love big. I like things that are grand and bigger than life and monumental, and that's certainly part of what I want *In the Meadows* to be. I want that grand and monumental part. And ironically, half of the show is little, very small pieces **(PL. 20–34)**. They're models, they're maquettes, meant to have this sort of monumentality. I don't think size really has anything to do with monumentality **(see FIG. 54)**. Again, Joseph Cornell is the perfect example of someone who can make truly monumental statements, and do it on a very meticulously small level, physically. But, my God, he may be one of the most powerful artists that's ever lived. He didn't have to make it fifteen feet high. I for some reason do. And I think that's just a part of artists. Artists have these sizes that they feel real comfortable with, they like. I like big art. Paradoxically, again, it's the hardest to do in the sense that it takes the most material, it takes the most kind of physical support system and tools and mechanism and devices and truck and cranes and boy, here you go with all this support system that you need to do art with **(FIG. 55 and FIG. 56)**. The payoff is that you get to have a certain awesome presentation, and I truly want that. I want the spectator to walk into the Meadows Museum, and from the time they start up those stairs, I want them to start kind of taking air, feeling, just feeling the presence of this. I think great art has a presence, and I certainly want mine to be there. I want it to do that.

GW: Do you enjoy the scale of your pieces in terms of the actual process, in terms of putting them together, of going from small to big, and assembling and seeing it for the first time on that scale? Are you aware of that?

JS: I think artists enjoy each one of their processes. You know, even if they grumble more about one than the other.

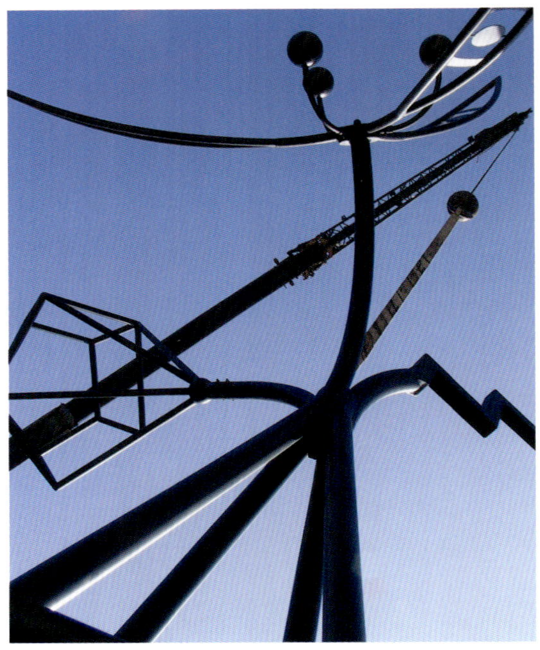

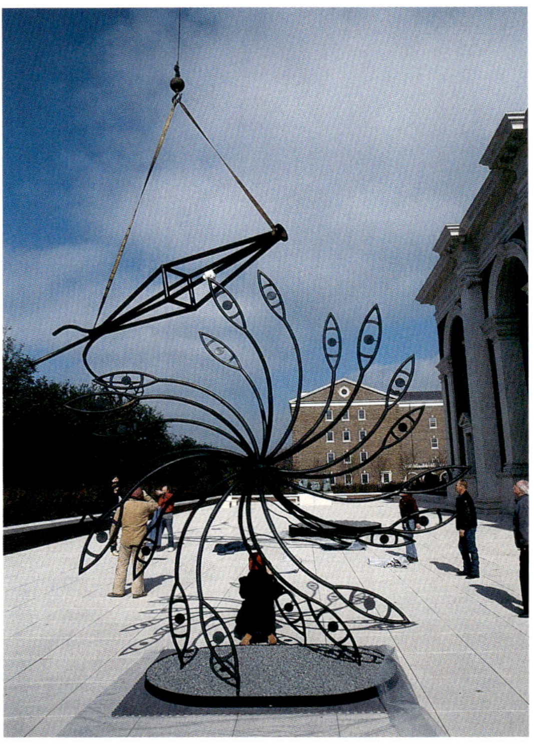

FIGURE 55
Exterior installation view of *Stairway to Heaven* **(PL. 19)**

FIGURE 56
Exterior installation view of *Reaching Out* **(PL. 18)** and *Walking See Flower* **(PL. 16)**

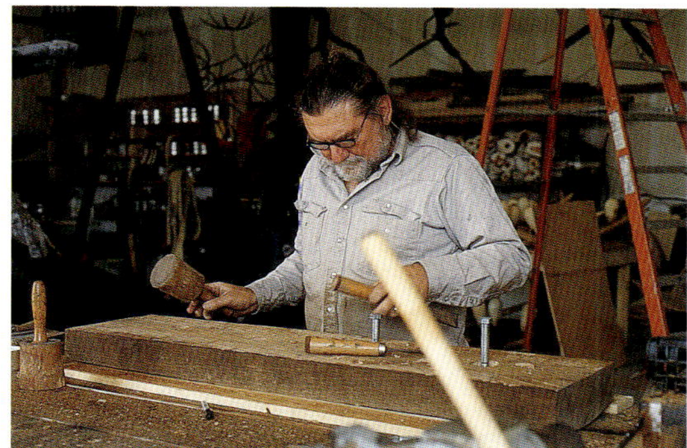

FIGURE 57
Surls working in his Silt, Colorado, studio

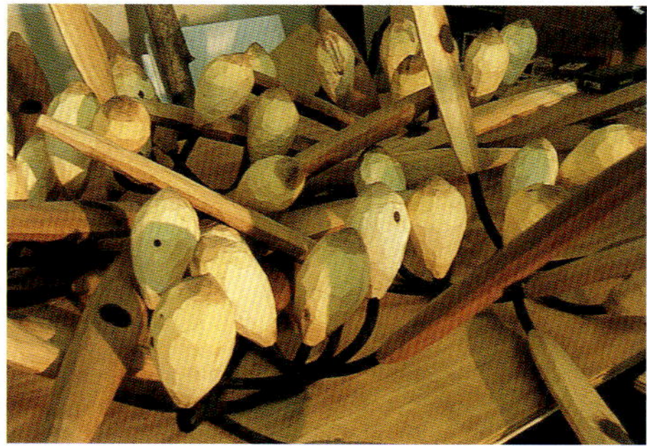

FIGURE 58
Elements for *Large Wall Flower* **(PL. 14)**

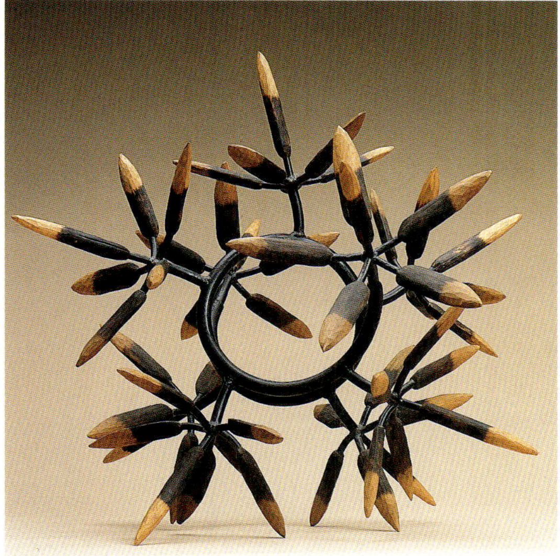

FIGURE 59
Star Flower (Maquette), 1994
Poplar, wood, steel
17 ¼ x 19 x 19 ¼

GW: Ah, the boring stuff, the grinding.

JS: Even the grinding part **(FIG. 57)**. If it was that bad, they'd figure out a way to avoid it. I can't imagine not liking their process. If they didn't like their process, they're in the wrong business. And, I think that there's an inherent flaw in the belief system about process. I actually wrote my thesis on process, thinking at that time that the process was the art, but on a mature, intellectual level; well, of course, the process is not the art. It's what you say with the process. I actually look at that like in a sports analogy about hitting the ball. You have to be able to hit the ball; you have to be able to catch the ball; you have to be able to throw the ball; I mean, you have to be able to do all that stuff just to get you in the game. That's all that'll do, that'll just get you in the game. Now, once you get in, what difference does it make if you come in through the front door or the back door? When artists are on their own, and regardless of whether they come from the so-called outsider world or the high intellectual world, once they get in the creative mode, then they're in. From that point on, it's not just about the process. The process is inherent. Of course, you have to be able to drive the nail.

GW: There are artists who would say, though, that the process doesn't matter at all. It's fine. You could have someone else do it for you. Your art, at least the way I read it, is all about your involvement in it. When you look at the textures of the wood, the oiling of the wood, the metal, the joins of the metal **(FIG. 58 and FIG. 59)**, even if you haven't done that little specific bit, there's a sense that you're there, that the textures and surfaces are part of what you put into it, and I don't think that every artist would agree with that.

JS: No, every artist wouldn't agree with that. I certainly could name you any number of artists who are…

GW: Quite happy to have other people just produce it.

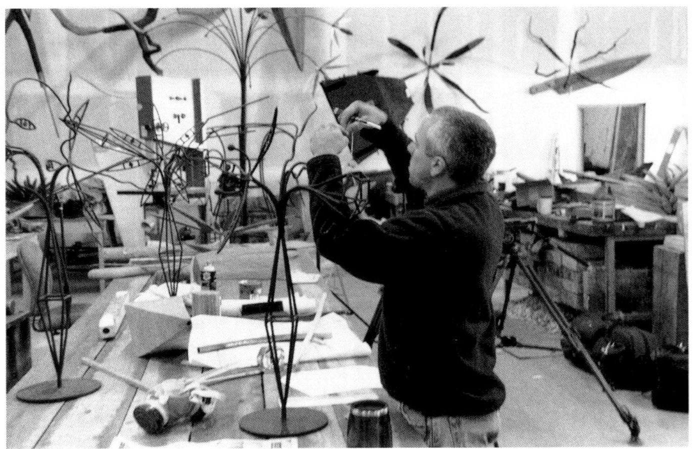

FIGURE 60
Tai Pomara working on *Maquette for Reaching out—Flower and Jewel* (**PL. 32**)

JS: Yeah, sure. I will tell you this: I don't necessarily know that I can make "big art" by myself. I certainly have to be there to set the tone, set the parameters, and if it ends up looking bad, I have to take the blame.

GW: But it feels as if you were there.

JS: I actually am there. Although, I don't necessarily know that I can take anything away from those who are not. That's the real beauty of art. I don't have to make one artist look bad for me to look good. I mean, that's a pretty nice field to be in. For instance, I could probably legitimately disagree with every single thing Donald Judd ever wrote. I mean Donald Judd has actually said things in print that's the stupidest stuff I've ever heard in my life. Yet, I can respect his perspective, totally respect where he came from, and totally understand what he's doing. That's intellect. Our intellectual abilities give us that, as a gift. I mean, I can understand the clean, the faceted, the absoluteness of—and where he says they come from—and I don't know that I'd disagree with him. They probably do only come from the head. He said they did come from his head. No nature. He'll tell you up front, or he did, he told us up front that this is really not about nature: all this came out of his head. Okay, I sometimes hear artists say things that I don't believe they believe. You know, as an example, I've heard artists say, "Well, I just make art for me." Well, no, you don't. We make art for people, for spectators, for the world. We want people to see it and to look at it and to visually read it. I don't know that there's any argument about that as an issue. I have help. Tai Pomara helps me an enormous amount (**FIG. 60**). He does a lot of stuff, and I have to tell you, in this show, he looms large. It's really important that he is here. I think artists inherently have a huge support system.

GW: Well, people wouldn't be seeing your work either…

JS: Oh, absolutely.

GW: If it wasn't for that chain…

JS: I wouldn't be making it, either, if it wasn't for that system.

GW: Well, that brings me to the next question, which is about the awareness of people who view your art, of the critical reception. You said just a little while ago that you don't want to plagiarize yourself, that you want to move and grow, but that you are in a different kind of place now. You have achieved a considerable amount of success in getting people to know your art, and people now have a certain view of you: this is the James Surls we know, this is the art that James Surls produces. And yet you're moving in a new direction. What are you thinking about as you do that? It's a risk in a way, and of course art is about taking risks.

JS: Well, I actually think that growing in art in the long run is not a risk. I think it's the only path that you can really take. Even monetarily or financially or marketability-wise, in the commercial world, even with all of those things as a consideration, you really have to, as an artist, operate under the premise that there is no market. There is no market? Come on, it doesn't really work that way. You're only looking for one person in the whole world to buy that one thing. That's as basic a ratio as you can get. You can't sell it to two unless they team up and act as one. You can sell it to a consortium, but still, they're acting as one. You're really only looking for one home, and most of the homes that are out there won't accommodate it anyway. So at every turn, you narrow that market. You're dealing with such an absolutely narrow band of humanity that can put a twenty-foot sculpture anywhere. I mean, what do they do with it? So, I don't think about the risk involved in making unique things. The act in and of itself is a risk. That's the risk, just simply saying you're going to be an artist. But once you cross the threshold into that world, then you're a free soul. That's part of being an artist, being a free soul. Free souls don't worry about all that other stuff.

GW: Do you worry about critical reception at all?

JS: It totally depends on who's writing. Ninety-nine percent of the time, it's not an issue. I listened to a lecture by Hilton Kramer at Virginia Beach. I like Hilton Kramer, I respect Hilton Kramer, I respect what he has represented, and what he still does represent, but again, like Donald Judd, Hilton Kramer said some things that were just absolutely ludicrous. One of them was that there are no modern masters. If he means modern masters in terms of "Modernism" then maybe he is right; they're all dead. If he means modern masters in the sense of what I would call masters in the here and now, then are there really none? You know, that's it—just peel off the top and say there are none. Well, that's taking it pretty far. I wouldn't go quite that far. I would back up a little bit on that.

GW: It's a little myopic.

JS: It's kind of cutting it close.

GW: Yes.

JS: And the other thing he said was that there can be no great art that deals with social-political issues. Picasso's *Guernica* just jumped up in my face, and I thought what about all the Spanish poets that got pistol-whipped down some dirt road? Just go through history. What I'm saying is, if Hilton Kramer gave me a bad review, I would smile and say, It kind of goes with the territory.

GW: You are, by that definition, never going to be considered a modern master, so there you go.

JS: Yeah, he's already blown me out, just by definition, so it just totally depends on who's writing it. I don't know that anybody should believe all that stuff. I think it's like the football coach. If you believe all that stuff they say when you win, then are you going to believe all that stuff they say when you lose? Somewhere in there there's a reality level. You're not the Devil on Friday night if you lose, but you're also not God on Friday night if you win. For me as an artist, what I make is so far back in the wake of my own personal world, I really have to be on point and creatively out in front of the criticism. Even the show that we're doing now, by the time it opens, it's all made. By the time the show opens, I've already stepped out a month or two or so out ahead of the game. I certainly want the show very much. I'm working incredibly hard for this exhibition. I want what the show brings psychologically. I want that reward. That is my reward, that's what I get out of it. That's the glory that you get. But man, how far are you going to go back to bask? Last week? Last year? Ten years ago? I mean, artists have to be ahead of the curve, at least in theory. I had a show in '79 and, boy, people were patting me on the back, telling me what a great show it was, what a great artist I was, and how wonderful I was. When the show was over, Charmaine and I went out to Greenville Avenue to go dancing, and we had enough money to get in the place and buy one drink each. So we went in, we each bought a drink and danced for an hour. We came back out, our car had been towed, and we had no money. And it was drizzling and 33 degrees, and I thought, two

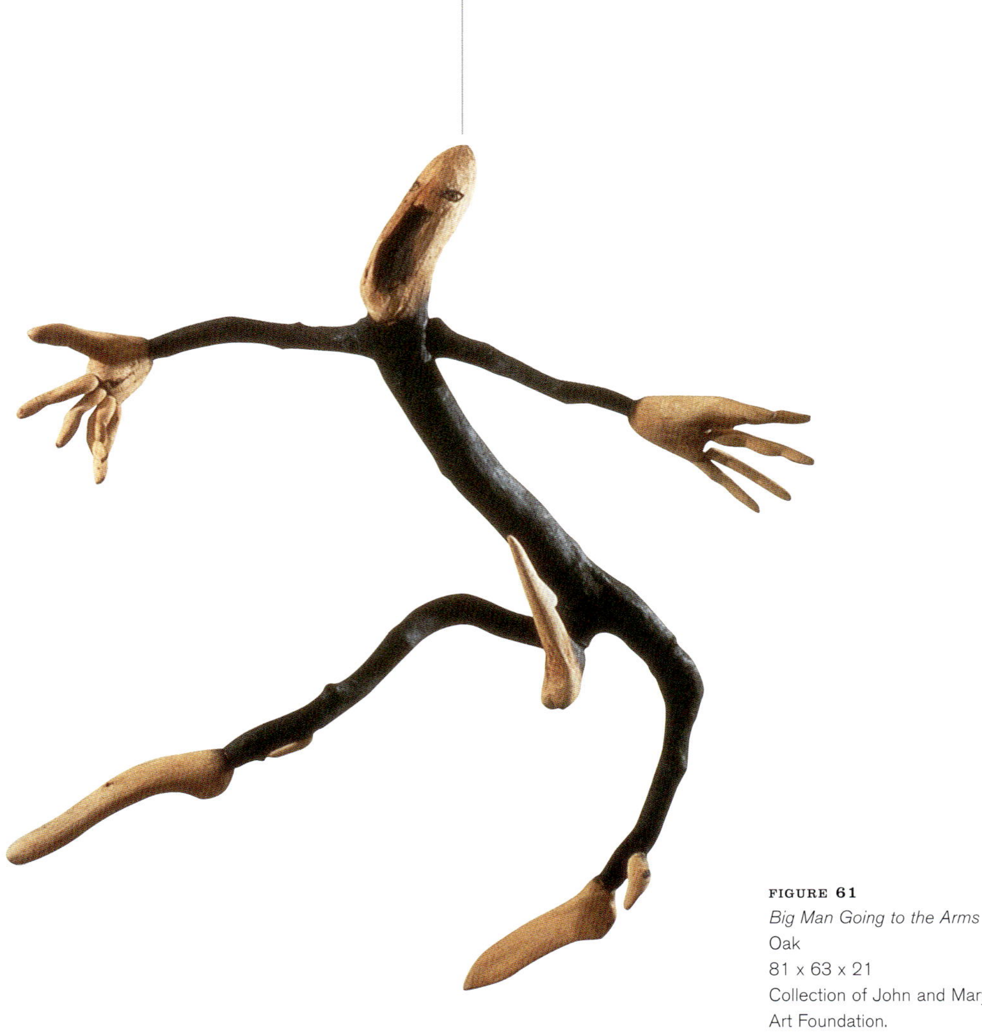

FIGURE 61
Big Man Going to the Arms Race, 1984
Oak
81 x 63 x 21
Collection of John and Mary Pappajohn Art Foundation.

hours ago I was this big shot. Now, I'm out on the street, it's cold, it's windy, it's raining, I'm broke and I'm mad as hell.

GW: And showing someone a review wouldn't have helped.

JS: It wouldn't have made any difference.

GW: Let's cover some old ground now. We've been talking about new things, but it strikes me that there is a lot that we can talk about that has been talked about before, but possibly not in this context. I'm interested in the personal and narrative side of your art. A little while ago you were talking about a story that went along with a piece. You are very interested in working with poets, working with other artists, and you are connected to this greater range of things. Is your art narrative and how so?

JS: I think that in a bizarre kind of way, all art is. Now, that's me trying to make the world fit my terms, and we've already established that that is not the case, so it's like my saying that all art is a self-portrait. I think you could validly say that. My art is a self-portrait. In what way? It's a slice of my personal world. You have to experience something personally if you are to speak of it. Otherwise you're speaking of it from a distance, you know, you're never there. So if I haven't done a certain thing, how can I really deal with it? Well, I've never been in war. Okay, so how can I write about that or speak about that? Well, I can't–not in the true sense—I'm not a veteran, okay, but

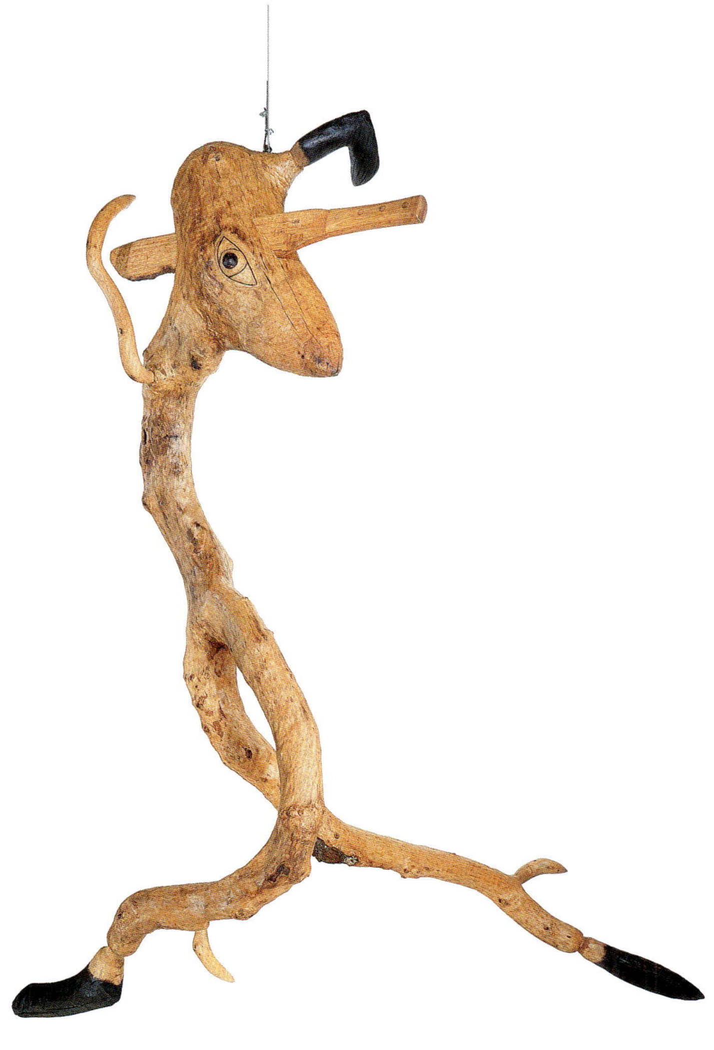

FIGURE 62
Man Doing War, 1984
White oak, red oak
176 x 96 x 72
The Museum of Fine Arts, Houston. Gift of Dr. and Mrs. Eric H. Scheffey.

I have been in what I would call personal wars—personal, real kind of tugs and pulls and fights in essence with yourself, with your spouse. It's really amazing that the person you love most in the whole world, that's the person you will get the maddest at, and vice versa. Your soul mate will get so mad at you that she will just want to cut your head off. That's just the way it is. Why? Because you are in this pull together. Here you are, you're two people moving in the same direction, working toward the same goal. That's not always an even flow.

It is possible to make the personal war applicable to a bigger picture. I've done any number of sculptures that were about that subject. One was called *Big Man Going to the Arms Race* **(FIG. 61)**, which was a very nasty piece of art. One was called *Man Doing War* **(FIG. 62)**, which is about self-inflicted pain, and one called *Me and the Butcher Knives* **(REF ESSAY FIG.)** is about my body being filled with butcher knives in a very riddled way. You could say, Oh, my God, that's incredibly dark. Well, what is that about? It's about self-inflicted pain; who is the worst enemy out there? It inevitably boils down to you. You are the enemy, and you are the one who has to work out things. You are the one who has to take the psychological journeys. You are the one who has to ask the questions about yourself, and you are the one who has to give yourself answers.

I am convinced that those so-called American primitives who hear this voice in the night, all of them have something in common, and that commonality is a voice that says something like, Margaret, you are a great artist. Who said that?

Who's the voice? I think that's her speaking to herself. I think that she is hearing this resonance from her own soul. They inevitably give it, the voice, a title—it's Jesus; it's an angel; it's a spirit; it's a deity; it's some greater power that comes. I think it's like body-knowing, it's like mind-knowing; it's like you having reached a certain point in your life where you're ready for something; you are receptive. You tell yourself to make the leap, to make the jump, to cross the threshold, to go, and to be there, and I came upon that early. I realized that, and that's a very freeing kind of phenomenon.

I mean, I don't necessarily know that college can give you that. I don't necessarily know that a Ph.D. would give you that. I think formal training is great stuff. I have a master's degree. I like that routing, the intellectual route. But if that's all you have, then you have been clipped. You are wounded. You're not full. You're not a whole, and it's really amazing that there are those who can make high intellectual things and be void of what I call the spiritual romance. There are those who can have this and be void of the intellectual, and they inevitably end up being what you call the American primitives, or the so-called folk artists. There's a world over there that encompasses those who are engaged in belief. I'm engaged in belief but also have been educated. You'd have an awful hard time calling me a folk artist, for obvious reasons. I really like them both. I like that sense of personal belief, that spiritual belief in something, and I think that's really what gave me my spark. Whether it's Walt Whitman or Wordsworth; whether you're writing about a train, a locomotive being this beautiful, powerful figure, you're talking about it in a very seductive way. Or whether you're talking about being a cloud in total and absolute drift through a field of daffodils. Either way you're over there. I like information. I like knowing things. It's fun. Now, does that make for narrative? In my art, it does. It is the story of things that happen to me.

GW: That brings us to the question of what informs you. Now, you say you'd have a hard time calling yourself a folk artist, and I agree entirely. You celebrate the vernacular, and you celebrate nature and other things as well, but when someone looks at your titles, and the way you approach things, there's a sense that there is a great deal below the surface. Was it when you were lecturing at SMU—I hope I'm not misquoting you here—that you said that you do look at Mexican art, but that what you're more interested in is the muralists than vernacular art? So what else has informed you that, perhaps, may not be obvious in your art but was influential in the making of it?

JS: I love Mexican folk art. I love that kind of Oaxacan clay, folky stuff. That's great stuff. I really love that, just like I love American folk art. I like folk art anywhere. I certainly like outsider art, I mean, boy, that's kind of gnawing and raw and very exciting stuff.

I don't really think that's what the Mexican artists were about; Frida Kahlo, Orozco, were very heavily into symbols, and content, and meaning, and representation. They were just literally one step away from the People's Revolt. They certainly played some very heavy roles in messaging the people. So their art was symbolic and very content-oriented. But where do you put that when you're looking up into a big, huge dome of a building? I'm talking about looking up, straight up, in a big, huge dome and seeing a swirling mass of a burning human, burning man. Orozco's painting in a dome—it's like a man on fire. I don't really look at that as if somebody doused somebody in gasoline and threw a match on them. It's a different kind of thing. It's purely a metaphor for the human triumph, and with that, being caught totally in desire. I don't mean that in just a sexual way. I'm talking about a way to create and grow and make. Lions and tigers and bears don't do that. Humans do that. I knew who Orozco was before I knew who de Kooning was. That's part of being from south Houston or south Texas. In the summer, I went to Pueblo on a school watercolor class, or a class would go down to Oaxaca for six weeks or something. That was incredibly informative early on. It showed me something. But you know, Charmaine and I go to museums. People who love art, where do they go? We go to museums. Where am I going to see ten little David Smiths, if I don't go to the Hirshhorn? Where do you get to see that stuff?

GW: One of the things you said earlier is that Merlin is the greatest sculptor. I know you were saying it somewhat facetiously, about someone who could magically make things happen, but there is this theme that runs through the way you talk about art, about the artist as magician or the artist as shaman, someone who transforms and interprets (see FIG 19). Do you think about that as you interpret, as you create?

JS: I do think about that. In terms of the Merlin comment, saying that Merlin perhaps was the best sculptor, I was being facetious to some extent, but why would I say that? Because, at least mythically, he had this power, this ability. That's what magicians do; they can just make things materialize. Poof, and there it is. I think, the poof is the process. We talked about process earlier. I think sculptors have a tendency to get caught and bogged and literally engulfed in their process because it's so tangible and physical and demanding and it's so tool-heavy, and by that I'm talking about the structural element of it. With a smile, I would say Merlin didn't have to do any of that. He could just simply make it materialize, and we all wish that we could do that. It is amazing that Einstein could ride on a beam of light. I mean, come on, you can't ride on a beam of light. How you gonna be sitting on a beam of light? What is it like at 286,000 miles per second or something? I mean, that's a little fast. So how can you do that? Well, how can you bore a hole through the Andes Mountains? What would the process be to bore a hole through the Andes Mountains? I mean, billions of dollars, man, how many people would you lose? How long? How many years? Or build the Verrazano Bridge or the Brooklyn Bridge or the Eiffel Tower? The process is just so arduous. Sculptors have their personal process, and Merlin didn't have to use any of this. So you can say, boy, he was the best one. I laugh and say I know the absurdity of it: you really cannot avoid process. I heard this lecture once on prayer, and the gist of it was, if you're hungry, instead of praying for a chicken,

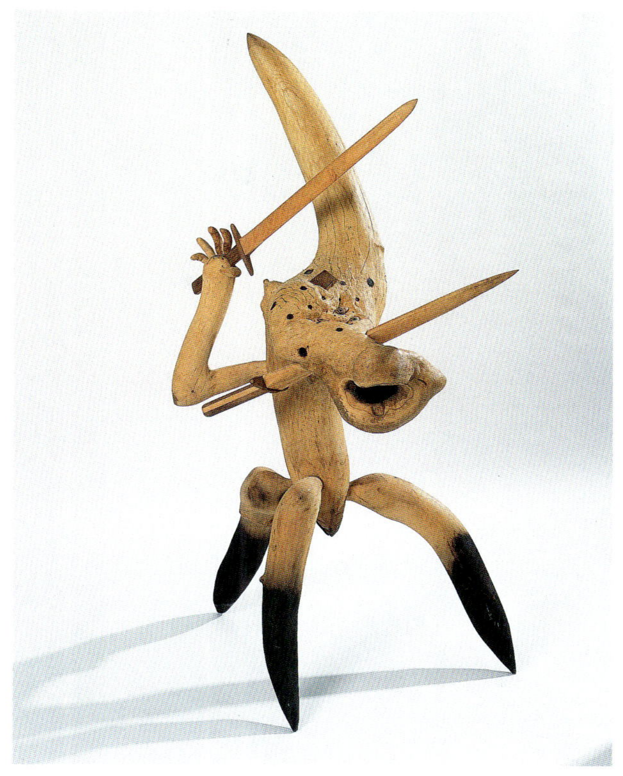

FIGURE 63
Me, the Dragon and the Sword, 1982
Live oak, maple
73 x 29 ½ x 34
Memphis Brooks Museum of Art, Memphis Tennessee. Gift of *Art Today* with matching funds from the National Endowment for the Arts, 82.9.

you better pray for a way to find the chicken, or pray for a way to go get the chicken. You know, you have to involve yourself. You have to put yourself into the mix, and that's what process does, and Merlin didn't do any of that.

GW: You do transform things, though, in a very magical kind of way, and you're very much aware of the material that you use and the quality of that material. We were talking earlier [not included in this excerpt] about the inherent quality of wood, and of stone, and certain things that just mean or carry a certain sense of soul. They animate. Just as you, in a way, animate those things (FIG. 63). What is that quality?

JS: Well, you're really looking for the soul of the art. What

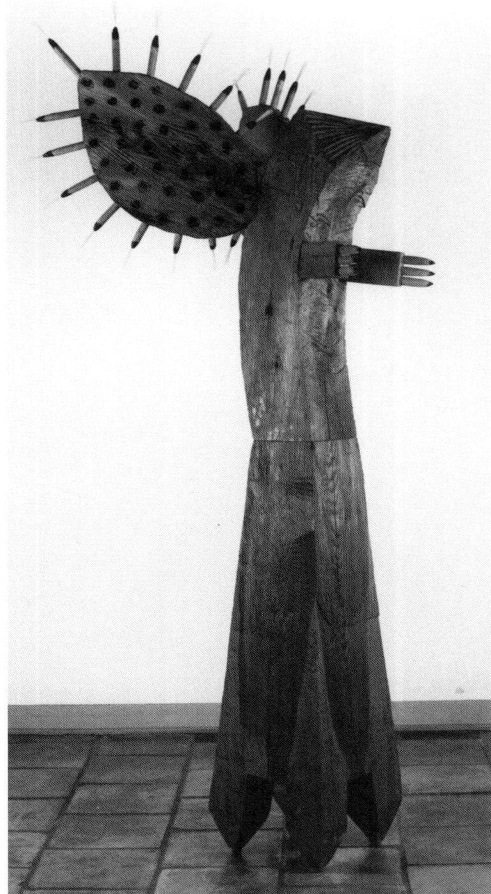

FIGURE 64
She Brings Gifts to Me, 1975
Pine, bristles, maple
72 x 28 x 42
Private Collection

gives art soul? What makes it have that sense of life about it? And, as its creator, you can say I am the parent, and I created this object, this thing. It's pretty amazing. When I wrote my thesis about process, my art basically was dead. Oh, my God, I talked about it in terms of how tall it was, how wide it was, what color it was, how much it weighed. I'm serious, I've gone to lectures, and I've heard sculptors talk about their art in these terms. They would click a slide and they would say, Here's a piece that I made in 1967. It's 18 feet tall; it weighs two tons; and it's brown. Click. Oh, wait a minute. Is that what you're going to say about this piece? Is that it? And that's what I said. Now, that's what graduate school is for. That's why you go to graduate school, so that you can kind of traverse that territory. You can find yourself. You're looking for something.

I actually had a revelation. That revelation was meeting Charmaine Locke. Now, this is about a muse, the spark, the life, the soul of something. Keep in mind, I was a young, physical kind of a workhorse. I had come out of that genre of the laborer family where you went to work on Monday morning; on Friday you got a paycheck, and if you didn't put in the hours you didn't get the paycheck. It was a one-to-one ratio of physical labor as it would relate to groceries on the table, and so I came out of that kind of background, and I did not come out of that introspective, social field of endeavor, of analysis. That's basically what it amounts to. Charmaine gave me that **(FIG. 64)**. She gave me that kind of introspective analysis of Why? What is it? What's it for? What does it do? Just falling in love with her made me ask those questions. It was not the most opportune time, in a sense, for me to be falling in love with somebody, but it happened. There was a certain kind of generative force that took place and for a good lot of years, she virtually showed up in every piece of art I made, in one form or another. When I spoke of "she" it was that particular "she." When I drew images of females, it was about that particular female. Now, the same thing was true with myself. I put myself in that mix a lot. That's what I mean when I say you want it to apply to a bigger picture, to a bigger world, and I think if it is truthfully told in a real, personal way where through a piece of art you've kind of laid your head on the chopping block, someone will take a chop, but someone will also say, Oh, oh, my God, look at that. They'll have a certain degree of understanding of it. I don't know if that answers your question.

GW: Not at all, not at all, but it was interesting.

(Both laugh.)

GW: I was talking about stones and wood and the power of those things. Well, you talked about another kind of power.

JS: Well, then let me at least have another shot at it.

GW: Okay.

JS: I think any material that is part of our inherent history, that's the organic stuff. That does not then necessarily include plastics or certainly the digital stuff—that's a new arena, but the wood and stone and dirt and earth, and the old four elements of the earth, wind, fire, and water, that's been with us for so long and is so deep in our psyche that I don't know if we could negate it. I grew up in the woods, literally. I mean, I grew up in a rural Texas setting where all of those things played a very prominent and immediate role. When I went to play, if I went outside to play, where did I go? I went to a creek bank, I went to the woods, I went out into a field. Why? That's what was around our house; we lived in the country, so I got to grow up playing games like chase or wild horse where you were the horse and someone chased you or vice versa, so you got to run free in that environment. My brother and I chopped down an oak tree with two hatchets, two handheld little hatchets, roofing hatchets, and the tree fell—took us all day to do it. I hadn't started in school. I was five. My brother was seven, and when my dad got home from work, we ran out to meet his pickup, and the first thing we had to do was show him the tree we'd cut down. Well, he didn't say, Why did you cut the tree? Why did you get into my toolbox? Don't you boys know you could've got hurt? None of that. All he said was, Boys, that's great. We can use that as a corner-post for a turkey pen, so I got a reward. I got a reward from my father—five years old—for chopping. Now, did that have an influence? Well, how could it not? Are you aware of it at the time? Of course not. Do you know it ten years later? No. Fifteen? When do you come to grips with that as a memory? I think people love wood. I mean, my God, Aspen is filled with these houses that weigh three hundred million tons. Buckminster Fuller would just turn over in his grave, you know, if he looked up there and saw that tonnage, but they love that big, heavy, raw stuff.

GW: They can feel it when they're living in it.

JS: Wood has done everything for us. It's played a real psychological role. That does not mean that because something is made out of wood, it will be good. There's a lot of ugly, bad, ridiculous stuff out there made out of wood, but assuming you've got something to say, assuming there is a reason, it does have symbolism and meaning and content and it does have a life about it. That's how I got off the subject a while ago, when I got to the life about it.

GW: Yes.

JS: Coming alive . . .

GW: Coming alive, you were becoming a Pygmalion of sorts.

JS: I drifted into some other world, away from the material, and into the muse.

GW: You use steel and bronze now?

JS: I do, but I don't necessarily use steel as raw material. I paint it black, so it just simply becomes a line in space. I can draw lines in space with steel. Tubing, hollow, light, strong. It's an answer to a physical issue. The way I integrate it is I just simply paint it matte black. It becomes almost an imaginary thing. It's just a line in space, and the line in space and wood work incredibly well together, and at one time I used vines. That's the way the steel got started; I was using vines **(FIGS. 65-66)**. I'd use a line in space, and then it became easier, the

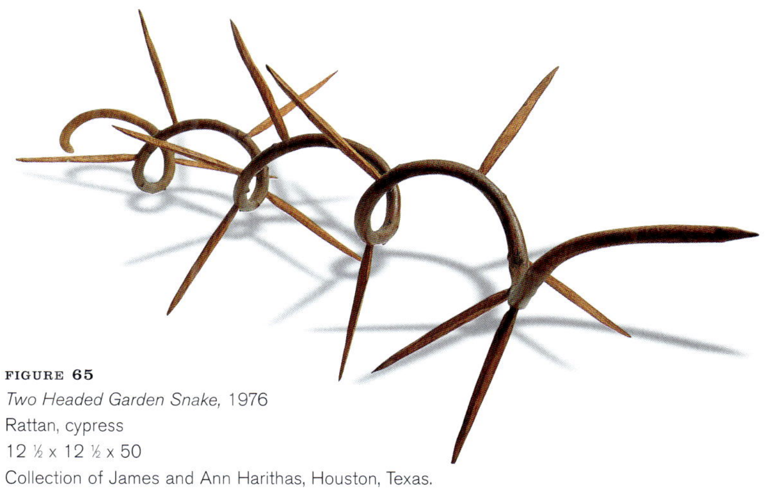

FIGURE 65
Two Headed Garden Snake, 1976
Rattan, cypress
12 ½ x 12 ½ x 50
Collection of James and Ann Harithas, Houston, Texas.

bigger it got, to duplicate the line another way. That's the way the steel got in there, but it plays an unbelievably important role now.

GW: Have you been tempted to use any other materials at all, or is the wood still the defining element?

JS: I would say that the wood is the defining element, although the steel is even to the point that now the outdoor pieces are all steel. They're just lines in space. You know, I painted at one time, but I haven't painted in thirty years, and why don't I paint? Well, hey, I work hard enough using what I use. I don't necessarily know that I'd want to be a person who uses all different materials and goes in many directions. I think that making your choice, saying these are the confines that I'm going to work within, these materials, these processes, these things that I do, if I use them to the fullest of their capability, and of mine, that pretty well eats a lifetime, so do I really want to start to carve Vermont granite? Well, that's not really for me.

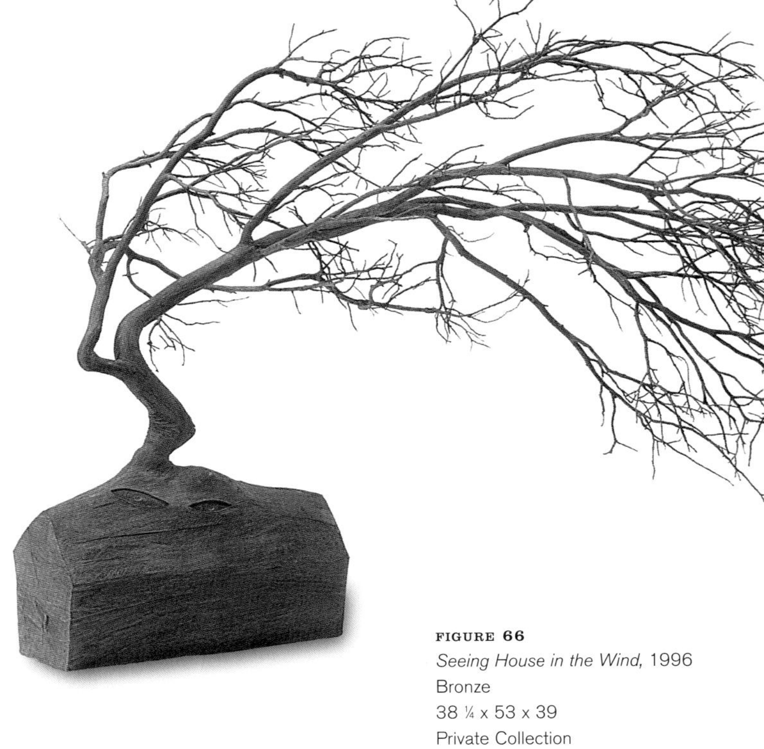

FIGURE 66
Seeing House in the Wind, 1996
Bronze
38 ¼ x 53 x 39
Private Collection

GW: No. Are you still drawing and making prints?

JS: Well, yes and no. I'm not really making prints now. I made prints from the late 80s to the early 90s very extensively. I did like 25 or 30 prints. That, in essence, took the place of drawing. Up to that point, the drawings were prevalent, lots and lots of drawing. Then in that period, there were lots and lots of prints, all of which had drawing in them. After that came a very emotional transition. What? Moving from the place that you had been in for twenty-five years to a whole new place, that's an emotional transition. Having your wife and children go ahead of you, that's an emotional shock. That's hard to do. Moving over a mountain, much like crossing a bridge, into a new place, a new world, a new space, a new situation. It's emotionally traumatic. Back in Texas to this day I have a 12,000-square-foot studio, huge, big, wonderful, great, my dream studio (see FIG. 6). I went from that to not having any studio. So that in essence is kind of being back to where I was. Well, I have at least come to grips with the reality that you can make art with a studio or without it. I mean, come on, if Joseph Cornell can work in a basement and make some of the most expansive art ever made on the planet, then from that point on there is no excuse. You don't have any excuses. Sculptors say I can't work today because... Then they list off all the reasons why they can't go work. I make art today because I can't do anything else. I'm like a lemming going to the ocean; I'm driven to do it. So, I do it. I've worked at Anderson Ranch, which has been incredibly good to me, about giving me a place to work, to help the landing and the transition. No place to put the art, but I can make it there, much like being back in graduate school, to tell you the truth, I mean, a little space with a whole lot of other people, but I've done very well. I just do it anyway.

GW: So you're drawing?

JS: *(Laughs.)*

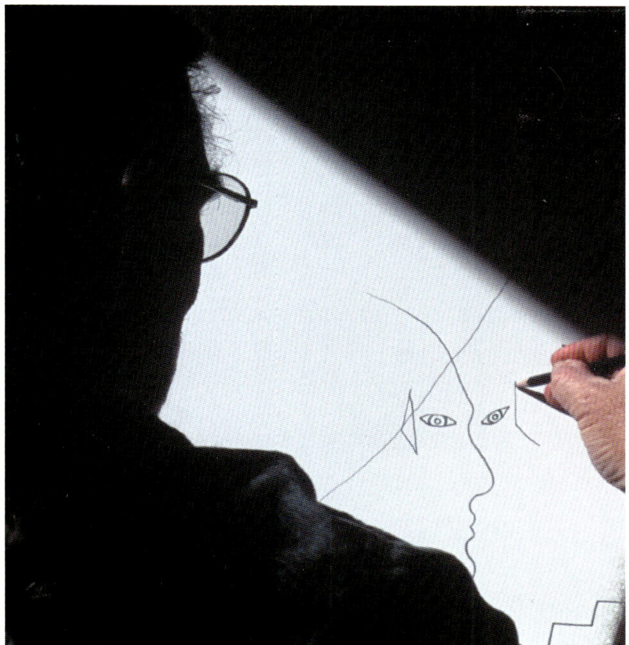

FIGURE 67
Surls drawing in Silt, Colorado, studio, 2003

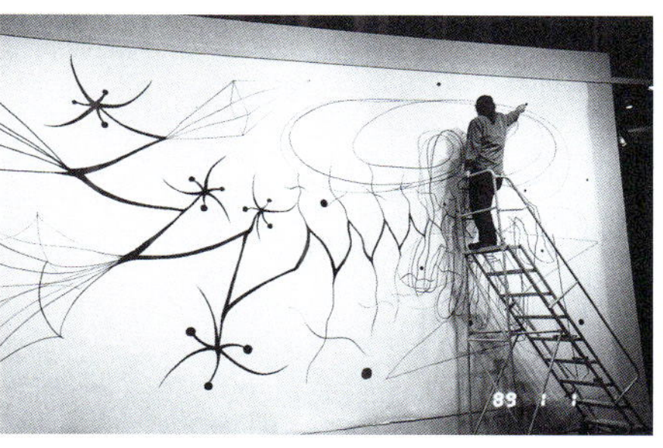

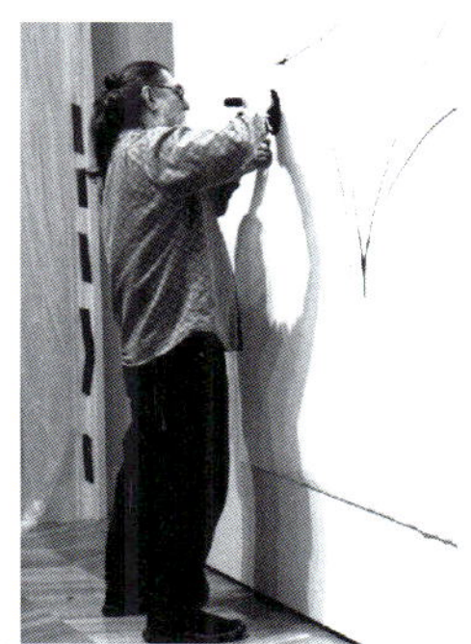

FIGURES 68-69
Surls drawing during installation for the *In The Meadows* exhibition

GW: Yes, you didn't answer that part of the question. Are you still drawing?

JS: No.

GW: No?

JS: No, I haven't been for the last couple of years, although I will for this exhibition, and I've got a couple of drawings done, but I still really haven't done the bulk of the drawings that will be in the show **(PL. 35–65)**.

GW: And you are doing a mural for us, too, aren't you?

JS: I'm doing two.

GW: Or something, a large piece?

JS: I'm doing two. *(Laughs.)* I hope I do stay on the subject of drawing, but I do want to make a lateral run at it. I use the analogy that any great surgeon could do incredible things physically to your body in a five-, six-, eight-hour period. They could take your heart out and put it back or put another one in; that's pretty amazing. Would it be better had they worked for three months on taking your heart out? No, it would have been worse, much worse as a matter of fact, so I don't know that if something takes a week it's better than if it takes ten seconds. I mean I don't really make that distinction, and I have to look at drawing in that light. That's the way I have to deal with drawing: I don't rub; I don't smudge; I don't smear; I don't use color **(FIGS. 67-69)**. There's thousands of things out there that artists make art with that I don't use. I use something that makes a dark line on a light ground, and that's it. That's it. If that's what you're doing, if you're dealing with a line on a ground, then the line better be pretty particular and have a very specific orientation, and it inherently has to be targeted very directly. I mean, the Oriental masters could paint a mountainscape with a single stroke. Oh, would it have been better if they had used thousands of strokes and worked on it for days and weeks

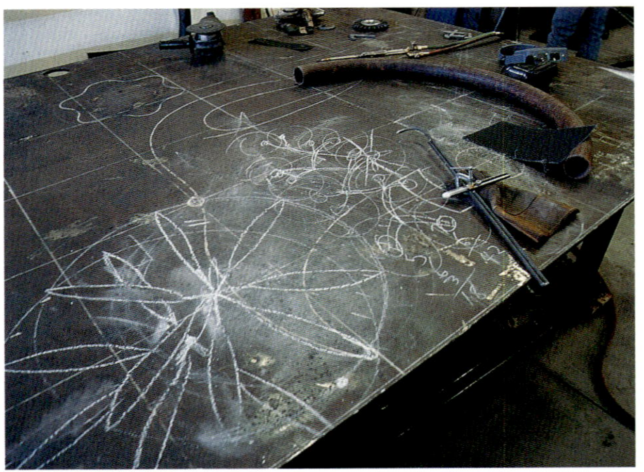

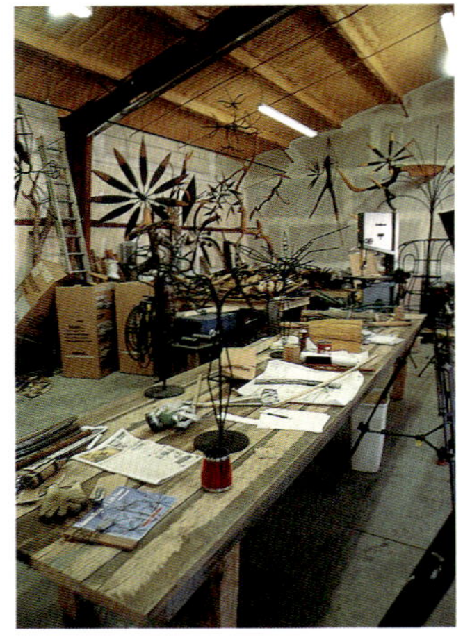

FIGURE 70
Metal worktable in artist's studio

FIGURE 71
Wood worktable in artist's studio

and months? I really don't think so. I mean, that's part of the beauty and the direct hit, so to speak. That's the way I have to deal with drawing, and I think it's probably one of the reasons I am so drawn to poets because I think that drawing to visual art is like poetry to literature. Poetry is as close to the bone as you're going to get. It's as direct a hit as you're going to get.

GW: Will the drawings be things that will lead you to other work later on?

JS: Well, I think all of the drawings led me to other work. The drawings are in a bizarre kind of way almost like kind of genealogical road maps that get you somewhere and are much, much more complicated than the sculpture, even though I'm known primarily as a sculptor. That's because they're tangible, physical. People can touch and walk around it and stuff. And they look at the drawings, they have to actually do a little more thinking, to tell you the truth, and they have to really listen. I have had people who have had drawings and prints, very knowledgeable people who were intellectual. They were connoisseurs, so to speak, who I would tell about something in the particular piece that they had, and they'd say, Oh, come show me. So we would walk in to where the piece was. I would point and look and show them something and, I'm telling you, I have seen people go *(gasps)*. You know like they've had it hanging in their house for two years, and they've never seen that. They've never seen that part of it. Drawings are totally spacey in that kind of mystic way, like poetry.

GW: I wanted to ask you about this piece of soapstone, and drawing on tables, that part of the design process. You were saying something about this worktable? [Referring to a large metal table in the studio on which Surls has sketched with the soapstone (FIG. 70 and COPYRIGHT PAGE).]

JS: The worktable is like the operating table. On that table, it's all fair game. The top of the table–you draw on the table, you sketch out on the table, you kind of work out dimensions and issues and things, you plan, you discuss. Tai and I have these kind of "how-to" discussions, so you draw it out. I actually have had any number of thoughts about the table. And that's really where this table, the idea for this table came from. This table [referring to the unfinished wooden table at which Surls and Warden are sitting, which will become a piece in the exhibit (FIG. 71, see PL. 11)] will be filled with imagery and forms: needles, knives, houses, diamonds, the heart out of Ponderosa, big knots that are very organic shapes. So, this table will formally say all that. The worktable, informally, says all that.

GW: The historian in me wishes you were preserving the

worktable as well and that you were doing some of those things on paper. But talk a little bit about the table as a symbol, what that means for you.

JS: Well, I think it means—I think it's a symbol for humanity—on the table. I mean, lay your cards face up, on what? On the table. You know, the table is a very formal ground for us. A lot of activity takes place and it's really pretty amazing that if you invite somebody to your house, inevitably, you will end up in the kitchen. Inevitably, you will end up around the table, you know, and it becomes kind of like *In the Meadows*; it's *On the Table*. It becomes metaphorically very powerful. So what is on this table? And I haven't titled this piece yet. This big pitcher will be on the table. What does the pitcher represent? There are historical treatises that you could spend literally a lifetime reading. There are a lot of books on the vessel in art, on the symbolism of the pitcher, the bowl, the receptacle, the thing that holds the liquid that gives the life; it's a pretty important thing. That's on the table, as a symbol. The needle is on the table as a symbol. So I'm putting a lot of big-picture symbols. The worktable has a lot of "work-as-a-process" stuff, and I actually tried to get my daughter who's in a photography class in high school to come over here and to photograph my worktable, literally. And she never did it, of course. A seventeen-year-old daughter doesn't want to go photograph her daddy's worktable. She's got other stuff to do out there in the world, but I think it would be an incredibly interesting thing for a photographer to get involved with, just in documenting the tracks of the hunt.

GW: It's quite photogenic. I think I've taken a roll of photographs of that table.

JS: Well, good.

GW: Yes, and the things on it were also quite interesting and revealing, I thought (FIG. 71). The table is a symbol you have worked with before and are working with now. The house is another one. The bridge is one that you mentioned a little earlier. Could you talk about those? The house has been written about a good deal; the bridge possibly not as much.

JS: No, no...

GW: As kind of metaphoric...

JS: Right, no.

GW: The bridge is new.

JS: The bridge has not been talked about or dealt with nearly as much. You know it is really amazing that if you pick a certain kind of symbolic reference, for instance, the house (FIG. 72). I have used the house a lot. The house has shown up over and over and over. Charmaine curated an exhibition called *The Image of the House in Contemporary Art*. She invited fifty or sixty artists across the country to be in this

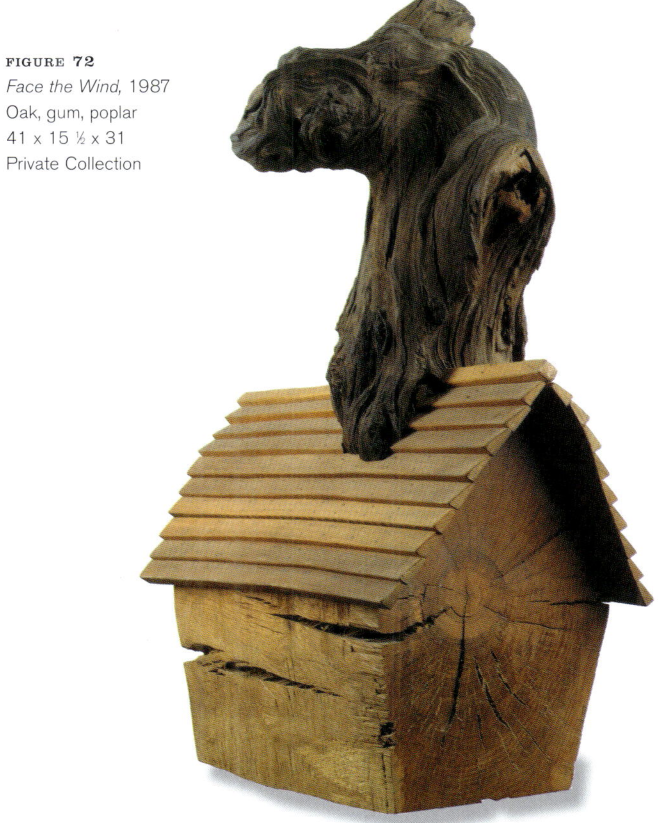

FIGURE 72
Face the Wind, 1987
Oak, gum, poplar
41 x 15 ½ x 31
Private Collection

exhibit; she invited architects to come and address the issue of the house. It really is an amazing thing. Charmaine wrote about and historically referenced how the house has been very humanlike. I mean, even the two windows are eyes, and the mouth is the door, the house is the head and the roof then becomes the top of the head or the hat, and even, in a symbolic sense, the pointy thing on top. Merlin wore one of those pointy things. I call it the aspiring symbol of this thing that goes on top of your head that actually becomes part of your head. It was pretty amazing formally, going through all of these processes of dealing with the house. There's been any number of other curators doing shows specifically dealing with the house. Charmaine actually wrote a very important paper about cutting off the head of the house, modernism, the reducing...

GW: Flat roof.

JS: The bringing everything back down to the so-called Bauhaus phraseology of starting anew. You kill everything that went before, and you start over with something brand-new, but when they started over they happened to have left off the head of the house, and it's pretty interesting when you think about it: they severed the head off the house. It actually became an issue even for people like Buckminster Fuller who talked extensively about who lived in the house. Now typewriters lived in the house, desks, phones; people didn't live in them anymore. You know, and the ones that people lived in, they were cut off from a certain kind of community level.

GW: It was no longer a home.

JS: It was no longer a home. Now it's simply a place that you stay, and that's so heavy in terms of the psychology around it and the philosophy around it, that, boy, you can't give all of those symbols their full and just due. You just can't. One artist can't do that, but I do use the vessel, the pitcher, the house. I also use needles: female, matriarchal. Knives: male. Males use needles and females use knives.

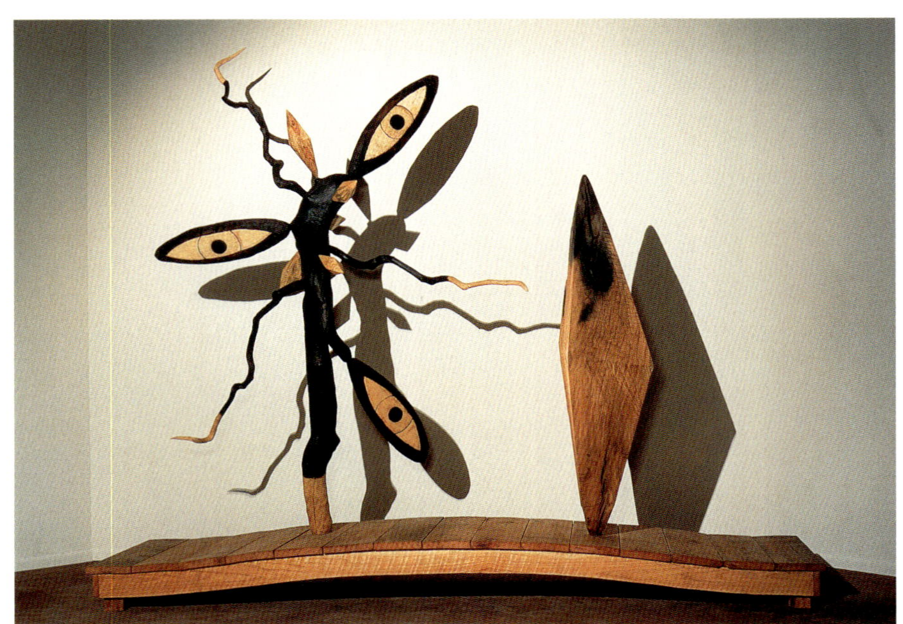

FIGURE 73
We Are Crossing Over, 1988
Oak and pine
166 x 48 x 143
Private Collection

Females peel peaches and males cut your head off. I mean, it's in the art of war. I mean, come on. There are whole, entire cultural schools based around the use of the knife. And it's back to that paradox again. This table will be riddled with paradoxes and very formal, very, very formal. The worktable is very informal. It's not even considered. It just inherently has these things that get built up and layered. It's almost like the dig for an anthropologist. The table is the dig. You're uncovering layers of stuff there. The table in the museum becomes absolutely formal, very formally presented, formally made, formally put together. It becomes representative and symbolic just like the needle becomes symbolic or all those other things become symbolic. Now the table in its total becomes symbolic. I think the bridge is the same way. The bridge is another way of representing the table. It takes you somewhere. The table you build on; you lie on; you put stuff on. The bridge you cross. Maybe both of them are means to an end, just like the house.

GW: Talk a little bit more about the bridge. Is it a one-way bridge? Is it a two-way bridge? Is that part of the attraction, that you can go back over the bridge (FIG. 73)?

JS: Well, it is certainly difficult to go back over the bridge. It's very, very difficult to go back over the bridge. The bridge in the garden you cross and you come back; you cross and you come back; you cross and you come back. If you look at it as past and present and future, then you can't really go back to the past. You can't really go back there, so in one sense, psychologically, you can't go back over the bridge. You've crossed. You're in the new place, the new space. Maybe you build another bridge. Maybe you keep the option of the bridge open. Maybe that's what the future is. I'm not real sure if you're talking about the bridge as taking you to the physical, like crossing the river.

GW: No, I wasn't. I was talking metaphorically as well. Even in terms of memory, you can bridge things by going back, by remembering, by bringing what was there back with you into where you are now. I was wondering if it was really just a one-way road or whether there might be ways to go back without circling around.

JS: Well, we certainly do go back. Humans go back all the time. I mean, they do go back into their own personal past, their personal history, their personal memory. So I guess, in one sense that is like crossing, you can go back over the bridge into it. It's really an interesting subject for me now personally because I made a transition. I went from that place to this place. I crossed the bridge, and I think . . . I just wrote Charmaine a letter because we got a new mailbox. We got a new place, you know. I wanted her to . . .

GW: To get a letter?

JS: I wanted her to get the first letter in the mailbox. It's like a way of saying this is our mailbox; this is our home; this is our place; and I wrote her a letter. I went to the post office and I mailed it so that it would be postmarked and stamped and everything, and basically the letter was about crossing the bridge coming to this new place, and . . . It's like the past is history. You can call it anything you want; you can visit it as much as you like; you can dig in it all you want to; you can uncover as much of it as is mentally possible for you to do. It's still history. It's history. It's gone. Now, you can reform it. You can reconfigure it. You can pull from it. You can draw from it. You can take the best of this. You can discard the worst of that. I have a friend who died last year. His name is Bill Simon, who was a sociologist, a really great sociologist. He wrote a paper about *The Man Who Shot Liberty Valance*, a black-and-white movie, and the reason he wrote about the movie is because there's a scene in it where a reporter said that when the myth is better, just print the myth. Well, that's your past. That's like your past. You do pull from your past, and hopefully you keep the best; you discard the worst; you learn from it and whatever. In one sense, you really can't go back; you don't get to go back. Okay, so at any rate, in one sense you really don't get to go back. And, in the letter, I said, what if we only have beginnings? That's a pretty interesting, philosophic way for me to deal with my life: it's a series of beginnings.

GW: It's a very healthy way, I would think, to deal with it.

JS: Well, I saw this thing once about centenarians. They took fifty people who were a hundred years old or older to find out what they had in common. What they didn't have in common was money; there were rich ones and there were poor ones. What they didn't have in common was diet; some of them didn't eat healthy, some of them ate totally healthy. What they did have in common was two things. One was genetics. They had, their families had, histories of living a long time. The other one was they had each lost or given up or let go of a lot. They had lost spouses; they had lost children; they had lost family; they had lost land; they had lost places; they had lost money, and it's really pretty amazing in the shamanistic sense to say that they didn't lose it. They just passed it on. I heard collector Ann Hudson say, about a person who had lost his fortune, that he didn't lose it; he spent it. It's not like he had it, and just suddenly he lost it. He spent it. Well, you spend your past. It's gone. I don't know that you can go back. You certainly get to go back in memory and pull things up. Wordsworth did; we all have that ability.

GW: So why did you go forward? What brought you over the bridge? What made you decide to cross it?

JS: Well, two things. One, you don't cross a bridge unless you need to. There's a reason. There is a reason that you do cross a bridge, and there's a premise about children leaving home. If everything is great, why are they gonna leave? Life's good. Inevitably, right before they leave, they'll have this turmoil. You know, they'll start fighting with their mother or something will happen and they'll say, Oh, I'm getting out of here. Why? They need to cross the bridge. Charmaine and I reached what you would call a psychological demise in Splendora. We had a dream. The dream came true. We wanted a house. We got a house with more bathrooms than you could flush. We wanted a big studio. We got the big studio. We wanted land. We amassed land. You know, it's really pretty amazing that you never should build what you can afford to build. You only should build what you can afford to maintain. Then you should do that with a certain discretion. How big do you want, when is big big enough? Our lives were so full—we filled them up. We traveled. We had shows. We got to curate. We got to do personal exhibitions. Our life was so full, psychologically and physically. We had stuff running out our ears. More stuff than you can imagine, like George Carlin, but we had more stuff than you could possibly maintain. It just became top-heavy and weighty and very difficult to deal with. We saw a land that we moved into in the mid-70s, we saw it reaching a certain kind of demise. Whole tracts of timber logged. Roads that you drove down where the canopy closed in at the top now were leveled just as far as the eye could see. East Texas has been butchered. Literally butchered. It was hard. It was very hard. We just reached the natural end, and I don't know how else to say that other than we simply reached the natural end. We had to get to open space, and Charmaine, bless her heart—I hate to use the term put her foot down—but she basically said, It's time; our time is here; this is now; I don't want to, in essence, live somewhere until I die. I want to go somewhere and live. So we went somewhere else. We moved. It was not easy. She came first. She came over the mountain first.

GW: How did you decide that this was the place to move to?

JS: We'd been to Anderson Ranch. We'd been to the valley.

We'd been all over Colorado. We'd already bought land in southern Colorado and we still own it. You know, we'd driven this state from one end to the other. We'd driven all over New Mexico. We knew the general terrain that we wanted, and I have to tell you, in all fairness to where we live now, it is filled with some pretty high-end people, and I don't mean just people with money. I'm talking about dialogue. There are photographers. There are writers. There are a lot of people who pass through. It's a very informed community. Yet, you get to have your cake and eat it too because you are engulfed in nature. You can have privacy. You can live in the sublime, you can live in solitude, and you have access to a lot of really terrific stuff. Affluence brings that. There's a lot of terrific stuff here. So, it wasn't by accident. We didn't throw a dart. I have often joked that Charmaine didn't ask me to move to Calcutta; she asked me to move to Aspen Valley. We had lived somewhere that I wanted. I was the person who for twenty years had my hand on the steering wheel of our world. She took control of the steering wheel, and turned it into a new direction, and, in all fairness to her, she didn't throw me off. She didn't sling me off; she didn't lose me on a curve, and she wrote me a really beautiful letter when she got out here. The gist of the letter was about crossing the mountain into the open space. Come fly with me, she said. You know, it's really romantic to tell someone I want you, I want to live with you: Come fly with me. I have to tell you that that letter sustained me for quite a period of time, when I was back there trying to keep things intact and functioning. It was one of the best things that's ever happened to me, and you asked the question earlier about the influence of space and terrain and this kind of visual territory. It's a very difficult thing to answer when you are making the change. It's much easier to answer later, a year or two or five or ten, after the fact, because you have that good judgment of hindsight. I may be still too close to be able to give you a definitive answer. I know my head has opened up. I now see things out there floating in space, whereas before I just saw them floating in my head. There was no space for them to float in. Now they go from head—concept—into real. It's like saying that in the show *In the Meadows*, I want them to read against the blue sky. Well, where did I get the blue sky? I live in the blue sky. That's my backyard. So now it's more of a natural place for me. I think the move has changed me a lot, and I feel it, and I think probably that the more important part of it is yet to come. I'm not sure.

GW: In terms of your art, at least, it may be something that you'll see a little further down the line. I think that it may be a little too soon, but how would you like to answer that question, How is it changing? You said you were thinking differently and visualizing your art in a different space.

JS: You know when really would be the time to answer that is walking through the Meadows, when you, when all the stuff is . . . For instance, *The Bridge*. I have not seen *The Bridge* assembled. I have not seen it all put together. I have not seen it complete. It may be the time to answer the thing about influence and terrain and head-set and mind-set maybe during, during the second phase of this, which would be the show itself. I had a worktable there; I have a worktable here. I lived in my head there; I live in my head here. I functioned on a high level there; I function on a high level here. The question is: how does terrain change constitute a head change? That's really what we're talking about, that transition. I think it is a subliminal change. I don't necessarily know that that is an absolute conscious change except after the fact, that it has subliminally been there long enough for you to consciously deal with it. You know, whereas beforehand, it may not necessarily be answerable. So, I don't know that I...

GW: It wouldn't even be a question that I would ask a lot of artists. But because you're so in tune with your environment, it's a question that comes to mind and that probably

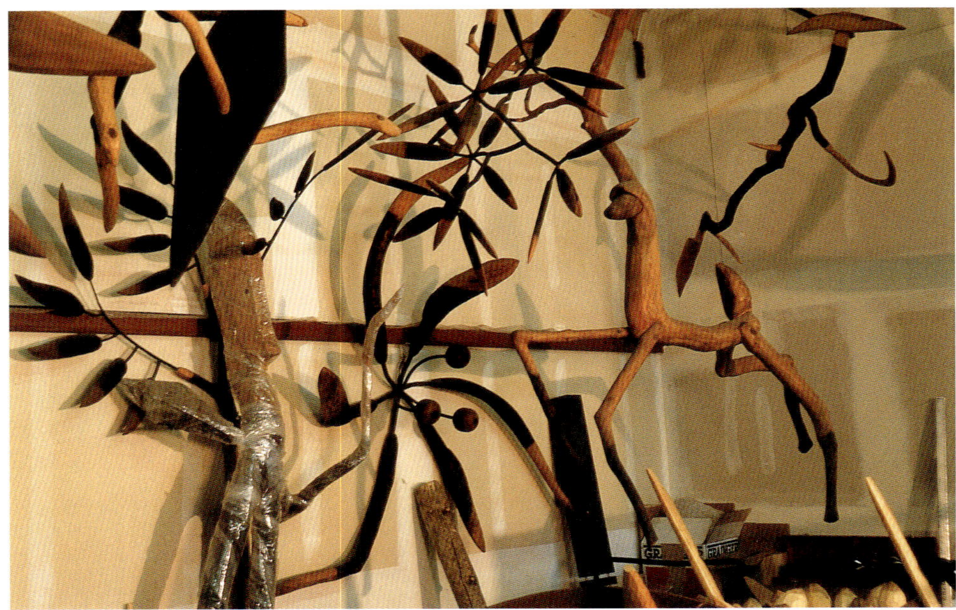

FIGURE 74
Studio view of miscellaneous sculpture

will be asked again. Let's come back to what is going to come. Let's talk a little bit about what you have done. We talked about a certain set of images: very, very broad symbols like the house and the table and the bridge. There is a lot more imagery there as well. There is a kind of human, animal imagery there, and then there's a more rational kind of imagery, a set of other symbols as well. Would you like to talk about those symbols in any order, not necessarily order of importance, but in the way they work?

JS: I haven't made too many sculptures about animals, a couple (FIG. 74). I've made a lot of sculptures about the human figure. I made a lot of art about figures, although I was thinking that there's really not very many in this show coming up. There is going to be one, it's called *Turning Around* (PL. 2); it's about looking back. It was one of the first pieces I made here. It's me as a figure turning around looking back at where I came from. It's very, very organic. It's figurative, although very few people may really know that. I think people who have any sense will know it. I've had curators turn figures with their face to the wall because they didn't really realize it was a face. So, to say I make figurative work needs a little qualifying in one sense. So, there will be one specific figure, but the needle represents a figure. The needle there is a she. You know, that's symbolic of a female, so that in a sense becomes figurative. The other stuff like the diamond, the prism, the pentagon, all of those shapes, the geometry is really about symbols of the intellect. The needle on the table is female. The knives are male. Now, as I've said already, the house is a very specific thing. I've done drawings called *Rasp and Hone, Build a Home*. I've used that kind of phraseology a lot about the hearth, the security, the psychological warmth, if you will, of just knowing of the existence of that and having that. That is inherently in us all. We all need that. It doesn't make any difference what continent you are on. It's a human need, so that's symbolic. A lot of times they get mixed. They get really put together. I'll put the knife, the house, and a flower together in some formal arrangement.

I've mixed a lot of these symbols together, and one of the earliest symbols was just the pyramid, just the head. It's almost like the alpha, the A, it was like discovering the beginning of an alphabet. Can you imagine if you discovered blue or red or yellow or circles or squares or triangles and then you claimed them as your own? That's what artists do, although there's a historical precedent for all of it. All those symbols, man, the

eye, I could take credit for the eye. The eye is mine. No one else can use the eye. Oh, yes, they can, on every continent, in every culture that's ever existed, they've used it, so it's very hard to claim it as mine. Well, wait a minute; that may make it universal. You know, that may actually put it out there in the realm of a certain universality. The circle certainly is, unless it's around your ankles, as shackles, or handcuffs, or you're chained to the dungeon wall. Then all of a sudden all that business about union and the continuation and all of the symbolicness that we've put into that goes out the window. It really does have a certain relativity to its symbols, how they're used. And that's why you get to use them over and over and over.
I mean, who's got a handle on the ABC's? Who gets to claim all those notes for them? The F note, that's my note; no one else gets to use that. Yes, they do. Everybody on the planet gets to use it. The same thing's true with symbols, particularly symbols that take on this kind of monumental referencing, like the needle, the axe, the knife, the house, the diamond, the table, the bridge, the window, the stairwell, the stairway, the...

GW: You barely mentioned the plant, the flower, or the leaf.

JS: Well, those things really came out of what I would call the mathematical in nature, our mathematical ability to assemble. Donald Judd used twos, fours, and squares and was very precise about it. I use threes and fives and sevens (PL. 5). I have recently started using even numbers, though, and finding a certain beauty in them that I really didn't in the beginning. All of those dot patterns in the drawings are all based around threes, which I just consider absolutely to be a certain magical number in nature, like the triple junction (FIG. 75). The number three: think what kind of role it plays in plants, in growth patterns, in different religions and different beliefs and, man, the Trinity. The three has a lot of power, and I think symbolically that in the count to three, the third one sets the pattern. It's like James Brown may have played on the one, but the idea of the three sets a certain pattern, pace, and I really like it. I like numbers. I like geometry. I like science.

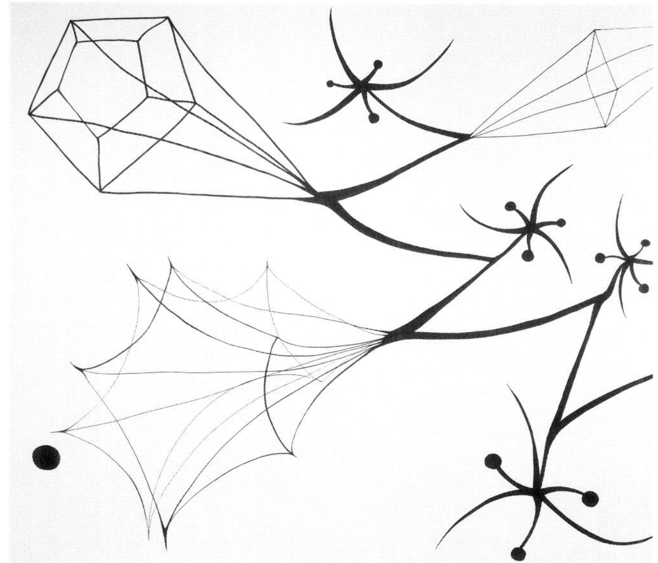

FIGURE 75
Me, God, Evolution, Love, Relationship and you (detail), 2003 **(PL. 48)**
Ink on paper
160 x 324

GW: Yeah. The art historian in me would say that moving from the medieval, the threes and the sevens, to the Renaissance, those even numbers. Maybe we've answered the Colorado question here about why your work is changing as well.

JS: I have not thought of that. I have not put that into any conscious expression, but why would I argue with that? I think that very well may be a point well made.

GW: I'll be counting the petals and flowers.

JS: The flower petals on the pitcher are six, and the pitcher's divided into six equal parts (see FIG. 76). It's based on a hexagon, which is like the honeybee. You know, there are a lot of structural things that are based around that. The pitcher is very even-numbered; very dividable in that axis, kind of symmetrical sense. I've never done that. That's not somewhere where I have gone, so maybe you're right.

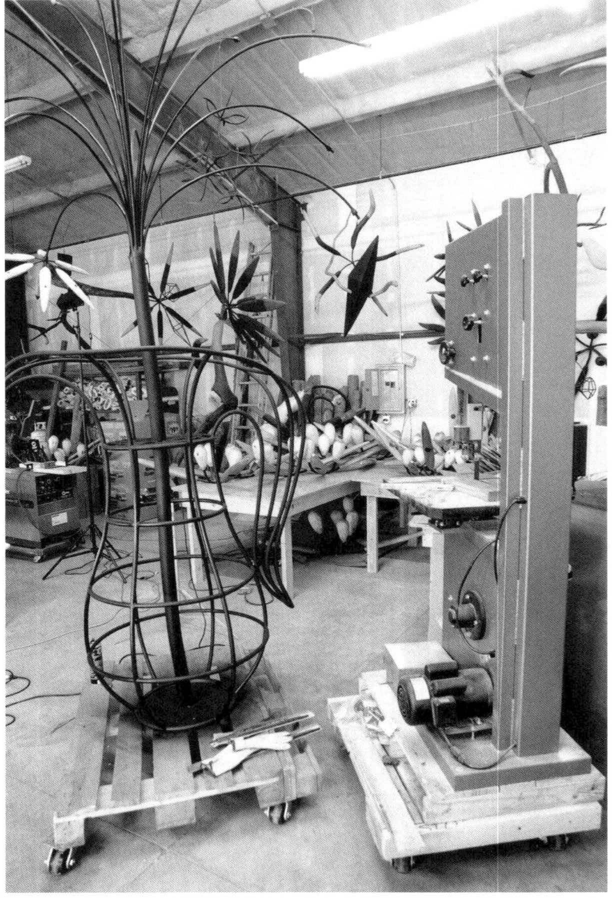

FIGURE 76
Studio view of *From the Pitcher*, 2002 (PL. 11)

GW: What's interesting is how conscious you are of these. What would be interesting to readers or to viewers is the kind of thought that goes into your art. Looking at your art, it looks so natural, it looks so easy. It looks as if it just came out of the subconscious.

JS: Hopefully it's a mix.

GW: Yeah.

JS: The free flow of the subconscious, I call it below the level of consciousness. God, what could be greater than consciousness? Consciousness should actually solve a lot of problems. Although I don't know that it solved Eve's problems when she discovered knowledge.

GW: I thought that was the whole problem.

JS: But she did give us a gift, that is consciousness, and, theoretically, if you can be conscious about something, you should be able to do a lot of healing, a lot of fixing of yourself and the world.

GW: Talk about symbolism in your work as it relates to your life in Splendora.

JS: The big house in this show is called *Forever Gone*. That's the title of that house, and I think that is applicable inasmuch as you ask about going back, about gone forever. How can I use titles like *Forever Gone*? What is gone forever? Well, that part of my past is gone forever. It's gone. I cannot do that part of my life over again. There are other symbols

FIGURE 77
I Never Knew (detail), 2003 (PL. 47)

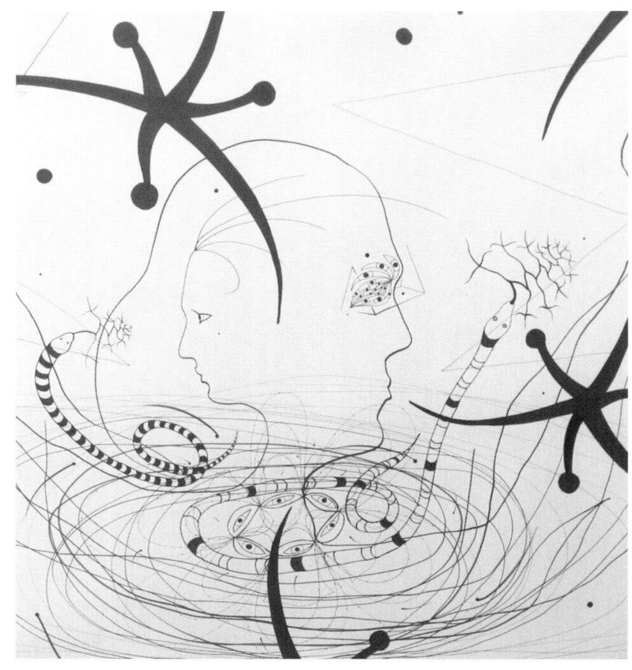

that I use. The snake has come to bear any number of times. Why would I use a snake? Personally, I would use a snake because we lived in a jungle. Snakes live in the jungle. We encountered a red and yellow killafellow in our kitchen. There it is, a coral snake crawling across our kitchen floor. We encountered snakes at the henhouse, at the chicken house all the time. Copperheads were everywhere. King snakes were everywhere. Chicken snakes were everywhere. Lots and lots of snakes live in the jungle.

So, why would I use a snake (FIG. 77)? Why would I use a house? I'm starting a life. I'm beginning anew. You know, it's like beginning anew. I'm ending one part of my life. I go from graduate school to SMU, that's beginning anew, that's crossing into a new territory. You know, I fall in love with a person, that's starting into a new territory. We move into a one-room house—we lived in a one-room house, for years—for almost four years, we lived in a twenty-foot-square house. We made our art in that house; we had our babies in that house; we cooked in that house; we entertained in that house. That was it. We made art in the front yard. Charmaine built a porch as an addition, and we slept on the porch. The porch became the living room. Why would we deal with the house? Because the house was huge; it loomed large in our personal life. We didn't have a house in the normal sense: no garage, no storeroom, no door on the bathroom, just, just one room. Life took place in there, much like in a nautilus, a shell, where the thing crawls in; it lives in it; it expands in it; and it gets too big for it; and then it has to go through a change. So, the house played a huge role. Plus, Charmaine was a psychology major at SMU. Charmaine analyzed a lot and showed me how to, and it really is pretty amazing about the whole idea about couples and the role they play with each other, and my feeling is the soul mate takes you somewhere you cannot get by yourself. You need that person to help you over the mountain, to help you across the bridge, to help you over the hump, in whatever metaphoric kind of language you want to cloak it in. Living in that house, dealing with those images, at that time. Flowers? That jungle was filled with flowers. We spent hours and hours and hours walking. And we spent Sundays walking in the woods, looking at everything from dogwoods, to honeysuckle, to lilies. The ditches had lilies in them; tiger lilies literally grew in the ditches. I mean, those woods are filled with some of the most primitive kind of succulent little things that caught water, just would catch water, and it would drain down into it; very, very beautiful things. How could that not be personal? Flowers? The house? The transition? I remember sitting on the porch out there remembering my parents and thinking of what my parents had done and thinking what I was choosing specifically to do or not to do in my life. That's consciousness. Consciousness allows you to make those very specific decisions as opposed to living your life by rote, not questioning, not asking why, not answering why.

Part II: October 15, 2002. The next morning I met with James Surls in his studio to discuss the content of the Meadows Museum exhibition. Much of the conversation concerned the mundane details of planning the exhibit and this publication, but some of the discussion is of broader interest.

GW: One of the questions I wanted to ask you today that I didn't get to yesterday is where did it start? Where did you...

JS: It actually started at SMU. It started about 1973 or '74. I'll tell you what happened when I went to Taos. This picture was taken of a piece I did; there's only three people there, and it was called *Five Minutes of Blue in Wind River* (see FRONTISPIECE #1). It's where I just kind of danced down through this meadow coming down the side of the mountain, and there's aspens on both sides, and there's a draw. The reason the draw is there and no trees are there is because of the wind, the prevailing wind. So dancing down in the wind like this, you get these little aspen trees, stripped of the bark, with yellow and blue torn pieces of rags, like ribbons, tied onto the poles. I used them as wings. The ribbons just flapped and blew and popped in the wind, and it was just magical. It was just great. It was during these years that I met Charmaine. She was a senior in the psychology department. I had made, my first year in Taos, a cradle out of aspen boughs, a fairly big baby cradle. I made it for someone; I gave it to someone, but I put it in the Faculty Show. Charmaine saw the cradle and decided to take a class. Well, one of the classes I taught was called Materials and Concepts, where we matched the concept with the material in the lab or we would pick a material and then find a concept to go with it. Well, I also taught a lecture class where that was discussed, and I took roll for that class by having my students turn in a one-page paper. Every week they had to turn in this paper. I would collect all these papers, and then after class I would read them. I would get to her paper, and it'd blow me away. You know, it was like, what? Who is this person? So, I put the paper and the face together in the sculpture class that she was in, and I was just moonstruck, man, I'm telling you, I was. God, I loved what she wrote.

GW: You fell in love with her writing first.

JS: I did. I fell in love with her right there, I did, just like she kind of fell in love with the concept of some guy who could make a cradle. That's a romantic beginning? Well, damn right it was.

GW: What happened to the cradle, by the way?

JS: Well, I gave the cradle to someone else. I mean, I had actually made the cradle for a friend, and I gave it to them. That was kind of the end of that. The cradle kind of opened the door to fly in the mountains, and then it's amazing that then I left and went to the jungles and then came back to the mountains all these years later, so there is a precedent for the mountains and being there and everything.

GW: And for Charmaine's role in it.

JS: It is truly, really amazing that my real, serious career started in the West, in and around northern New Mexico, in the Kit Carson National Forest. Charmaine and I moved to Splendora in '76.

GW: And you met Charmaine?

JS: No, I met her in about '72 or '73, but…

GW: So, after graduating in '69, you ended up in SMU? Immediately afterwards?

JS: Well, pretty close. I moved back to Dallas, and I was working as a welder over in Oak Cliff. Well, Bill Verhelst was the sculpture teacher at SMU. I went to a blues bar on Lovers Lane called the Black Out, and I was sitting there—this was 1970—beside this guy who turned out to be Bill. I sat there for an hour, just drinking, shooting the breeze, just talking, and finally he said to me, Well, what do you do? And I said, I'm an artist, and he said, Oh, so am I. He said, What kind of art do you make? I said, Well, I'm a sculptor. He said, So am I. Then, he said something that was staggering. He said, Well, do you have a degree? I said, yeah, I went to Cranbrook. He said, You went to Cranbrook? Do you have an MFA? I said, Yeah. He said, You want my job for the summer? I went up the next day. I went to talk to Bill Jordan; he was the chair at the time. Bill Jordan, Bill Verhelst, and I sat in a room, and Bill Jordan hired me on the spot. I took him a portfolio of stuff—now, this is all from graduate school—and he basically then hired me to teach a summer class. I taught that summer class. The following semester he hired me to teach a couple of more classes, and from there I got on full-time, as a professor. I got hired at SMU from sitting in a goddamn bar. I mean, I never wanted to teach.

GW: If only they knew now…

In the Meadows: Recent Sculpture, Drawings and Prints by James Surls

An Exhibition at the Meadows Museum,
Southern Methodist University, Dallas, Texas
January 24–April 20, 2003

This exhibition not only examines the grandness, beauty, and artistic creativity present in James Surls's most recent works, it also constitutes the first major museum exhibition of Surls in almost twenty years. Through the installation, lectures, educational programs, and this publication, our goal has been to further the understanding and knowledge of Surls's life and work. This comprehensive exhibition, featuring thirty-four sculptures, twenty-two drawings including a monumental mural, and five prints, has provided an unparalleled opportunity to witness Surls's latest work and to understand his influences and aspirations.

Most of the works in this exhibition were done after Surls moved to Colorado from his home in East Texas, concluding a transitional period that lasted five years. The museum space, inside and out, has provided the inspiration for several pieces, including the work installed above the staircase (PL. 10) and the three monumental sculptures in the outdoor plaza (PLS. 17, 18 and 19). The artist created these pieces expressly for the museum's space and surroundings. The great drawing on paper in the main gallery, *Me, God, Evolution, Love, Relationship and you* (PL. 48), was inspired from a poem written by Surls in 2002 (see page 14) and created after the installation of the sculptures in the exhibition space. This mural is the largest drawing ever done by Surls, and as a draftsman, he achieves the same monumentality and grandeur of his sculptures. A smaller drawing, titled *I Never Knew* (PL. 47), which reveals a stronger interest in detail, is exhibited in one of the interior corridors of the museum.

All sculptures in this exhibition, ranging in size from twenty-two inches to thirty feet, testify to Surls's artistic evolution over the last years. As Surls remarks, "Growing in art is the only path that you can really take." Although many of the symbols found in his new works are still as vivid as his earlier examples, such as flowers, eyes, houses, diamonds, one can say that these symbols have now become more refined and stylized. The wood, the basic material in most of his sculptures, is being treated with more interest and care. Metal is being applied more in his work, not as much as a structural element, but as a fully integrated part of the sculpture and a relevant step in the artistic creative process. The dialogue between wood and metal has been intensified.

Known primarily as a sculptor, James Surls also proves to be an accomplished draftsman and printer. Because our intent has been to explore the different facets of James Surls's latest work and highlight the beauty of his artistic achievements, the museum chose to include an important representation of models and works on paper. These works are clearly related to his sculpture and they are integral parts of the artistic process for Surls.

Maquettes and preparatory drawings

Surls's monumental sculptures are the conclusion of an artistic creative process in which drawing and models are crucial elements. Usually he fleshes out his first ideas through a fast sketch, either using white chalk on his working table or graphite on a sheet of paper. The process continues with a more elaborate drawing that is often accompanied by notations including the title and dimensions of the future sculpture. Surls does not need to make many preparatory drawings before beginning to work on a piece; in most cases, he can begin after meticulously elaborating just one drawing. The surety with which he traces the lines on the paper, sometimes denting the surface as if he were chiseling a piece of wood, reflects his confidence as a draftsman.

For most sculptors, as with James Surls, these preparatory drawings are considered mere working tools that lead up to the desired result, the sculpture. For this reason, once the sculpture has been finalized, many of Surls's drawings were put aside, lost or simply destroyed. Included in the exhibition are some rare examples of his preparatory works, none of which has ever been exhibited before. Several drawings are directly connected to pieces in the exhibition, while others relate to other projects or are simply ideas **(PLS. 49-61)**.

On the other hand, in some cases the maquette constitutes the basic model for a future major work. The preparatory drawing then becomes a three-dimensional piece. Although Surls says, "I like big. I love big. I like things that are bigger than life and monumental, and that's certainly part of what I want *In the Meadows* to be. I want that grand and monumental part," the artist is well aware that the enlargement of a model or the assembly of a large sculpture does not mean that his maquettes are less relevant works of art. They have their own monumentality. Surls adds, "Ironically, half of the show is little, very small pieces. They're models, they're maquettes, meant to have this sort of monumentality. I don't think size really has anything to do with monumentality."

Drawings and prints

As the artist notes, drawings and prints were undertaken during different stages in his life: "I'm not really making prints now. I made prints from the late 1980s to the early '90s very extensively. I did something like 25 or 30 prints. That, in essence, took the place of drawing. Up to that point, the drawings were prevalent—lots and lots and lots of drawings. Then in that period, there were lots and lots of prints, all of which had drawing in them. After that came a very emotional transition." When Surls speaks about a transition, he is referring to his family's move from Texas to Colorado, a period that lasted from the mid-1990s until 2002, when they fully adapted to their new home.

The subjects of Surls's drawings and prints, as in his sculptures, are strongly charged with symbolism. The simplicity of the line that moves lightly and freely across the paper hides a complex superimposition of images such as facial profiles, hands, geometric objects, flowers, and figures. As a result, there is a profound and metaphorical dialogue on the surface of the paper that requires the full attention of the viewer. Surls says, "The drawings are in a bizarre kind of way almost like genealogical road maps that get you somewhere and are much, much more complicated than the sculpture, even though I'm known primarily as a sculptor. That's because they're tangible, physical. People can touch and walk around it and stuff. When they look at the drawings, they have to actually do a little more thinking."

As Surls remarks, his drawing technique is reminiscent of Asian art. He likes to make continuous silhouettes while dragging his pencil over the paper, lifting the pencil as little as possible and therefore exploiting to its maximum the refinement and beauty of the line. The artist says of his technique, "I don't rub; I don't smudge; I don't smear; I don't use color. . . . I use something that makes a dark line on a light ground, and that's it. I mean, the Oriental masters could paint a mountainscape with a single stroke. Oh, would it have been better if they had used thousands of strokes and worked on it for days and weeks and months? I really don't think so. I mean, that's part of the beauty and the direct hit, so to speak. That's the way I have to deal with drawing, and I think it's probably one of the reasons I am so drawn to poets because I think that drawing to visual art is like poetry to literature. Poetry is as close to the bone as you're going to get. It's as direct a hit as you're going to get."

As a printer, Surls has completely changed direction with his technique and has gone from working primarily with woodcut and linocut to lithographs. As a result, the importance of the drawing has intensified, covering most of the surface of the paper, and there is a stronger interest in balancing the composition. The contrast and depth, which were obtained using color and perspective, are now achieved through delicate changes in the tonalities of the lines.

This exhibition of Surls's latest creations links the artist to his past and his future. His move to Colorado prompted the freedom to explore new ideas such as combining metal with wood, resulting in a sharper and more refined finish to his sculptures. Even the exhibition itself inspired Surls to create new works. The massive mural, done in less than one day and without any preparatory drawings, is not only a marvel of fluidity and grace, it also exemplifies his confidence as a draftsman and maturity as an artist. These new sculptures and works on paper all testify to Surls's love affair with monumentality, beauty, and meaning.

Mark A. Roglán
Curator
Meadows Museum
Southern Methodist University

JAMES SURLS

1943 Born in Terrell, Texas

EDUCATION

1969 M.F.A., Cranbrook Academy of Art, Bloomfield Hills, Michigan

1966 B.S., Sam Houston State College, Huntsville, Texas

AWARDS

1993 Living Legend Award, Dallas Visual Art Center, Texas

1991 Texas Artist of the Year, Houston Area Art League

1979 National Endowment of the Arts Fellowship

SELECTED SOLO EXHIBITIONS

2003 *In the Meadows: Recent Sculpture, Drawings and Prints of James Surls,* Meadows Museum, Dallas, Texas (catalogue)

2002 *James Surls: A Life Force,* Pillsbury & Peters Fine Art, Dallas, Texas

1999 *James Surls, Recent Sculpture,* Barbara Davis Gallery, Houston, Texas
James Surls: Sculpture and Drawing, Gerald Peters Gallery, Dallas, Texas

1997 *James Surls: Swimming in Forever,* The University of Texas at Tyler

1996 *James Surls: In the Garden,* Gerald Peters Gallery, Dallas, Texas
James Surls: Carved Icons, The Savannah College of Art and Design, Georgia
Sculpture, Drawing, Prints – New Works, Milagros Contemporary, San Antonio, Texas

1994 Gerald Peters Gallery, Dallas, Texas
Marlborough Gallery, New York, New York (catalogue)

1991 The Contemporary Museum, Honolulu, Hawaii (catalogue)

1990 Jan Weiner Gallery, Kansas City, Missouri
University of Tulsa, Oklahoma

1989 Hiram Butler Gallery, Houston, Texas
Barry Whistler Gallery, Dallas
Arthur Roger Gallery, New Orleans, Louisiana

1988 L.A. Louver Gallery, Venice, California
Art Museum of Southeast Texas, Beaumont (catalogue)

1987 Cranbrook Academy of Art Museum, Bloomfield, Michigan
Fuller Gross Gallery, San Francisco, California
Pittsburgh Center for the Arts, Pennsylvania; traveled to Allan Frumkin Gallery, New York, New York

1986 Allan Frumkin Gallery, New York
Hiram Butler Gallery, Houston
Arthur Rogers Gallery, New Orleans, Louisiana

1985 Santacafe, Santa Fe, New Mexico
L.A. Louver Gallery, Venice, California

1984 Dallas Museum of Art, Dallas, Texas; traveled to La Jolla Museum of Contemporary Art, California; Seattle Art Museum; University of Oklahoma Art Museum, Norman, Oklahoma (catalogue)
Fuller Goldeen Gallery, San Francisco. California
Honolulu Academy of Art, Hawaii
Delahunty Gallery, New York, New York
Delahunty Gallery, Dallas, Texas

1982 St. Louis Art Museum, Missouri
Allan Frumkin Gallery,
New York, New York
Akron Art Museum, Ohio

1981 Daniel Weinberg Gallery,
San Francisco, California
Delahunty Gallery, Dallas, Texas

1980 Allan Frumkin Gallery, New York,
New York (catalogue)

1979 Robinson Galleries, Houston, Texas
Delahunty Gallery, Dallas, Texas

1977 Contemporary Arts Museum,
Houston, Texas
Delahunty Gallery, Dallas, Texas

1975 Contemporary Arts Museum,
Houston, Texas (catalogue)

1974 Tyler Museum of Art, Texas
(catalogue)
Delahunty Gallery, Dallas, Texas

SELECTED GROUP EXHIBITIONS

2001 *Alexander Calder & James Surls,*
Pillsbury & Peters Fine Arts,
Dallas, Texas
Beeville Art Museum
Sculpture Garden,
Beeville, Texas
Sculpture on the Grounds,
Contemporary Art Center of
Virginia, Norfolk, Virginia
Inside & Out – Contemporary
Sculpture,
Bass Museum of Art,
Miami Beach, Florida

2000 *Monte Carlo 2000,*
Monaco
On The Edge,
El Paso Museum of Art,
El Paso, Texas
Crossing State Lines,
Museum of Fine Arts,
Houston, Texas

1999 *Faultlines: Drawing on/off paper,*
ArtScan Gallery, Houston, Texas

1998 *Link,*
Gerald Peters Gallery,
Dallas, Texas

1997 *Link,*
Gerald Peters Gallery,
Dallas, Texas
Finders/Keepers,
Contemporary Arts Museum,
Houston, Texas
Fresh Ink: Austin Print Workshops,
Austin Museum of Art, Texas
37th Annual Art Faculty Exhibition,
Gaddis Gesslin Gallery,
Sam Houston State University,
Huntsville, Texas
Schemata: Drawings by Sculptors,
The Glassell School of Art,
The Museum of Fine Arts,
Houston, Texas

1996 *C3,*
Cerrillos Cultural Center,
New Mexico
In the Warehouse: Large Works,
Meredith Long Gallery,
Houston, Texas
Art Faculty Exhibition,
Lowman Student Center,
Sam Houston State University,
Huntsville, Texas
Anne Reed Gallery,
Sun Valley, Idaho
Bucking the Texas Myth,
Austin Museum of Art, Texas
Schemata: Drawing by Sculptors,
The Glassell School of Art,
The Museum of Fine Arts,
Houston, Texas
Establishment Exposed: Part I,
Dallas Visual Art Center, Texas
Surls, Moroles, Manjarris:
Three paths in our garden,
Irving Arts Center, Texas
Link,
Gerald Peters Gallery,
Dallas, Texas
32 Texas Artists,
Fifth Floor Gallery, Health
Science Center, The University
of Texas, Houston

1995 *Link,*
Gerald Peters Gallery,
Dallas, Texas
Magic and Mystery,
Laguna Gloria Art Museum,
Austin, Texas

1994 *Outside:In,*
Laguna Gloria Art Museum,
Austin, Texas (catalogue)
Illusion-Allusion,
Florida State University
Museum of Fine Arts,
Tallahassee
Second Annual Sculpture
on the Green,
Omni Houston,
Houston, Texas
Ideas and Objects: Selected
Drawings and Sculptures from
the Permanent Collection,
Whitney Museum of American
Art, New York, New York
Eight Contemporary Sculptors:
Beyond Nature, Wood Into Art,
The Lowe Art Museum,
Miami, Florida (catalogue)

1993 *It's A Beautiful Thing,*
Savage Fine Art,
Portland, Oregon
Wood,
University Art Gallery,
Staller Center for the Arts,
State University of New York,
Stoney Brook, New York
Virgil Grotfeldt, James Surls,
Joe Havel,
Hiram Butler Gallery,
Houston, Texas
Eye to Eye,
Art Center of Corpus Christi,
Texas (catalogue)
Seeing the Forest Through the Trees,
Contemporary Arts Museum,
Houston, Texas (catalogue)
Summer Invitational,
Jan Weiner Gallery,
Kansas City, Missouri
Summer Stock,
Gerald Peters Gallery,
Dallas, Texas
Figure,
Marlborough Gallery,
New York, New York
(catalogue)
Installation,
Nations Bank Plaza,
Charlotte, North Carolina
Here's Looking at Me,
Contemporary Self Portrait,
Elac, Lyon, France (catalogue)

1992 *Roy Slade, James Surls,*
Deloss McGraw,
Robert Kidd Gallery,
Birmingham, Mississippi
20th Anniversary Exhibition – 1972-1992,
The Art Center, Waco, Texas
Some of Houston's Known
and Underknown,
Allen Center Gallery,
Houston, Texas
Summer Invitational,
Jan Weiner Gallery,
Kansas City, Missouri
Thirty Prints,
Barry Whistler Gallery,
Dallas, Texas
Art and Nature,
Hiram Butler Gallery,
Houston, Texas
Cork Marcheschi, James Surls,
Braunstein/Quay Gallery,
San Francisco, California

1991 *Creative Partners,*
Sewall Art Gallery,
Rice University, Houston, Texas
Texas, The State I'm In,
Dallas Museum of Art,
Dallas, Texas
A Celebration of Friends,
Hiram Butler Gallery,
Houston, Texas
Sticks & Stones,
Katonah Museum of Art,
New York (catalogue)
Retrieving the Elemental Form,
Schmidt Bingham Gallery,
New York, New York; traveled
to Lakeview Museum of Arts
and Sciences, Peoria, Illinois;
Fresno Art Museum, California
Art As A Healing Force,
Bolinas Museum, Bolinas,
California (catalogue)
The Eyes of Texas, Prints
and Unique Works,
Jan Weiner Gallery,
Kansas City, Missouri
Image & Likeness,
Whitney Museum of American
Art, New York, New York;
traveled to Whitney Museum of
American Art, Fairfield County,
Stamford, Connecticut
(catalogue)

1990 *Direct References: Drawings*
by Texas Artists,
The Glassell School of Art,
The Museum of Fine Arts,
Houston, Texas
Deep in the Art of Texas,
Art Gallery, Visual Arts Center,
California State University,
Fullerton
The Artist's Eye,
Diverse Works, Houston, Texas
Forty Texas Printmakers,
Modern Art Museum of
Fort Worth, Texas
Word As Image: American Art
1960-1990,
Milwaukee Art Museum,
Wisconsin; traveled to
Contemporary Arts Museum,
Houston, Texas
The 4th International Shoebox
Sculpture Exhibition,
Manoa Art Gallery, University
of Hawaii, Honolulu (catalogue)

1989 *Singular Spaces,*
Phenomenal Places,
The Contemporary Arts Center,
Cincinnati, Ohio
JAMES SURLS—sculpture,
PILIP WOFFORD—paintings,
PETER SAUL—paintings,
Arthur Roger Gallery,
New Orleans, Louisiana
The Boat Show: Fantastic
Vessels, Fictional Voyages,
Renwick Gallery, The
Smithsonian Institution,
Washington, D.C.
Past/Present,
Allan Frumkin Gallery,
New York, New York

1988 *Sculpture Inside Outside,*
Walker Art Center,
Minneapolis, Minnesota
(catalogue)

Figure as Subject: The Revival of Figuration Since 1975,
Whitney Museum of Art,
New York, New York (catalogue)

Art for the Museum: A Legacy,
Art Museum of Southeast
Texas, Beaumont (catalogue)

The 3rd International Shoebox Sculpture Exhibition,
The University of Hawaii,
Honolulu (catalogue)

Direction & Diversity,
The Museum of Fine Arts,
Houston, Texas

Texas Art,
The Menil Collection,
Houston, Texas

Contemporary Art from Texas,
Groninger Museum,
Groninger, The Netherlands

Current Vision: Sculpture & Sculptors' Drawings,
Joy Emery Gallery,
Bloomfield Hills, Michigan

One+One: Collaborations by Artists and Writers,
The Glassell School of Art,
The Museum of Fine Arts,
Houston, Texas

1987-88 Ancient Aspirations: Six Figurative Sculptors,
Stedman Art Gallery,
Rutgers University Gallery,
Calgary, Alberta; traveled to
Alexandria Museum,
Alexandria, Louisiana;
The Bass Museum of Art,
Miami Beach, Florida

1987 *The Eloquent Object,*
The Philbrook Museum of Art,
Tulsa, Oklahoma (catalogue)

Structure to Resemblance,
Albright-Knox Art Gallery,
Buffalo, New York (catalogue)

Sculptors on Paper: New Work,
Madison Art Center, Wisconsin;
traveled to Pittsburgh Center
for the Arts, Pennsylvania;
Kalamazoo Institute of Arts,
Michigan; Sheldon Memorial
Art Gallery, Lincoln, Nebraska

Bert Long, Jesse Lott, James Surls: An Inaugural Exhibition,
Barry Whistler Gallery,
Dallas, Texas

Don't Knock Wood – A Group Exhibition: Works of Wood,
Helander Gallery,
Palm Beach, Florida

The Importance of Drawing,
Fuller Goldeen Gallery,
San Francisco, California

1986 *75th American Exhibition,*
The Art Institute of Chicago,
Illinois (catalogue)

A Sense of Place: Contemporary Southern Art,
Minneapolis, Minnesota

Sculpture/Aspen,
Aspen Art Museum, Colorado

Texas Exhibition,
McIntosh/Drysdale Gallery,
Washington, D.C.

Group Show,
National Museum of American
Art, Renwick Gallery, Barney
Studio House, Washington, D.C.

Works on Paper: Artists Working in Texas,
Barry Whistler Gallery,
Dallas, Texas

Market Square Proposals,
DiverseWorks, Houston, Texas

Outdoor Sculpture by Texas Artists,
Laguna Gloria Art Museum,
Austin, Texas

Figure as Subject: The Last Decade,
Whitney Museum of American
Art at the Equitable Center,
New York, New York (catalogue)

America: Art and the West,
Art Gallery of Western
Australia, Perth, Australia;
traveled to Art Gallery of New
South Wales, Sydney, Australia

1985 *Biennial Exposition,*
Whitney Museum of American
Art, New York, New York
(catalogue)

Chuck Dugan: New Paintings/ James Surls: New Sculpture,
Allan Frumkin Gallery,
New York, New York

Gallery Artists: Recent Work,
Hiram Butler Gallery,
Houston, Texas

American/European Painting & Sculpture, 1985,
L.A. Louver Gallery,
Venice, California

Works in Wood: A Survey of Contemporary Sculpture,
Monterey Peninsula Museum
of Art, Monterey, California

Body and Soul: Aspects of Recent Figurative Sculpture,
The Contemporary Arts Center,
Cincinnati, Ohio (catalogue)

1984 *Visions of Paradise: Installations by Vito Acconci, David Ireland and James Surls,*
Hayden Gallery, Massachusetts
Institute of Technology,
Cambridge, Massachusetts
(catalogue)

American Art Since 1970: Painting, Sculpture and Drawings from the Collection of the Whitney Museum of American Art,
New York, New York; traveled to La Jolla Museum of Contemporary Art, California; Museo Tamayo, Mexico City; North Carolina Museum of Art, Raleigh, North Carolina; Sheldon Memorial Art Gallery, University of Nebraska, Lincoln, Nebraska; Center for the Fine Arts, Miami, Florida (catalogue)

Face to Face/Back to Back,
The Main Gallery, Visual Arts Center, California State University, Fullerton, California (catalogue)

Painting, Drawing & Sculpture, American and European,
Louver Gallery, Venice, California

Contemporary Wood Sculpture, Crocker Art Museum,
Sacramento, California (catalogue)

Cranbrook Contemporary,
CDS Gallery, New York, New York

Inaugural Exhibition,
Hiram Butler Gallery, Houston, Texas

1983 *A Century of Modern Sculpture: 1882-1982,*
Museum of Fine Arts, Houston, Texas (catalogue)

Fact and Fiction,
Aspen Center for the Visual Arts, Colorado (catalogue)

Minimalism to Expressionism: Painting and Sculpture since 1965 from the Permanent Collection,
Whitney Museum of American Art, New York, New York (catalogue)

The House that Art Built,
The Main Gallery, Visual Arts Center, Cal State University, Fullerton, California (catalogue)

New Art from a New City: Houston,
Salzburger Kuntsverein, Salzburg, Austria (catalogue)

Southern Fictions,
Contemporary Arts Museum, Houston, Texas (catalogue)

Update: Cranbrook, A Survey Exhibition 1925-1983,
Robert L. Kidd Associates Galleries, Birmingham, Alabama

1982 *Cranbrook, U.S.A.: Painting and Sculpture,*
Cranbrook Academy of Art, Bloomfield Hills, Michigan

A Sense of Spirit,
Lawndale Art and Performance Center, University of Houston, Texas (catalogue)

20 American Artists: Sculpture 1982,
San Francisco Museum of Modern Art, California (catalogue)

Scott Burton, Joel Shapiro, James Surls,
Daniel Weinberg Gallery, San Francisco, California

Lucero, Scanga, Surls,
Texas Gallery, Houston, Texas; traveled to Delahunty Gallery, Dallas, Texas (catalogue)

Art from Houston in Norway,
Stavanger Kuntsforening, Stavanger, Norway

1981 *The First Annual Abilene Outdoor Sculpture Exhibit,*
Abilene Cultural Affairs Council and the Abilene Fine Arts Museum, Texas

Childsplay: Wit and Whimsy in Contemporary Sculpture,
The Queen's Museum, Flushing, New York

The Image of the House in Contemporary Art,
Lawndale Art and Performance Center, University of Houston, Texas

1980 *First Person Singular: Recent Self-Portraiture,*
Pratt Manhattan Center Gallery, New York, New York

Response,
Tyler Museum of Art, Texas (catalogue)

Charmaine Locke and James Surls,
Stephen F. Austin University, Nacogdoches, Texas

Inside Texas Borders,
South Texas Artmobile, Corpus Christi State University, Texas (catalogue)

10 Abstract Sculptures: American and European, 1940-1989,
Max Hutchinson Gallery, New York, New York (catalogue)

Two From Texas,
Gallerie Simone Stern, New Orleans, Louisiana

Couples,
Fendrick Gallery, Washington, D.C.

Houston Exchange Show,
500X, Dallas, Texas

Surls/Locke,
University Center Art Gallery, Louisiana State University, Shreveport

Visions and Configurations,
Fullerton Art Gallery, California State University, Fullerton (catalogue)
The Texas Invitational,
Contemporary Arts Center, New Orleans, Louisiana
The Eleventh International Sculpture Conference,
International Sculpture Center, Washington, D.C.
Fine Art for Federal Buildings, 1972-79
National Collection of Fine Arts, Smithsonian Institution, Washington, D.C.

1979 *Whitney Biennial Exhibition,*
Whitney Museum of American Art, New York, New York
Fire,
Contemporary Arts Museum, Houston, Texas (catalogue)
Made in Texas,
Archer M. Huntington Gallery, University Art Museum, University of Texas, Austin (catalogue)
18 Texans,
Weil Gallery, Corpus Christi, Texas (catalogue)

1978 *One Person Exhibitions: Janis Provisor, Jim Richard, James Surls, Casey Williams,*
New Orleans Museum of Art, Louisiana
Art of Texas,
The Renaissance Society at the University of Chicago, Illinois
Texas in Chicago,
Marion Deson Gallery, Chicago, Illinois
The Spirit of Texas,
John Michael Kohler Arts Gallery, Florida State University, Tallahassee
Four Houston Artists,
University Fine Arts Gallery, Florida State University, Tallahassee

1977 *Texas Today: Three Exhibitions,*
Fort Worth Art Museum, Texas (catalogue)
Nine Artists: Theodoron Awards,
Solomon R. Guggenheim Museum, New York, New York
Installations for Corner Spaces,
Fort Worth Art Museum, Texas
1977 Artists' Biennial,
New Orleans Museum of Art, Louisiana (catalogue)

1976-77 *Philadelphia-Houston Exchange,*
Institute of Contemporary Art, University of Pennsylvania, Philadelphia; traveled to Contemporary Arts Museum, Houston, Texas (catalogue)

1976 *Tex/Lax: Texas in L.A.,*
Union Gallery, California State University, Los Angeles
The Permanent Collection: A 75th Anniversary Retrospective,
Fort Worth Art Museum, Texas
ARTPARK,
The Program in Visual Arts, Lewiston, New York

1975 *Tarrant County Annual,*
Fort Worth Art Museum, Texas
Exchange DFW/SFO,
Fort Worth Art Museum, Texas; traveled to San Francisco Museum of Modern Art, California
Texas Tough,
Witte Memorial Museum, San Antonio, Texas
Monumental Sculpture,
Main Street Festival, Houston, Texas

1974 *Houston Designer-Craftsmen '74,*
Sarah Campbell Blaffer Gallery, University of Houston, Texas
First Biennial Invitational Painting and Sculpture Exhibition,
Beaumont Art Museum, Texas
12/Texas,
Contemporary Arts Museum, Houston, Texas (catalogue)

1973 *Tarrant County Annual,*
Fort Worth Art Museum, Texas
16th Annual Delta Art Exhibition,
Arkansas Art Center, Little Rock, Arkansas
Two Man Show,
829 Exposition, Dallas, Texas

1971 *14th Annual Delta Art Exhibition,*
Arkansas Art Center, Little Rock. Arkansas

SELECTED COMMISSIONS

2002 Hall Financial, Frisco, Texas
Kathryn Hall Vineyards, Napa Valley, California

1992 *Family,*
Mariposa Park, Corpus Christi, Texas (collaboration with Charmaine Locke)

1991 *To the Point,*
GTE Telephone Operations World Headquarters; Hidden Ridge; Irving, Texas
Points of View,
Market Square Park Project; Houston, Texas

1988 *There Used To Be A Lake,*
(collaboration with poet Robert Creeley), Poets Walk; Citicorp Plaza, Los Angeles, California

1986 *The Brazos Flower,*
The Brazos Center and
Arena/Pavilion Complex;
Bryan, Texas

1979 *Pine Flower,*
Buford TV Inc., Tyler, Texas

1978 *Sea Flower*
(steel and pine),
New Federal Building;
New Bedford, Massachusetts

PUBLIC COLLECTIONS

Albright Knox Gallery,
Buffalo, New York
Arkansas Art Center,
Little Rock, Arkansas
Bennington Museum,
Bennington, Vermont
The Contemporary Museum,
Honolulu, Hawaii
Centro Cultural Arte
Contemporaneo,
Mexico City, Mexico
Dallas Museum of Art,
Dallas, Texas
El Paso Museum of Art,
El Paso, Texas
Solomon R. Guggenheim Museum,
New York, New York
High Museum,
Atlanta, Georgia
Katonah Museum,
Katonah, New York
Los Angeles County Museum,
Los Angeles, California
Meadows Museum,
Southern Methodist University,
Dallas, Texas
Memphis Brooks Museum of Art,
Memphis, Tennessee
Metropolitan Pier and
Exposition Authority,
Chicago, Illinois
Modern Art Museum of
Fort Worth,
Fort Worth, Texas
Montgomery Museum of
Fine Arts,
Montgomery, Alabama
Museo de Arte Contemporaneo
de Caracas,
Caracas, Venezuela
Museum of Fine Arts,
Houston, Texas
Museum of Modern Art,
New York, New York
McNay Art Museum,
San Antonio, Texas
Nelson-Atkins Museum,
Kansas City, Missouri
Pittsburgh Center for the Arts,
Pittsburgh, Pennsylvania
San Antonio Art Museum,
San Antonio, Texas
San Francisco Museum of
Modern Art,
San Francisco, California
Seattle Art Museum,
Seattle, Washington
Stedelijk Museum,
Amsterdam
University of Nebraska Art
Galleries,
Lincoln, Nebraska
Waco Art Center,
Waco, Texas
Whitney Museum of
American Art,
New York, New York

1974

Contemporary Arts Museum. *12/Texas.* Houston: Contemporary Arts Museum. 1974.

Holmes, Ann. "CAM Show Bristles with Texan's Art." *Houston Chronicle* (October 5, 1974, section 3): 5.

Knight, Betsy. "Texas School—a different dozen." *The Houston Post* (October 13, 1974, section Spotlight): 36.

Kutner, Janet. "Houston challenges in 12-Texas Show." *The Dallas Morning News* (October 13, 1974, section C): 14.

——. "Tyler Shows Surls' Sculpture." *The Dallas Morning News* (November 7, 1974, section A): 45.

1975

Crossley, Mimi. "Sculpture by the ton." *The Houston Post* (November 2, 1975, section Spotlight): 29.

Haacke, Lorraine. "Surls and his wood sculpture." *Dallas Times Herald* (April 1-7, 1975, section C): 3.

Kutner, Janet. "Life in artist's garret isn't what it used to be." *The Dallas Morning News* (March 23,1975, section F): 1.

——. "Surls' Sculptures on View in Houston." *The Dallas Morning News* (April 10, 1975, section F): 1.

——. "Witte show is tough on Texas." *The Dallas Morning News* (October 12, 1975, section C): 7.

——. "Mocking myths, nachos, nostalgia." *ARTnews* (December 1975): 88, 90, 92.

——. "Art for dog's sake." *The Dallas Morning News* (December 7, 1975, section C): 1.

Rabyor, Joanne. "James Surls at Delahunty." *Art in America* (March-April 1975): 107.

Samuels, Michael. *James Surls: Sculptor.* Houston: Contemporary Arts Museum, 1975.

1976

Ayres, B. Drummond. "Cultural Activities in the South Grow with Its Economy." *The New York Times* (November 1, 1976, section C): 24.

Contemporary Arts Museum and Philadelphia: Institute of Contemporary Art. University of Pennsylvania, 1976.

Dunham, Judith L. "Bay Area, Texas Art Exchange." *Artweek* (February 28, 1976): 1, 16.

Frankenstein, Alfred. "Impressive Texas Art in Exchange." *San Francisco Examiner & Chronicle* (February 8, 1976, section The World): 28.

Kutner, Janet. "From coast to coast." *The Dallas Morning News* (November 7, 1976, section F): 3.

Smith, Roberta. "Twelve Days of Texas." *Art in America* (July-August 1976): 42-48.

"Texas artists in TV special." *The Dallas Morning News* (January 25. 1976, section C): 5.

1977

Fort Worth Art Museum. *Texas Today: 3 Exhibitions.* Fort Worth: Fort Worth Art Museum, 1977.

Haacke, Lorraine. "Surls finds his subjects in wood." *Dallas Times Herald* (January 28, 1977, section C): 3.

Kutner, Janet. "From Piney Woods to Gotham." *The Dallas Morning News* (February 20, 1977, section Scene): 18-20.

——. "Five Artists, four shows, three dimensions." *ARTnews* (March 1977): 95–98.

New Orleans Museum of Art. *1977 Artist's Biennial.* New Orleans: New Orleans Museum of Art, 1977.

Russell, John. "James Surls" *The New York Times* (March 20, 1977, section D): 27.

The Solomon R. Guggenheim Museum. *Nine Artists: Theodoron Awards.* New York: The Solomon R. Guggenheim Museum, 1977.

1978

Tucker, Marcia, and Gallander, Cathleen S. "James Surls." *Contemporary Art Southeast*, vol. II, no. 1 (1978): 24.

1979

Archer M. Huntington Gallery. *Made in Texas.* Austin: Archer M. Huntington Gallery, University Art Museum, University of Texas at Austin, 1979.

Hughes, Robert. "Roundup at the Whitney Corral." *Time* (February 26, 1979): 72-73.

"James Surls." *Artefact* (summer 1979): 32-33.

Kutner, Janet. "James Surls beats the brushes for art." *The Dallas Morning News* (February 18, 1979, section C): 5.

——. "'Fire' brings hope for art." *The Dallas Morning News* (February 24, 1979, section F): 3.

Lippard, Lucy R. "Texas Red Hots." *Art in America* (July-August 1979): 30-31.

Marvel, Bill. "'Fire' in Houston: Whetting a Texas-sized appetite for art." *Dallas Times Herald* (March 4, 1979, section C): 1.

——. "America's Art Scene Spreads Out from New York." *The Wall Street Journal* (June 8, 1979, section Leisure and the Arts): 19.

Platt Susan. "Dallas/Houston." *Artforum* (summer 1979): 75-76.

Rifkin. Ned. "'Fire or Flood?" *Artweek* (March 10, 1979): 1.

——. "James Surls." *Artweek* (March 24, 1979): 3.

Stevens, Mark. "The Dizzy Decade." *Newsweek* (March 20, 1979): 88-91.

Surls, James. *Fire!* Houston: Contemporary Art Museum. 1979.

Whitney Museum of American Art. *1979 Biennial Exhibition.* New York: Whitney Museum of American Art, 1979.

1980

Allan Frumkin Gallery. *New Sculpture, James Surls.* New York: Allan Frumkin Gallery, 1980.

——. "James Surls Makes New York Debut." *Allan Frumkin Newsletter* (spring 1980): 1-2.

Crossley, Mimi. "Hard by the freeway, a warehouse of creativity." *The Houston Post* (November 9, 1980, section AA): 8.

Kramer, Hilton. "10 Abstract Sculptures: American and European. 1940-1980." *The New York Times* (April 4, 1980, section C): 18.

——. "James Surls." *The New York Times* (May 23, 1980, section C): 27.

Kutner. Janet. "Abstract sculptor puts 'Flower' power in Dallas." *The Dallas Morning News* (April 21, 1980, section C): 1.

Marvel, Bill. "Texas backwoods mystique joins grit 'n' glitter in N.Y." *Dallas Times Herald* (June 8, 1980, section C): 1.

Max Hutchinson Gallery. *10 Abstract Sculptures: American and European 1940-1980: Ronald Bladen, Louise Bourgeois, Alexander Calder, Eduardo Chillida, Mark di Suvero, Charles Ginnever, Joan Miro, Alan Saret, George Sugarman, James Surls.* New York: Max Hutchinson Gallery, 1980.

Rifkin, Ned. *Response.* Tyler: Tyler Museum of Art, 1980.

Schjeldahl, Peter. "Art and Money in the City of Future-Think." *Houston City Magazine* (February 1980): 46-54.

Staniszewski, Mary Ann. "James Surls." *ARTnews* (November 1980): 215.

Stevens, Mark. "Sculpture Out in the Open." *Newsweek* (August 18, 1980): 70-71.

Zimmer, William. "James Surls." *The SoHo News* (May 14, 1980): 54.

1981

Kalil, Susie, and Freudenheim, Susan. "A Survey of Texas Art." *Arts + Architecture*, (winter 1981): 20-31.

Kutner, Janet. "Poet with an axe." *The Dallas Morning News* (June 13, 1981, section C): 3.

——. "Sculptor James Surls' work now deemed 'Ultra' special." *The Dallas Morning News* (December 7, 1981, section C): 9.

Lawndale Annex. *The Image of the House in Contemporary Art.* Houston: Lawndale Annex, University of Houston, 1981.

Schwartz, Ellen. "Strangeness is the Bait." *ARTnews* (May 1981): 80-81.

Tennant, Donna. "Beyond Carved Objects." *Artweek* (October 31, 1981): 5.

1982

Allan Frumkin Gallery. *James Surls.* New York: Allan Frumkin Gallery, 1982.

"As Others See Us." *Museum News* (March-April 1982): 16-18.

Cowart, Jack. *Currents 16. James Surls.* St. Louis: St. Louis Art Museum, 1982.

Daniel Weinberg Gallery. *Scott Burton, Joel Shapiro, James Surls.* San Francisco: Daniel Weinberg Gallery.

Kalil, Susie. "Texas Ranges: Houston—From Boogyman to 'The End Result of Constructivist Theory'." *ARTnews* (December 1982): 82-85.

Kutner. Janet. "Three Spirits: Scanga, Lucero and Surls: Sculpture opens new Delahunty Gallery." *The Dallas Morning News* (September 17, 1982, section C): 1.

Platt, Susan. "Personal, Modern, Eccentric." *Artweek* (August 28, 1982): 3.

San Francisco Museum of Modem Art. *20 American Artists: Sculpture 1982.* San Francisco: San Francisco Museum of Modern Art, 1982.

Zimmer, William. *Michael Lucero, Italo Scanga, James Surls.* Houston: Texas Gallery and Dallas: Delahunty Gallery, 1981.

1983

Camfield, William. *New Art from a New City—Houston.* Salzburg: Salzburger Kunstverein, 1983.

Contemporary Arts Museum. *Southern Fictions.* Houston: Contemporary Arts Museum, 1983.

Johnson, Patricia Covo. "James Surls." *Artspace* (winter 1983-1984): 20-21.

McCandless, Judith. *A Century of Modern Sculpture: 1882-1982.* Houston: The Museum of Fine Arts, 1983.

The Museum of Fine Arts, Houston. *A Century of Modern Sculpture: 1882-1982.* Houston: The Museum of Fine Arts, 1983.

Peterson, William. "Fact & Fiction at the Aspen Center for the Visual Arts, Aspen, Colorado." *Artspace* (summer 1983): 66-67.

Robert L. Kidd Associates. *Update: Cranbrook A Survey Exhibition 1925-1983.* Birmingham: Robert L. Kidd Associates/Galleries, 1983.

"Sculptors International." *International Sculpture Center*, vol. 2, no. 1 (1983): 23.
Whitney Museum of American Art. *Minimalism to Expressionism: Painting and Sculpture since 1965 from the Permanent Collection*. New York: Whitney Museum of American Art, 1983.

1984

Bourdon. David. "Whirled Without End." *Vogue* (December 1984): 78.
Choate, Part Stave. "James Surls." *Flash Art* (summer 1984): 68-69.
Crocker Art Museum. *Contemporary Wood Sculpture.* Sacramento: Crocker Art Museum, 1984.
Everingham, Carol J. "James Surls' works evoke fairytale images with a wicked wooden twist." *The Houston Post* (December 23, 1984, section F): 3.
Glueck, Grace. "James Surls." *The New York Times* (March 16, 1984, section C): 21.
Graze, Sue. *Visions: James Surls, 1979-1984.* Dallas: Dallas Museum of Art, 1984.
Hays, Joanne Burstein. "A bold lyricism." *Artweek* (November 24. 1984): 3.
Hughes, Robert. "Intensification of Nature." *Time* (April 2, 1984): 80-81.
Kutner, Janet. *James Surls.* Dallas: Delahunty Gallery, 1984.
——. "Texan Surls' inner visions." *The Dallas Morning News* (February 11, 1984, section F): 2.
——. "Stigma of the Lone Star." *The Dallas Morning News* (April 20, 1984, section C): 1.
——. "Corporate Collecting." *The Dallas Morning News* (July 14, 1984, section F): 1-2.
——. "The Grain of James Surls' Art." *The Dallas Morning News* (December 22. 1984, section F): 1.
Marvel, Bill. "James Surls Carves His Niche." *Dallas Times Herald* (February 1, 1984 section C): 1.
MIT Committee on the Visual Arts. *Visions of Paradise: Installations by Vito Acconci, David Ireland and James Surls.* Cambridge: Committee on the Visual Arts and Massachusetts Institute of Technology, 1984.
Whitney Museum of American Art. *American Art Since 1970: Painting, Sculpture, and Drawings from the Collection of the Whitney Museum of American Art.* New York: Whitney Museum of American Art, 1984.
Wilson, William. "Whitney Spirit Comes to La Jolla." *Los Angeles Times* (March 25, 1984, section Calendar): 81.

1985

Berger, David. "Obsessed Sculptor Has Personal Touch." *Seattle Times* (September 27, 1985, section Tempo): 16-17.
Drohojowaka, Hunter. "Surls Carves Wood in His Own Image." *Los Angeles Herald Examiner* (October 14, 1985, section B): 5.
Ennis, Michael. "Sterling Surls." *Texas Monthly* (February 1985): 124-126.
Flam, Jack. "The Museum as a Funhouse." *The Wall Street Journal* (March 27, 1985, section Leisure and the Arts): 32.
Freudenheim, Susan. "James Surls: The Power of Singular Belief." *Artspace* (spring 1985): 10-13, 79.
Gangelhoff, Bonnie. "The Private World of James Surls." *The Houston Post* (July 28, 1985, section The Magazine): cover, 8-11.
Hackett, Regina. "Whittler's Eccentric Sculptures Have a Plain-Talkin' Texas Flavor." *Seattle Post-Intelligencer* (September 27, 1985, section What's Happening): 7
Johnson, Patricia C. "James Surls: in his craft and sellin' art." *Houston Chronicle* (January 6, 1985, section C): 16.
Kutner, Janet. "Visions: James Surls, 1974-1984." *ARTnews* (March 1985): 106+.
Larson, Kay. "The Bad-News Bearers." *New York* (April 8, 1985): 72-73.
Marvel, Bill. "Texas Sculptor Refines Rough, Powerful Style." *Dallas Times Herald* (January 5, 1985, section C): 1.
Muchnic, Suzanne. "Artist Plants His Style with Roots in East Texas." *Los Angeles Times* (October 12, 1985, section Part V): 1.
Whitney Museum of American Art. *1985 Biennial Exposition.* New York: Whitney Museum of American Art, 1985.

1986

The Art Institute of Chicago. *75th American Exhibition.* Chicago: The Art Institute of Chicago, 1986.
Block, Gay, Carlozzi, Annette, and Jones, Laurel. *50 Texas Artists.* San Francisco: Chronicle Books, 1986.
Chadwick, Susan. "Surls' Pencil Drawings Offer Look into Creative Psyche." *The Houston Post* (May 18, 1986, section F): 16.
Johnson, Patricia C. "Drawings and sculptures." *Houston Chronicle* (June 8, 1986, section Zest): 16.
Loughery, John. "James Surls: Allan Frumkin Gallery, New York." *Arts Magazine* (May 1986): 121-122.
O'Conner, Colleen. "James Surls." *The Dallas Morning News* (March 15, 1986, section High Profile): 1-3.
Whitney Museum of American Art. *Figure as Subject: The Last Decade.* New York: Whitney Museum of American Art at the Equitable Center, 1986.

1987

Albright-Knox Art Gallery. *Structure to Resemblance: Work by Eight American Sculptors.* Buffalo: Albright-Knox Art Gallery, 1987.
Gambrell, Jamey. "Art capital of the third coast." *Art in America* (April 1987): 186-203.
Heartney, Eleanor. "James Surls: Allan Frumkin Gallery, New York." *ARTnews* (October 1987): 1-2.

"James Surls at Allan Frumkin Gallery." *Art in America* (April 1, 1987): 73.

Kutner, Janet. "Bert Long, Jesse Lott, James Surls: An Inaugural Exhibition." *The Dallas Morning News* (March 13, 1987, section Preview): 31.

——. "Artists bare their souls." *The Dallas Morning News* (March 14, 1987, section C): 1.

Morgan, Robert C. "American sculpture and the search for a referent." *Arts Magazine* (November 1987): 20-23.

Perreault, John. *James Surls: Sculpture and Drawings.* Pittsburgh: Pittsburgh Center for the Arts, 1987.

Zimmer, William. *Ancient Inspirations: Six Figurative Sculptors, Magdalena Abakanowicz, Reuben Kadish, Diana Moore, Linda Peer, Italo Scanga, James Surls.* New York: Independent Curators. Inc., 1987.

1988

"Art exhibition at museum in Netherlands will showcase works by eight Texans." *Houston Chronicle* (February 2, 1988, section D): 10.

——. *Art for the Museum: A Legacy.* Beaumont: Art Museum of Southeast Texas, 1988.

Greene, Alison de Lima. *Texas Contemporary: Art from Texas.* Groningen: Groninger Museum, The Netherlands, 1988.

Johnson, Patricia C. "Something old and something new, combining words and pictures, too." *Houston Chronicle* (February 14, 1988, section Zest): 18.

Houston: The Glassell School of Art, The Museum of Fine Arts, 1988.

Larson. Kay. "Outpost for Art: James Surls and Charmaine Locke in Splendora. Texas." *Architectural Digest* (June 1988): 154-157, 216.

"Twosomes collaborate for 'One + One,'" *Houston Chronicle* (January 2, 1988, section Weekend Preview): 5.

Walker Art Center. *Sculpture Inside Outside.* New York: Rizzoli, 1988.

Whitney Museum of American Art. *Figure as Subject: The Revival of Figuration Since 1975.* New York: Whitney Museum of American Art, 1988.

1989

"All Eyes on Texas." *The Houston Post* (January 10, 1989, section D): 1, 3.

Chadwick, Susan. "Working in the Woods: Artist sculpts life out of love, steel at isolation's edge." *The Houston Post* (April 10, 1989, section D): 1, 3.

Gerstler, Amy. "James Surls at L.A. Louver." *Art Issues* (April, number 3, 1989): 26.

Hammond. Pamela. "James Surls." *ARTnews* (March 1989): 186.

Hendricks, Patricia D., and Reese, Becky Duval. *A Century of Sculpture in Texas, 1889–1989.* Austin: Archer M. Huntington Art Gallery, College of Fine Arts, University of Texas, 1989.

Kutner, Janet. "The Artistic Poetry of James Surls." *The Dallas Morning News* (January 20, 1989, section C): 1.

"New Work by James Surls." *Houston Chronicle* (December 4, 1989, section D): 4

"Pining for Surls." *The Houston Post* (March 26, 1989, section H): 2.

1990

Chadwick, Susan. "Texas Art Offers Perspective on Life." *The Houston Post* (February 11, 1990, section H): 14.

——. "Two museums Acquire Major Texas Artist's Works." *The Houston Post* (July 9, 1990, section C): 4.

Johnson. Patricia C. "An exhibit that draws attention/Collection shows diversity of Texas artists." *Houston Chronicle* (October 18, 1990, section D): 3.

Milwaukee Art Museum. *Word as Image: American Art 1960-1990.* Milwaukee: Milwaukee Art Museum, 1990.

1991

"Art League plans tribute to Texas sculptor." *Houston Chronicle* (October 10, 1991, section D): 3.

Chadwick, Susan. "A Friendship Set in Stone." *The Houston Post* (June 2, 1991, section H): 16.

Creeley, Robert. *Looking Out: Drawings and Prints by James Surls.* Honolulu: The Contemporary Museum, 1991.

"Daughter's birth inspires Texas artist's woodcut." *The Houston Post* (February 9, 1991, section F): 3.

Johnson, Patricia C. "Celebration of friendship Project pulls in poet, sculptor and painter." *Houston Chronicle* (June 7, 1991, section D): 33.

——. "Art by collaborators, couples offers contrasts." *Houston Chronicle* (September 11, 1991, section D): 3.

Kimmelman, Michael. "In Westchester, Sculpture Meets Nature." *The New York Times* (July 19, 1991, section C): 19.

Kutner, Janet. "State of the Art: DMA's Texas exhibit covers a lot of territory, but omissions are many." *The Dallas Morning News* (August 8, 1991, section C): 1.

Paris, Wendy. "James Surls." *Sculpture* (January-February 1991): 18-19.

Raynor, Vivien. "From Twigs, Leaves and Mud, a Show of Landscape." *The New York Times* (July 14, 1991, section 12): 22.

Whitney Museum of American Art. *Image & Likeness.* New York: Whitney Museum of American Art, 1991.

Wilson, William. "Poetry and art marry in sculpture garden/'Poet's Walk' whimsical, thought provoking." *Houston Chronicle* (June 6, 1991, section Zest): 10.

1992

Baker, Kenneth. "James Surls at Braunstein/Quav." *San Francisco Chronicle* (May 26, 1992, section E): 3, 5.

Chadwick, Susan. "Artists Winningly Complete Market Square Park." *The Houston Post* (July 1, 1992, section D): 2.

Colby, Joy Hakanson. "Cranbrook Trio Adds Up to Good Chemistry." *Detroit News* (October 30, 1992, section C): 10.

Methner, Ellen Rosenbush. "James Surls." *Museum and Arts Houston* (August 1992): 27–28.

1993

Art Center of Corpus Christi. *Eye to Eye.* Corpus Christi: Art Center of Corpus Christi, 1993.

Chadwick, Susan. "Understanding Excellence at Hiram Butler Gallery. *The Houston Post* (October 5, 1993, section D): 2, 5.

Ennis. Michael. "Local Color. Once, artists sought fame in the East. Now they find rich rewards here." *Texas Monthly* 20th Anniversary Edition (February 1993): 212-213.

Espace Lyonnais d'Art Contemporain. *Here's Looking At Me, Contemporary Self-Portraiture.* Lyon: Centre d'Exchanges de Perrache, 1993.

Herbert, Lynn M. *Seeing the Forest Through the Trees.* Houston: Contemporary Arts Museum, 1993.

Jones, Kathryn. "What's Doing in Dallas." *The New York Times* (August 29, 1993, section 5): 10.

Lawndale Art and Performance Center. *Lawndale Live! A Retrospective 1979-1990.* Houston: Lawndale Art and Performance Center, 1993.

Marlborough Gallery. *Figure: Contemporary Sculpture.* New York: Marlborough Gallery, 1993.

Miller, Robert. "Living Legend to be honored by D-Art." *The Dallas Morning News* (June 23, 1993, section D): 3.

1994

Borum. Jenifer P. "James Surls: Marlborough Gallery, New York." *Artforum* (summer 1994): 92.

Creeley, Robert. *James Surls.* New York: Marlborough Gallery, 1994.

Kutner, Janet. "Texas artists more than local phenomena." *The Dallas Morning News* (March 6, 1994, section A): 37.

——. "Texas sculptor throws himself into his work." *The Dallas Morning News* (September 18, 1994, section C): 1, 4.

The Lowe Art Museum. *Eight Contemporary Sculptors: Beyond Nature, Wood Into Art.* Miami: The Lowe Art Museum, 1994.

Mahoney, Robert. "James Surls." *Cover* (February 1994): 22.

Taplin, Robert. "James Surls at Marlborough Gallery." *Art in America* (June 1994): 96.

1995

de Estrada, Uyolanda Batres. "James Surls." *New Art Examiner* (September 1995): 54–55.

Johnson, Patricia Covo. *Contemporary Art in Texas.* Roseville East, Australia: Craftsman House in association with G+B Arts International, 1995.

——. "Shows of unchanging images, black board forms." *Houston Chronicle* (May 18, 1995, section D): 1.

Kutner, Janet. "New face among big names at Gerald Peters." *The Dallas Morning News* (July 28, 1995, section A): 39.

1996

Cuellar, Catherine. "Views of the Muse. Artists reveal origins of their work." *The Dallas Morning News* (September 1, 1996, section C): 10.

——. "Top Texas artists 'Exposed' at Visual Art Center." *The Dallas Morning News* (November 1, 1996, section C): I-?

Kutner, Janet. "Cultivating artists. Art center's sculpture garden starts to bloom." *The Dallas Morning News* (June 21, 1996, section C): 1.

——. "Sculptor's Poetic spiritual impulses are on display." *The Dallas Morning News* (August 23, 1996, section A): 41.

——. "Lone Star art stars. Dallas Visual Art Center showcases state's top talent." *The Dallas Morning News* (November 2, 1996, section A): 43.

Olsen, Valerie Loupe. *Schemata. Drawings by Sculptors.* Houston: The Glassell School of Art, Museum of Fine Arts, 1996.

Villani, John. "A Natural Force." *Southern Accents* (July-August 1996): 78-83.

1997

Contemporary Arts Museum. *Finders/Keepers.* Houston: Contemporary Arts Museum, 1997.

1999

El Paso Museum of Art. *Monumental Limbs.* El Paso: El Paso Museum of Art, 1999.

"James Surls: Interview by Valerie Loupe Olsen, Assisted by Kristin Fields." *Artlies* (Fall 1999): 88-89.

2000

de Turenne, Auzias, Curator. "Monte-Carlo International Sculpture Festival: Contemporary American Sculpture." *Monte-Carlo* (July to October 2000): 50-51.

Kalil, Susie. "James Surls: A Restless Magician." *Sculpture Magazine*, vol. 19, no. 5 (June 2000): 18-25.

2001

Annas, Teresa. "Artist Meets Critic." *The Virginian Pilot* (May 30, 2001).

McGhie, Juliet. "...compelled to create images and tell tales." *Citilites* (Summer 2001): 13-18.

Strunck, Juergen, and High, Tim. "Texas Prints 2001: Contemporary Prints by Thirty-One Prominent Texas Artists." Essays by Mark Smith, Ph.D. 14.

2002

"James Surls: A Life Force." *Pillsbury and Peters Fine Art* (March 22–May 4, 2002), essay by Edmund Pillsbury, Ph.D.

2003

Kutner, Janet. "Natural Selections." *The Dallas Morning News* (February 5, 2003).

McBride, Elizabeth. "Thinking About Art, Writing About Art, Making Art." *Artlies,* vol. 38 (Spring 2003): 14-17, cover.

Tennant, Donna. "James Surls make it BIG." *Houston Chronicle* (February 15, 2003).

——. "James Surls, Meadows Museum, Southern Methodist University", *Artlies*, vol. 38 (Spring 2003, section Dallas Review): 77, cover.

Wash, Brendan. "Statues planned for art garden." *Corpus Christi Caller Times* (May 1, 2002).

PHOTOGRAPHY CREDITS

All works owned by the Artist, unless noted i n the text.

All Photography by Michael Bodycomb unless noted below.

Frontispieces: 1. Shell Hirshhorn; 2–4. © P. Gregory Warden, Dallas, Texas; **Title Page:** © Tai Pomara, San Jose, California; **Copyright page:** © P. Gregory Warden, Dallas, Texas; **pp.13-14:** Courtesy Dallas Museum of Art, © Daniel Barsotti, Santa Fe, New Mexico; **pp. 16-17:** © John Alexander, New York.

Figures: *fig. 1:* Courtesy Dallas Museum of Art Archive, © John Alexander, New York; *fig. 2:* Courtesy Dallas Museum of Art Archive, © Charmaine Locke, Basalt, Colorado; *fig. 3:* photographer unknown; *fig. 4:* photographer unknown; *fig. 5:* Shell Hirshhorn; *fig. 6:* Mary E. Nichols, Courtesy *Architectural Digest*, copyright © Condé Nast Publications; *fig. 7:* Courtesy Dallas Museum of Art Archive, © Nan Vroom; *fig. 8:* © James Paussa; *fig. 9:* © James Surls; *fig. 10:* © James Paussa; *fig. 12:* Mary E. Nichols, Courtesy *Architectural Digest*, copyright © Condé Nast Publications; *fig. 13:* Courtesy of Gerald Peters Gallery, Dallas, Texas, and Santa Fe, New Mexico, and James Surls, © Joe D'Alessandro; *fig. 14:* © Meadows Museum; *fig. 15:* Courtesy of Arkansas Arts Center Foundation Purchase: 14th Annual Delta Art Exhibition, 1971, © Cindy Momchilov; *fig. 21:* Tom Van Eynde; *fig. 24:* Tom Jenkins; *fig. 28:* Robert Millman, Aspen, Colorado; *fig. 34:* Courtesy of L.A. Louver Gallery, Venice, California; *fig. 36:* Sandak, Inc.; *fig. 39:* Courtesy Dallas Museum of Art Archive; *fig. 40:* Mary E. Nichols, Courtesy *Architectural Digest*, copyright © Condé Nast Publications; *fig. 43:* Vickie S. Kirby; *fig. 44:* Courtesy of Diverse Works, © Diane Barber; *fig. 48:* © Tai Pomara, San Jose, California; *fig. 49:* © Meadows Museum; *fig. 50:* Courtesy of Gerald Peters Gallery, Dallas, Texas, and Santa Fe, New Mexico, and James Surls, © Joe D'Alessandro; *fig. 52:* Courtesy Dallas Museum of Art Archive, © Hickey-Robertson, Houston, Texas; *fig. 53:* © P. Gregory Warden; *fig. 54:* Courtesy of Gerald Peters Gallery, Dallas, Texas, and Santa Fe, New Mexico, and James Surls, © Joe D'Alessandro; *figs. 55-56:* © Meadows Museum; *fig. 57:* © James Paussa; *fig. 58:* © P. Gregory Warden; *fig. 59:* Courtesy of Gerald Peters Gallery, Dallas, Texas, and Santa Fe, New Mexico, and James Surls, © Joe D'Alessandro; *fig. 60:* © P. Gregory Warden; *fig. 64:* Courtesy Dallas Museum of Art Archive, © Connie Moberley, 1984; *fig. 67:* © James Paussa; *figs. 68-71:* © P. Gregory Warden; *fig. 73:* Courtesy of L.A. Louver Gallery, Venice, California; *fig. 74:* © P. Gregory Warden; *fig. 76:* © P. Gregory Warden; *fig. 78:* James Brundige.

FIGURE 78
James Surls with wife Charmaine Locke at their Colorado home

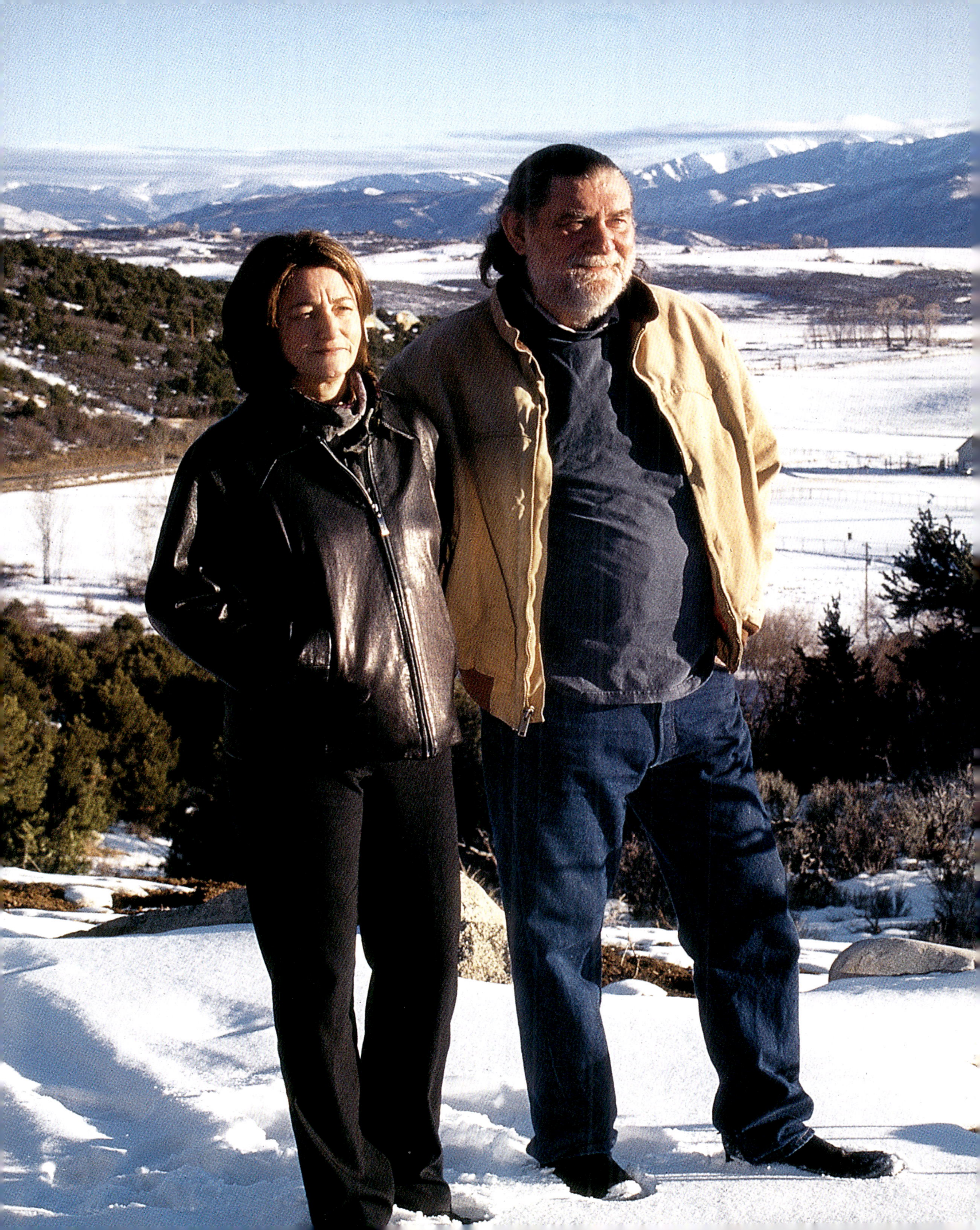

INDEX

Note: page numbers in boldface refer to illustrations.